# the corporate intranet

## Create and Manage an Internal Web for Your Organization

### RYAN BERNARD

WILEY COMPUTER PUBLISHING

John Wiley & Sons, Inc.

New York ◆ Chichester ◆ Brisbane ◆ Toronto ◆ Singapore

Publisher: Katherine Schowalter
Editor: Philip Sutherland
Managing Editor: Susan Curtin
Text Design & Composition: North Market Street Graphics

Designations used by companies to distinguish their products are often claimed as trademarks. In all instances where John Wiley & Sons, Inc., is aware of a claim, the product names appear in initial capital or ALL CAPITAL LETTERS. Readers, however, should contact the appropriate companies for more complete information regarding trademarks and registration.

This text is printed on acid-free paper.

This publication is designed to provide accurate and authoritative information in regard to the subject matter covered. It is sold with the understanding that the publisher is not engaged in rendering legal, accounting, or other professional service. If legal advice or other expert assistance is required, the services of a competent professional person should be sought. This publication is sold without warranty of any kind. Neither the author nor the publisher assumes any liability for any damages arising from the use of or the inability to use the information in this publication.

*Library of Congress Cataloging-in-Publication Data:*
Bernard, Ryan.
     The corporate intranet : create and manage an internal Web for your organization / Ryan Bernard.
        p.     cm.
     Includes index.
     ISBN 0-471-14929-2 (paper : alk. paper)
     1. World Wide Web (Information retrieval system)    2. Business communication.    I. Title.
     TK5105.888.B47    1996
     650'.0285'575—dc20                                                              986-15479
                                                                                           CIP

Printed in the United States of America
10  9  8  7  6  5  4  3

# contents

## Chapter 2    A New Kind of Information System    30

## Chapter 3    The Birth of the Information Center    72

## Chapter 4    The Intranet in Practice    132

## Chapter 5    Toward the Paperless Office    166

## Chapter 6    Harnessing the New Media    210

## Chapter 7    Serving Data and Applications    244

## Chapter 8    Interfacing with the Internet    288

## Chapter 9    Managing the Web Explosion    314

## Appendix A    HTML Quick Reference    339

## Appendix B    Cool Tools for the Intranet    357

## Appendix C    Glossary    367

## Appendix D    User Authentication    377

## Index    381

# preface

This book is like an open letter to the managers and employees of any organization in the world. Over the last 20 years, I have worked with many different companies and have seen—especially in the last decade—a great drive to continuously cut costs and improve productivity. Systems have been reengineered *en masse* and organization charts have been streamlined to a fare-thee-well. And yet, despite this tremendous effort, we are still facing many of the same problems that we did 10 or 20 years ago: how to communicate and manage the vast streams of data and information created daily by millions of office workers, manufacturing facilities, design teams, dealers, sales reps, customers, and suppliers worldwide.

It's amazing sometimes, despite the unending improvements in our technology, how little has really changed. When you walk down the hall of any modern corporation, you can still hear the *pop* of the three-ring binder echoing against the walls. Then you turn the corner and immediately stumble across a more recent development: the perpetually gorged recycling bin, where thousands of pages of unwanted information have finally come home to roost.

Despite massive investments in office automation over the years, and persistent dreams of the "paperless office," corporations continue to devour trees at an incredible rate. And, of course, any paper-based information delivery process is something straight out of the Victorian age.

The three-ring binder is only a small part of the problem, but it is a prominent symbol of what we're fighting against. Another part of the problem is that traditional corporate information systems deal with only a small part of the data processed by the typical business. If we want to automate the rest of the process, we will have to make room for the extra traffic in our systems and make it easier for people to use computers for these purposes. In many ways, it will mean making our data networks as open and easy to use as the in-house phone system.

As it happens, recent developments have conspired to put these goals within reach. Over the past 20 years, I have personally seen many technologies come and go, from the keypunch card, to the dedicated word processor, to the CD-ROM drive. More recently, technological solutions like electronic data interchange (EDI) and groupware have helped put a dent in the paper glut. But none of them quite matches the potential of what I will be calling here "web technology" or "the Intranet" to streamline the information flow, democratize our internal networks, and help free us from the oppressive burden of paper we generate everyday.

In late 1994, when I first started circulating the draft proposal for this book, web technology was not a practical way to deliver large volumes of information online. In the early systems, you had to code the information by hand using a text editor, the same way we once used word processor codes to change fonts or start new paragraphs. The early web servers were plain vanilla: They just sat there and served files. Early browser tools like Mosaic were severely limited: You couldn't do tables, centering, or special positioning of inline graphics—the kind of thing that's second nature for any run-of-the-mill word processor. WYSIWYG authoring, of course, was out of the question. And if you wanted to do advanced applications, such as database access, you had to hire a programmer with expertise in an arcane mechanism called the Common Gateway Interface (CGI).

There were other impediments as well to acceptance of this new technology. Until very recently, many large organizations still had not integrated their individual LANs into wide area networks, so that users could communicate and share files across the enterprise. Others were only starting to reach the point where desktop computers were widely available in their organizations—and well understood. It wasn't that long ago we were still explaining *simple* things to people, like how to use windows and a mouse.

What a difference a year or two can make. Most of the tools mentioned in this book were conceived, developed, and brought to market within the past year. Whereas the web was until recently only a question mark in many peoples' minds, now it's a thriving development environment. And, since many organizations already have the infrastructure in place to make an internal web practical, it's clear that the time for this technology has finally arrived.

## A Personal Epiphany

Like many people who've been captivated by the Intranet, I can still remember where I was and what I was doing the first time I laid eyes on Mosaic. I had been asked by one of my clients, a large international services firm, to help develop a way to share information and documentation between various workgroups. The idea was that by sharing information, they might more easily standardize their work methods and avoid many of the integration problems involved in merging the efforts of different groups.

We started planning the project in late 1993 and early 1994, at a time when Mosaic was still practically unknown and groupware like Lotus Notes was just beginning to penetrate the market. To put all the information online, we decided to use FrameViewer, a tool we had already used successfully before for other online publishing projects. The idea was to create a "toolkit browser" that the company's in-house software developers could use to view programmer documentation, specifications, and other information online.

I already had an approved design for the browser format worked out and ready to go when some colleagues pulled me into an office one day and asked me to take a look at "this new Mosaic thing." It was one of those hot summer days in Houston and traffic was oozing through the morbid humidity on Westheimer Street 700 feet below. They had sitting on the desk a Sun SPARC 10 running the old Alpha version of NCSA Mosaic for X Windows, with a direct connection to the Internet through the company firewall. Of course, I was amazed as we proceeded to surf the World Wide Web (WWW), browsing through documents located on computers as far away as Chicago, Silicon Valley, and Geneva, Switzerland.

What amazed me was not the *content* of the Web—it was mighty slim pickings then, compared to now—but the *concept*. Here was a browser that would let users not only view information online, but do it transparently across a network. Instead of having to maintain copies of the material at various sites and have users log in to get it, we could serve it from a single node and have *any employee access it automatically worldwide* through the company's internal wide area network. Not only that, but in addition to publishing documents we could also publish interactive forms and actually capture feedback or data from the users. Most importantly, we wouldn't be limited to a certain file type: We could use this tool to provide users with any type of computer object or resource, including not only documents but programming tools, libraries, and software—even sound, video, or live data. And we could serve it to browsers located on any platform: PC, Mac or UNIX.

It all sounded too good to be true. Certainly there had to be a catch. What would happen, for instance, if we didn't want just *anybody* to have access to the information? Suppose we wanted to limit it? No problem, we could password-protect just about anything. Suppose we still wanted to use a publishing tool like FrameMaker to create the content? No problem, there were conversion tools that could automatically generate the web content from our FrameMaker documents using a single batch command.

Needless to say, I was sold on the idea. We immediately threw out the FrameViewer design—lock, stock, and barrel, as they say—and adopted the web as our platform of choice. It's been nearly two years since that first web experiment, but we've had no regrets about our decision, and we never looked back.

## Who Needs This Book

You will find this book most useful if your job description fits one of the following profiles:

- *Managers/department heads.* Web technology works best in an environment where upper-level managers clearly understand the technologies and issues involved. This includes not just information technology (IT) managers, but department and division heads who may end up blindsided not only by the power of the technology, but also by how large these systems can grow and how fast they can become unmanageable. If you are a manager, this book will help you understand the value of the technology and the key management issues involved. If you are not a manager, but are involved in a haphazardly planned or controlled internal web system, please make sure someone upstairs sees this book.

- *Communicators.* Nearly everyone in the business world fits this description, since we all have something to communicate with others. However, this technology will be extremely helpful to those who regularly provide information or services to the rest of the organization, or those who would like to. In particular, those involved in corporate communications, marketing communications, or technical communications may find the Intranet an ideal way to distribute information to employees, customers, distributors, or suppliers.

- *Data guardians.* Those who manage large databases or data warehouses may find the Intranet an ideal way to get more mileage out of the data by serving it to a wider audience of employees, customers, or suppliers. This book describes both the database publishing aspects and the security angles.

- *Work groups.* An Intranet is an ideal way for work groups and teams to publicize their efforts within an organization. In particular, teams using client-server groupware applications like Lotus Notes may find in this technology an intriguing alternative.

- *Systems analysts, developers.* A web interface may be the best way to cut down on the work involved in developing graphical user interfaces (GUIs) for client-server applications. In particular, you will learn how the Intranet allows developers to create a single point of access for a wide variety of applications, and how you can roll out self-documenting applications online without much of the effort previously required in introducing a new system.

◆ *Corporate trainers and seminar leaders.* Peoples' understanding of Intranet technology is clouded by their confusion over the Internet. Most companies will see a necessary period of adjustment similar to what happened shortly after the introduction of Windows 3.1 and other mouse-and-window interfaces. To help ease people into the new Intranet technologies, this book may provide an excellent background text.

◆ *Re-engineering teams.* Teams dedicated to the task of improving or re-engineering internal processes may find that web technology provides an excellent way to streamline and eliminate many of the costs associated with paper-based information delivery systems.

## Where Web Technology Fits

Web technology is not the best solution for every problem, but it's always amazing to see so many companies using it in the various ways they do. In particular, the technology is a natural fit for companies where the following conditions exist:

◆ *Internal network running TCP/IP.* Web technology is designed for use in a networked environment containing desktop computers, whether they are Macs, UNIX workstations, or PCs (and especially if the network supports a mixture of these operating systems). Web technology is device-independent and works well in a cross-platform environment. The main requirement is that the network support TCP/IP communications. This is not as uncommon as it may sound. Even if your network runs Netware, SNA, or any of the other widespread protocols, it may already have a TCP/IP overlay on it, especially if there are UNIX machines being used as servers anywhere on the network. The best way to find out is to check with the closest network administrator, examine your networking configuration or look for programs running on your local machine with names that include words like TCP or Winsock.

◆ *Dispersed but connected work groups.* You can use web technology productively for the benefit of individual work groups as small as a dozen people working in the same suite of offices. But it's most useful for improving communications between widely separated work groups—especially those that operate on separate but interconnected LANs or WANs spread across an office building, a campus, or around the globe. The key word here, however, is *connectivity*. Web technology will not work in parts of the network that are isolated and not addressable through TCP/IP. Later chapters will explain how this works.

◆ *High ratio of desktop computers.* Since it is completely online, this technology is of course best used in organizations with a high ratio of computers to employees. To a certain extent, you can work around this by using kiosks in work areas (such as a dedicated or shared web client at the packing station in a warehouse). The user base should be familiar with use of a mouse, but few other skills are needed with a well-designed interface.

## What's in This Book

In case you haven't figured it out yet, let me clarify. This book is emphatically *not* about the Internet or the World Wide Web per se—although you will see them mentioned many times herein. (If you've been to the bookstore lately, you know there are already far too many books on those subjects, anyway.)

Instead, it is intended to show anyone with a little technical savvy how to apply *the same technologies* used on the Internet and WWW to the typical business enterprise LAN, WAN, or Internet gateway. Why? To help you automate and streamline the flow of documents, data, and other mission-critical information in ways they've never been streamlined before. And to share important business data with *all* the people who are vital to the success of your business; not just customers but also employees, dealers, and suppliers. This *includes* the idea of using the technology on the Internet, but it is by no means limited to that use alone.

To avoid the familiar traps—and provide a fresh viewpoint on the subject—this book takes the position that the Intranet is perhaps the highest and greatest use of web technology. The idea comes rather late to the publishing world, which has had its attention riveted by the Internet. At a time when up to 70 percent of all Internet products sold were being used for Intranet, exactly 0 percent of the books were dedicated to the concept. That is an imbalance it is time to correct. Typical books on the Internet and the World Wide Web are of little help when it comes to understanding or designing Intranets. In fact, the ground rules change considerably when you apply this technology internally versus externally, which is why few of the traditional Internet providers and Web design houses get involved in Intranet work. And because of these differences, internal webs require a completely different approach to the technology, as you will see.

As an added fillip, this book tries to take a holistic approach to the concept of communication within an enterprise. Too often, people take a simplistic approach to technology that looks at the individual limbs without seeing the whole tree. What they end up with is a system that is harder to use and maintain than it should be. For instance, we are already beyond the point where people should have to learn something obscure like Hypertext Markup Language (HTML) to be able to publish web documents, just as no one has to code raw PostScript these days to get a nice-looking printout. We are also near the point where we will no longer need programmers to connect web systems to external applications like databases.

The other challenge is to take a balanced approach to the use of web technology. Organizations that have rushed onto the World Wide Web while ignoring internal applications suffer from a sort of myopia induced by all the Internet hype. Suddenly, they've found a way to provide their customers with in-depth information online, but somehow ignore the fact they could use the same technologies to benefit their employees, dealers, and suppliers. This book will help restore balance by offering an integrated business model that gives proper weight to both the internal and external uses of a web.

Even for organizations that have started their own Intranets already, there is still a sort of myopia involved. The people who are entrusted with web development, while usually the most technically savvy, aren't always the best communicators. We must never forget that data is information, and information requires communication—especially in a web environment where we can now apply desktop publishing techniques on-the-fly and present even the rawest, ugliest data in a pleasing document-like dinner coat. So even if you are one of those technosavvy webheads, this book can help you learn how to communicate your data more clearly to end users.

Although many people already understand HTML and how to create web documents, they may not fully understand the new approaches to document creation and management this will make possible. Many people instinctively want to apply old paradigms without rethinking the requirements of the new medium. Once we start taking our documents online, the way we structure them will inevitably change to match the unique capabilities of the new publishing medium. Because webs and the entire Intranet environment make it possible to present some information *exclusively* online, we also need to take a look at how that will change the whole way we go about creating, presenting, storing, and retrieving the information. This book explores the idea that documents could become more like data—and data more like documents—so that eventually there may be a merger between the two.

Finally, many people who dabble in web technology still don't understand the full power available for delivering high-value information resources. Consequently, this book has several chapters devoted to the concept of advanced content delivery, including database, multimedia applications, and more. And it makes the assumption that—to get full use out of Intranet technology—you really need to understand how it compares to and interacts with other computing technologies, such as mainframe-centric, groupware, and client-server.

This book was written to address all these concerns in ways that nearly anyone with a little computer savvy should be able to understand. There's something here for everyone, including writers and communicators, trainers, system developers, designers, network administrators, and managers of every hue and stripe. That's because the web itself covers all these disciplines and more. And everyone—management especially—can benefit from a complete overview of both the science and the art involved in creating an internal web.

## A Quick Tour

Chapter 1, "What Every Business Can Learn from the Internet," explains how the Internet model applies to business and gives a first glimpse of the concepts involved in the Intranet.

Chapter 2, "A New Kind of Information System," explains the developments in technology that have made Intranets feasible for the enterprise and discusses how it may change the way we all do business in the future.

Chapter 3, "The Birth of the Information Center," explains how any department in an organization can use a web server to create its own "information center."

Chapter 4, "The Corporate Intranet in Practice," provides examples of how companies like DEC, Chevron, Sun, and Nortel are already using web technology for internal applications.

Chapter 5, "Toward the Paperless Office," explains how to use an internal web as a publishing medium, including how to create web documents and bring large publishing groups online.

Chapter 6, "Harnessing the New Media," covers the issues and concepts of delivering multimedia over an internal web.

Chapter 7, "Serving Data and Applications," explains how the internal web can be used to serve information from databases and other client-server applications.

Chapter 8, "Interfacing with the Internet," explains the relation between an internal web system (the Intranet) and an external one delivered over the Internet.

Chapter 9, "Managing the Web Explosion," explains how to manage the inevitable growth that will occur as your first Intranet applications evolve into large-scale web systems.

## Acknowledgments

This book wouldn't exist without the aid and encouragement of many people who helped light the way. First credits go to my colleagues John Foster and David Lineman, who originally showed me the wonders of Mosaic, as well as Steve Sidney, Bill Calcote, Sara Stewart and others at Western Atlas International, who gave me the opportunity to help develop that first internal web so many months ago. My original book proposal in the fall of 1994 would have gone nowhere without the vision of Matt Wagner of Waterside Productions, who saw the subject's potential at a time when virtually no one had heard of the Intranet, and when few wanted to take a chance on a book about it. Without his constant promotion and followup, the original proposal might still be sitting on the shelf.

Special thanks goes to Phil Sutherland at John Wiley & Sons for seeing the book's potential in the summer of 1995, slating it for production, and waiting patiently during the fall and winter as the first draft took shape. Special credit to Sue Curtin, Frank Grazioli, and the other members of the Wiley team for their excellent help in editing the book and bringing it to press in a timely manner.

Key portions of this book would not be possible without the help of participating companies and individuals who opened doors, answered calls, and shared their knowledge and insights on Intranet technology and many of its key components and applications. In particular, I'd like to thank Carl Meske and Hassan Schroeder at Sun Microsystems; Nick Schonhut at DEC; John Hanten, Sharon Sloan, and Debbie Scott at Chevron PTC; Herschel Miller, Chris Koehncke, and Walter Oldham at Nortel; Chris Holten, Len Feldman, and J.F. Sullivan at Netscape Communications; Mike New at InfoAccess; Dan Plasse at EOR; and Peter Dicerbo at Burson-Marsteller.

Naturally, we all owe a debt of gratitude to the unsung webmasters who are responsible for publishing the online information that makes all web knowledge possible. But without doubt the greatest technological kudos go to master inventors Tim Berners-Lee, Marc Andreessen, Eric Bina, and all the others who gave us the technology that make the Intranet possible.

As always, my final most heartfelt thanks go to my family, Diana, Evan, and Claire, whose patience and unfailing support make possible my continuing adventures in the publishing world, and to the Creator who—working diligently behind the scenes—gives us all our opportunities and inspirations.

Ryan Bernard
Houston, Texas
March 1996

*rbernard@wordmark.com*
*http://wordmark.com/*

# the corporate intranet

## Chapter One at a Glance

This book explains all you need to know about the design, building, and management of corporate Intranets. But before we delve into the details of the Intranet, it's useful to start with the same point of reference that everyone else does: the Internet and the World Wide Web (WWW). Because it's only by understanding the Internet and WWW that you will come to understand how the Intranet and internal web systems can also work on private corporate networks. This chapter explains:

- Why the Internet and World Wide Web can serve as a model for business communications, teamwork, and collaboration
- How an Intranet works, and why it is useful
- What kinds of "hidden tools" already exist on most computers that make it possible to create internal webs
- Why a data network is like a phone network, and why one is free while the other is still restricted
- How web technologies can open up the data channels and make them as easy to access as the phone system
- How Intranets may save companies millions of dollars by making it easier for employees to share information, data, and other computer resources online
- Why web technologies will put us light-years ahead on the road toward the "paperless office"
- Why companies need to take a more integrated approach to the design and delivery of Intranet systems.

# What Every Business Can Learn from the Internet

*The growth of the Net is not a fluke or a fad, but the consequence of unleashing the power of individual creativity. If it were an economy, it would be the triumph of the free market over central planning. In music, jazz over Bach. Democracy over dictatorship.*

—THE ECONOMIST

You've heard the hype, and it's true. When all is said and done, the Internet will be counted among the greatest success stories in history. Its rise from virtual nonexistence to over 30 million users in the past decade is a growth curve unequaled by any other organization or medium in history.

This network of networks is like a biological organism that is entirely self-replicating, self-sustaining, and self-governing. No one plans the Internet; no one works to make sure it is properly staffed, managed, or budgeted. It simply happens through a kind of serendipity and the cooperative action of millions. The people who make it happen are scattered throughout the globe, are generally unknown to each other, and have little understanding of exactly what the total network looks like or how it truly operates. And yet there has arisen from the Internet the kind of community and culture that can serve as a model for business and other cooperative enterprise well into the next century.

*Wait a minute!* What kind of heresy is this? Someone is saying that business—the paragon of efficiency, profitability, and rigorous management—has something to learn from the wild and woolly Internet? Yes, that's exactly right.

At first glance, the Internet would seem to be the antithesis of everything that business stands for. In the standard school of thinking, business is orderly; the Internet is chaotic. Business is well-planned and managed; the Internet is a free-for-all. Business has leaders, shareholders, and a clearly defined management structure; the Internet, like some kind of asylum for lost souls, has no one in charge and no one to answer to. All these things are certainly true, to a certain extent. But let's take a closer look.

## The Ghost in the Machine

Over the past few years many major corporations and private organizations have developed their own worldwide networks to tie together remote offices no matter where they're located in the world. In most cases, these networks have all the characteristics of the Internet and are capable of carrying the same kinds of traffic, too.

Even local or regional businesses with widely scattered branches, offices, or sales networks have their own LANs and WANs that can carry Internet-like communications. And in most cases, the users of these networks have little idea of what the whole network looks like, how it truly operates, or even that it may already have some components of Internet technology embedded in it—ready to use.

In particular, any computer running UNIX, Windows 95, Windows NT, or Macintosh System 7 has certain Internet tools already built in, or easily added, including TCP/IP networking, web server software, and web client software that can help users do just about anything currently being done on the Internet. But in most cases, these tools lie dormant because most businesses do not understand how to use them in a productive way to enhance network communications within their organization. And this is mainly because they misunderstand the fundamental nature of the Internet.

The Internet represents the first truly large-scale experiment in creating a global public network like the phone system, but one devoted to exchanging data rather than voice communications. When you get a phone, you don't have to ask anyone for special permission to call Paris, London, Melbourne, or Tokyo. No one has to reconfigure the system so you can reach remote areas of the world and chat with tribesmen in Borneo, burghers in Zurich, or *gauchos* in Argentina. You automatically get access to the entire globe. You can call anywhere in the world and anyone can call you (Figure 1.1).

When you pick up the phone and call Timbuktu, you don't see the complex set of connections made by all the intervening phone companies, state bureaucracies, satellite relays, and fiber-optic links. You don't think of all the treaties that had to be negotiated and technical problems that had to be hurdled to get

**Figure 1.1**  The phone system.

your voice from Point A to Point Z. The connection just happens automatically. This is now so easy, we all take it for granted. No one sits around all day and wonders, "How do they do that?"

The Internet is a lot like that (Figure 1.2). If you have a computer and an Internet connection, you get access to the entire worldwide public data network without restriction. You can get data and information from Microsoft, IBM, AT&T, Ford, the *New York Times,* the White House, the Library of Congress, the Australian Parliament, the Vatican, or the World Bank without any additional setup and without asking anyone's permission. If you have the proper equipment on your computer, you can also *provide* information to the rest of the world. Thus, the Internet, through its World Wide Web feature, supports the same kind of direct point-to-point communication we already get from the phone system.

It wasn't necessarily planned this way. That's just how it happened. The public data networks have evolved—just as free markets evolved—based on their enabling architecture and the way human beings naturally decided to use them. Nowadays, connecting to and exchanging data with a random computer halfway around the world is as routine and easy as clicking your mouse.

## The Business Mindset

In the private world of business, on the other hand, there is a curious (though understandable) dichotomy between the data networks and the phone system.

**Figure 1.2**  An Internet (or Intranet).

When you're hired to do a job, there's a phone already sitting on your desk. You can immediately pick up the receiver and dial human resources, marketing, or any other internal department without further ado. If you want to call a customer or supplier outside the company, you can just dial "9" and call outside, too. It's all very simple and it's all done automatically. No one has to give you permission or set you up specially to communicate with other departments or customers over the phone system.

Why do you communicate with other departments? Because you have information to share, and most of it is vital to the business. Some of the information comes to you verbally through the phone network and some through the paper-based communication systems: the copy machine, the fax, the repro department, or the mail room. Together, these communication systems are the glue that holds together any business operation. The ubiquitous presence of these tools in our daily lives shows the amount of importance we attach to them as means of communication. No one would ever imagine running a business without them, and no one questions their value.

Things have not always been the same for the computer and the corporate data network, however. Not too long ago, it was a privilege to have a computer on your desk. Network connections were even harder to come by. The situation is improving so that now, when you report to work, chances are you'll have a computer sitting on your desk, as well as a network connection that plugs you into the local area network (LAN), or even a wide area network (WAN). Unlike the phone network, however, you can't use the data network to automatically communicate or share data with just *any* department. In fact, you may not be able to share it with anyone at all, except for a few people in your immediate area.

## Locked into the Loop

Typically, you may start out being limited to your own local programs and the data on your local hard drive, then have network access added little by little, as you need it. Or, you may be logged automatically to a set of hard drives or *file servers* on a LAN, where data and applications are stored for employees in your group or division. But in most cases, you are locked into your own department or divisional loop. And, if you want to get information from human resources, marketing, or some other department or division of the company, chances are you'll have to rely on the trusty old phone-and-paper system to take care of it (or something slightly more advanced, like a floppy diskette shipped through the interoffice mail).

Most companies are trying to remedy this problem using client-server applications like database management systems (DBMS) and groupware. The idea is that people can share files and data using applications that serve as a traffic cop, keeping track of user changes and resolving them in the final version of the data. For example, Oracle software lets multiple users view and edit the same set of data; Lotus Notes does roughly the same thing for documents. This is much more productive than giving people access to a document or database one user at a time, or keeping different versions of the same information on each user's machine.

Still, these new client-server systems tend to operate in a closed loop. It's as though you had a phone system where you could only talk to the people in your own department or the team members who work on the same project, without being able to connect to the rest of the company down the hall; or as though someone built an artificial barrier in the middle of the hallway, and you had to ask a gatekeeper for permission to walk through.

Things are starting to change now, thanks to the success of the Internet and the World Wide Web. Due to the torrent of publicity in the media and trade press in recent years, computer manufacturers and software companies like IBM/Lotus, Microsoft, Novell, DEC, Sun, and Oracle have started building increasingly powerful Internet features into their operating systems and software. And many of these same companies are leading the way in applying the technologies to their internal and external business communications.

At first, the idea of installing Internet tools on corporate networks was daunting. Though universally available on UNIX systems, the tools were not available on PC and Macs until recently. Now, every new operating system or computer sold in retail stores is equipped with basic tools like Web browsers, TCP/IP networking, and other Internet components included as standard features, or easy add-ons. Because of these developments, we are already seeing a second Internet revolution—one that promises to bring true and lasting benefits to the enterprise by *bringing the information superhighway in-house.* This is what we mean when we talk about "the Intranet."

## The World Wide Web We All Know and Love

It's important to make a distinction between the global phenomena we know as Internet/WWW and the related concepts of *Intranet* or *internal webs.* The words *Internet* and the *World Wide Web* are now drilled so firmly into our brains that we have a hard time separating the original technology from its newest implementations.

The Internet has been around for well over a decade, but the World Wide Web is a recent phenomenon that only started seeing widespread use in 1994. Soon after the invention of advanced graphical browsers like Mosaic and Netscape, businesses and their customers started flocking to the World Wide Web in droves. These new tools made it possible for any company to transfer graphically rich information—with real type fonts and full-color graphics—across the Internet at the click of a button. Since the browsers were inexpensive, anyone with a computer, a modem, and an Internet connection could easily access the information.

The advent of these new tools, along with the removal of previous government-imposed restrictions on commercial use, created a massive explosion in business activity on the Web. The total number of registered domain names (the unique Internet aliases like *microsoft.com* and *ford.com*) climbed from 17,000 in June 1994 to 70,000 a year later, a growth rate of nearly 150 companies a day. And that's only the companies that have registered. Possibly twice that number are hosted unofficially by third-party Web services like Webcom Communications, The Well, America Online and others. By some estimates, there are over 20 million pages of information currently available on the Web, with thousands of pages being added every day.

Currently, the Web provides a home for all types of enterprises from the greatest to the smallest. There are scores of Fortune 500 corporations online, including names like Ford, IBM, Time Warner, and Microsoft. There are smaller but influential companies like the Big Six accounting firms, the major television networks, and most major newspapers.

You can use the Web to connect to banks like Wells Fargo, Bank of America, Toronto Dominion, NationsBank and many others. You can do business with giant investment firms like Merrill Lynch and Charles Schwab. There are major retailers and mail order firms online with names like JCPenney, Target, Land's End, and Sharper Image, plus any number of tiny boutiques.

You name it and the Web has it: lawyers, architects, air chartering services, career headhunters, publishing houses, manufacturers, advertising agencies, pharmaceutical companies. You can already read the full text of many newspapers, computer mags, and financial journals on the Web. There are also businesses created specifically for the new medium, like Security First Network Bank and many of the online cybermalls created to do nothing but connect businesses and customers in the cyber-realm.

When customers "visit" a company's Web site, typically the first thing they see is the *home page* (Figure 1.3). This is usually a greeting or a main menu that welcomes them and shows them what is available at the site. Once they reach the home page, they can point and click to access any information at the site.

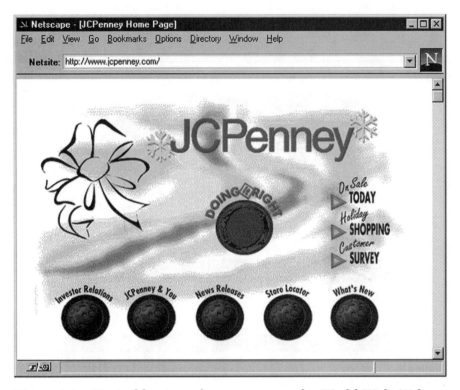

**Figure 1.3**   Typical business home pages on the World Wide Web.

Most businesses use the Web strictly for marketing purposes, since it provides an ideal way for companies to connect with real or potential customers through cyberspace. Many companies have extensive product information online, including not only the information you normally find in brochures but other details like press releases, case studies, testimonials, demonstrations, and feedback forms. Some have investor information, like a copy of their SEC report and current quotes on their stock price. Smaller companies may have pictures and bios of the staff, and many companies of all sizes advertise their current job openings online.

More advanced sites, like Microsoft Corporation (http://www.microsoft. com) and Digital (http://www.digital.com/), have migrated their extensive knowledge bases to the Web, with detailed product reports and troubleshooting information. Others, such as mail order firms and software discount houses, actually let you order products online using a credit card or purchase order number. In the case of information products like software or investment

**Figure 1.3**   *(Continued).*

newsletters, you can not only *buy* the goods online but you can also *download them* directly through the Internet.

To provide these kinds of services, a company must be set up a certain way. When we say that a company is "on the Web," it usually means it is connected directly to the Internet through a full-time hookup, which might be either a leased line or dedicated dialup connection to a local Internet provider. The information content served to customers over the Web is stored on a desktop computer either at the company's local site or off-site with a third-party "hosting service." The only requirement for doing this is some type of web server software such as Website, Netscape Communications Server, Purveyor or any of the other commercial or shareware server packages available for UNIX, PC, and Mac systems. Once a site is set up like this, customers can access it anytime from anywhere in the world (Figure 1.4).

To access the business site, customers must have their own Internet connection. For the average consumer, this is a dialup modem connection provided by a local Internet provider or an online service like America Online or CompuServe. Customers pay from $10 to $40 a month for an account they can

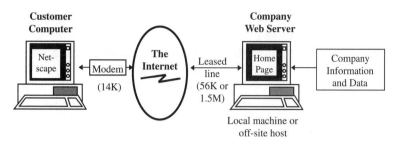

**Figure 1.4**    Typical Business WWW Connection.

use to dial in and connect to the Internet. Once the connection is made, the customer can use a Web browser, an e-mail program, a newsgroup reader, or other tools to get information from the Internet. Some users have Internet connections at work, which are made through a modem or dedicated lease line.

Thanks to the phenomenal growth figures, no one can argue that the World Wide Web hasn't been a complete success. There just hasn't been anything like it to come this far, this fast in a long time—if ever. Not television, radio, telephones, automobiles, or copying machines.

## Problems in Paradise

So what's wrong with this picture? How could we possibly find fault with the success of the World Wide Web? Well, several problems should be immediately obvious to anyone who uses the Web or provides content for others to use.

The first major problem is that, in a sense, web technology is currently wasted on the World Wide Web, the way Great Art and gourmet food is wasted on teenagers. A major problem is the connection speed or, as some people call it, the *bandwidth.* The Internet backbone itself—the main channel that links most components of the system—is very fast, passing data along at a rate of 45 megabits per second (45 Mbps). This is like transmitting the entire contents of Tolstoy's *War and Peace* in the single tick of a wrist watch. Most major commercial Web sites also have a relatively fast Internet connection, on the order of about 1.5 Mbps.

When the information reaches the customer's modem, however, it's like hitting a brick wall, as the bandwidth narrows considerably. Most users with new home computers have a modem speed of about 14.4 kilobytes per second (Kbps), which is about half a book page per second. Some are slower still, at 9600 or the old 2400 Kbps standard. Even if users want to plunk down extra cash for a fast modem, 28 to 36 Kbps is the maximum speed handled by a standard phone line. This makes it superfast for downloading pages of text, but deathly slow for anything else, including simple graphic illustrations. Faster speeds are available through other technologies, such as *integrated services digital network* (*ISDN*), but technical complexity and high costs put these beyond the reach of most consumers.

Business users who access the Internet at work benefit from the greater bandwidth of their corporate connections (T1 speed is common, or 1.5 Mbps), but may find their connection slow because it is shared by so many people. So the true speed of any WWW transaction is only as fast as the bandwidth at the customer end, which can be mighty slow indeed.

The data bottleneck at the customer end effectively reduces the Web's power to the lowest common denominator (Figure 1.5). Web site developers must constantly make sure they're not overloading their users with too much graphic information. Customer-conscious site developers check and recheck file sizes and find themselves working overtime to optimize graphics. At 14.4 K or even 28.8 K, servercentric applications like online databases work fine, but multimedia effects like real-time sound and video are impractical since they are so garbled or low-resolution as to be unusable.

A new class of startlingly powerful tools, like Sun Microsystem's Java development language, are stifled by the limitations of the present environment. If a site has the admirable trait of being graphic-intensive (pictures being, as we all know, worth a thousand words) it becomes insufferable when filtered through the standard computer modem.

Another problem with the WWW is the sheer unpredictability of what lies at the other end of the connection. Customers may be accessing a Web site using a wide variety of hardware and software, including Macs, PCs, and UNIX workstations of varying monitor resolutions. There are now dozens of different web browser packages on the market, each interpreting web pages slightly differently than the next one. Some customers may not even be using a graphical web browser at all—undoubtedly some of the old character-based browsers are still being used in places on the Internet.

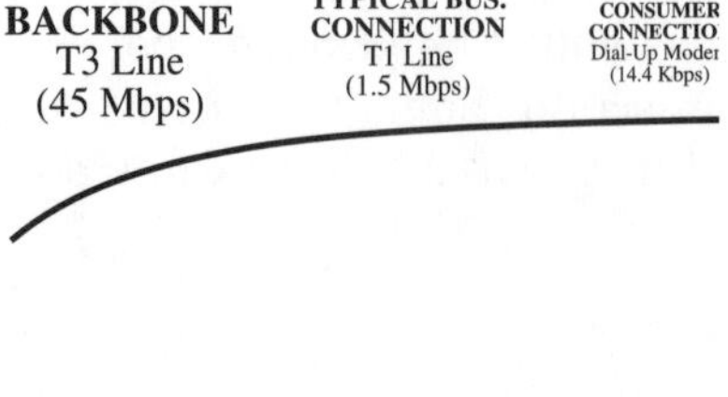

**INTERNET BACKBONE** T3 Line (45 Mbps)    **TYPICAL BUS. CONNECTION** T1 Line (1.5 Mbps)    CONSUMER CONNECTIO Dial-Up Modem (14.4 Kbps)

**Figure 1.5**  The Internet data bottleneck.

The final problem is that the entire business model represented by current WWW use is lopsided (Figure 1.6). The customer is supreme in the business pantheon, and current WWW models rightfully put the customer first. But what about the other people involved in making businesses successful—the employees, suppliers, and dealers who form the organizational food chain that keeps the business alive and kicking? If we can use web technology to smooth the information flow to customers, can't we do the same to benefit these other groups?

## The Hidden World of the Intranet

As it happens, the answer is "yes." One concept that often gets lost in all the Internet hoopla is the idea that many corporate LANs and WANs are already turning into miniature versions of the Internet, delivering home pages, data, services, online documents, and other vital information across departmental boundaries to headquarters, manufacturing sites, and field offices throughout the enterprise. This is happening because companies are finding ways to take

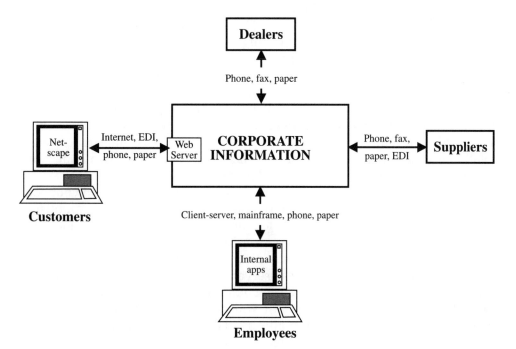

**Figure 1.6**  A lopsided business communications model.

advantage of Internet tools already built into their desktop computer systems. When it happens, we call the result an *Intranet* because the communications system exists solely *within* the organizational network, whereas the *Internet* is more of a communications system *between* networks. Both the Intranet and Internet, however, use many of the same tools and techniques.

The Intranet is so promising it is already heavily used by corporate giants like Nortel, Eli Lilly, Levi Strauss and National Semiconductor, as well as many other smaller, technically savvy organizations (Figure 1.7). You never see these sites on the World Wide Web, because they are entirely private and shut off from the rest of the world. These companies may *also* have Web sites on the Internet, but each company's internal web is a separate realm that exists behind the "firewall"—that is, behind the protective layer of security mechanisms that separate the company's internal LANs and WANs from the Internet.

An important concept to remember about Intranets is that *an Internet connection is not required.* Your company can have an internal web or Intranet without ever having an Internet connection or home page on the World Wide Web. All you need is a network and a set of desktop computers running the correct protocols and software that enable the Intranet to operate (as described in the next two chapters of this book). It's natural that some companies might want *nothing to do* with the Internet, given the horror stories about security, pornography, and the like. If so, fine: They can still use an Intranet for their own internal purposes, without exposing their private networks to the threats posed by full Internet connectivity.

Companies that have taken the plunge and created their own Intranets are finding new ways to cut through the communication snags that traditionally shackle their operations. Once grasped, the potential for this approach is truly amazing. Unlike other client-server applications, which require hands-on involvement by system administrators and programmers, an Intranet allows instant, random, and totally unfettered point-to-point communication between any two nodes on a network without login, setup, or special programming.

By installing a web server on a local computer, any department in your company can become an ad-hoc "information center" broadcasting published materials and data to the rest of the network on demand. The published information can then be accessed by any user in the network using web browsers like Netscape and Mosaic. For instance, much of the information now being delivered through expensive client-server applications like Lotus Notes, or through special media like CD-ROM, could be delivered easier and cheaper through an internal web system. All you need to get started is about $500 worth of software, a few commonly available software tools, and a clear understanding of how web technology works (Figure 1.8).

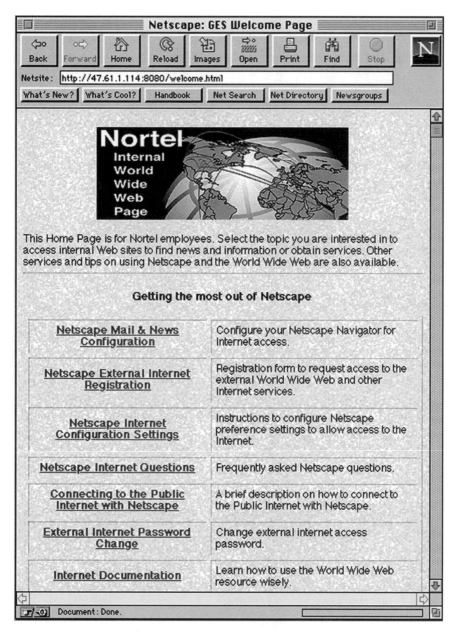

**Figure 1.7** Example of internal home page.

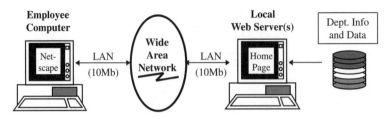

**Figure 1.8**  Typical internal web setup.

Even more powerfully, the Intranet promises to liberate many traditional mainframe and client-server applications by allowing easy access to data from any seat on the network. Instead of creating special programs to access your company's product database, for instance, you could quickly create a web front end that gives any user instant access at the click of a button. And you can do it on any platform: UNIX, PC, or Mac.

## Visionary Applications

Imagine then, an enterprise in which there is a human resources web server, a manufacturing web server, a legal department web server, an information systems (IS) web server—or even a web server for each team or employee who generates information of value to the corporation (some companies using this technology already have thousands of web servers installed throughout their organizations). Then imagine a creative webmaster weaving all these different blossoming resources into a central home page with menus and access mechanisms that allow any user to easily browse unimpeded through the company's vast pool of information. You start to get the picture of what a corporate Intranet is all about. Here are a few examples of potential applications:

- Mechanics in an aircraft hangar in Dallas view a drawing of a jet engine and click on any part of it to see detailed maintenance procedures for that part. The information they access is taken from the company's engineering web server in Seattle, where it is being updated daily with new information including information captured from troubleshooting reports.

- A new employee clicks into a set of pages including an online company orientation seminar, job-specific training, and a follow-up quiz with results automatically graded and forwarded to the employee's electronic file in human resources.

- The company support center is automated by giving users direct access to troubleshooting information. Instead of getting the information over the phone, they can retrieve it by searching the internal web.

- The company distributes an online survey to employees nationwide, gathers the results automatically, and stores them in a database for further analysis.

- The company IS department provides a web front end to many of its legacy databases, allowing users to search for information or access computer reports online.

- The company legal department provides position papers on important topics like sexual harassment in the workplace, drug testing, and so on.

- Recent addresses by company executives are made available online to all company employees in text, audio, or video format.

- Training videos and manuals are provided on demand through a web-based menu.

- The company sets up a special web server that dealers can access over the Internet. The server is set up to only accept requests specifically from authorized dealer locations, thus creating a *virtual private network* just for dealers.

This is not as blue-sky as it may sound. Many such applications are already being created using a variety of commercial software packages like Lotus Notes and MacroMedia Director. But notice that all the listed applications can be delivered to end users easier through a web system. Web technology, therefore, is the first low-cost, easy-to-use, cross-platform, open-standard-based, integrated set of tools that will allow users to access an entire menu of applications through a single interface and do so randomly and universally, on a user-initiated basis, across an entire network.

## The Other Shoe Dropping

In fact, the web-based Intranet could be considered "the other shoe dropping" in the Internet revolution. While all the media attention has been focused on the Internet and World Wide Web, many companies have been quietly applying this technology behind closed doors, finding ways to improve internal communications and cut costs in the bargain. The web revolution behind the firewall has not gotten a lot of attention because often it is a grassroots effort led by a few visionary information technology (IT) managers, or applied scattershot by technically savvy employees with a passion for innovation.

One of the reasons for the grassroots nature of this sea change is the fact that web technology is based on open standards and usually inexpensive tools that are not the proprietary product of a major hardware or software company. For this reason, the Intranet registered barely a blip on the radar of most corporate MIS departments during 1994–95, the first two years of the World Wide Web's most explosive growth. The reasons why this happened are easy to see. There was no sales force for the Intranet, like there were sales forces for Oracle databases, Microsoft Office products, or Lotus Notes (though many of these vendors have now leaped full-tilt onto the Intranet bandwagon). As this book went to press, there were not yet any computer journals devoted to Intranets (though many will likely emerge soon, and even mainstream computer journals are dedicating increasing editorial space to the subject). There were very few schools or seminar courses where you could send staff members for training. And there weren't any squads of consultants from Anderson, Deloitte, et al. swarming across the organization and urging upper management to pour millions of dollars into development of internal web systems, like they did for other proprietary client-server technologies.

So, unlike previous IT paradigms, web technology is not being promoted from the top down; it's growing from the bottom up. Most of the technologies involved in web development are not the kind of big-budget items that can make or break corporate MIS departments. They are often simple add-ons or extensions to existing products that make them capable of operating in a different way, like Microsoft's Internet Assistant, which lets Microsoft Word users save their documents in web-compatible format, or the NOV*IX network firmware products that make it easier to provide Internet-like services over Netware-based networks, or the new TCP/IP networking features built into Windows 95. Some components—including web servers themselves—are shareware that can be freely tested and evaluated at no cost to the corporation.

Since there were no major budget dollars or vendor profits at stake, web technologies at first rated barely a mention on the agenda of many corporate MIS departments. For that reason alone, web technologies didn't get the kind of respect that proprietary products did within the IT community. You get what you pay for, goes the common wisdom. And if these tools were so cheap and easy to acquire, some people felt they couldn't be worth a plugged nickel.

By early 1996, there was strong evidence this attitude was beginning to change. A *WebWeek* survey of 50 Fortune 500 companies found that even though just 16 percent of the surveyed companies had an Intranet, another 60 percent were either planning one or "considering it." In addition, companies like Microsoft began announcing massive restructuring of their organizations around the concept of the Intranet. And prestigious periodicals like *Business Week* were carrying cover stories on the Intranet. The attention paid to the Intranet was long in coming, but when it struck it was with gale force.

## Guilt by Association

Web technologies also suffered from a poor reputation in the MIS community, since they were mainly known for their association with the wild and woolly Internet. A typical reaction came during a presentation I once gave to upper management of a midsized sales and supply firm. After hearing a half-hour talk on the potential internal applications for this new technology, the company CEO had one pressing question. "Is it *really true* that *children* can actually see *pornography* on the Internet?" he asked, his voice shaking with outrage. The Internet burden looms so large that sometimes it's impossible for people to separate the raw technology from its most unflattering applications, in peoples' minds.

Until recently, the only way an Intranet could be built in a company was if someone took a keen interest in Internet technologies, had a gut feeling for the communications issues involved, had noticed the arrival on the market of these various tools, and then had a vision of how to put them all together in a way that could facilitate the transfer of data and information across the enterprise. All of these elements had to coalesce first in the mind of an individual or team, and then the people involved had to sell it to management in a way that management could understand.

This, it turns out, was the greatest hurdle for the Intranet: getting management to understand the concept and buy in. The successful implementation of an internal web requires a not-too-hard-to-perform, but occasionally difficult-to-understand paradigm shift in the way information flows across an organizational structure. And it often requires the vanguard team to be empowered in a way that cuts across feudal-era departmental structures. But more about this later.

Despite the grassroots nature of the internal webolution, the building of internal web in corporate networks is apparently proceeding at a rapid pace. In fact, most traditional Internet-related companies like Netscape Communications and Process Software report that well over half their product sales are made within the corporate arena. If these statistics are true, it indicates that *more computing power is being devoted now to internal webs than to the World Wide Web itself.* And yet these kinds of news items—when they appear at all—still rate second billing behind the ever-popular Internet.

## Why the Web Works Better in Private

When you think about it, you realize that private networks are a far better place to use web technology than the World Wide Web itself. Unlike the Internet, where you quickly run up against the brick wall of 14.4 K modems, corporate LANs have a bandwidth 300 to 700 times greater, on average, than the typical consumer modem (10 Mbps for the typical Ethernet LAN, versus 14.4 Kbps for the average consumer modem). That means not only that text and graphics can move faster through the pipeline, but that it is suddenly much more practical to serve up exotic content types like sound, video, Java applets, and Adobe Acrobat files.

Of course, network bandwidth is always at a premium, even on private networks. There may be a concern from management that web traffic—and especially multimedia traffic—might unduly burden an already overtaxed infrastructure. But this is a case where costs and benefits must be carefully scrutinized and weighed fairly against each other. If management hasn't realized it yet, they will soon be aware that in the future the network will increasingly be the lifeblood of business and it will have to evolve rapidly to support the advanced modes of communication the information superhighway will deliver.

For instance, even if you don't see video being transmitted across your corporate network now, it undoubtedly *will be* in the not-too-distant future as networks undergo natural growth cycles and advanced new technologies like desktop videoconferencing increasingly make a dent. Within a few years, you should be able to make conference calls on your computer and see all the participants talking in separate windows on your screen.

To accommodate these new technologies, networks will have to be rescaled accordingly and grow with the traffic, just as desktop systems have advanced from the dumb terminals and 640 K RAM computers of the early 1980s to the power workstations we have today. Any technology that helps shift us from a paper-based model into an online model should be given all the support it needs, because the potential for cost savings are astounding (as shown by the examples later in this chapter). Admittedly, bandwidth over 10 Mbps is prohibitively expensive right now, but prices will certainly come down. Many companies are evaluating and installing Fast Ethernet and Asynchronous

Transfer Mode (ATM) network technologies that will bump bandwidth up to 100 Mbps and higher. So, if your company has to invest to upgrade its network, it may find that the savings and productivity gains of the Intranet will make it worth the cost and effort.

Surprisingly, unlike other new technologies to recently hit the market, web applications may actually *reduce* the drain on network resources because web documents are up to 10 times smaller than their current desktop publishing counterparts. Remember that web technology was originally optimized for transport over much less bandwidth-intensive public networks. So the typical web document is stored in a plain text (ASCII) format without all the spare baggage of traditional binary file formats like Microsoft Word and FrameMaker. Web-compatible graphics likewise also are stored in the highly-compressed GIF and JPEG formats, which are 10 to 100 times more compact than their BMP, PCX, XWD, TIFF, or EPS cousins. As an additional benefit, installing an Intranet significantly reduces the number of redundant copies of information across a network. With web server technology, only one copy of the information is needed for distribution company-wide.

Unfortunately, some corporate networks are not much more homogenous than the Internet itself, supporting an unwieldy mix of PCs, Macs, and UNIX workstations. But on internal networks, you have a much better shot at creating an integrated system by developing specifications, standards, and preconfigured installations. You can create templates and style sheets for web authoring, develop a coherent structure for managing the information flow, and automate much of the process of gathering, converting, and distributing information content.

For example, you could conceivably specify that everyone on the Intranet use a certain version of a certain type of browser, like Netscape Navigator. If they don't, you could easily supply them with it. The installation disk (or network installation utility) could also include other advanced components needed, such as an Adobe Acrobat Amber, RealAudio player, or media.splash. Once everyone is on the web, you could easily broadcast announcements when system requirements change and provide users with new software components they can download directly through the web browser.

There's no doubt that security is much easier to deal with on an Intranet than on the Internet. Of course, sabotage can be done easier from within than from without, but it is less likely to happen in a controlled environment. Most internal web systems I've seen are open to all comers, with little concern for hiding or protecting any of the data that is served. That in itself is a powerful indicator of the conceptual paradigm shifts that web technology can bring to an enterprise, opening up the system and exposing to light all the dark, secret corners of the organization. "We're opening up silos," is how one company puts it—and that's exactly how it is. At last, an internal web can be used to exhume all those old disk drives and filing cabinets and expose long-hidden information to the light of day. Although there are proprietary data sources that must be protected within a corporation, such as customer records and employee files, it is also quite easy to design a web system where database integrity is fully protected.

## Toward a More Well-Rounded Business Model

Putting Intranet applications at the forefront—and recognizing their value—is the first step your company can take toward developing a more well-rounded business model. As mentioned earlier, current web business models focus on the World Wide Web and customer-centered applications, which is great, because customers really *should* be the central focus of any business model. But the model is a bit lopsided when you consider all the other ways web technology can be used within the enterprise.

When you look at the whole picture, then consider the Internet as just a *component* of the overall web system, you have a better stab at restoring balance to the business model, as shown in Figure 1.9. The complete model takes into account not only the customer but all the other players who can benefit from better communication with the core of an enterprise, including employees, dealers, and suppliers.

As this model shows, instead of having a single server devoted to customer-oriented marketing applications, the organization might have a group of low-level servers created by different departments of the company to open their channels of information to the rest of the enterprise. At some higher level within the web management structure, the system would be configured so that data from the various servers could be funneled off through different channels to the appropriate constituent groups that have a stake in the organization.

For instance, most Human Resource data would go only to employees—except job listings, which might be publicized both internally over the LANs and externally over the Internet. Marketing data might be mainly targeted to dealers and customers, but also could be used by employees internally for reference. IS legacy data and transaction processing systems could be brought into the loop to provide automated information on current business operations to anyone who needs it—with appropriate safeguards to keep parts of it out of the hands of unauthorized users. And external Internet access could be

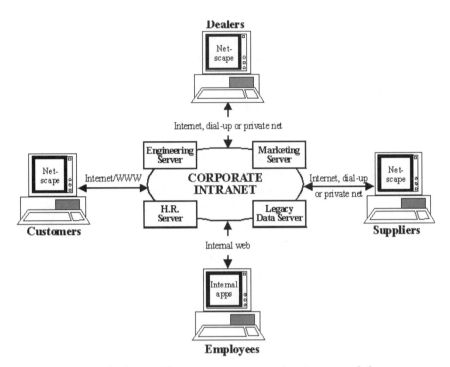

**Figure 1.9**    A balanced business communications model.

provided to employees for use in researching business topics or competitor information.

## An Example: How Web Technology Saves Publishing Costs

Companies that use web technology to distribute documents may experience momentous gains in productivity and incredible cost savings. Like the reengineering craze that has marked the other half of the client-server revolution, converting many paper-based systems to web systems can save both labor and overhead costs within an organization.

Take the simple example of distributing a company policy and procedures manual to employees. Some companies distribute tons of them: enough to fill an entire wall of shelves. Typically, the author creates the manual using a program like Microsoft Word, saves it to disk, then prints a master copy on a laser printer.

That is just the beginning of a labyrinthine process that would make Rube Goldberg blush. The master copy is sent to the local repro center or an outside company for printing, where hundreds of copies are made. After the document goes through the printing process, it still may need special collating, binding, or handling. Often it is shrinkwrapped, stuffed into a three-ring binder, and boxed for delivery. Once that happens, a forklift advances, scoops up the pallet and loads the boxes onto a truck, where they are whisked off to the mail center to be prepared for delivery (Figure 1.10).

At the mail center, someone must prepare an address label for each box and stick it on before it can be delivered. The boxes are sorted by delivery zone, and then loaded onto another forklift and truck for delivery through the company's internal mail system, the national postal system, or a private carrier like UPS. The end result is that the individual manuals are *hand-carried*—across the building, across town, across the nation, or around the world—to the individual employees who need them.

When the document reaches its destination, what happens then? It goes straight up on the shelf, where it may or may not be consulted for days, weeks, or months. Since your company doesn't ever stand still or quit improving its operations, procedures keep changing and soon the manual is out-of-date. Going through an update cycle starts the whole process over again—still with no guarantee the information is being used.

Meanwhile, look at all the effort and cost—all the paper used and time spent by the mail room and repro center, not to mention your own time and effort—on the chance that the user *might* need (or want to read) the manual or the updates.

If you've passed the recycling bin on your floor lately, you've seen the results of many such efforts. In some companies, the recycling bins are getting to be the size of small Volkswagens. This is great, because it finally brings the problem out in the open and makes totally visible and obvious to everyone the absurd amounts of paper we are wasting *on the contingency* that someone might have the time or interest to read what we have to say.

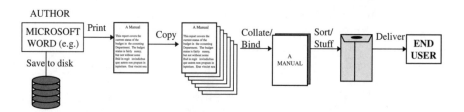

**Figure 1.10**    Traditional document distribution example.

## The Alternative: Instant Document Delivery

Of course, many forward-looking companies have already discovered the benefits of electronic distribution using advanced media and tools like CD-ROM, WinHelp, Adobe Acrobat, and others. But the Intranet offers a new dimension to the online equation, going beyond traditional electronic publishing to integrate documents, multimedia, data, and applications into a dynamic cross-platform environment that bridges the gap between the world of PCs, Macs, and UNIX machines.

With an Intranet (to continue the previous example), the author can still create the document using Microsoft Word or any other desktop publishing tool. But as soon as the document gets saved to disk, *it's immediately accessible to anyone in the company.* Joe Schmoe down in engineering can pull it up on his screen and read it anytime he wants to. Jill Schmill in cost subaccounting can read it when she has the time, or when she has a special question. If Joe prefers to read it on a printed page, he can print it on the spot. And if Jill finds the information useful and wants to add an excerpt to one of her memos, she can save a copy to disk or cut-and-paste at will.

The only difference is that when the author saves the final document, it's saved in a web-compatible format using the Save As feature in Microsoft Word (Figure 1.11). And instead of saving the document just anywhere on disk, it's saved in a directory managed by a *web server*—a background process that allows anyone to access the file over the network using a *web client* (also called a *browser*) like Mosaic or Netscape Navigator. The server is just a piece of software that handles the job of serving documents across the network. It could be easily installed on a special dedicated machine, or even on the author's local hard drive.

Individual users do not have to be set up or configured to "see" the web server as a local drive mounted on their computer, because the web browser can automatically find the information no matter where it's located on the net-

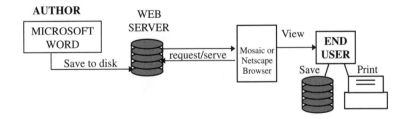

**Figure 1.11** Web document distribution.

work. So you can hire a new employee in the Seattle office and no one has to remember to make sure to connect him or her to every web server in the company (no more than Internet users need to be configured to see each of the thousands of web servers on the World Wide Web). The employee just starts the browser, selects the manual from a menu, and there it is.

Meanwhile, the author can update the manual anytime, and as soon as changes are made and saved to disk they are immediately visible to anyone reading the document *at that moment.* You don't have to worry about whether Joe or Jill bothered to snap their changes into their three-ring binders, because they don't have three-ring binders anymore. The information exists online and no longer needs to be printed. So basically, you can achieve the same goal as before—getting information from the author to the end user—but without using all that paper, ink, and mailroom time or without worrying whether users have local server access.

But look what also happens when you start "serving" documents, instead of printing and mailing them. Suddenly you've gone from an information delivery model based on chance to one based on demand. (You might also say that you've gone from a model based on "supplier push" to one based on "customer pull.") Instead of supplying information to people *just in case* they need it, you're making the information available *when they actually need it,* which could be immediately (i.e., as soon as you save it to disk), next week, or maybe never.

If you take this simple example and multiply it times all the manuals, reports, and newsletters your company produces, imagine the tremendous savings in cost, time, and previously wasted resources. Some companies produce literally tons of technical manuals, procedures, specifications, work instructions, and training materials that end up doing little more than taking up space on people's shelves. Imagine sweeping all those shelves clean and making the information available to people online—*whenever* they need it. We are not talking just the cost of a few reams of paper. We are talking major savings in time, money, and frustration.

The question then becomes: If we can publish information universally over a corporate network, what further use do we have for the fax, the three-ring binder, or the copy machine? If we can publish material cross-platform, what use do we have for machine-specific tools like WinHelp? If we can update online and provide all users with network connections, why limit ourselves to a static version on a CD-ROM? If we can serve compact HTML and other file types through the same browser, why limit ourselves to Acrobat's proprietary file format? If we can serve data and online forms, why use Lotus Notes?

Although there are valid and specific reasons for using any or all of these other tools, the fact is that the Intranet now gives us a single technology that can replace all of them with a single, more powerful solution. Of course, there are things WinHelp and Acrobat can do that the typical web browser cannot, and of course there are things Lotus Notes can do that the typical web server cannot. But overall, the Intranet—and specifically the web technology that supports it—is something bigger than any of these other limited solutions. It is a universal information delivery environment that will ultimately devour or co-opt them all.

## Another Example: The Living Catalog

One of my oldest and best clients is a nationwide U.S. distributor of laboratory supplies. Until recently, they spent several million dollars every few years to print a 400-page full-color catalog of all the products they sell. The catalog was typed into a publishing program called PageMaker, which was used to create a master layout for the book. The typeset pages went to a printing company, where each picture was put through a color separation process, inserted manually into the layout and burned onto multiple plates. Once the plates were finished, the book went through a process where it was printed, cut, collated, bound, shrinkwrapped, stuffed into boxes, and loaded onto trucks headed for the company's activity centers nationwide. From there, stacks of the catalogs were loaded into the trunks of company salesmen, who went out on the road and hand-delivered them to individual customer sites.

The interesting part of this scenario was that *these incredibly expensive catalogs were already out of date the minute they went to press.* Product prices could change weekly or monthly, and items were continually being added to or dropped from the company's available inventory. By the time the book reached the customer, it was grossly inaccurate. And yet it sat on the shelf for another two years, serving as the customer's main reference to the company's products and prices until the next catalog could be compiled and printed. Not surprisingly, a large amount of the company's telephone-based customer support effort went into answering questions about product availability and pricing. So, in addition to the millions of dollars spent on catalog printing, you could add the millions of dollars spent on telephones and customer service operations as the total financial penalty for using this incredibly inefficient system.

The system was ripe for change, and specifically change in the direction of web delivery. Imagine customers being able to view the entire catalog online and see updates as they happened. Imagine them being able to see full-color pictures of products at the click of a button, read supporting technical literature in full detail, connect to automated demos, and even order products online with a point and a click.

A catalog delivered this way would be even easier to use than the original. Customers would start with an icon on their screen that they could double-click to start Netscape. The Netscape software would open directly at the catalog table of contents, or at a home page where the catalog was prominently featured. Once the catalog appeared, users could enter a catalog number or product description and immediately see a list of matching products and prices updated daily on the company's computers. At that point, they could print or save the information locally, or follow the ordering process to send an order back to the company directly through their web browser! (See Figure 1.12.)

On the company's end of things, the entire information delivery process would be re-engineered to make it easier and more manageable. Instead of locking catalog data into PageMaker files, which can only be used by layout artists, the same data would be collected in a database that could be continually edited and maintained online by the company's product managers. The database would be stored on a computer alongside the web server software, so that information could be transferred directly from the database to the web server, and from there across the network to the user's web browser.

As the information leaves the database and proceeds to the customer, each field could be wrapped in codes that cause the entire page to display in an appropriate format inside the customer's web browser. In effect, the customer would be looking at a fully formatted "catalog page" that had been assembled and published on-the-fly from the company's product data repository.

Not only could the company save millions of dollars on catalog printing and delivery costs, it could also scale back its customer support burden, cut back significantly on sales calls, avoid the wasted effort dealing with orders for nonexistent inventory, and keep happier customers in the bargain. The main problem, of course, would be how to connect all those customers to the company's catalog web server. But with the millions saved, they could easily *buy each customer an individual Internet account* or set up local points-of-presence in each city where customers could connect to the company's private network.

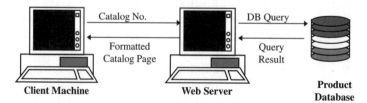

Catalog No.

Formatted
Catalog Page

DB Query

Query
Result

**Client Machine**          **Web Server**          **Product Database**

**Figure 1.12**   Catalog page retrieval process.

## Lessons Learned from the Internet

As you can see from these examples, there are many ways to apply web technology to business problems, and you will learn about more of them as you progress through this book. It should be obvious by now that Internet/Intranet technologies will have a major impact on the way we use corporate networks. The results of this transformation will be interesting, because modern corporations can learn a lot from the Internet and its culture. What the Internet can teach private business, among other things, is:

- How to integrate diverse types of information online in a multimedia environment
- How to finally achieve the much-heralded but yet-to-be-seen "paperless office"
- How to conduct sales and business transactions automatically, without human intervention
- How to design and implement systems that encourage collective action
- How to create collaborative structures that transcend corporate or governmental boundaries
- How to leverage proprietary business knowledge and consulting expertise for external use, business promotion, and financial gain

Models for all these applications already exist in embryonic form on the Internet and in various sectors of the business world. This book shows you how we can bring these to the forefront and provide new paradigms for business reengineering well into the twenty-first century.

## Where Do We Go from Here?

If all this sounds interesting, and you want to start creating web applications on your local network, it's really best that you understand how web technology works and how it fits into the current thinking on client-server applications. Chapter 2 starts at the beginning and gives you a technological grand tour that will bring you up to speed on web technology from a corporate networking point of view.

## Chapter Two at a Glance

Most people have a hard time understanding the true value of web technology because they don't understand all its components. Some understand the publishing part, others the network and programming part, still others the communication and information management part. But few understand the whole picture. This chapter reviews the trends in management and information technologies that have transformed business over the past two decades, and shows how web technology fits in. In particular, you will learn:

- How the PC revolution brought computing to the desktop
- How the business management revolution helped foster teamwork and information sharing
- How the desktop publishing revolution made it possible for the average person to become a sophisticated publisher
- How the online publishing revolution made it possible to share published documents in electronic form
- How the networking revolution made it possible to share printers, disk drives, and the files contained on them
- How the client-server revolution made it possible to share data and applications across a network
- How the Internet revolution helped expand the coverage of information systems while reducing the administrative burden
- How the web revolution combines all these trends into a single phenomenon and a single solution
- How the standards of HTTP and HTML made web systems possible
- Why web browsers can be used as universal playback devices for any file type and as universal clients for any client-server application
- How web systems invert the traditional client-server models, open up network access, and reduce network administration
- How new improvements in web server technology will significantly expand the capabilities of future web systems

By learning all these different aspects of information technology, you will be in a better position to evaluate and use web systems as a possible solution to various common business problems.

# A New Kind of Information System

The dawn of the Information Age happened a long time ago, by today's hyperactive standards. And it's only nanoseconds since the World Wide Web was invented. But already, it's High Noon on the Infobahn and things are getting hotter by the minute, with new technologies coming down the pike at an alarming rate of speed. With so much to learn and so much to evaluate, how do you sort the valuable technologies from all the drivel?

The question is especially crucial in light of phenomena like the Internet and World Wide Web, which are clearly unlike anything we've ever seen before. The problem is not just "How does it work?" but "How can you use it to do anything productive *at all?*"

Things have been this way for a long time, it seems. Surely you recall the story about Alexander Graham Bell and his rival Elisha Gray, who both invented the telephone (independently) at about the same time in the latter half of the nineteenth century. The reason we remember Bell—but not Gray—is because he correctly predicted that people would use telephones to talk, while Gray figured he had just invented a better version of the telegraph. For that error, Gray sank into the mire of history, while Bell went on to stardom. Yet even Bell, with all his vision, could not have imagined the incredible phone networks of the late twentieth century, with integrated fax, cellular, videoconferencing, voice, and paging services.

Web technology is a lot like that. When it first started out, it was intended—and most people perceived it—primarily as a way to transmit information across the Internet. But others saw that you could use it on internal networks, too. Many see it as a way to serve "home pages" with documents, text, and graphics. Others see it as a front end for multimedia, data warehouses, and more. Like the argument between Bell and Gray, it's an incredible telegraph, but it's one heck of a telephone, too. You can use it on the Internet or on the Intranet.

Anyone who has worked with this technology for a while knows that it is incredibly deep, and we have just begun to imagine all the ways we may eventually use it. Just as the old crank telephone was the precursor to the modern fax, PBX, and pager, so the webs of today are just rough kludges of tomorrow's cutting-edge information technologies.

Despite all its depth, web technology is not that complex. In fact, the reason for its power and popularity is that it can make things incredibly *simple.* This is the one technology that finally brings it all together and gives anybody a way to serve *any kind of information to anyone.* In a way, web systems help make possible the grand unification of all forms of information, helping us blend documents, data, sound, pictures, movies, messages and computer applications in ways we never imagined before.

Web is also the only technology to come along so far that simplifies the user's task down to the single click of a mouse. You see something, you like it, you click on it. It's like a romp in the candy store. Designers have been working for years to make user interface this simple and friendly, to the point that some Macintoshes actually grin as they start up. But you can't get much simpler than a *single mouse click.* This, in many ways, represents the end of the road in software design—the Holy Grail of information technology.

In fact, web technology may change the entire face of systems development, particularly in the area of user interface design. Web systems will make it possible for people who know nothing about programming to control the way information is presented to the user—a chore they previously had to farm out to programmers who barely understood the specifics of the application or the requirements of the end user.

To help you understand how we got to this point, and how web technology will take us beyond, let's take a tour of recent trends in business information technology. As you will see, web technology neatly ties together the loose ends of many trends and developments of the last two decades, and points the way to a very interesting future ahead. Even if you already understand a lot about the World Wide Web and Hypertext Markup Language (HTML), you will find the view completely different when you look at it from the point-of-view of the corporate Intranet.

## Revolutions of the 1980s

If you've watched the rollercoaster ride of business over the past two decades, you can be excused for feeling a bit queasy. During that time, the modern corporation was wracked by a series of earth-shaking tremors that nearly tore it apart—yet paradoxically left it more sound and viable than ever before. In particular, several trends that began in the late 1970s and early 1980s caused major aftershocks that are still being felt well into the 1990s.

The first major trend was the personal computer revolution. Until the PC came along, the computing world was dominated by the large room-sized computers called *mainframes* and a smaller class of refrigerator-sized machines called *minis.* These are the systems that inhabit everyone's nightmares and that, along with the early PC's disk operating system (DOS), are responsible even today for the phobias that lead people to reject computers out-of-hand.

The problem with mainframes and minis is that they were just this side of inscrutable. Anyone who held a job in the 1970s and early 1980s can remember the phosphorescent green glow of the early CRTs,[1] which often displayed nothing but mind-deadening rows of numbers. (If you go a bit further back, like me, you may even remember when data went in as a deck of cards and came out on a sheet of paper a yard wide.)

The CRT was the centerpiece of a unit called the *dumb terminal,* which in those days was the only way you could communicate with the mainframe (Figure 2.1). These terminals were called *dumb* because they had no brains. All the brain power, memory, and data storage was handled by the mainframe—the terminal just gave operators a way to type in the data and view it on the screen.

---

[1] Cathode ray tubes, just one more bit of evidence proving these were the tools of an alien conspiracy.

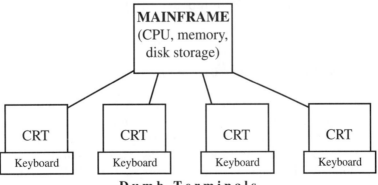

**Dumb Terminals**

**Figure 2.1**    Mainframe systems in the era before PCs.

The early dumb terminals were a vast improvement over the days when you had to carry data around in a box and shuffle it like a deck of cards. But the information they provided wasn't a whole lot easier to understand. In those days, computer manuals looked like they had been written by sea otters, and online help was a joke (if you had any at all, it looked like this: PF1=ENTER, PF2=DELETE, PF3=GIVE UP).

When the first personal computers or *PCs* hit the desktop circa 1981, they were hailed as a force that would revolutionize business by putting incredible brain power on every user's desk. The PC was revolutionary because it united the useful elements of the big computers (processor, memory, disk storage) with the useful elements of the dumb terminal (keyboard, screen) and put it all into a single package that would fit on anyone's desktop.

The problem with early PCs was that they had minuscule computing power compared with their larger counterparts, and barely enough power to do anything useful at all. In fact, early PCs had only a few thousandths of the memory and disk space found on the average machine sold at computer stores today. It wasn't until the development of powerful networked workstations using mouse and windows that desktop computers finally started living up to their original promise and the PC revolution finally reached its peak.

Companies also used the early desktop computers in clunky and unimaginative ways. For instance, they used them to simply replace older technologies like typewriters with newer technologies like the word processing program, with barely a thought given to whether they actually made people more productive. They did other things that were even dumber (in the sense that we now know better), like using PCs as dumb terminals for mainframes. With special software called 3270 terminal emulation, it was possible to create a mainframe display on a PC screen, and use the PC keyboard just like the keyboard on a dumb terminal. It wasn't until networks and new types of software came along that we would find better and more productive ways to use the PC.

## The Search for Management Formulas

The second major trend of the 1980s, running concurrently with the PC revolution, was what we might call the *business management revolution.* Starting in the mid-1970s and accelerating in the 1980s, corporate managers began taking a hard look at the way they did things, and questioning the standard business models of the past. Various schools of thought arose and vied for prominence on the corporate podium.

In the late 1970s and early 1980s, the predominant business religion was management by the *bottom line.* Like everything else, it made sense at the time. In this line of thinking, companies were divided into cost centers, and each department or cost center was judged by its total contribution to the bottom line (that is, to the company's overall profitability).

But this mode of thinking was soon challenged by developments in the international marketplace. In the mid-1980s, Japan was the undisputed leader in marketing its goods to the rest of the globe. Japanese autos and electronics flooded showrooms worldwide and put some U.S. and European manufacturers out of business. By the late 1980s, with a major recession brewing, Western business started fighting back by giving Japan a dose of its own medicine. The magic ingredient was called *quality,* and it was the quality movement that first introduced the now-popular trend toward flattening management structures and empowering employees.

The quality movement didn't exactly save business from all its follies, and many might argue that it failed to achieve many of its lofty goals. But what it did accomplish was to help companies break with tradition, reexamine how they do business, and focus on improving discrete processes. More specifically, it helped companies understand how important it is to empower employees and improve the lines of communication between departments, and between the organization and its customers, suppliers, and dealers.

Remnants of the quality movement can still be seen in the current emphasis on interdisciplinary *teamwork* and *collaboration.* Not surprisingly, desktop computers fed these trends, networks catapulted them, and web technologies will launch them into the stratosphere.

## The Growth of Desktop Publishing

With all this going on in the background, yet another revolution was taking place: this one in the publishing arena. When I started my first job in the data processing department of the local power company in 1972, we used IBM Selectric typewriters, Rapidograph pens, scissors, glue, and Scotch tape to deliver information to the end user. The copying machine had just been invented, but already was a major part of our effort. Back then, "cut and paste" really meant "cut and paste" and the final draft of a document might well look like one of the stabbing victims at the county morgue.

Over the years, our publishing tools changed rapidly and relentlessly with the development of new technologies. The IBM Selectric gave way to the IBM Mag Card, and the Mag Card gave way to dedicated word processors like the

IBM DisplayWriter, the Wang, and the Lexitron. Then the PC was invented and $25,000 dedicated word processors died a quick death at the hands of $250 software like WordStar, WordPerfect, and Microsoft Word.

In the 1980s, PostScript was invented, and along with it laser printers and window-based desktop publishing systems like PageMaker, Ventura Publisher, Interleaf, FrameMaker, and Quark. Instead of using pens, scissors, and paste to draw and insert illustrations, you could now draw them on the screen using a mouse and drag them around to any position you wanted in the text.

The new publishing systems brought the ancient art of typesetting directly to the desktop. As recently as 1969, about the time the Internet was being invented, typesetting was still done using something called *hot type.* If you wanted special fonts you had to arrange the letters by hand, set them in a mold, and then pour on a nice steaming batch of hot molten lead.

In the mid-1970s, if you wanted to change fonts in midsentence, you had to open up the back of your typesetting machine, change a few gears and pulleys, wrap a different photostrip around the drum, close the machine, go back to the keyboard, type a few words, then repeat the process all over again. By 1980, we had found ways to automate this process, by putting font change codes and formatting codes into text like this:

```
[Single Space][Helvetica,14,bold]
A Short Report on the Current State of Publishing[Return]
[Times Roman,10,bold]by Haiku Kirby[Return]
[Extra Leading 12 pt][Times Roman,10,regular]
Does this look confusing to you? It does to me, too! There
simply [italic on]must[italic off] be a better and easier
way to publish our documents.[Return]
```

Some popular word processors of the mid-1980s, like WordPerfect, let you choose whether to hide or reveal the codes. But the result was still rather unenlightening, since you often had to guess how the final result might look on the printed page. There was a "preview mode" where you could see an approximation of the printed page on the screen, but you couldn't edit the text in preview mode. So formatting a document often involved a lot of switching back and forth between preview mode and editing mode.

One of the greatest advances in authoring technology was the development of WYSIWYG, which means "What You See Is What You Get." Instead of seeing a mess of codes like the example above, or a monospaced approximation of the final printed result, you could see the document displayed on the screen exactly as it might finally look on the printed page. This seems like a no-brainer now, but amazingly there are still a few holdouts using the old character-based WordPerfect 5.1.

The advent of WYSIWYG was helped by the development of PostScript and software font packages like TrueType and Adobe Type Manager. These made it finally possible to do typesetting right on the screen. Instead of pouring on hot lead, or projecting celluloid alphabetic images onto photosensitive paper, each alphabetic character could be molded individually and instantaneously out of the glowing phosphorescent pixels on a computer screen.

## The Birth of Hypertext and Online Publishing

Once WYSIWYG was invented, this brought up an interesting new question. If you could make text look the same way on the computer screen as it does on the printed page, why use the printed page at all? Why not just publish it online and let people read it there? If they wanted to read it in printed format, they could still print it from the screen image. But if not, why bother?

Online publishing had other advantages, like the ability to use a nifty new feature called *hypertext.* First proposed by Ted Nelson at Xerox PARC in 1965, hypertext was appropriately named because it is a good way of dealing with hyperactive readers. You can read it in a linear fashion like a book, or you can "jump around" reading it in bits and pieces like a puzzle. Key concepts can be highlighted in a such a way that when you click on the highlighted concept, it automatically jumps to a different document (or page) where the concept is discussed in greater detail (Figure 2.2).

Hypertext is great for tables of contents and indexes, because you can browse through them, click on the topic you want to read, and *voila!* you're at the correct page. It's great for cross-references, too, because you don't have to turn to page 42 anymore. You just click on the hyperlinked cross-reference and suddenly *you are at* page 42, the same way Mr. Spock used to step inside

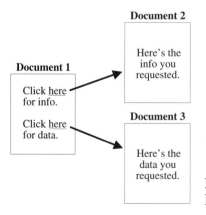

**Figure 2.2** Online document with hypertext links to other documents.

the flux capacitor and suddenly appear on the surface of the alien planet Remulak. (Okay, so I got *Star Trek, Back to the Future,* and *Saturday Night Live* a little mixed up—you get the idea.)

Hypertext started appearing on desktop computers with the creation of window systems like the Macintosh and Microsoft Windows for the PC. Macs had a feature called *HyperCard* and PCs running Windows had a built-in feature called *WinHelp.* The latter was simply a viewing utility that let you display any appropriately formatted file directly on the screen. Though it was first used to provide online help for PC-based programs, many people now use it to produce online newsletters, reports, manuals, and many other types of documents.

The nice thing about these tools was that they were bundled with the operating system, so they required no other special hardware or software. For example, if everyone in your company is running Windows 3.1, you can distribute a WinHelp file (.HLP) and they can open it and read it—even without having a speck of any other kind of software on their computer. In a way, a WinHelp file is like a self-displaying document, since it contains not only the document content, but all the buttons and pull-down menus you need to browse through it (Figure 2.3).

The problems with WinHelp were several. First, formatting a document for display is an incredible chore, and even involves a final step where you have

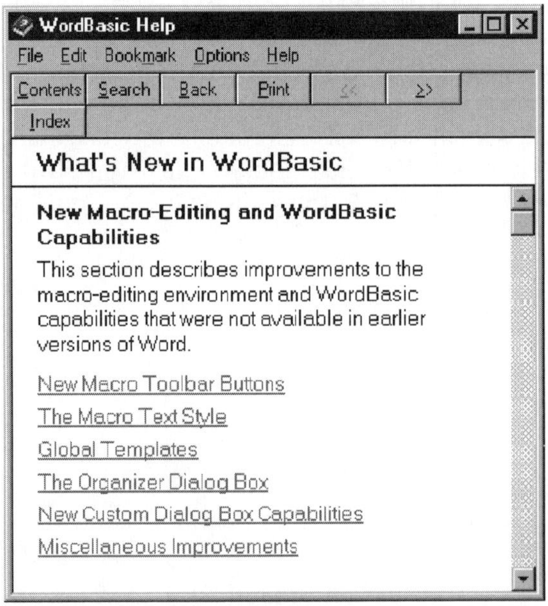

**Figure 2.3** Typical WinHelp page.

to run everything through a compiler, just like software developers do to their programming code. To solve these problems, third-party vendors created online publishing tools like Doc-To-Help and RoboHelp, which worked inside of Microsoft Word to automate these tasks. You could create a document in Microsoft Word, select an option that says "Make Into Help" and then, after about half an hour of moaning and groaning, your computer would spit out a finished online help file that you could pass around like candy. This was an indisputable improvement, but it's still quite a pain for the author who has to create the help files.

The other problem with WinHelp, of course, is that it only works under Microsoft Windows. If everyone has a PC, that's great. But what about companies where some people use a Macintosh and others use UNIX workstations? Both WinHelp and HyperCard suffered from a lack of what we call *cross-platform connectivity.* Systems running UNIX didn't even have a built-in online help feature (unless you count the incredibly rudimentary *manpage* utility).

## The Move to Cross-Platform Technologies

The market always has an answer to every problem, of course, and it wasn't long before some companies started taking the cross-platform issues into account. During its heyday, Frame Technology Corporation (now a part of Adobe Systems) was one of the leaders in cross-platform connectivity for both desktop and online publishing. With Frame, you could create a desktop-published document on a UNIX workstation, copy the file to a floppy diskette, and then—incredibly—pop it into a PC or Mac and view or edit it with no (apparent) conversion involved. What's more, you could create hypertext links and push buttons directly on the text page. Just underline a word or phrase (or draw an invisible box over a graphic), insert a hidden marker telling where the link should jump, and *voila:* hypertext.

FrameMaker also eliminated the dreaded "compile" step. With a few key-strokes you could lock down the document, hide the regular FrameMaker menus, and create a neat little self-contained online document window. So, with Frame, the desktop publishing file and the online publishing file often were one and the same (Figure 2.4).

Nothing is perfect, of course, and Frame was no exception. Though it beats WinHelp in the cross-platform category, it loses on ease-of-distribution. If you wanted to distribute your files to a wide audience, you had to buy each user a special tool called FrameViewer, which can be used to open, view, and print the online hypertext file—but not edit it. Still, this is better than nothing, as many online authors will readily admit. If all you have to deal with are strictly

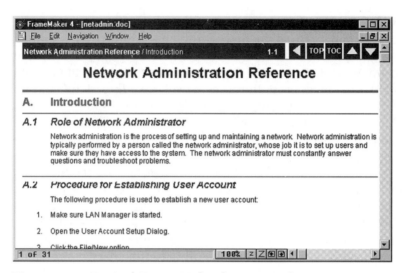

**Figure 2.4**   Typical FrameMaker hypertext document.

Macs or strictly PCs, no problem. But in a UNIX or cross-platform environment, there were few alternatives to proprietary products like FrameViewer and Interleaf's World View.

## The Viewer/Author Split

Though these products created an extra expense, and added another layer of software to the configuration burden, it was a profoundly interesting development. With the advent of inexpensive tools like FrameViewer, software designers were starting to realize the need for a separation between two distinctly different functions: *authoring documents* and *viewing them online* (Figure 2.5).

In the case of Frame Technology, for instance, they offered two distinctly separate products: FrameMaker as their main *authoring tool,* and Frame-Viewer as their *online viewing tool*—also known as a *browser.* Though you might pay $500 to $1,000 for a copy of FrameMaker with all its bells, whistles, and advanced editing features, you might only pay $30 for a copy of Frame-Viewer, which would let you directly view the finished document online but not edit it.

Other desktop publishing products followed this model, in some cases offering a browser for free. In early 1995, for instance, Microsoft Corporation made

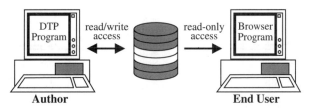

**Figure 2.5**   The dichotomy between authoring and online viewing.

available a free document browser called the Microsoft Word Viewer. This tool lets you open, view, and print (but not edit) Microsoft Word documents—even if you don't have a copy of MS Word on your machine. Theoretically, authors equipped with MS Word are no longer limited to the WinHelp system for online presentation. But, unlike WinHelp or even FrameViewer, the Word files viewed online using this tool are just flat documents with no hypertext features built in at all (which is probably the reason why Microsoft gives it away free instead of charging for it).

## The Tricks Performed by Acrobat

A more interesting approach came with the release of a product called *Adobe Acrobat* from Adobe Corporation, the company that developed PostScript in the 1980s and purchased Frame Technology in the mid-1990s. The people at Adobe recognized that their PostScript technology had opened up the field of desktop publishing by providing a freely accessible, widely available way to print richly formatted documents on any PostScript-enabled device. But PostScript was not easy to view online. The file sizes can be massive (especially when they include bitmapped color graphics), and there was no support in the original PostScript language for hypertext.

To solve these problems, Adobe created a new file format called the *Portable Document Format* (PDF). Unlike PostScript, PDF is highly compact format that includes hypertext features. So, like WinHelp, you can not only view the .PDF document file online, but also hyperlink from one file to another (including web pages, in recent versions of the product) (see Figure 2.6).

The most useful aspect of PDF is that it makes it possible to go online from nearly any kind of word processing or desktop publishing program. To do this, you print the document to the PDF format using a special print driver furnished with the Acrobat Exchange program. Another program called Acrobat

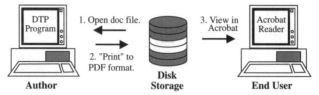

**Figure 2.6** How Acrobat documents are converted and used.

Distiller lets you actually convert raw PostScript files to PDF format. Tools like Exchange and Distiller also let you add hyperlinks to the final PDF documents, including hyperlinks to the World Wide Web.

Once the document is in PDF format, anyone can view it if they have a copy of the (free) Adobe Acrobat Reader. The Reader not only lets people display and print the document, but also navigate through it by clicking hyperlinks.

Acrobat and its native PDF format are interesting because they represented the state-of-the-art in online desktop publishing about the time the World Wide Web exploded onto the scene. In fact, you might say that WWW stole some of Acrobat's thunder, since it provides not only many of the features of Acrobat, but other useful features such as the ability to access *any* file type (including PDF). Intriguingly, Adobe seemed to be trying at first to position PDF as a possible replacement for HTML and the WWW—but now offers a "plug-in" for Netscape that lets users view PDF *inside* the Netscape browser window.

---

**Pause for an Intermission**

Are you about revolutioned out yet? Sorry, but there are about three more revolutions to go. But we take this opportunity to pause for a moment. If you'd like to step away for a coffee break, a powder, or a short nap, please do so. Then rejoin us just in time for the next revolution: the one that has to do with networking and sharing data over long distances.

---

## The Networking Revolution

During the 1980s, while executives were inventing new management styles and PCs were proliferating like rabbits, more new technologies were emerging that would profoundly change information technology. In particular, networking technologies have probably done most to make desktop computers the machine of choice for any business application.

PCs and Macs were fine sitting on your desk, but unlike the old mainframe dumb terminals they were isolated standalone machines—cut off from the central repository of data hoarded by the MIS department's gargantuan mainframes. Cut off, that is, until companies like Apple and Novell found ways to connect desktop computers and mainframes together into *local area networks* (LANs).

The LAN was a convenient way to connect machines on a single floor, or in a small building. But a large organization might occupy dozens of floors in an office building, be spread out over a campus, or have geographically dispersed activity centers around the world. Each location might have its own LAN, but these were isolated from the rest of the organization until someone figured a way to connect them together into a *wide area network* (WAN). (See Figure 2.7.) Typically, this was done by simply leasing a line from the telephone company and hooking the LANs together through the leased-line connection.

The WAN made it possible to put the entire company on the same network, no matter how scattered its locations. The network could be spread across a state, a country, a continent, or around the world. Thus, it was possible for global multinational companies like IBM, Digital, and Chevron to have their own private worldwide networks tying together business locations in the United States, Europe, South America, the Middle East, Australia, the Far East, and the Pacific Basin.

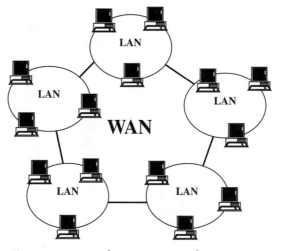

**Figure 2.7**   Wide area network.

LANs and WANs made it possible for business to save money by letting widely dispersed desktop computers share expensive resources. The first things they shared were just hardware components like hard drives and printers. For example, instead of buying an expensive laser printer for each desktop computer, the company might buy one expensive high-speed printer, connect it to a central *print server* on the network, and let everybody print to it the same way they might print to their local printer on their PC. Companies also set up central hard disks or *file servers* that could be used to save data the same way you do on your local hard drive. Instead of being called Drive C, the network drive(s) might be called D, E, F, P, X, or any other letter of the alphabet.

The diagram in Figure 2.8 shows a simplified view of a typical print/file server configuration. Notice that the applications using the server are all self-contained and run strictly on the users' local computers. The print or file server may not run any applications at all, except the utility programs that control the transfer of files to and from its disk drive(s) and printer(s). Notice also that this kind of setup implies that entire files would have to be shipped across the network for printing or storage.

The creation of file and print servers begged the question: If you could share hardware like printers and drives over a network, why not share software and

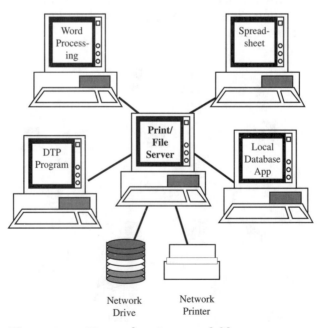

**Figure 2.8**    Network printer and file server.

data, too? Of course, it wasn't long before people found a way to do that. The result was a new kind of software application known as *client-server*.

## The Client-Server Model

Client-server is a way of designing software that takes advantage of the ability to distribute data and processing chores across a network. And in fact, it is the technology that made the Internet and World Wide Web possible and so successful.

The idea with client-server is that, along with the data itself, you can spread out or "distribute" the pieces of software that handle the data. Even though different parts of an application are scattered across the network, they can still work together very much like a single standalone program used to do. (This isn't hard to imagine, since most standalone computer applications are just a group of different programs or *subroutines* masquerading under the guise of a single product.)

Compare the client-server setup to the file server configuration discussed in the previous section. With a file server, you might run a database program on your local computer and save the files to the network drive. But this causes problems, since you need a powerful computer to run the database locally, and you must transport the database file *en masse* across the network every time you want to use it (slowing everybody else down in the process). Compared to client-server, this is a very inefficient way to run a network.

With client-server, instead of running a database locally on each user's machine, you could install the database application and data files on a remote networked computer, then let users access it remotely over the network, as needed. This is what we mean by client-server.[2] The main part of the application runs on a centralized *server* in another part of the network, and any user can control it using special *client* software designed for this purpose. Instead of transporting the entire database across the network for you to work on it, the server *just sends the records you request,* and your client software displays them on the screen. If you change the records, your changes are sent back to the server for processing and inserted into the database.

In the diagram in Figure 2.9, notice that any server can have multiple clients, and any client can be set up to access multiple servers. Thus, if you

---

[2] Notice the term *client* can refer to just the software that makes this possible, or the entire combination of local machine, software, and user. Likewise, *server* can refer to just the application running on the remote machine, or to the entire combination of machine, application, and database.

were using both Oracle and Lotus Notes, you would typically have one client program that works with Oracle and another to work with Lotus Notes. As you will see later in this chapter, this entire model may change significantly on an Intranet, because you can use a single web client like Mosaic or Netscape to access both (see "The Web Browser as a Universal Client").

In one fell swoop, client-server seemed to solve many of the problems of networked computing using desktop machines. Network traffic was reduced because large database files stayed in one place, instead of being shunted across the network. Managers could spend their money on a few powerful servers instead of having to buy everyone the software, drive space, and computing power to run the full application locally. Centralizing the database made it easier to back up mission-critical data at the network level. In effect, client-server optimized both the network and the individual desktop computers running on it.

Better yet, client-server fit right in with the burgeoning management trend toward employee empowerment, teamwork, and collaboration. Client-server systems and networks became key elements in the *re-engineering revolution* that took the business world by storm in the early nineties. Corporate planners found they could use these new systems to re-engineer processes, eliminating many unnecessary steps—and jobs—along the way.

The key concept with client-server is the idea of *distributing the work* and *sharing the resources.* Perhaps you've seen the computer company ad that says "The network *is* the computer." What they mean is that now the business

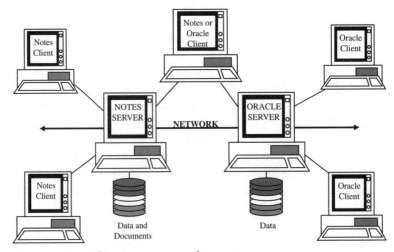

**Figure 2.9**    Client-server configuration.

network has become like a single giant computing organism with users, desktop machines, clients, and servers all interconnected and working in tandem. Instead of everyone toiling away at their own isolated workstations, everyone is now interconnected and sharing data, documents, and many other types of computer resources. In fact, some of the newer client-server applications like Lotus Notes are called *groupware* because they foster this sharing, collaborative approach to computing.

## The World's Biggest Client-Server Experiment

As it happened, the Internet turned out to be an experiment in collaborative client-server computing on a massive scale. That's because all the applications that run on the Internet are based on the client-server model, including the World Wide Web. To understand why this is so, you have to understand a little bit about the history of the Internet.

As far back as the mid-1960s, during the dark days of the Cold War, the U.S. government was looking for ways to connect important research centers together in such a way that the network could take a direct hit from a nuclear attack and still "keep on ticking." Up to this time, many of these centers—mainly on university campuses—had their own room-size mainframe computers working on different parts of the American defense puzzle. But they were isolated from each other just as the first desktop computers were in the days before LANs. Since these organizations often collaborated on defense projects, it made sense to find ways they could connect their computers together, share data, and communicate with each other over a network.

The first stab at such an idea was called the *ARPAnet,* since it was developed by the U.S. government's Advanced Research Projects Agency (ARPA). When it first started in 1970, this fledgling network connected only four universities: Stanford, Utah, and two branches of the University of California. Within a couple of years, the number of connected organizations had increased tenfold, to 40.

Based in part on the ARPAnet model, other special-purpose networks formed over the next two decades, with names like Bitnet, CSnet, Usenet, FidoNet, NSFnet, and CompuServe. But it wasn't until the early 1980s that someone had the idea of connecting these expanding networks together so that data and messages could be shared freely between them. As these networks began to merge, they formed the beginnings of what we now call the Internet.

In this sense, the Internet is simply an agglomeration of different networks that once existed on their own but now are all connected together (Figure

2.10). When you think about it from a business perspective, you might say all these different networks were like separate, isolated LANs until someone connected them together into the WAN called the Internet. In this sense also, any WAN can be considered an *internet*, because it connects various subnetworks together into a unified system. But if the WAN exists solely inside a private company, it's more likely to be called an *intranet.*

Connecting networks together into an internet or intranet typically doesn't affect the way people work inside each of the individual subnetworks. It just makes it possible for them to communicate freely with others across the internet (or intranet). It's similar to the idea of placing a phone call between different regions of the United States or different parts of the world. Though each region is served by a different telephone company, the local networks are all connected so that the call goes smoothly from a point on one regional network to a point on a different regional network.

The same thing happened in late 1994 when companies like CompuServe, Prodigy, and America Online connected their private networks to the Internet. Now, people who subscribe to America Online can exchange messages with Prodigy or CompuServe users. And, when they do, the Internet serves as the bridge between the two systems. The same thing happens every day as more and more individual companies link their own private Intranets to the global Internet. When that happens, the people in those companies can send messages to anyone else with an Internet hookup, including not only subscribers

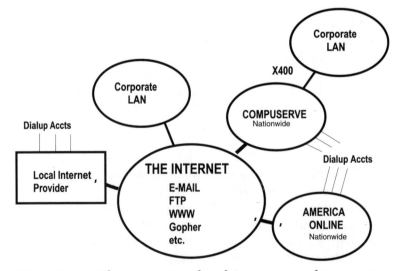

**Figure 2.10**    The Internet as the ultimate network connector.

to CompuServe and America Online but also people who are connected to the Internet through direct-access accounts at home or work.

## Don't You Ever Forget It

Before we go any further, there are a couple of key points you need to remember about the Internet. I put these here to help avoid some of the most common misconceptions people have about the Internet.

- ◆ *The Internet is nothing but a bunch of wires.* At the core, it's nothing but data paths connecting computers, the same way wires connect your computer to others in your office. It's not the idea of wires that's important. It's what we *do* with the wires. It's the fact that *the wires allow us to communicate* between computers, because information cannot leap from computer to computer through thin air. (Okay, technically it can. For instance, there are certainly parts of the Internet supported by satellite links. But in this case, the satellite link is simply a kind of *virtual wire.* It is part of the mechanism that connects computers.)

- ◆ *Nobody "runs" the Internet.* The individual networks that came together to form the Internet were based on a decentralized, collaborative model in which each network node is a *peer* to all the others. There *are* administrative organizations controlling individual subnetworks, and there is an organization that handles domain name registrations, but all these administrative structures are quite loosely organized and under no type of central control. What's more, parts can be added without having to reconfigure the whole system. And individual messages or data files exchanged between computers can find their way from source to destination automatically, on their own, without requiring an administrator to make sure the two computers are connected or that the data successfully reached its destination. I call this a *self-administering network.* In some ways, it's like a self-replicating, self-sustaining metabiological organism.

## How Computers Talk to Each Other

The whole purpose of the Internet is to support independent communication between computers. To understand how this works, you need to understand how a network operates and how computers communicate. Every type of communication—whether people-based or network-based—requires a *protocol* to support it.

When you make a phone call, for instance, you always follow a well-known protocol. First, you dial the number and make a connection. The person on the other end answers the phone by saying "Hello." You greet the person, state your name and the reason for your call. Then, you take turns speaking until you're through. Finally, one person says, "Good-bye," the other says, "So long," and you both hang up.

Of course, the more complex the communication, the more protocols may be involved. Imagine the mass of protocols that surround the meeting of high-level delegations at the UN. There are different protocols for the heads of state, the negotiating teams, the translators, the limo drivers, and so forth. Everybody knows what to say, what not to say, when to shake hands, when to bow, and when to all start dancing.

On a computer network, there may be dozens of protocols operating simultaneously. One protocol controls the physical transmission of electronic signals. Another opens and closes sessions between the chatting computers. Another controls the way data is packaged and handled. Each component of the transaction bows, pauses for a nanosecond, then takes a turn in the dance. These things happen whether the communication occurs on a private LAN or on the Internet.

The key protocol for Internet communication is called *TCP/IP,* which stands for *Transmission Control Protocol/Internet Protocol.* This sounds excruciatingly technical, but it's not hard to understand.

- *TCP* handles the packaging and reassembly of data. It splits large messages or data files into smaller *packets* or *datagrams* that can be sent across the network more easily and independently. Each datagram has a size and sequence number stamped on it, so the computer at the other end will know how large it's supposed to be and where it fits in the puzzle.

- *IP* creates the "envelopes" which carry each datagram to its destination. On each envelope, it stamps the address of the computer sending the message and the address of the computer that must receive it.

Each datagram is like a paper airplane that one computer wafts toward the other. Once released, each packet must find its way to the target on its own, the way sperm cells find their way to the egg. This happens whether the communication occurs on the real Internet, or on the internal kind. It is also employed regardless of the type of data or application that you use.

The process is helped along by intelligent machines called *routers*. A router contains an internal map of the network, recognizes where the packet is headed, and does its best to send it down the shortest or fastest route to its destination. All of this happens so fast and seamlessly, it looks like the two computers simply connect, exchange data, and disconnect.

A key point to remember is that TCP/IP communications are not limited to the Internet. It is a native protocol that has been used in UNIX-based networks for years, and more recently has started appearing on other platforms such as PC and Mac. Once you have TCP/IP capability on a network, it is possible to run any of the Internet applications discussed later in this chapter.

## Calling All Computers

The only part of the TCP/IP you may run across in your daily life is the IP part. Occasionally, when you are using an Internet or Intranet, you may have to use an IP address to make a connection between two computers. What does this address look like? Well, it looks a lot like a telephone number—and works like one, too.

For instance, when you call a friend in Paris, you dial a number like this, which includes a country code and a city code:

011-331-8765-4321

The phone system uses this number to locate the instrument you're calling and make it ring. Likewise, every computer on the Internet (there are millions) also has a unique "phone number" (IP address) that looks something like this:

193.10.128.45

So if you want to connect to a computer and send it data, the IP address plays a key role in making the connection.

To make things simpler, computers also use unique monikers called *domain names*. For example, on the Internet, a computer named *sam.abc.com* might be the computer named "sam" at the ABC Corporation. On an Intranet, the computer named *cust-serv* might be the database server in customer service.

Domain names were invented to make computer addresses easier to memorize, the same way people use catchy phrases on their license plates. For example, it's much easier to remember *cust-serv* than *193.10.128.45,* even though both refer to the same computer. If you have a choice between using a name or a number, which would you pick? Of course, whenever a domain name is available, few people bother with the IP address.

Even better, the domain name can refer to a permanent logical function, rather than a specific computer. So if the customer service data moves to a different computer (at a different IP address), you might still be able to refer to it as *cust-serv,* assuming the network routers are reprogrammed correctly.

## What Is an Internet Application?

So far I've talked a lot about how computers communicate, but not *what* they communicate. When we say that networks were created to share data, what exactly is it they share?

Think again of the phone system. When you use the phone system, you are connecting two instruments and using them to exchange information. What type of information? Well, anything encoded as sound. This might be the sound of two people talking, the sound of your company's Musak lulling a customer to sleep, the warbling of a fax machine as it transmits bitmaps across the line, or the squalling sound of a computer modem. The main forte of a phone network is simply this: It transmits sound (or *analog data* as computer geeks might say).

A data network, on the other hand, is primarily organized to handle *digital data,* which is usually transmitted as discrete messages or *files,* but which also can include random *character strings* or *commands.* Files can contain anything you want to share with other people, including messages, documents, graphics, sound, video, data, and more. How do you share it? Well, a client-server application is ideal. And there are different client-server applications for sharing different kinds of files.

Remember that, on the traditional standalone desktop computer, you use specific programs to handle specific applications. You use a word processor to create documents, a spreadsheet program to create financial statements, an accounting program to do billing, and so forth. Likewise, various programs were developed that help people transmit data across Internet-style networks. These include:

- ◆ *E-mail*—a way of transferring messages from one computer to another
- ◆ *Usenet news*—a way of transferring messages to a central server, where they can be read by many people in a group

- *Telnet*—a way of logging in to a remote server and running programs
- *File Transfer Protocol (FTP)*—a way of logging in to a remote server and copying files back and forth
- *Gopher*—a way to automatically retrieve text stored in files on remote servers
- *Web (HTTP)*—a way to automatically retrieve documents, graphics, sound, video, data, and other computer resources or objects stored in files on remote servers.

Interestingly, all of these are client-server applications that involve using a *server* program on a remote computer and a *client* program on your local computer. When you use e-mail, for instance, you are using an *e-mail client* to send a message to an *e-mail server,* which routes it to the person you are addressing. For example, a message to *john@abc.com* goes to the mail server at *abc.com,* which stores it in John's mailbox. Likewise, you can use a gopher, FTP, or web client to communicate with gopher, FTP, or web servers.

How does this work? Let's look at a generic FTP session on a UNIX system, which may look something like this:

| User Commands | What Happens |
|---|---|
| `ftp bigfoot` | Login to the FTP server on the host computer named *bigfoot* |
| `userID: your_name` | Enter user ID and password. |
| `password: your_password` | |
| `(connected)` | |
| `cd directory_name` | Change to the directory containing the file. |
| `get file_name` | Copy a file from the host computer to your computer. |
| `quit` | End the session and disconnect. |

Notice in this example that the user actually has to log in and open a session on the remote computer using a unique ID and password. This is typical of most client-server applications in traditional computing environments, because they tend to be tightly controlled. But it's also a lot of trouble, since the person who maintains the server has to authorize a separate user ID and password for each person who might want access to the files.

On a global network like the Internet, this kind of server administration is impossible, so people don't even mess with it. Imagine the administrative nightmare involved if you had to authorize and keep track of a separate password for each of the millions of users who might want to access your site over the Internet. In most cases, it shouldn't be necessary because the information—your resume, for example—is probably something you want to share with everybody. The same should be true of a business sharing product information, a government agency sharing census data, or a university sharing research results within the academic community.

Since the Internet is so massive, ways were devised to make the administrative burden significantly easier. For instance, most public FTP servers support a mode of communication called *anonymous FTP*. With this technique, you must still log in, but you can use the word *anonymous* as the user ID and just about anything else as the password.

Thus, instead of having to get into the business of saying *yea* or *nay* to every user that comes along, the administrator of an FTP site can let people retrieve information at will, without bothering to ask for permission. As you will see, web technology boils this process down even further and makes it easy as a single click of a mouse.

## The Basics of Web Technology

Tools like e-mail, telnet, gopher, and FTP turned the Internet into a success, with millions of users already happily communicating away by the early 1990s. But all that success would pale in comparison to what lay just around the corner.

The birth of the World Wide Web in 1990 came and went almost totally unnoticed by the rest of the world. As far back as early 1989, Tim Berners-Lee, a then-unknown researcher at the European Particle Research Center (CERN) was writing proposals about a new method people could use to transfer information between computers. The new method took advantage of the *hypertext* concept proposed years earlier, and already being written into online publishing applications like WinHelp.

The innovations that Berners-Lee and his colleagues proposed came in two parts:

- ◆ *Hypertext Markup Language (HTML)*—a way of marking text so it could be published easily online with embedded hyperlinks, font changes, and other features
- ◆ *Hypertext Transfer Protocol (HTTP)*—a communication method that could be used by clients and servers to exchange hypertext documents over a network.

It was just an idea, but it had promise. At first, no one even called it the World Wide Web, but Berners-Lee recognized that if such documents were scattered across the Internet, they would create a "web" of interconnected information that would stretch around the globe.

To understand HTML, think about the codes that we used to see in word processors and typesetting machines (see "The Growth of Desktop Publishing" on pages 35–36). That's sort of what HTML is like. For instance, a document coded with HTML might look something like this:

```
<TITLE>Short Report</TITLE>
<H1>A Short Report on the Current State of Publishing</H1>

<B>by Haiku Kirby</B><P>

HTML still involves coding, but the codes are much
<I>cleaner</I> because most of them specify functional
components of the document, such as headings and emphasis,
rather than specific font changes, spacing, etc. <P>
HTML lets you add graphic illustrations to your documents,
like the one shown here: <P>

<IMG SRC="picture.gif"><P>

You can also add imbedded hyperlinks, such as the one
<AHREF="resume.html">here</a></A>.
```

HTML provides a way to mark up a document with common desktop publishing elements such as headings, bullet lists, numbered lists, bold/italic font changes, and so forth. It also provides a way to insert graphic images and hyperlinks which can reference other files on the same computer or even on remote computers. For instance, the <IMG> tag in the above example inserts an image stored in the file *picture.gif.* The <A HREF> tag turns the word *here* into a live hyperlink that retrieves the file *resume.html* when selected.

Like the word processors of old, these codes can be inserted by the author, but are not visible to the reader. For instance, if you saved the above example as a file, then displayed it in a web browser, it might look like Figure 2.11 when displayed on the user's screen.

But HTML is only half the picture. Once you create a document using HTML and store it in a file, you still need a way to transfer the file between computers. That's where HTTP comes in. HTTP provides an easy way for a client and server to communicate and transfer hypertext files. This is done using a standard request format called a *Universal Resource Locator (URL).*

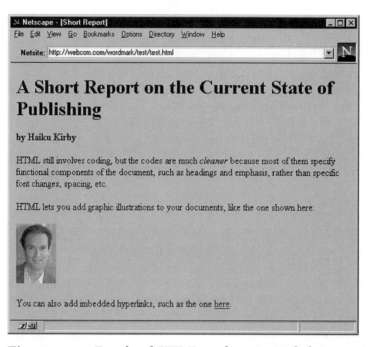

**Figure 2.11** Result of HTML coding in Web browser window.

Anyone who has used UNIX or DOS is familiar with the concept of a *path-name.* In DOS, for instance, the pathname

```
c:\personal\letters\john.doc
```

indicates that the file named *john.doc* can be found on Drive C in the directory *personal* and the subdirectory *letters.* A URL works the same way, except it specifies a server type, server name, path, and filename. For instance, the URL

```
http://sam.com/webpages/home.html
```

indicates that the file named *home.html* can be found on the HTTP server named *sam.com* in the directory *webpages.* (Notice that URLs use a forward slash, like in UNIX, rather than the backslash found in DOS.)

When sent from a web client to a web server, the URL tells the server where to find the document. If you're the person on the client end, you just type in the URL and hit the Enter key to retrieve the file—the server returns it automatically. The nice part is that any hyperlink can have a URL embedded in it, so you don't even have to know the file location *or* its name. All you have to do is click the hyperlink and the file is retrieved automatically (Figure 2.12).

## How the Web Changes Things

It doesn't strike you how simple HTTP makes everything until you compare it with the way we *used to* find information on a computer (in fact, many people *still* do it this way):

- Determine where the file is located and what format it's stored in (a process that can take hours, if not days).
- Log in to the computer where the file is stored (if you can).
- Start an application like Microsoft Word that can display the file in its native format.
- Find the directory where the file is located.
- Open the file.
- Page down to the desired information.
- View the information (print it if desired).
- Close the file.
- Log out.

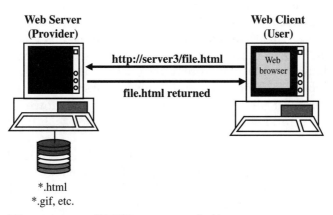

**Figure 2.12**   HTTP server and client.

Notice how these typical steps are a lot like the FTP session shown earlier in this chapter (see page 53). In a web system, *all these steps are collapsed into the single click of a mouse,* including the login/logout process. Since the pathname is contained in the URL, there is no interactive session involved in which the user has to tell the server what directory to change to and what file to retrieve. The URL already contains all that information. It's like a fully loaded guided missile that goes straight to the target and extracts the file in a single step. So what once took minutes or hours now takes only seconds. And the information log jam has been loosened like never before.

## The Real Impetus Behind the Web

During the first years of its existence, a few adventurous souls used the new HTML/HTTP standards to publish documents on the Internet. But the response from the rest of the world community was a resounding "ho, hum." By early 1993, two years after Berners-Lee's original proposal, there were still only about 50 web servers online. Within another two years, however, there were nearly 100,000 with a volume growing exponentially. Obviously, something happened to catapult web technology to prominence in the period between 1993 and 1995.

It's clear that web technology would not exist without the HTML and HTTP standards first proposed by Berners-Lee. But the web, as a technology, did not really kick into high gear until a number of refinements occurred, including more feature-filled versions of HTML and more advanced browser tools like Mosaic and Netscape Navigator. (It also helped that most government-imposed commercial restrictions on Internet use had melted away by late 1994.)

Mosaic and Netscape weren't the first web browsers, but they are certainly the best known. In fact, Berners-Lee and his colleagues had created a web browser for the NeXT computer system as far back as 1990 (the fact that NeXT systems never sold widely obviously didn't help things). Over the next few years, other browsers came along with long-forgotten names like Viola, Midas, Cello, and Lynx. Of all the browsers that emerged, however, Mosaic and Netscape are the products most credited with lifting web technology off the launching pad.

Mosaic was designed by Marc Andreessen and Eric Bina at the National Center for Supercomputing Applications (NCSA) in early 1993. Within a year, the NCSA staff had created versions of the browser for PC, Mac, and UNIX platforms. But Andreessen left NCSA for work in Silicon Valley, and eventually ended up partnering with Silicon Graphics founder Jim Clark to form a new company called Netscape Communications. The rest—as they say—is history.

The main reason for Netscape and Mosaic's success is that they were in the right place at the right time. New versions of HTML and a standard called CGI (Common Gateway Interface) were making it possible to create advanced web-based applications like online forms that could indirectly interface with databases. Mosaic and its predecessors could do these kinds of things and a lot more.

## How Web Browsers Beat the Old Internet Tools

The new browsers included a number of advanced features that made them especially powerful information gathering tools. Unlike other types of client programs, which could only be used with a certain type of server, these were *multipurpose clients.* That means they could communicate with not just web servers (HTTP), but with FTP servers, gopher servers, and others. You didn't really need an FTP or gopher client anymore to access those kinds of services. Instead, all you had to do was change the URL to reflect a different server type, for instance:

```
ftp://server_name/path/file.ext
gopher://server_name/path/query_string
telnet://server_name
news:news.group.name
mailto:person@server_name
```

What's more, each additional URL type could be built right into hyperlinks so that users didn't even have to understand that they were using different kinds of servers. If something was available on an FTP server, for instance, the Web page might include a button or a hyperlink that says "get this file" and a single click would bring it straight to your computer.

It's hard to overstate how important this one feature was. Not only could the new web browsers do things better than the old Internet tools, they could actually *even replace* the old tools. As a result, the web browser became the vehicle of choice for cruising the Internet.

Web browsers added a new level of convenience to file access that had never been seen before. For instance, a Web document could contain links not only through words but pictures, too. You could a click on a map of the world, and see a picture of the selected continent, then click on a country, a region, and a city, zooming in closer with each click to the site you want to visit. Imag-

## A Buyer's Guide to Web Technology

The authors of the Mosaic Handbook once called Mosaic "the Swiss Army Knife of the Internet" because of its wide range of features. But as we all know, you don't need the Internet to use a web browser. Imagine then that you are the purchasing agent in a large company (maybe you really are) and imagine for a second that the Internet doesn't even exist (admittedly hard to do). Then pretend you have someone from IBM trying to sell this to you as an online browsing tool for your next report, online help project, or database application. These are the sales features they would likely mention:

- Inexpensive shareware or freeware
- Intuitive graphical user interface that reads like a book, menu, or guided tour
- Requires little or no training (just point and click on interesting topics)
- Universal browser for any file type (reads file extensions and spawns external viewers, when necessary)
- Supports full-color inline graphics
- Supports multimedia (sounds, video, and other multimedia objects)
- Supports hypertext links to local or remote documents, including links inside graphics (virtual pushbuttons, clickable maps)
- Supports compound documents and reusable images
- Supports SQL queries or other interactive retrieval, display, and updating of database information
- Supports retrieval/display of reports generated by other applications
- Supports direct access to mainframe legacy data
- Supports on-line forms, data entry, and interactive communications
- Supports integration with e-mail applications, including list servers
- Supports the automatic spawning of shell scripts, batch files, or operating system commands

- Capable of spawning remote server or mainframe sessions (telnet, rlogin, or 3270)
- Supports automatic downloading or transfer of computer files at the click of a button
- Contains security features including node access authorization, user access authorization, and encryption
- Supports Internet services like FTP, gopher, and newsgroups, even on local networks
- Supports flexible document/database searches with rank-ordered, clickable, automatically hyperlinked search results
- Supports central or decentralized document management philosophies
- Allows "democratization" of online document publishing
- Supports on-demand printing of desired documents on local or remote printers
- Supports usage tracking/analysis (server log)
- Nonproprietary, platform-independent, open document architecture based on ISO standards
- Client-server architecture for optimum performance across networks
- Saves disk storage by requiring only one copy of a file or image to exist organizationwide
- Displays appropriately on any resolution monitor (user adjusts fonts locally for easy viewing)
- Works on standalones, LANs, WANs, or global networks, whether public or private (any network using TCP/IP)
- Configurable as an embedded front-end browser for CD ROM apps
- Cross-platform compatible (PC, Mac, Sun, SGI, DEC, HP, IBM, etc.)

As this list shows, what may have looked like a simple tool really holds a considerable amount of power for information delivery and user/provider interaction.

ine this feature being used in a parts manual, where you could click on an engine, then on a fuel injector, and finally on an individual component part and see its exact specifications.

The browsers came with other helpful features, like the ability to keep track of all the links traversed in a hypertext session and go back to previous links. If you wanted to make a note of an individual page you found useful, you could easily add it to a pull-down menu for later selection.

The last convenience came by way of font selection. In the old publishing paradigm, the *author* was the one who selected the fonts, specifying for instance 14-point Palatino as the user's font. In an online environment, this doesn't make as much sense because the same font might appear differently on different monitors. Most browsers let the *user* select a typeface and font sizes for the visible documents, so that people could adjust the type size for consistent easy viewing at their unique monitor resolution.

But these were just the simple cosmetic things that web browsers could do. For those who understand the technology and how to make it work, there is a lot more depth and power involved.

## The Web Browser as a Universal Playback Device

One of the most powerful features of tools like Mosaic and Netscape is the ability to recognize file types by their extension and trigger "helper applications" capable of displaying the files (Figure 2.13). In some file manager programs, for instance, you can associate a file extension like ".DOC" with an application like Microsoft Word, so that when you double-click a .DOC file it opens up the file inside its associated application.

Advanced web browsers do something similar: They can recognize and directly display certain "native" file formats directly inside the browser window, including ASCII (plain text), HTML (marked up hypertext), GIF, and JPEG (inline graphics). But if the URL accesses a different file type, the browser can automatically kick off the correct application to display it.

For instance, you might have a button on a web page hyperlinked to a sound file (AU, or any other format). When you click the button, the web server retrieves the sound file and sends it to your client window. The client in turn recognizes the .AU extension on the incoming file, opens up a sound player, and plays the sound so that it can be heard on your end. Of course, the ability to play back files assumes that the proper playback devices are installed on your local computer. But new technologies now coming down the pike will eventually change that, too.

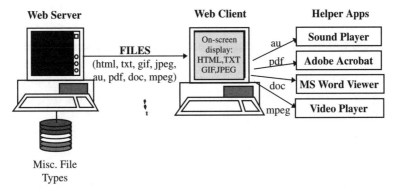

**Figure 2.13** HTML native formats and common helper applications.

This kind of technology not only brings the potential of multimedia to the web universe, but also makes it possible for a web browser to serve as a universal playback mechanism for just about *any file type.* A relatively new concept called *plug-ins* takes this all a step further, by allowing helper applications to run *inside the web browser.* For instance, the Adobe Acrobat plug-in (called *Amber*), works a lot like the helper application called *Acrobat Reader,* but it works entirely on the inside of the Netscape Navigator window. Later sections of this book will contain more detailed information on the available plug-ins (see Chapter 5).

## The Web Browser as a Universal Client

The last feature that made web systems so different was the incredible flexibility built into the HTTP protocol. Earlier, I explained how URLs can retrieve *files* stored on a remote computer. But, in fact, URLs can carry nearly any kind of information that you want between the client and server side of a web system. For instance, just as a file extension can kick off a helper application on the client side, there are also ways to kick off programs or "scripts" on the server side. You can even pass data freely in both directions between the server and the client.

The feature that makes this possible is a mechanism called CGI (Common Gateway Interface). The gritty details of CGI are covered in more detail in Chapter 7, but suffice it to say that CGI makes it possible for a person sitting at a client workstation to control various applications on the server side. For example:

◆ *Online content search.* Anyone who has used the World Wide Web knows about this one. Many web sites provide a search field you can use to search for information on the server, such as all documents that deal with "cost accounting." The typical result of a search is a clickable list of all the document titles, displayed in your browser. When you click a title, the corresponding document is retrieved and displayed in the browser window.

◆ *Interactive database queries.* Web pages could be connected to a customer database, so that if you wanted to view all records for account number 12345, you could type the number, hit Enter, and have all the records retrieved. The retrieved records could be formatted in such a way that you could edit them and have the changes written back to the database.

Both examples involve server-side applications that are controlled from the client side. And in both cases, the communication with the remote application is totally transparent to the user because it is handled through the background mechanism of HTML and CGI. (See Figure 2.14.)

The interactive nature of this communication is made possible through a feature called *HTML forms* (Figure 2.15). HTML form tags let the web system designer set up pages that look just like a standard dialog box. An HTML form can include most of the standard dialog box components you see in windows-based applications, such as text boxes, radio buttons, pop-up menus, and more.

Information typed into a form (called the *form output*) is passed to the web server as a URL string or environment variable, and from there it is handed off to the CGI, and then to the server-side application. The reply from the application can come back as straight text or as HTML-formatted text. So the result could be a simple data table, or it could be a data table wrapped inside an explanation, or it could be data with another form embedded for even more feedback from the user. This type of communication can go on indefinitely.

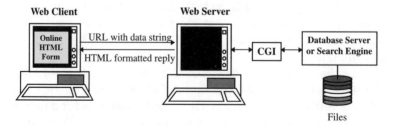

**Figure 2.14** Typical CGI configuration.

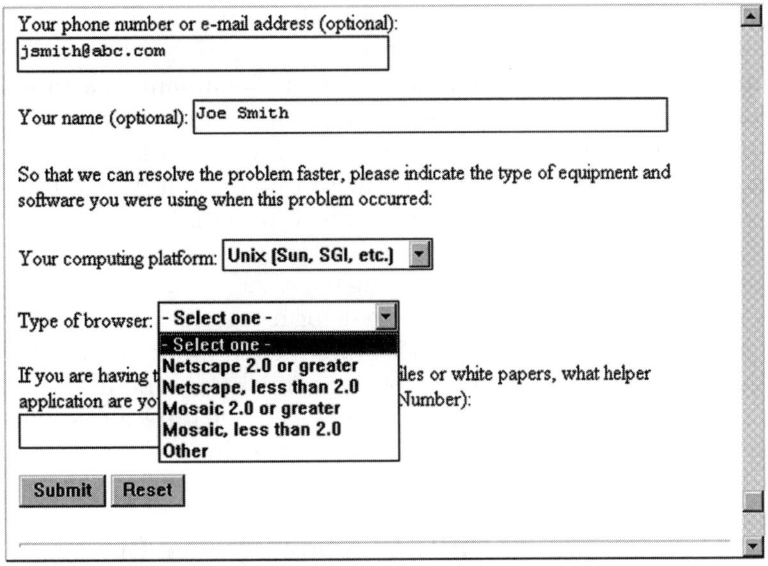

**Figure 2.15** Standard HTML form.

But look what's also happening here. The applications being controlled on the server side may have nothing to do with web technology. They may have been designed for some other purpose entirely. That means you can use the web browser as a *universal client:* a dynamic interface for just about any kind of remote server application on the network.[3]

Even more interesting, the response from the application can be wrapped in HTML codes and accompanying text on-the-fly as it is sent back to the viewer. This means that, in effect, the output from a database or interactive process can be published instantaneously online in response to any user query. Instead of getting a flat data readout or a bare-bones dialog box the way we used to, we can now provide the user with data that is self-explanatory, and dialog boxes that are, in effect, *self-documenting.*

What's more, all of this can be controlled from the server end in such a way that the user interface can change week-to-week, day-to-day, or even minute-by-minute in response to ongoing changes in business needs—*without requiring anyone to change their software, reinstall applications, or retrain on a new system.*

---

[3] That is, any application or server that allows communication with other applications or servers through a programming interface (API).

When used this way, web technology will blur the already fuzzy lines between what we think of as *data,* and what we think of as *documents.* Suddenly, online data can be presented within a document-like interface and online documents can be accessed just like data. So data will become more like *documents* and documents will become more like *data.*

Compare this to the static user interfaces you commonly see in most computer programs. These interfaces are the result of months of laborious efforts by highly trained and specialized programmers who have to invest a considerable amount of effort and time tweaking massive amounts of computer code until it works just so. Now consider that form tags let anyone with a little knowledge of HTML create a dialog-like interface in minutes. And that a form interface can be wrapped around data dynamically on-the-fly as it emerges from applications anywhere on the network. This feature alone will revolutionize the way networks are used to get our work done.

## On Democracy, Totalitarianism, and Administrative Burdens

Another key concept to understand about web technology—perhaps *the* key concept—relates to the way that users access the system. Unlike other client-server technologies, a web system provides universal access across a network to anyone with a web browser, regardless of whether they are authorized to log in to the computer where the server is located. That's not to say that a web site can't be protected from unauthorized users, because it can. It just means that a web site is open to all comers *by default,* unless you specifically protect it.

During the Cold War, people thought of the difference between democratic and totalitarian societies this way: In a free and open society, everything is allowed unless it is specifically prohibited by law. In a totalitarian society, on the other hand, everything is prohibited unless it is specifically allowed.

That's kind of how you should think of the difference between web systems and their more traditional counterparts. In a traditional client-server system, people can't access the server unless they are specifically *permitted* to do so—they must either have an account on the server, or it must be installed so that it appears as an accessible application or drive on each user's machine. A web server, by contrast, is automatically visible to anyone on the network who owns a web client like Mosaic or Netscape. Thus, anyone can access a web server unless they are specifically *prohibited* from doing so.

This fundamental shift in the client-server model has had an important effect on the way networks are used and administered. In the past, the more users you had for a networked application, the greater the administrative burden. Network administrators had to open an account for each user, or configure their systems specifically to access each server they needed to do their work. If a company has hundreds or thousands of users who need server access, this becomes an incredible administrative chore. (That's one of the major reasons why network administrators, as a class, tend to be a bit grouchy.)

The typical network administrator these days is a bit like the old-style Soviet bureaucrat. The system is rigged in a way that the more services are provided, the more work it creates for the administrator. With a web system installed on a TCP/IP network, however, server access becomes totally transparent and begging a network administrator for access becomes totally unnecessary. It's like *perestroika* breaking out all over, because the system is suddenly free and unburdened by bureaucratic control.

Again, since the technology was originally designed for the Internet, it *had to be designed that way.* Imagine how hard it would be to set up a web site on the Internet if you had to individually authorize each of the 30-plus million users around the globe who have Internet access. Companies like Netscape and Microsoft could not possibly field the millions of requests for information that they get *every day.*

## The New Communications Model

The ability to field massive numbers of requests and disseminate incredible volumes of information is a function of the way web clients and servers communicate. A web server, once installed and started up, really just sits there and "listens" for requests coming across the network. Thus, any web client like Mosaic or Netscape can locate a server no matter where it is located on a network, even if it is halfway around the world. The URL request sent out from the client contains all the info it needs to find its way to the server on its own. The information retrieved by the server returns the same way: like a guided missile turned right back around and targeted at the client. The key idea is that the data travels through the network independently, without any direct connection between the server and the client being made.

Notice how this communication model differs from traditional client-server communication. In the traditional model (even with Internet services like telnet and FTP), there is a live connection made between the client and the server. The user may manually log on to a server (or a logon may occur automatically on boot up), and when this happens a *session* begins. If you were sitting at the keyboard on a UNIX server machine, for instance, you could use the *who* command to see all the people currently logged onto the system. The connection between the client and server remains open until the user closes it by logging off (or turning off the machine).

On a web server, typically no such connections occur. Instead, communication between a web server and its clients is more like a set of *discrete transactions.* The server receives a URL from the client, processes the request embedded in it, and returns the requested data to the client. The server is occupied only as long as it takes to fulfill the request and complete the transaction.

The payoff for this approach can be seen when you compare how the web works on a typical server platform. Windows NT, for instance, is becoming one of the most widely used server platforms in the world today. To set up a Windows NT server, your company might buy an ordinary PC (486, Pentium, or better), install the Windows NT operating system on it, connect it to the network, and stage a traditional client-server application on it.

For each client-server application that you install on the NT server platform, there is likely to be a separate charge for each individual application server and each client. Furthermore, the issue of *scalability* applies. The client-server application you install, such as Lotus Notes, may have an upper limit of simultaneous clients it can handle per server. A Lotus Notes R4 server supports 1,000 users; if your users exceed the number allowed, you will need to purchase additional servers to make up the difference. Furthermore, you may need a separate server for each LAN, so that users can easily log in for local access.

Now think of how it works on the Internet. A single web server located in Boston or Tokyo or Madrid can handle all the users in the world; not all at once but possibly many hundreds or thousands of simultaneous accesses (depending on the brand of server you use). Thus a web application is *instantly scalable worldwide.* And instead of purchasing separate server and client software for each individual application, the same server and client can support a host of applications. Of course, if it works this way on the Internet, it will easily work the same way on your corporate Intranet.

## The Role of Authors in a Web System

The last point to understand is how people supply information to a web system and how they use it. Earlier in this chapter, I explained how client-server systems were invented to let users share data and applications over a network. A web system can be used for this purpose, too. But the way it goes about it is quite different from the traditional client-server model.

In a client-server application like Oracle or Lotus Notes, the system exists for the benefit of a defined group of users (Figure 2.16). Often, the people who use such a system are both the *authors* and *users* of the data. In Lotus Notes, for example, people can share documents, which means they can view the documents, or edit them. If different people edit the same document, the

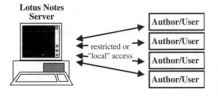

**Figure 2.16** Traditional client-server model.

Lotus Notes software reconciles the various changes made by the user community to the document database.

In a web system, there is a clear distinction between the *authors* or providers of the information and the *users* of it (Figure 2.17). In this situation, an author develops the information for the benefit of the users. The author has direct access to the server, and can use the server directories to store documents and data that will be made available to users online. In this model, however, the users are both more passive and more numerous. Typically, the users can read the information on the server, but they cannot edit it unless the author(s) set up some type of interactive mechanism. While this may seem like a limitation, it works quite well for information-delivery models where people want to provide free access to their data across a network, but don't want just anyone to be able to edit it.

Fortunately, web technology lets us have our cake and eat it, too. The diagram in Figure 2.18 shows an example of a web system that is integrated with a traditional client-server application like Lotus Notes. In this case, the Lotus Notes server is still being used by a restricted group of people to author and edit a set of documents. But the presence of a web server on the back end allows the documents to be published across a network to all interested users. The connection between the application server and the web server is handled through a gateway interface like the Lotus InterNotes Web Publisher that automatically converts Notes documents to HTML format, which allows them to be served across an Intranet and to be viewed anywhere on the network using a web browser.

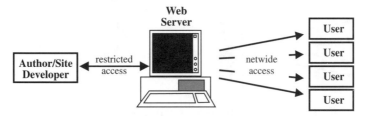

**Figure 2.17** Typical web client-server model.

Increasingly, vendors of client-server applications are providing web gateways that will make it easy to connect their applications to the Intranet. Oracle is just one example, providing web connectivity through its WebServer software. Thus, instead of a team or department having to take their information offline and publish it through paper or other media, widely distributed web users can peer directly into the database and retrieve their own.

## Future Strides in Web Technology

All the web features we've seen so far are just the most basic features already built into the current HTTP and HTML standards. But these are by no means all the tricks that web technology is capable of. Due to the success of the Internet, dozens of companies are now vying for ways to improve the technology and make it into even more of a "killer app" than it is already.

Interestingly, most of the initial strides in web technology were made on the client side, as companies like Netscape and Spyglass developed successive versions of their web browsers with increasingly sophisticated features. Almost overnight, browsers went from a point where they could do little more than publish straight ragged-right text, to a point where they could display sophisticated tables, centering, positioned graphics, blinking text, inline color controls—even foreign alphabets. New versions of Netscape's famous browser seem to appear every month now, with many new features per release.

The great untapped potential of the web, however, lies on the server side. And that part of the market, though slow coming to life, has now blossomed and is on its way to fulfilling its promise. Here's what we have seen so far, and what we will be seeing in the future:

- *More security*. The first server improvements came in the area of security, as Netscape and others added encryption protocols that

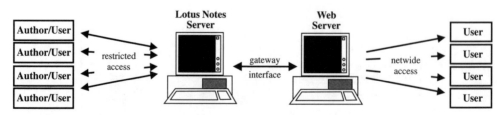

**Figure 2.18** Extended web client-server model.

would allow information to be transmitted across a web in encoded format. These security features were essential to support online commerce on the World Wide Web, but may also be useful for communication of highly confidential data across corporate networks.

◆ *More connectivity.* Several servers are now coming to market with their own built-in search engines and database management tools. So, instead of hooking the web server to a back-end application, the application might actually be integrated into the server. Many of the back-end application providers, like Oracle and Lotus, have also come out with their own web connectivity tools that let users more easily serve data over webs.

◆ *Collaborative tools.* Netscape's late 1995 acquisition of Collabra was a dead giveaway that they want to create a web system that provides integrated groupware features. Other companies are moving in the same direction, so expect to see more web-based groupware products soon.

◆ *Less programming.* Moves are underfoot to reduce the amount of CGI programming involved in interactive applications or eliminate CGI altogether. In particular, tools like JavaScript will make it easier to build web applications.

◆ *More programmability.* Look for browsers and servers with application programming interface (API) hooks that allow other applications to control them. For instance, you might want to press a Help button in one application that brings up online help in a web browser window.

Appendix B of this manual contains a survey of some of the more promising web development tools available as this book went to press.

## Where Do We Go from Here?

Now that you understand how web technology works and how it fits into the current thinking on client-server applications, you're ready to set up your own web system. The next chapter explains the tools you will need and how to set them up.

## Chapter Three at a Glance

When used on a corporate LAN or WAN, web technology will empower people to set up autonomous *information centers* to provide data, documents, and multimedia to the entire enterprise. If your company doesn't yet have an Intranet, this chapter will show how to set one up. If your company already has an Intranet, this chapter will help new people understand how to set up a server and join the action. In particular, you will learn:

- What an information center is and what is needed to set one up
- How to tell whether your network can support an Intranet
- What approach to take when planning or enhancing an information center
- How to set up a test server and a *proof of concept* for an internal web site
- What types of information you can share, and the different types of users you can share it with
- Basic tools you can use to prepare content for the web
- How to structure information on the server
- Basic tips on web page design
- How to connect your users to the information center
- Problems you may encounter and how to fix them

# The Birth of the Information Center

Do me a favor. Before you do anything else, pull out a sheet of paper and write the following words in big block letters. While you're at it, draw a few flowers around the edges, too.

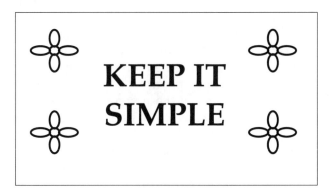

**KEEP IT SIMPLE**

Now take that sheet of paper, frame it, and hang it on the wall over your computer. This should be the mantra for the Intranet, because no web system will succeed unless you keep things as simple as they can possibly be.

Remember that you are not creating an Intranet just because you like web technology and think it's cool. You're creating one because it will satisfy human needs and it will make things *easier for everyone*. This means that the system should be easy to use, easy to access, easy to participate in, and easy to administer. Above all it should be easier and cheaper than the current alternatives: the copy machine, mail system, and the bureaucracy-laden network management schemes we use today. Otherwise, nobody will want to use it.

That doesn't necessarily mean it will be simple for the person who sets up the first few sites (although it can be, if you use the right tools). There has to be someone who does the work of reading this book, getting up to speed on all the concepts, and leading the way. As simple as I try to keep things in this book, there are still some subjects that are inherently technical. But the idea is that, given this knowledge, you can go out and create a system that will be easy to use *by everyone.*

If you're still stuck in a bureaucratic frame of mind, maybe you'll understand it better if I say we need to create systems that are *inclusive, empowering,* and *decentralized.* This is, after all, what the Internet has proven already: that you can build a field of dreams and the entire world will come, as long as you open it up to everyone and keep the bureaucracy at a minimum.

Empowerment is the key to making a web system inclusive and decentralized. Empowerment means people being able to help themselves, which means they have the knowledge, tools, and techniques to do what needs to be done to make the system work. In this chapter and the following, I will try to impart that knowledge to you and show you how to think when you impart it to others.

If this were like other books, I would jump right into the most technical part of the argument, scare the pants off everyone, and proceed from there. Instead, I am here to tell you that anyone can create an Intranet from scratch—or participate in one that already exists. And anyone can provide content that can be served over an internal web. When I say anyone, I mean secretaries, accountants, your boss, people who can't program a VCR, and people with six thumbs on each hand. Not that any of these people will be interested necessarily in setting up their own web sites; but with proper encouragement and a little hand-holding it can be done.

Above all, I hope to demystify the process of setting up a web site. If there is anything web systems require right now, it is demystification. When approached in the right frame of mind, setting up and using an internal web server should be no harder than installing and using any other kind of software. Of course, there may be complications along the way. But let's assume that everything will go right and that you will be successful, then we can talk about what might go wrong.

If we take this approach, and treat the Intranet like any other run-of-the-mill business application, we can empower any individual, department, or group in the company to become an autonomous *information center,* communicating with users across the enterprise the same way people do it on the World Wide Web. This chapter explains what an information center is and how to set one up. And it will show you why we should let many of these centers blossom and grow on their own.

## What Is an Information Center?

An information center is the term I use to describe a web site on an Intranet. As such, it is the basic unit of organization in an internal web. It can be a person, a group, a department, or a division of a company. The main qualification is that the people involved: (a) work together on the same LAN, (b) have access to the same hard drives, and (c) want to share information with other people inside or outside of the company (accessed through the same LAN, through a WAN, through dialup connections, or across the Internet).

Typically, this will probably happen at the departmental level, since each department has a common set of information to share and a common place to store it. For instance:

- *Human resources* may want to publish employee-orientation materials, benefits programs, company policy programs, and newsletters over the internal web, rather than going through the standard paper distribution system.
- The *documentation and training* group may want to provide its manuals online through a web rather than in three-ring binders, on CD-ROM, or using other media or tools.
- *Engineering* may want to set up its own servers to communicate product development plans, schedules, and other information.
- *Marketing* may want to distribute continuously updated product information for general reference by employees, dealers, suppliers, or customers.
- *Tech support* could provide troubleshooting tips, access to the knowledge base, and interactive services.
- *Legal* could offer online access to legal guidelines such as those on sexual harassment in the workplace.
- Even *MIS* could use it to deliver legacy data from large mainframes or other traditional computing systems, without the traditional programming efforts required.

You could say that each of these traditional company divisions is, by its very nature, *already* an information center. However, an information center doesn't have to be a department or a traditionally organized group. For instance, a cross-functional team charged with improving productivity in the manufacturing division may have data, meeting notes, and progress reports it wants to share with the rest of the company. Thus, the team itself can become an ad-hoc information center to the rest of the enterprise.

At one company where I worked a few years ago, there was a guy who did nothing but cross-reference lists of catalog numbers. For every catalog number the company used, his list showed the corresponding catalog numbers for similar products in competitor catalogs. This information was always in demand, because it was useful not only to customers and customer service people involved in the ordering process, but to product managers, sales reps, and even system developers in the company's internal organization. If web systems had existed back then, the guy who maintained that list would have been a natural-born information center.

Maybe *you personally* have some particular information you would like to share with the rest of the company, such as scores of the company volleyball teams, recent sightings of the company president, historical information, troubleshooting tips, software reviews, hard-to-find statistics, or contact information for your department. If you have anything at all you want to share with others in an organization, *you* should consider becoming an information center (Figure 3.1).

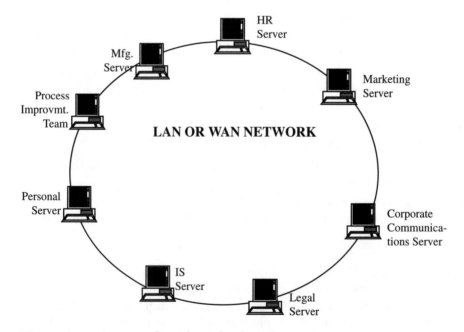

**Figure 3.1** A network with multiple information centers.

## What Does It Take to Be an Information Center?

With an internal web system, it doesn't take all that much to set yourself up as an information center: just a computer and the right tools. The main component of a web-based information center is a *web server,* which includes the following components:

- *Hardware*—a network-connected desktop computer on which to install the web server software. This would probably be the computer you're using right now.
- *Software*—the appropriate web server software that can be used to automatically send information to any user who requests it. You can get several different types of web servers off the Internet for free evaluation and testing (see the sidebar on page 84).
- *Content*—the information you will serve to the rest of the organization. This depends on what you have available, but it could be documents, database records, or multimedia files.

Notice the one thing missing from this list that you would need if you were setting up shop on the World Wide Web: an Internet connection. Since no Internet connection is required, this considerably simplifies the process of setting up an internal web site.

## How Easy Can It Be?

Setting up a web server isn't as hard as it may sound. For example, I was recently asked to demonstrate the Intranet concept to a potential client. I brought with me two floppy diskettes. One was a zipped copy of a fairly obscure web server I had retrieved from the Internet (win-httpd). The other was an evaluation copy of Netscape Navigator, the popular web browser. Neither of these cost me a dime to use for demonstration and evaluation purposes. I didn't preload them or preconfigure them in any way. Here's what I did to get the web started:

1. I copied the zipped server file onto a PC running Windows 3.1. Then I unzipped it, and fired up the server.
2. I created a few simple demonstration files in HTML and saved them in the server document root directory.

3. I went to the manager's office, installed Netscape Navigator on his hard drive, started Netscape, and let him read the demonstration files I had created. Keep in mind the files were still back on the server computer and he was reading them *over the network.*

Three steps, about 30 minutes worth of time, and *voila*—instant Intranet. A little installation, a little typing, and that was it. Of course, that was the end of the demonstration—and the start of what would become a much longer, ongoing development process. But, at that moment, the Intranet already was a *fait accompli.* The only work left to be done was to populate it with information that would be interesting and valuable to users.

Anyone could have come behind me and used that server to begin providing information to the rest of the company (and some people did). Plus, if they wanted to set up more servers to create more information centers in the company, they could have done that too, just as easily as I did.

Server installation is usually not much harder than unzipping the files or going through a standard installation routine. So just about anyone can set up a web server anywhere on a computer network. And once the server is installed and content is prepared, anyone using a web browser can read it from any location in the network.

The art is not in the mechanical part, it's in the informational part. The art is presenting information to users in a way that provides value, getting people interested in using the system, and then managing the communication explosion that follows.

The importance of these last two factors cannot be overestimated. I know of companies now where the web is so popular that some people are using it to put pictures of their dogs online. The managers at these companies should be happy (but aren't) because at least their web systems are being used. There are other places I know where money has been spent and extensive development work has been done on an internal web, but the employees don't use it at all, mainly because they haven't even been told about it. But all that will be discussed later.

## How to Tell if Your Network Can Support an Intranet

One reason why it was easy for me to install an internal web site on the client's network is because the network already "had what it takes" to support a web system. The what-it-takes part is the protocol known as TCP/IP. I knew that the network supported TCP/IP before I started, or else I wouldn't have bothered. Not all networks support TCP/IP, especially if they don't have UNIX components. But increasingly, most of them do.

As you may recall from Chapter 2, TCP/IP is the native protocol that all Internet applications use to communicate. This doesn't mean you need an Internet connection to use it—just that your network must have TCP/IP embedded in it to run Internet-style applications like web browsers and servers. Without TCP/IP, you cannot create an Intranet. So the first thing you may want to do before you even begin to install a server is find out whether the network supports TCP/IP.

Actually, my client was not sure if the network used TCP/IP or not. Keep in mind that this was an IT manager, who normally should know things like this. Originally, he said, "the network uses SNA and Netware." But a quick check with key network administrators confirmed that TCP/IP had also been installed recently to support *other* client-server software (a popular financial program called SAP).

Some people make the mistake of assuming that just because a network uses one type of protocol, it can't support others. For instance, just because your network uses Netware doesn't mean it can't also have TCP/IP. In fact, TCP/IP can sit right on top of Netware without anyone knowing the difference, and web applications can glide across the network on the TCP/IP layer without even causing a ripple in the Netware environment (see the accompanying sidebar on page 81).

That's why it's important—even if someone tells you there's no TCP/IP—to check it out for yourself. Because some of the most knowledgeable people in your organization may not know for sure. When in doubt, it may be easier just to run a quick server test like I did (see the "Hello World" test later in this chapter). But there are also several fairly quick and easy ways you can find out whether TCP/IP is available:

- *People are already using Netscape or Mosaic.* If you know people are already using web browsers or web servers on your network, skip the rest of this section. That's obvious, isn't it?

- *People are already using UNIX servers.* If you or a coworker already use a UNIX server, this is usually a clear sign your network supports TCP/IP. When I say UNIX server, I mean something like Sun, Silicon Graphics, DEC Alpha, IBM RS/6000, or some variant of these. There's also a machine called an X-terminal that is a dead giveaway you're working on a TCP/IP network.

◆ *Your PC/Mac has TCP/IP.* If none of the above conditions apply, and your network supports primarily PC or Macintosh computers, the situation may be a little murkier. First, check the Networking section of your Control Panel for TCP/IP. Then check the list of programs that are currently running on your computer (for example, press Ctrl-Esc in Windows 3.1, look at the task bar in Windows 95). If you check the list of running programs and see a name containing the words *winsock, tcp, newt,* or *ping,* there's a good chance your machine is already running TCP/IP. At one time there were dozens of different shareware and commercial utilities that performed this function, with names like Chameleon, SuperTCP, MacTCP, Trumpet Winsock, and others. Nowadays, TCP/IP is included as a standard networking option in systems like Windows 95.

   If you find a TCP/IP component, open it up and see if you spot an IP address for your machine: a four-part number such as 196.5.43.154. If you see a null IP address of 0.0.0.0, this is suggests that the TCP/IP option, though present, is not being actively used.

◆ *Your network administrator says so.* The preceding tips were easy ways to find out if your network supports TCP/IP. Of course, the easiest way may be to check with your local network administrator. Keep in mind that even he or she may not know. Also, don't be surprised if your network administrator turns to you with a quizzical look and says, "What do you want to know *that* for?" If he presses you for details, get ready to defend your actions. Remember that many old-line system administrators are notoriously suspicious of Internet technologies. Some consider them downright dangerous, and others will dismiss your efforts out of hand, saying "you don't need a *web server* to do *that.*" If this happens, read the next section for details.

If any of these methods turns up clear evidence of TCP/IP, or if you have the barest suspicion it may be present, then you have no problem. Go ahead and run a server test, as explained a bit later in this chapter. This assumes, of course, that you can foresee no active opposition to your doing so.

However, if you verify that there is no TCP/IP on the system (and a network administrator tells you, furthermore, that there is no chance you'll ever have it) then you've got a somewhat larger problem. Not only do you have the chore of creating an Intranet, you also have to convince the network people to adopt the basic tools you need to make it work. The main problem here is that you are getting into an argument with people "who know the network." Let's take a quick look at how that works.

## How to Handle Surly Network Administrators

One of the biggest problems you may have launching an internal web—especially if your network does not support TCP/IP—is getting it past a class of person I will call "the surly network administrator." Don't get me wrong: I don't mean that *all* network administrators are surly, because most of them are quite friendly and helpful people. But I will say this about network administrators: They are some of the most overworked and underappreciated people I

---

### Running an Intranet on Netware

As you can see in this section, TCP/IP is a required component of an internal web system. And traditionally, the hardest place to find it was in PC networks based on Netware or one of the other popular PC network operating systems. There are several important trends underway in this arena, as listed below. WWW sites are also listed for more details and reading.

- Many companies have already installed TCP/IP on top of their Netware networks. Web applications can use this built-in TCP/IP to communicate independently of the Netware system. For a list of TCP/IP utilities, see:

  For PC: http://www.northernc.on.ca/wasted/stacks/

  For Mac: http://www.intercon.com/newpi/TCP-Connect-Mac.html

- Systems are being developed, such as NOV*IX, that give TCP/IP capability to Netware networks.

  For NOV*IX info: http://www.firefox.com/product/novix.htm

- Netware has developed a web server of its own that works on Netware networks.

  Netware Web Server: http://corp.novell.com/announce/web-serve/

know. So if they seem a bit grouchy and uncooperative at times, you can understand why. They're under a lot of strain.

For some reason, the grouchiest administrators also tend to be the most opinionated about subjects like the relative merits of this or that operating system, and this or that client-server technology. And the really, down-deep-mean network administrators are the ones who *hate the Internet with a passion.* Just the very mention of the word *web* may send them into a tizzy.

Fortunately, most savvy administrators have heard about the Intranet by now, but the occasional overburdened administrator may not. The thing to remember, of course, is that you are dealing with a new way of using technology that many people don't understand yet—*especially* if they have a traditional networking background.

If you encounter resistance from the network people, remember this: The people who run your company's network do it *all the time,* which means they are the best at what they do. On the other hand, being involved in the nitty-gritty of network administration 24 hours a day means they rarely get involved in regular business processes, such as online publishing, management, or data analysis. In other words, they spend a lot of time dealing with the *mechanics* of network technology, but not as much time thinking about *applications and uses* of the technology.

The best person to decide how to use the network is a person like *you.* After all, the network was not created for the benefit of network administrators. It was created for the benefit of *all employees,* especially those who use it as a conduit for data and information. So, if the argument comes down to what goes on the network, the average employee should win that argument any day. And if not the average employee, then the average employee's boss.

Another important point to remember is that you are not defenseless in such an argument. For instance, you've already read Chapter 1 of this book and have cleared your mind of any confusion between the Intranet and the Internet. You've read Chapter 2 and understand that this technology can be used internally in myriad ways. So maybe you *do know a thing or two* after all. If good arguments fail you, hand this book to someone with clout and let the book make the argument for you.

The truth is, I've seen companies adopt TCP/IP in a sparrow's heartbeat when it was needed for mission-critical applications like SAP financial software or Oracle databases. But, as I said before, those are products that have considerable sales forces standing behind them. IT managers and network people already have the benefits of those applications drilled deep in their heads, because they are the subjects of myriad magazine articles and conferences. The Intranet—since it is a *phenomenon* rather than a *product*—has no sales force gunning for it. So *you* may need to step in and fill those shoes for the time being.

## How Wired Is Your Network?

One last issue before beginning a server test is the level of integration on your network. Previously, I explained that many companies have taken all their separate *local area networks* (LANs) and wired them together into a single *wide area network* (WAN). To install an internal web, it doesn't matter whether you are dealing with a LAN or a WAN, as long the network supports TCP/IP.

The question of LANs and WANs is not just academic, however. It directly affects how wide your audience will be. If you install a web server on a LAN that is connected to a WAN, then anyone on the WAN should be able to "hit" your server (assuming TCP/IP is in force through the entire system). But if your company has not interconnected its LANs, your potential audience will be limited to the people on the same LAN where you install the server. It's like living on an island: You can drive anywhere you want to on *your* island, but you can't drive to *other* islands unless there's a bridge already built between them.

That's not to say web technology is useless on a LAN. I've seen work groups as small as a dozen people use a web system effectively to store and retrieve information. But, of course, the more is always the merrier, and web systems are no exception. Also, if the group down in cost subaccounting are the prime target for your web, you'd better make sure they're on the same network that you are before you start building a web site to serve them.

How can you tell if your company is integrated into a single WAN? Of course, the quickest way is to ask a friendly and knowledgeable network administrator. Knowledgeable is the key. But if you can't get a straight answer, it may be time for a quick server test.

## The "Hello World" Server Test

So now you know—or suspect—that you have TCP/IP on your network. And you want to perform the same kind of server test I mentioned earlier in this chapter. Here are the complete steps you need to make it successful:

1. *Find a networked computer where you can install the server.*
   This could really be any desktop computer connected to the network. Most people use their own. At the very least, you can install

## Software for the "Hello World" Test

The type of software you use for the server test depends on the type of operating system you have. Different web servers are recommended for different operating systems, and the Netscape browser (web client) is recommended for all operating systems. The following software may not be what you end up using, but it should work fine for initial development and testing of your internal web site. You can move on to more powerful or feature-filled server packages as your needs grow, without having to redo a lot of the material you have developed. Each of these software packages can be downloaded from the Internet at the URL listed below. In each case, make sure you just get an "evaluation" or "demo" copy. You still have plenty of time to buy the software, once you verify it's what you want to use.

**Freeware, shareware, or demo servers for different platforms:**

MS Windows 3.1

   Win-httpd Server  http://www.city.net/win-httpd/

Windows 95

   Website Server    http://website.ora.com/checkitout/demo.html

Windows NT

   EMWAC Server    http://emwac.ed.ac.uk/html/internet_tool-chest/https/CONTENTS.HTM

Macintosh

   Various offerings  http://www.comvista.com/net/www/server.html

UNIX

   NCSA Server    http://hoohoo.ncsa.uiuc.edu/docs/Overview.html

**Browser (all platforms):**

   Netscape Navigator http://home.netscape.com/

**TCP/IP software:**

   For PC: http://www.northernc.on.ca/wasted/stacks/

   For Mac: http://www.intercon.com/newpi/TCP-Connect-Mac.html

the server software on your own computer for initial testing and serving, and leave it on your computer indefinitely (unless you notice a significant drag in performance). Once your web site becomes very popular, or you prove the value of your web site to the appropriate management, you can then consider buying a special machine dedicated to this purpose. Again, most people who install servers on internal webs do not buy special machines—they just use their own. The main requirement is that the computer have appropriate disk space and power to run the server. Surprisingly, web servers typically don't require all that much power. Any recent desktop model is probably up to the task, such as a 486 or Pentium PC, a PowerPC or any reasonably powerful Mac, a Sun SPARC 10, or any equivalent computer. You should consider a more powerful machine only if you have a very large user base and a very popular web site. Server software usually won't take up more than 10 to 20 MB on your hard drive. If you are not installing on a UNIX computer, make sure the computer you're using has TCP/IP networking already installed, as discussed earlier in this chapter.

2. *Find a networked computer where you can install the client.*
Any computer on the network will probably do, as long as it uses a mouse. This is the machine you will be using to install the Netscape software and test the server response (i.e., "hit" the server across the network, the same way people hit servers on the World Wide Web). For this reason, it should *not* be the same machine where you are going to install the server. Again, if this is a PC or Mac, make sure it has an appropriate TCP/IP utility on it.

   *Tip:* If there isn't another convenient computer, or you don't want to bother anyone with your testing, you can install the client on the same machine as the server. It's just not as much fun to hit the server on the same machine as it is when you're in a different room or on a different part of the network.

3. *Obtain the appropriate software for the test.*
You can get the appropriate software directly off the Internet, or by contacting the manufacturer. To run the test, you need a web server like the ones listed in the sidebar on page 84 and a web client like Netscape Navigator. The software you retrieve depends on the machines you will be using for the server and client end of the test.

4. *Install the server software on the chosen platform.*
Most of the software you get off the Internet comes in a zipped or compressed format. Installation may involve something as simple

as unzipping or untaring the file (when you do, use the "recursive" option to preserve the directory structure). More likely, after you unzip or untar the file, you may have to run an installation program, such as *setup.exe* (on PC) or *make* (on a UNIX machine). Installing software on a PC or Mac is simple; nontechnical people do it all the time. On a UNIX workstation, you may need help from a network administrator unless you install it in your home directory (which may be appropriate for testing purposes, just so you won't have to bother the network administrator).

If you're installing on a PC, the installation routine should automatically create a set of icons on your desktop (Figure 3.2). It should also create a set of directories (i.e., folders) containing the server software and various utilities, including such things as sample CGI scripts, icons you can use on your web pages, and possibly some extra web administration tools (depending on the individual server you select).

For instance, if you install the Website server on a Windows 95 or NT machine, the entire installation will go under a directory like C:\WEBSITE (Figure 3.3). Different subdirectories will contain different types of supporting files such as the server scripts (\cgi-win or \cgi-bin), server information content (\htdocs), and web administration utilities (\admin).

5. *Create a "Hello World" test file.*

   Use a text editor (such as the vi editor on UNIX systems or the Notepad editor in Windows) to create a file named *test.html* (or *test.htm* on a PC). Enter the following content verbatim, or modify it as desired:

```
<HTML><HEAD>
<TITLE>Test File: Hello World</TITLE>
</HEAD><BODY>
<H1>Hello World!</H1>
This is a test page for my new information center at
   AnyCompany, Ltd. Here's a bullet list of reasons why I'm
   creating this site:
<UL>
<LI>Easier publishing of information over the network.
<LI>Cost savings over old publishing and information
   systems.
<LI>Ego gratification.
<LI>Excitement/boredom (select one).
</UL>
```

**Figure 3.2**    Startup icons for the Website server and tools.

```
If you see this test page, give me a ring at my_ext or send
  me an e-mail at my_address.
<HR>
Last updated today's_date. My_Name.
</BODY></HTML>
```

Of course, be sure to change all the italicized parts above to the
appropriate values for your situation. Feel free to change any of the
text, but be careful about the stuff in angle brackets (< >). This
should be all the HTML coding you have to do. Later on, I'll show
you some tools you can use to avoid HTML coding.

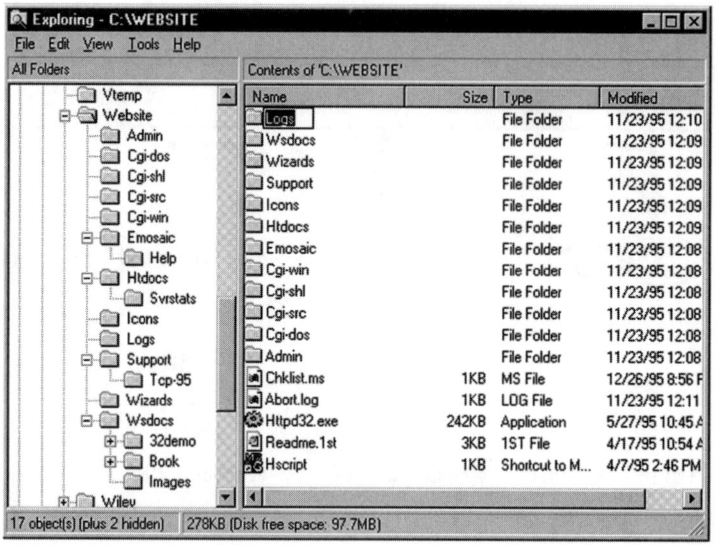

**Figure 3.3** Typical server directory structure.

6. *Save the test file in the appropriate server folder.*
   The server will not serve files from just any directory (i.e., folder). Typically, there is only one directory under the server that can be used for this purpose. This directory is called the *server document root* and anything you want to serve must be placed in it. For instance, for a Win-httpd server installation on a Windows 3.1 computer, the document root directory name is *htdocs*. So, if the server is installed on Drive C, you would save the test file as:

   ```
   c:\httpd\htdocs\test.htm
   ```

   Notice that, if you're using Microsoft Windows 3.1, the file should be named *test.htm* instead of *test.html* because Windows 3.1 supports only three-character file extensions. On most other operating systems, the four-letter file extension *.html* is okay.

7. *Fire up the server, if it isn't started already.*
   Usually the server software is just a background process, which means either that it *has no real user interface,* or that the user interface—such as it is—is *iconized* as soon as you start it. You will see it running in the list of programs, but you will not see it on the screen (other than possibly as an icon).

Starting the server may occur in different ways. On a PC or Mac, the installation should have left behind a program group and startup icons on the desktop, and you can double-click the server icon or executable filename to start the server. If not, you can use the computer's built-in file manager utility to click into the server installation directory and start the executable server program. On a UNIX system, you may need to change to the server installation directory (or add it to the PATH), and start the server executable from the command line.

8. *Determine the IP address or name of the server.*
This is a key bit of information that will make it possible for people to hit your web site. In a TCP/IP network, every machine has a unique numeric IP address such as 197.34.125.14, and possibly even a name such as *sparky* or *viper.* If you are working on a UNIX system, for instance, you probably already know your machine name and see it on the screen right at the command line, such as:

```
sparky>
```

On most UNIX machines, you can also see the IP address by looking at the /etc/hosts file and reading the line that contains the word *localhost.* For example:

```
more /etc/hosts
```

On a PC or Mac, check the configuration section of the TCP/IP networking utility. Unlike the server software, the TCP/IP utility should actually have a workable user interface you can see on the screen. You can search the menus for configuration information, and usually in there somewhere you will see the IP address of the local host (i.e., the server machine) and even a host name. Once you have the machine's IP address or name, write this number down and tape it to the machine, because you don't want to have to go looking for it again (Figure 3.4).

9. *Install the web browser on the client machine.*
By now, you should have some other machine picked out to test the client-server interaction. Go and install the Netscape Navigator software on that machine. Just like the server, if you are using a PC or Mac, the client machine should also have TCP/IP networking.

10. *Hit the server.*
Now pretend you are on the World Wide Web and try to access the server site across the network. To do this, fire up Netscape, then select

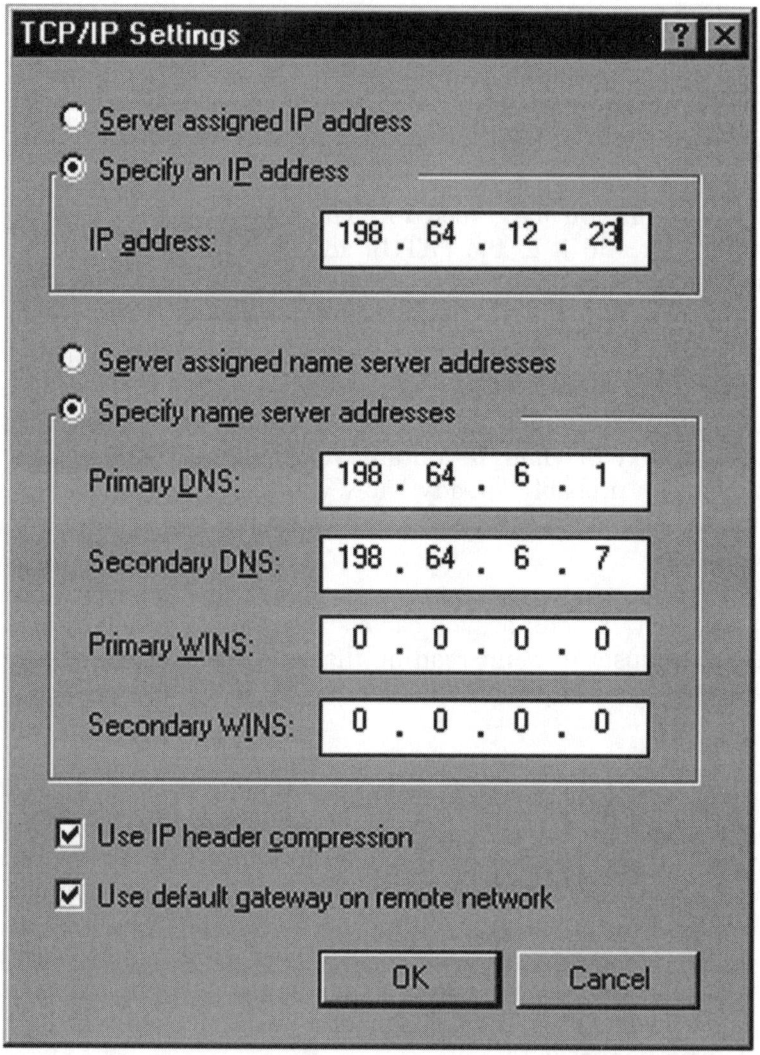

**TCP/IP Settings** [?] [X]

○ Server assigned IP address
◉ Specify an IP address

IP address: | 198 . 64 . 12 . 23 |

○ Server assigned name server addresses
◉ Specify name server addresses

Primary DNS: | 198 . 64 . 6 . 1 |

Secondary DNS: | 198 . 64 . 6 . 7 |

Primary WINS: | 0 . 0 . 0 . 0 |

Secondary WINS: | 0 . 0 . 0 . 0 |

☑ Use IP header compression
☑ Use default gateway on remote network

[ OK ] [ Cancel ]

**Figure 3.4**   TCP/IP configuration panel.

the Open Location option in the browser's File menu, or use the Location field in the browser main window. Type in a standard World Wide Web URL, but using the server's IP address. For instance, if the server IP address is 197.31.123.14, you would enter:

```
http://197.31.123.14/test.html
```

or, if you know the server name is *sparky,* you might try:

```
http://sparky/test.html
```

If the server is installed on a PC running Windows 3.1, try shortening the file extension to three letters. For instance:

```
http://197.31.123.14/test.htm
```

If you have done everything correctly up to this point, you should see the server test page (created earlier) appear in the browser window, fully formatted and without the HTML codes (Figure 3.5). (If you see any angle brackets, by the way, go back and check your coding.) If you see this, the server test is complete. Congratulations, you now have a working internal web site.

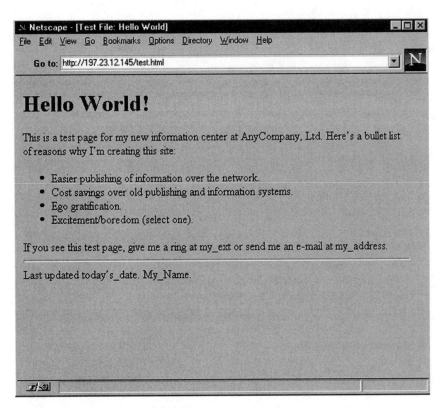

**Figure 3.5** Browser window with test page.

## What to Do if the Server Test Fails

If you perform the server "Hello World" test as shown on the previous pages and saw the test page display correctly, skip this section. If not, you may want to consider what might have gone wrong.

### No TCP/IP, or Inadequate Connectivity

The most likely culprit here is the TCP/IP connectivity, or lack of it, in the network. This is especially true if you get absolutely no sign of response from the server and never had any real evidence of active TCP/IP usage on the server anyway. For instance, if you did not see TCP/IP-networking in the control panel, there is good reason to believe the machine is not actively using TCP/IP.

It may also be possible that you found some type of TCP/IP utility, such as Trumpet Winsock, on the computer and started it up, hoping it would do the trick. Not all TCP/IP utilities are designed for communicating over a network, however. Some are designed to establish serial line (SLIP or PPP) connections over dialup phone lines. This is not the same type of connection you typically have across a network.

If you think the TCP/IP connection may be the problem, there may be no recourse but to involve the network administrator. Usually, a good administrator can pinpoint in a minute whether you have the correct software running to do the job, and whether the IP addresses are mapped correctly at the server. I have seen cases where the TCP/IP utility was configured for one IP address, then someone physically moved the machine to a different location and failed to reconfigure the TCP/IP utility to reflect the new address.

Remember that an IP address is location specific, so if the machine moves to a new location it usually gets a new IP address. (This, by the way, is the best argument for using host names instead of IP addresses to refer to machines—*sparky* will always be *sparky,* no matter which IP address it is located at. Unfortunately, though names are almost always available for UNIX machines, they may not be implemented for PC and Mac machines unless the people who set up the network were very thorough.)

### Server Name or IP Address Wrong

You may have read the wrong IP address off the TCP/IP configuration menu, or you may have typed it in wrong. Double-check it and try again.

If you used a name, instead, it's possible the name is incorrect or spelled imprecisely. On a UNIX or Mac system, for instance, the name is case sensitive. Thus, *Sparky* and *sparky* are considered two different names.

### Part of URL Wrong

Recheck the URL that you entered into the web browser. It may be that you did not type it in correctly. In particular, be sure to use only forward slashes (/), not backslashes (\)—*even on a PC.* Be sure to place a colon and two slashes after the *http.* For instance:

> http://197.34.127.24/test.htm

### Test File in Wrong Directory or Named Wrong

The other problem is that you may have saved the test file to the wrong place or using the wrong name. If this happens, you are likely to get a message back from the server saying it cannot locate the file. If you get such a message, at least you are doing something right, because this indicates the client and the server are actually communicating and the server is trying to find the file.

If you get such a message from the server, there may be several causes. On a UNIX or Mac system, for instance, the filename is case-sensitive. So if you save it as *test.html* then try to access it as *Test.html,* the server may not recognize the switch in case. You may also have used *.htm* for the extension, when in fact the actual filename uses the extension *.html,* or vice versa. On a PC, try shortening it to .htm.

The server may also not be able to find the file because it is saved in the wrong path. If you are unsure which directory to save the file to, you might want to read the server README or Help files to figure out which subdirectory is the server document root. Then move the file to the document root directory and try the test again.

### Server and Client Not on Same Network

Unless you know for sure, there is a chance that the machine where you installed the server and the machine where you installed the client are not on the same network. Remember earlier where we talked about LANs and WANs? It may be that you are dealing with two separate LANs that are not interconnected via a WAN. A friendly and knowledgeable network administrator can help you figure this out.

## What You've Accomplished . . .

If the server test succeeds and you see the test page on the client machine, a hearty congratulations is in order. You can break out a quick bottle of champagne, just don't let the boss see it. You now have a server platform working as part of an Intranet that you can start using to build your information center. This means that anyone on the same network should also be able to access the information on your server, as soon as you have some useful information to present to them.

The rest of this chapter shows the different types of information you may want to consider serving, and various tricks you can use to improve the quality of your offering and your own productivity. It also talks about connecting users to your information center and encouraging their participation. Later chapters will give you in-depth examples of how other people are using internal webs and how to serve various types of sophisticated content over the web, such as desktop-published documents, multimedia, and data.

## . . . and What's Left to Do

To finish setting up your information center, however, you will have to take each of the following steps:

- ◆ *Provide content.* So far you just have a single test page on your web server. Next, you will want to start creating (or converting) documents or other information to be served from your site. In the next part of this chapter, I'll show you how to get started. I'll also cover this concept in greater detail in later chapters.

- ◆ *Empower your users.* People will not be able to use the information at your site unless they have web browser software installed like Netscape Navigator or Mosaic. If your company already has an Intranet, this problem may already be solved. If not, you will have to arrange for them to get a copy of the software installed on their computer. I'll explain how later in the chapter.

- ◆ *Notify your users.* One thing you need to understand about a web system: Just because it exists doesn't mean it gets used. Either the system is a regular part of people's lives, or else they need to be reminded to use it. In a later part of this chapter, I will explain ways you can do that.

The most important thing to realize is that you have your own information system started here, which doesn't (or shouldn't) require the ongoing involvement or approval of people in other parts of the organization. In other words, you are now *empowered*.

The web system you installed is now coasting along *on top of* (or should I say *above*) all the other network applications, and should not affect or interfere with other network uses, other than to add a slight additional burden to the overall load of traffic. In a sense, you have actually hotwired the regular network. And you can use this new system to instantaneously and automatically distribute information across the whole enterprise.

## What Can You Share with Users?

Once you've set up a web server, the first question naturally is: What do I do with it? (Actually, this question should have occurred to you sooner, but for the sake of argument I will pose it here.)

The answer to this question, of course, is to provide information to users. When you look at the sheer volume of information stored by corporations today—including reams of printed information like computer documentation, procedures, specifications, and reference documents—you quickly see plenty of information you can start taking online. Users no longer have time to wade through a shelf full of manuals to find some obscure tidbit of information. And chances are you can no longer justify the cost of printing all this information without any guarantee that users are actually reading it. Then there is the problem of keeping all that printed information up-to-date. So there are a number of information resources and transactions that are potential candidates for your new web site.

### Documents

Every company has reams of business information that it must distribute to internal employees or external customers and suppliers. The following list provides examples of the types of documents that companies traditionally distribute:

- Policy and procedure manuals
- Quality manuals
- ISO 9000 work instructions

- Employee benefits programs
- Orientation materials
- Software user guides
- Hardware manuals
- Quick reference guides
- Online help
- Style guides and other standards
- Training manuals and tutorials
- Seminars
- Company newsletters and announcements
- Scheduling information
- Maps and schematic drawings
- Computer reports
- Customer data
- Sales and marketing literature
- Specifications
- Price lists
- Product catalogs
- Press releases

Your web site gives you a way to put all of these documents online for instantaneous access by authorized users.

## Electronic Resources

Companies also have a number of electronic resources stored on computer that are traditionally distributed by transportable media or by copying across network nodes. These may include:

- Test data
- Customer data
- Spreadsheet templates
- Documentation templates
- Software applications and utilities
- Programmer toolkit components

In the past, many of these resources may have been hidden away in rarely accessed cavities of the network. With a web browser like Netscape or Mosaic, you can catalog these resources online for user review and automatically distribute them—through a single mouse-click—across a network to any authorized user who requests them.

### Interactive Communication

Finally, there are various kinds of two-way communication within a corporation that can be facilitated by the new technologies. These include:

◆ Surveys and feedback
◆ Program notification and enrollment
◆ Progress inquiries and reporting
◆ Memo distribution, comment, and reply
◆ Spontaneous data entry and data collection
◆ Interactive database queries
◆ Product promotion and ordering

Web browsers give us a way to communicate with employees, customers, or suppliers, present information, capture feedback, and process the feedback automatically through databases or scripting mechanisms. They also support spontaneous user searches of information archives or databases. In Chapter 7, we'll delve extensively into how these applications are set up.

## How to Share Information with Users

By this time, you probably have a good idea what kinds of information you want to share with users. The question now becomes: How do I share it? You may have noticed that the test page created for the "Hello World" server test was coded entirely using HTML. That's fine for a server test, but you probably shouldn't be doing a lot of raw HTML coding. Content for a web system can be created using any number of standard word processing, desktop publishing, and illustration tools. But in some cases, you may need or want to adopt additional tools that make it easier to prepare your information for presentation over the web.

The table beginning on page 98 summarizes various kinds of information you might serve over a web. For each content type, it shows how to prepare the information for the web and some typical tools you might use to do it (see Appendix B for a detailed list of web tools). It also shows the kind of file you

| Content Type | Preparation Methods | Examples of Tools | Save As* | Best Used For . . . |
|---|---|---|---|---|
| Documents (layout converted) | Create text with imbedded HTML codes. | Text editor or HTML editor (HoTMetaL, HTML Assistant, etc.). | .html | Menus, web-based forms, short documents or messages. |
| | Prepare as usual; save directly to HTML format. | MS Word, WordPerfect, FrameMaker, others. | .html | Individual documents with straight-forward layout using style tags. |
| | Prepare as usual; use web tools to convert document set to a complete web. | Normal authoring tools (Word, FrameMaker, etc.), with conversion programs like Cyberleaf, WebMaker, or HTML Transit. | .html | Large document sets with consistent layout that conforms to a style guide. |
| Documents (layout preserved) | Prepare as normal; print to PDF output. | Acrobat Distiller or Exchange (author); Acrobat Reader (installed on user machines). | .pdf | Short docs designed for printing or use "as is" (white papers, forms requiring signature, brochures, newsletters, specs, etc.). |
| | Prepare as normal, serve on web in native format (e.g., MS Word). | Appropriate viewer must be installed on user machines, such as MS Word Viewer. | .doc (or other) | Limited delivery of docs to small groups, where everyone has correct viewer. |
| Static lists, catalogs, directories | Store information in database or table. Generate static HTML output and store as a document. | Mail merge or database report writer with HTML code wrapped around output fields. | .html | Staff phone directories, small catalogs, price lists, etc. |
| Real-time data | Store information in database or table. Allow user to query directly using HTML form. | CGI scripting language (perl), programming language (C, VB), or CGI data access tool (Cold Fusion, dbWeb). | .html (form) .pl or .exe (script) | Large databases or catalogs. |
| Static illustrations | Create as usual; store as GIF or JPEG. Add to final doc "by reference" or use alone. | Freehand, AI, Corel, PhotoShop, etc. | .gif/ .jpeg | Standalone illustrations or inline illustrations. |
| | Create inside WP/DTP program; autoconvert to inline web format. | Standard WP/DTP tools (Word, Frame, etc.) converted through WebMaker, HTML Transit, others. | .gif/ .jpeg (saved auto) | Illustrations in large docs where DTP/WP tool is primary means of creating illustration. |

| Dynamic illustrations (clickable imagemaps) | Create as usual; also create map file indicating pixel coordinates and hyperlinks. | Imagemap Editor, Mapedit, Webmap. | .gif/.jpeg (image), .map (map file) | |
|---|---|---|---|---|
| Sound/video files | Convert to standard sound/video formats. | Media conversion tools (RealAudio Encoder). Suitable sound/video players must be installed on user machine (NA Player, RealAudio, Stream-Works, mpegplay). | .wav, .au, .mpeg, .mov, etc. | Film clips, recorded interviews, etc. |
| Multimedia | Create as usual, process for web. | Macromedia Director, ShockWave, media.splash | .dir, .dcr, .dxr | Training programs, tutorials, demos, special effects. |
| Applications | Create as usual, but design interface using HTML. | CGI/API programming in C, C++, Java, etc. | .html (form), .exe (CGI app) | Server-based apps with programmable APIs and function calls. |

*On a Windows 3.1 system, use three-letter file extensions such as .htm, .mpg, .jpg, etc.

might be saving (.html, .doc, etc.) and the types of situations where the methods are best used.

Notice that in many cases, the second column of the table says something like, "Prepare information as usual, then do *something extra.*" If you belong to a group where many people will be contributing to the web, the "prepare as usual" part could apply to the entire group, so that people don't have to give up their regular tools and start learning new ones. The "extra" part could be reserved for a single person who specializes in final-stage preparation of materials for serving over the web, and who makes the extra effort to learn the tools. Such a person is often called a *webmaster* (although there are quite a few *webmistresses,* as well).

In later chapters, I will show you not only detailed procedures on how to prepare each content type, but also ways you can introduce web production methods while minimizing the disruption to your workgroup.

## Setting Up a Home Page

So far in this chapter, you've created one HTML file: a test page called *test.htm.* At this point, if you wanted to send this file over the network, you would need to type in a URL that includes both the IP address and filename, such as:

```
http://197.34.127.24/test.htm
```

As you create more and more material for your information center, however, you'll need a way users can automatically access all your stuff. But it would be impossible if users had to memorize the name of each separate file you create. Instead, users should have a clickable list of all the information available at your site. Such a list would be like a *main menu* or—to use a bit of World Wide Web terminology—a *home page.*

Remember that on the World Wide Web a home page is the first thing people see when they get to a site. That's the same concept you should aim for here. Your information center should have a home page that is the first thing people see when they visit, and it should contain links to all the information available. You can do this by creating either of the following types of menus:

- *Single main menu.* You could fill the home page with direct links to every resource available at your site. Clicking a link brings up a document or other resource. A single-page menu can be a problem if you have lots of information to access (i.e., if the menu covers a lot of categories and fills several screens).

- *Menu hierarchy.* Categorize the various types of information, then create a separate submenu for each category of information. The home page would list the categories and provide a link to each submenu. The submenus, in turn, would contain links to more submenus or to actual documents or server files.

The examples on the following pages show how each type of menu structure might be created.

## Creating a Single Main Menu

When you set out to create a web menu, you need to have a good idea how you want it to look. For instance, let's say you wanted to create a document menu listing some of the first documents you created. You may want the user to see something like this:

---

**Welcome to My Test Server**

Here you can get access to all the documents I have created so far while testing out the server. In particular, you may want to see:

- My first test page (the "Hello World" server test).

Select the document you want by clicking on it.

Coded in HTML, the same information might look like this:

```
<HTML>
<HEAD>
<TITLE>Test Server Home Page</TITLE>
</HEAD>
<BODY>
<H1>Welcome to My Test Server</H1>
Here you can get access to all the documents I have created so far
while testing out the server. In particular, you may want to see:
<UL>
<LI><A HREF="test.html">My first test page</A> (the "Hello World"
server test).
</UL>
Select the document you want by clicking on it.
</BODY>
</HTML>
```

Notice in HTML coding that the <A HREF> and </A> tags create a hyperlink by bracketing the clickable hypertext and naming the file to be retrieved when the user clicks on the link. For example, when the user clicks on *My first test page,* it will retrieve the document file named *test.html* and display it in the client browser.

Instead of coding the home page in HTML, you can easily create it using a tool like Microsoft Word Internet Assistant (see page 182 for more details):

1. Use the File/New option to open a new HTML document.
2. Type in the text of the home page, without using HTML codes. Instead, use the following style tags on the toolbar to format non-body paragraphs:

    Heading 1,H1    The main heading (Welcome To My Test Server)

    List Bullet,UL    Bullet list

3. Save the file as *index.html* in the server's document root directory, using the SaveAs option on the File menu (or *index.htm* if the server is on a PC). Make sure you save the file as the type HTML. Don't close the file, however. Leave it open for the remaining steps.
4. Drag the cursor over the hypertext link to be created (shade the words "My first test page . . .").
5. Click the Hyperlink button on the toolbar (Figure 3.6).

Hyperlink button

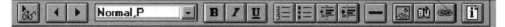

**Figure 3.6** Word IA toolbar with hyperlink button.

6. When the Hyperlink dialog opens, select the tab titled "To Local Document" (Figure 3.7).

7. Use the Directory and Filename boxes to select the server document root folder and in it the filename *test.htm*.

8. Click the OK button. This will create a hyperlink between the selected words and the selected file.

9. Select the HTML Document Info option on the File menu and enter the document title: *Test Server Home Page* (Figure 3.8).

10. Close and save the completed home page.

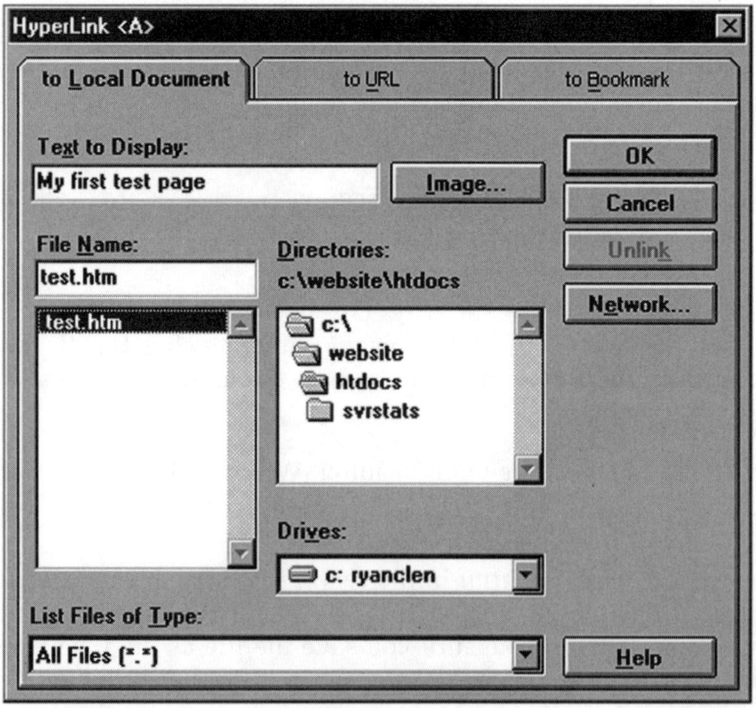

**Figure 3.7** Word IA HyperLink dialog.

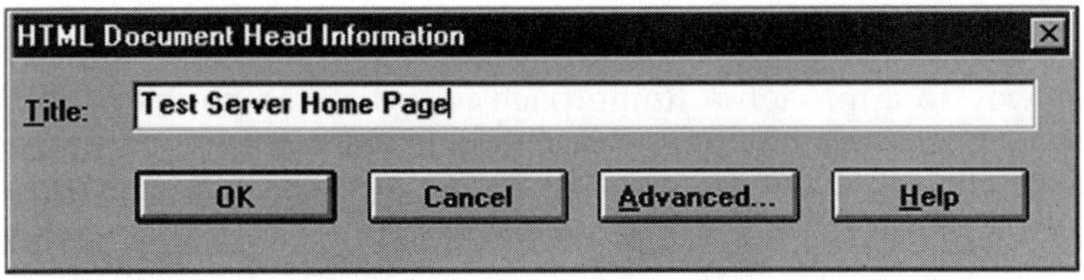

```
┌─────────────────────────────────────────────────────────────┐
│ HTML Document Head Information                            [X] │
├─────────────────────────────────────────────────────────────┤
│ Title:  │ Test Server Home Page│                             │
│                                                               │
│      ┌────────┐  ┌────────┐  ┌───────────┐  ┌────────┐       │
│      │   OK   │  │ Cancel │  │ Advanced..│  │  Help  │       │
│      └────────┘  └────────┘  └───────────┘  └────────┘       │
└─────────────────────────────────────────────────────────────┘
```

**Figure 3.8**    Specifying the document title in Word IA.

## The Importance of a Default Filename

Notice in the last procedure that you saved the home page as a file called *index.html* (or *index.htm* if the server is on a Windows 3.1 PC). This is the default name of the home page for many web servers, although some servers may use a different name, such as *default.html* or *welcome.html.* The home page is defined in the server *by default* so that users can access a site without knowing the exact filename of the home page.

For instance, to see the Microsoft home page on the World Wide Web, you can just type in:

http://www.microsoft.com/

When you do this, the Microsoft server automatically retrieves the default home page for Microsoft, because its name has already been defined in the server configuration. Likewise, on an internal web, you want to be able to just type in an IP address or server name to access your home page, such as:

http://197.34.123.14/

or

http://sparky/

For your server to work this way, you will have to use the actual default home page name defined by the server. A good way to check this is to go to the client after you have created a home page and hit the server using only the IP address or name. If the home page comes up, it works. If not, you may have to use a different default name. Check the server's online documentation (or help system) to find out what this name might be, or look in the server document root for an existing HTML file with a name like *default* or *welcome.*

## Creating Multilevel Menus

The other way to approach a home page is to list categories of information, and have each category open up a submenu. For example, suppose you are creating an information center for the Corporate Communications Department, and you have three types of information available: press releases, brochures, and newsletters. Your home page might look like this:

### Welcome to Corporate Communications

We maintain a repository of all the information you would expect to get from this department including:

- Press releases
- Brochures
- Newsletters

Select the type of information you want by clicking on a category.

When users click on the Newsletters category, they might see:

### Company Newsroom

These are the newsletters available on our web system. Select the one you want to see:

- The ABCer—our external newsletter for customers
- ABC Profiles in Courage—our in-house employee newsletter.
- ABC Down Under—the special newsletter for our Australian divisions.

Select the newsletter you want by clicking on a title.

If users select Profiles, they might see another menu listing all issues of that newsletter for the past two years. Clicking on an issue would open the actual document.

Notice that this multiple menu structure implies a hierarchy that looks something like Figure 3.9. In this case, each different menu and submenu is represented by a separate HTML document. In the home page, there is a set of hyperlinks that point to the files containing the submenus. The links in the submenus either point to actual documents (such as the December 3 press release) or still more submenus (Profiles). A standalone document like a press release might be contained in a single HTML file, but a newsletter might start with a table of contents file, which links to individual files for each section or article.

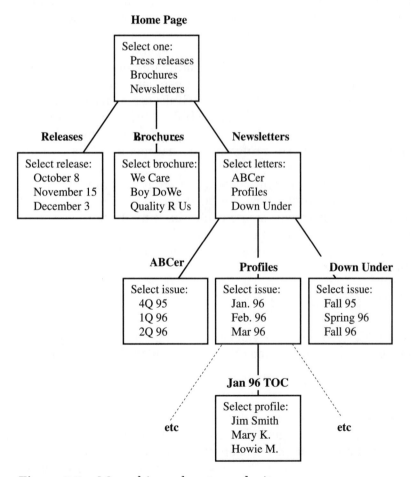

**Figure 3.9**  Menu hierarchy at a web site.

As you can see, with this type of arrangement, the number of interlinked documents begins to proliferate rapidly. The previous diagram implies 16 different menu files (including TOCs), plus about triple that amount of actual documents that can be browsed. This is a fairly simple web site, yet there are already close to 40 separate documents to keep track of (not to mention any illustration files that might be associated with the documents). You can see why people call this thing a "web."

File clutter like this screams out for some form of management, especially as more information continues to be added to the site. Though there are many advanced tools for site management discussed later in this chapter, you can start out with the simplest of all: arranging related files into folders (subdirectories).

The diagram in Figure 3.10 shows the same document structure, but instead of a functional view you are now seeing the actual filenames and link names that might be used. Each box represents a separate menu file, and the label over each box shows the filename for that menu and its location in the path from the server root. Inside the box, you can see the actual reference name used in the hyperlink. Notice that relative links can be used, and a default filename can be used in each directory. So a link to "nws" on the first level would retrieve the default menu file in the /nws folder, which happens to be /nws/index.html. Likewise, a reference in that menu to "abc" would retrieve the default menu file in the /abc folder.

If you looked at this same document hierarchy in a more traditional directory tree structure, it might look like the diagram in Figure 3.11. In this directory tree, notice that as you create each file, it might be saved to a different path. For instance, the table of contents for the January 1996 issue of ABC Profiles might be saved in the following path (assuming the server document root is c:\httpd\htdocs on a PC):

```
c:\httpd\htdocs\nws\prf\96ja\index.htm
```

But the URL used to directly access the same file from a user machine (or via a hyperlink carried on some other server) might be something like this:

```
http://197.34.127.14/nws/prf/96ja/
```

since the /httpd/htdocs part of the path is already implied as the document root, and *index.htm* is recognized as the default opening file for any path. These long URLs are just given as an example, to show the difference between the path when it is referenced on the local hard drive versus when it is accessed through a web URL. You need to understand how these URLs work to be able to

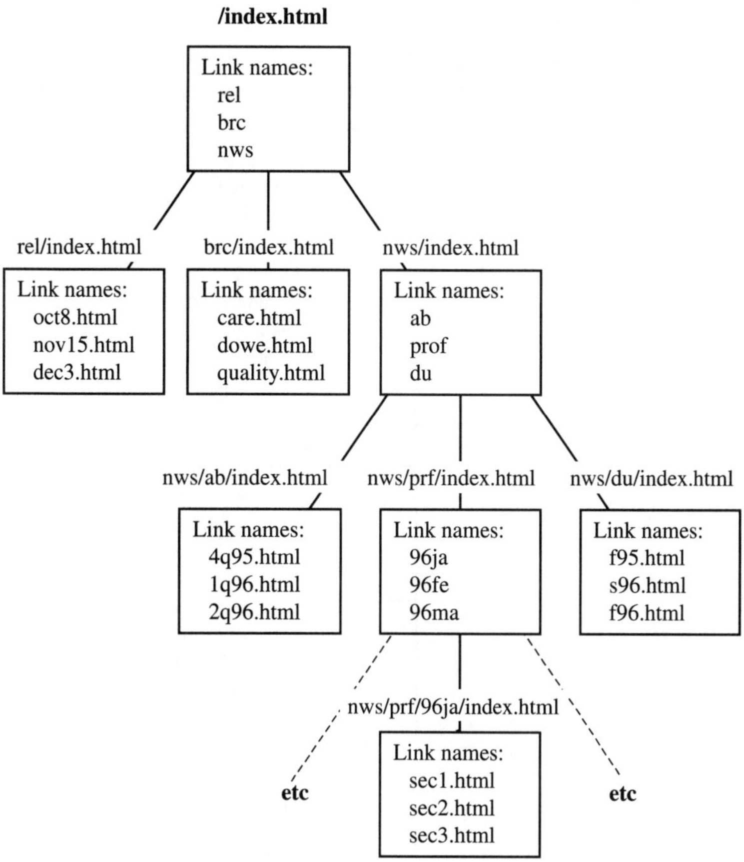

**/index.html**

**Figure 3.10** Web site hierarchy shown with file and hyper-link names.

create appropriate hyperlinks. But the user doesn't need to understand them because all URLs should be hidden inside the hyperlinks you create.

Now you're asking: *What happened to the idea of simplicity?* The truth of the matter is, when you set up a web system, you want to think about file and folder configuration because it will make things simpler later on, once you get into a production mode. This complex folder structure might seem to be con-fusing at first, but once you install a web publishing system (as shown in Chapter 5), your publishing tools will automatically remember where you store your brochures and where you store your newsletters. And when you create links between documents in different levels of a directory tree, even a

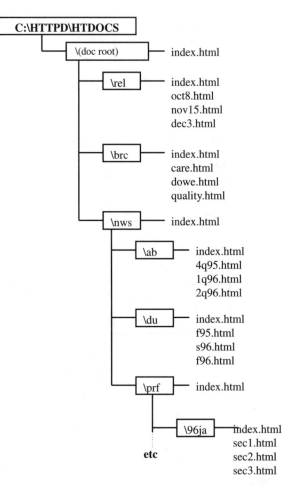

**Figure 3.11** Directory tree view of server structure.

tool as simple as Word Internet Assistant should code the relative path changes correctly.

If you plan to do extensive web publishing and site building, however, chances are you will soon need some sort of site management tool. Many web publishing packages now come fully equipped with site management tools, as do some servers. For instance, Adobe's SiteMill, Microsoft's FrontPage software, and Netscape's Livewire all have them. The main idea behind most of these tools is to provide a graphical view of the web site, and an easy way to configure and reconfigure the different files and folders at the site. Netscape's Site Manager (Figure 3.12), which is available as part of its Livewire package, lets you use the drag-and-drop capability of most windowing systems to move files and folders around, then it automatically repairs all the hyperlinks between the files. For example, if you move a file named *brochures.html* from the root directory to the folder named *promo*, the site manager tool would correct any hyperlinks at the site to reference the full path *promo/ brochures.html.*

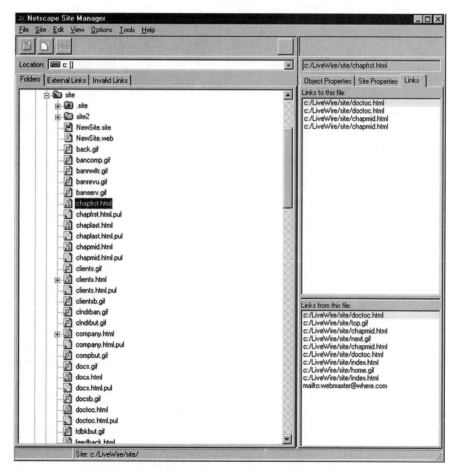

**Figure 3.12**   Netscape Livewire Site Manager

## Secrets of Successful Web Sites

At the beginning of this chapter, we plunged right into the thick of things without much thought being given to long-term planning or overall site design. That's fine, because I wanted to cut to the chase and let you see how easy it is to get a server up and running.

Now that your server's running and you understand how to create web content, it's a good time to step back and take a good look at where you're going. You may have something already in mind that you want to start serving from your new information center. Before you get too far into it, there are certain quality control issues you'll have to confront.

Remember that the main thing you're trying to do with an information center is to communicate information. That involves a lot more than just slapping your content online and seeing who reads it (or who doesn't). It's more of an art, like painting or ballet. None of us are born doing the *pirouette* or the *grande jetée.* But we can learn these with a little practice, and improve as we go along (I'm still working at it).

To truly master the art of communication on the web, you may want to study extensively in the subjects of writing, publishing, illustration, graphic design, user interface design, database management, client-server technology, and more. *Oh really,* you say? Yes, the ultimate webmaster has a bit of all these skills. But that's no reason to get discouraged; there are some fairly basic tricks you can use to make sure your information is well organized, easy to access, and easy to use (remember that mantra). Here, then, are the most basic requirements for successful web sites.

### 1. Plan Ahead

The best way to plan is to make a list of all the different types of information you could conceivably share over a web. Then go to the nearest white board, get some colored pens and an eraser, and start organizing the information into a hierarchy. Think in terms of big categories instead of specific documents— you will be collecting many documents over time, your big challenge is how to organize them into categories the user will understand.

For instance, in our previous example of a Corporate Communications web site, it didn't take a genius to recognize that the department produces essentially three types of information: brochures, press releases, and newsletters. If I'm a user, chances are this is how I'll see it, too. I'll want to see press releases, brochures, *or* newsletters. I'm not likely to want to see a press release *and* a newsletter on the same menu, unless both are related to a specific product. In that case, maybe the site should be organized by product type instead—or by *both* product type *and* document type.

To help with your organization, a storyboard often helps. Draw some pictures showing how you want the different menus to look and work. Spread them out on a table and pretend you're moving from one screen to the next. Show the sketches to users and get feedback. This is usually a lot quicker than setting up each major screen, testing it, then reorganizing it after the fact. Creating a good design on the front end will save a lot of work later on, once your site starts accumulating information. The one thing you don't want to have to do is reorganize everything after the fact and have to rebuild all the links between documents (although a site management tool like the ones discussed earlier in this chapter would certainly make the reorganization task much simpler).

### 2. Chunk, Layer and Nest Your Subjects

Notice that the Corporate Communications example on page 104 takes a rather large and diverse set web of documents and breaks it down into nested categories. It even takes an individual document like a newsletter and subdivides it into sections that can be browsed one at a time. This layering actually helps make things easier for the user. Imagine if you put all the documents at the site on a single menu, and didn't even try to arrange them by category. The user would have to scan the entire list to find the desired material, and might not realize that there are only three types of material at the site: brochures, newsletters, and press releases.

Dividing large documents into smaller files also helps them load faster. Though this is not as much a concern on an internal web, very large documents like a technical manual should definitely be chunked into separate files: one per chapter or even one for every major heading. On an Intranet, the problem is not loading time, it's scrolling. With a long document file, the user might have to continuously scroll through page after page of detail, looking for the desired passage, only to find that it isn't in this part of the book. How much easier, then, to have a quick table of contents for a manual, or even for each chapter, and click straight into the part of the document you want to read.

One way to improve access within a long file is by putting a table of contents or menu bar at the top, then linking the entries to specific headings in the document. This is accomplished in HTML using the <A NAME> and <A HREF> tags together:

```
Table of Contents:

<A HREF="#intro">Introduction</A><P>
<A HREF="#sect1">Section 1</A>
etc.
<A NAME="intro"></A>
<H1>Introduction</H1>
This is the introduction section. Clicking the Introduction
   link under the TOC will get you here.
<A NAME="sect1"></A>
<H1>Section 1</H1>
This is the first main section of the document. Clicking
   the Section 1 link under the TOC will get you here.
```

In this case, <A NAME> defines markers in the document that you can hyperlink to using the <A HREF> tags. The way to hyperlink to a marker is to put a pound sign (#) in front of the reference name.

You could do the same thing using a WYSIWYG authoring tool like Word Internet Assistant. In Word IA, for instance, you would insert a "bookmark" at each place where you want a marker, and then create a hyperlink from the TOC to the referenced bookmark using the toolbar Link button and the Hyperlink dialog (Figure 3.13).

### 3. Minimize Clicks; Maximize User Convenience

The danger with dividing your information into categories is that you may end up with too many layers, so that it becomes tedious for the user to select category after category of information. On closer inspection, it's easy to see that the Corporate Communications example on page 104 suffers from this problem. Instead of having separate submenus for press releases, brochures, and newsletters, wouldn't it be easier to just chunk them all into a single organized menu (Figure 3.14)?

Organized this way, the home page eliminates an entire layer of complexity, including three separate submenus. If the separate submenus had been retained, it would take six separate user clicks to see everything that you see in this one page. Though this adds convenience for the user, it's important to strike a balance. If a menu like this eventually expands beyond a few dozen entries, it might be harder to use than three separate submenus.

On the other hand, if the nature of the information is such that the user will always travel vertically in one direction, without a need to travel horizontally

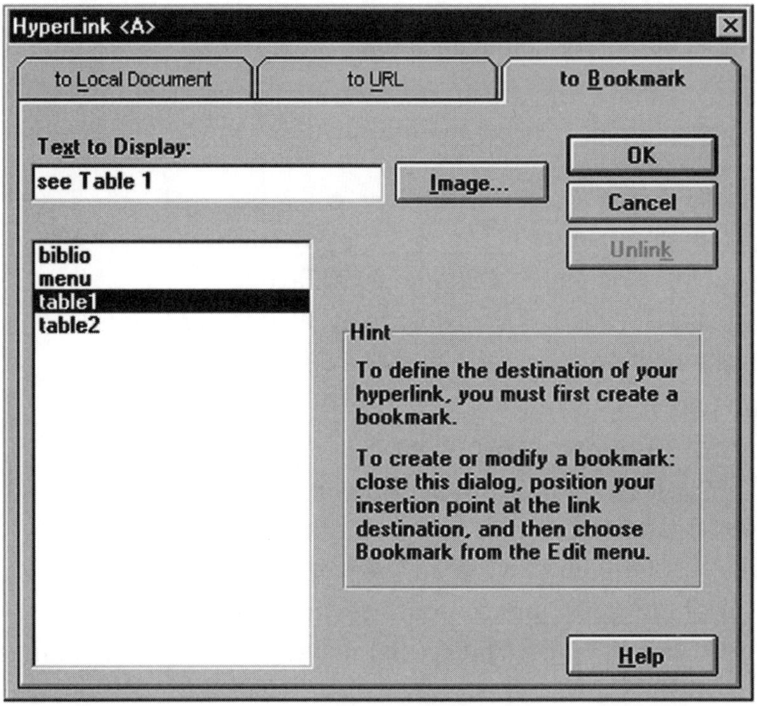

**Figure 3.13**  Example of Word IA HyperLink dialog with bookmark selected.

across categories, then separate menus might not be so bad. The only way to settle the issue is with rigorous *usability testing.* This sounds difficult, but is actually quite easy to do. Just show it to some typical users and get their opinion. Then put those opinions to work improving your site.

## 4. Tell Them What's New

The What's New section is a standard feature of any World Wide Web site, and it should be a standard feature on any Intranet site as well. Think about it from the users' viewpoint. Each time users access your information center they probably see the same menu. There's no way to peer beyond the familiar façade of your home page and guess what might have changed since the last time they visited. The only way is to go poking around through all the submenus, looking for clues. This is not a fun thing to do.

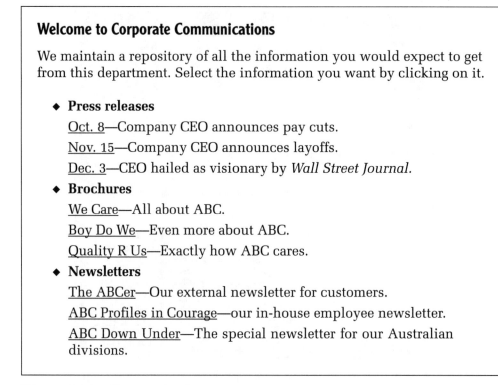

**Figure 3.14**    Reorganized menu.

A What's New section puts all the most recent information right up front so the user can see it all at a glance on a single page. The entries in this section should provide a link to new resources *in addition to* the links already provided on the regular menus and submenus. Of course, going to a What's New page is yet another click for the user, and there is no way to guarantee that every user will do it. Better yet, why not consider just putting all the new stuff right there on the home page (Figure 3.15)? A chatty, newsy introduction is a good way to draw readers into your site. Also check the Netscape homepage on the Internet (http://home.netscape.com/) for a great example.

## 5.  Make It Searchable

Telling them what's new is nice, and it quickly gives users the latest information. But searching is the best way to guarantee that users will locate exactly what they need quickly and easily. There are some easily implemented web

---

**Welcome to Corporate Communications**

Check out our latest <u>press release</u> on the subject of our CEO's nomination to the Business Council . . . or browse our latest <u>newsletter</u> with pictures of the board's golfing tour through Belize . . . a new <u>company brochure</u> explains all the ways ABC has learned to maximize shareholder return . . . and while you're at it, visit our fast-growing library of:

- <u>Press releases</u>
- <u>Brochures</u>
- <u>Newsletters</u>

Select the category of information you want to view.

---

**Figure 3.15**   Telling the user what's new up front.

search strategies. However, since searching is a somewhat more advanced application, it is covered in more detail in Chapter 7.

## 6. Provide a Master Table of Contents or Index

The greatest problem with using any large web site is making sure that you haven't missed anything important. Thus, once your site becomes sizable the best thing you can do for your users is to provide a single alphabetical, sequential, or hierarchical listing of everything at the site. I've seen some webs with multiple indexes sorted in different ways, such as by department, by information type, and even by author. Each entry should provide direct clickable access into the material.

## 7. Make It Look and Feel Consistent

On an internal web, your web pages don't have to be anything fancy. Unlike the World Wide Web, you're not being judged by a global audience—just by the people in your organization. So before you spend a lot of time on snazzy graphics or mind-boggling applications, spend some time giving your pages a consistent "look and feel."

A consistent web page design makes your site eminently more readable and usable, and helps make sure your readers never get disoriented. You'd be surprised how much difference it can make if you pay attention to the following details:

◆ *Consistent chunking.* In a web system, larger documents might be split into multiple sections for faster retrieval and scrolling. Each section is stored in a separate file that displays as a separate "page" on the screen. Chunking should be done in logical units, and should be done consistently throughout the document (Figure 3.16).

◆ *Unique titles on every page.* Each page at your site should have a unique title to identify it, such as "HR Policy Manual, Section 1." Unique titles are absolutely essential to easy navigation. Keep in mind that the user may come to this page in an entirely nonlinear fashion, and the title should answer the question: "Where am I?" Also, in many browsers, page titles accumulate on a special menu (such as the Go menu in Netscape) as the user moves through your site. The purpose of the Go menu is to let the user easily backtrack to any previously visited page. If all pages have the same title, it will be hard to tell one page from another (Figure 3.17).

◆ *Consistent heads within a page.* Each page should have an opening heading that indicates the subject matter on the page. The heading and title may be the same or may complement each other. But a separate opening heading is required because not every user will notice the title at the top of the window (or wherever it happens to be displayed in the browser). For consistent presentation from page to page, the heading should always be positioned the same way on each page and should always use the same heading level in HTML coding (usually H1). Heading levels should also be used consistently. For instance, never use H3 level directly below an H1; use heading levels in the hierarchy they were intended.

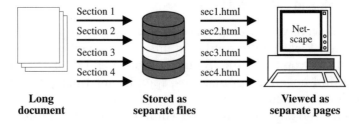

**Figure 3.16** How long documents are chunked.

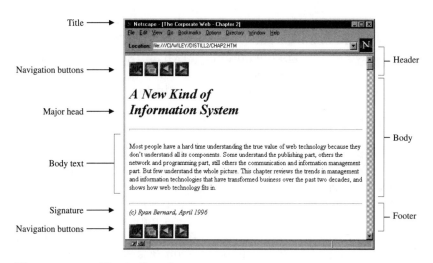

Title →

Navigation buttons →

Major head →

Body text →

Signature →

Navigation buttons →

— Header

— Body

— Footer

**Figure 3.17**  Typical web page components.

Many people flaunt these rules, but the result may be visually confusing to the user.

♦ *Consistent headers and footers.* In an HTML document, just as in a print document, the header and footer are the consistent elements that appear at the top and bottom of the page. The only difference is that a complete web page may not all fit into a single window, so that you nearly always see the header as soon as the page loads, but you often don't see the footer until you scroll to the bottom of the page (i.e., file). Certain elements are commonly included in the header, the footer, or in both. These may include a toolbar, navigation buttons, a simple slug that identifies the originating department or group, the date the page was last edited, and the e-mail address of the person to contact for more information. You should always use header/footer elements, and if so they should be consistent throughout your site.

♦ *Consistent navigation buttons.* Most browsers include simple menu controls that let a user go back to previous links or jump to new URLs. But suppose that a user links into the middle of one of your documents, and wants some way of going backward and forward in the document, or returning to the table of contents (TOC) or opening page. There should be buttons that allow this kind of linear movement or reference, such as a next page/previous page button, a TOC button, or even separate buttons for each major section in the document. Navigation buttons are easy to create in HTML (assuming you already have pictures of the buttons drawn and saved as GIF or JPEG images). This is done by inserting the button image (IMG tag) into the middle of the hyperlink (A HREF tag), for instance:

```
<A HREF="file.html"><IMG SRC="picture.gif"></A>
```

A more advanced way of providing navigation buttons is by using a *toolbar* or a *frame.* A toolbar is a row of buttons that is saved as a single image and then mapped to a standard set of links using the web's image-mapping feature (discussed in Chapter 5). The problem with this arrangement—as with individual navigation buttons—is that the buttons may scroll off the screen and not be easily accessible. This problem is effectively solved by the frame feature of Netscape (see http://www.netscape.com/assist/net_sites/frames.html), which lets you display the toolbar or navigation buttons in a stationary window segment that always stays in the same place, even as the user scrolls through the text. The use of toolbars, frames, and image mapping will be discussed in more detail in later chapters.

If you're using an HTML editor to construct web pages, it's hard to maintain consistency, especially when multiple authors are involved. The only way to do it is to publish a style sheet or template and hope that everyone follows the rules.

As it turns out, however, the best way to ensure consistency may be to quit using HTML editors and automate the process of document creation. Some web publishing systems (discussed in Chapter 5) now let you *automatically* include predefined headers, footers, titles, and navigation buttons within every page generated.

## 8. Make It Easy to Print

Web systems make it incredibly easy to print online documents, as long as the entire document is in a single file. But what if the document has been split into different files, as suggested earlier? To print the entire document, you would have to go to each section and print it individually. For a long document with dozens of sections, this would be prohibitive.

There are several ways to avoid this dilemma. The simplest way would be to produce a print file for the entire document, which can be accessed through a hyperlink, downloaded, and shipped to a local printer. A more advanced way might be to create a simple form that the user can use to request print jobs. A CGI script attached to the form could kick off a batch print job or notify the local secretary or administrator to kick off a print job and forward the document to the requesting party (see Chapter 7 for details on forms and CGI).

### 9. Test, Test, Test . . .

You did everything you were supposed to do. You dotted your *i*'s and crossed your *t*'s. But if you don't test your finished pages, you'll never know for sure. There'll always be that little nagging suspicion that something is wrong. So as soon as you are finished creating new pages—or even if you made a few tiny edits—use your browser to quickly review what you've done. Make sure all the hyperlinks still jump correctly. Make sure the illustrations display properly. Make sure the paragraphs all break the way you intended. You never know, you might have forgotten something.

### 10. Ask for Feedback

You may think you are a web page designer *extraordinaire,* but why not ask other people what they think? You might be surprised. And you might also be surprised how following up on the critique makes your web site even better.

## Power to the Users

An old question goes like this: If a tree falls in the forest and there's no one around to hear it, does it make a sound? A more up-to-date question might read like this: If you create an information center, and no one knows about it or uses it, does it really exist?

Sure, you can install a server, save your documents to it, and think up nifty new ways to deliver content to end users. But the web server is just half the equation. You're just spinning your wheels unless you have people actually using the stuff. And the more users you have, the more value you are providing to the entire organization. One of the main tricks to developing a successful information center is capturing the attention of people in your organization (or around the world, in the case of external web servers) and keeping them coming back. To get there in the first place, they will need certain kinds of tools and access methods, as discussed below.

## What Software People Need to Reach Your Site

Naturally, no one is going to be able to use your information unless they have the proper tools. Here's what they need:

- ◆ *A browser.* The user needs a web-compatible browser such as Netscape Navigator or Mosaic. If you have anything to say about it, recommend Netscape. As a simple example, a client of mine recently decided (against my recommendation) to use Mosaic as the standard browser for their Intranet. This was before browsers began to support tables. Once they started including tables in their documents, they found that the Netscape browser dynamically adjusted the table columns to fit the window size, whereas Mosaic didn't. A minor point if you are a web developer, perhaps, but a major one for people who have to use the information all the time. Even despite the furious pace of progress in the browser market, it will probably be a long time before any other browser matches the features of Netscape (I'm keeping my fingers tightly crossed on this one).

- ◆ *A network connection.* The user must be connected to the same TCP/IP network (LAN or WAN) that you are. For users on UNIX workstations, this is no problem. But users on PCs or Macs may also need to install *TCP/IP* networking to support the communication. (Check out the discussion of TCP/IP networks earlier in this chapter, and the introduction to TCP/IP in Chapter 2.)

Thus, setting up an Intranet may be—at first, anyway—a matter of distributing software. If you work in a company that already has an Intranet, or where the employees have the ability and knowledge to retrieve their own browsers from the Internet, you are in luck. (In the near future, many new computers will come with a web browser as standard equipment.)

If not, you will have to consider different ways of providing users with the software. In many companies, software can be retrieved and installed directly through the network using various installation utilities. Or there may be a support crew that does nothing but go around and install software for people. At worst, you may have to create your own installation diskettes, or put the software on various network file servers where people can grab it or run it.

Keep in mind that many browsers available for downloading off the Internet are free for short-term evaluation, including Netscape (see the sidebar on page 122). However, long-term dedicated use (typically anything over 30 days) requires licensing and payment. Netscape runs about $50 a seat, with lower unit prices for site licenses. Although this is somewhat of an expense, it is still considerably cheaper than almost any other business software you can buy. And once people have it, you will be able to use it in many different ways.

Also, regardless of how you distribute the software, be sure to take into account any helper applications that may be needed with the browser software. For example, if you plan to supply multimedia or Adobe Acrobat files from your information center, you may need special viewer software or plug-ins to make it work. These will be discussed in more detail in later chapters.

## What People Must Do to Reach Your Site

Remember how we hit the server during the "Hello World" server test earlier in this chapter? That's exactly the way all users will be accessing your system. If an internal web does not already exist, and there is no way to point users to your location from other hyperlinks elsewhere in the web, then users will have to type in the IP address or hostname of your server.

For instance, someone with Netscape might use the File/Open Location feature to type in the following:

```
http://197.14.123.35/
```

assuming 197.14.123.35 is the IP address of your server, or:

```
http://shorty/
```

if the computer where your web server is installed has a hostname of *shorty*. Assuming your opening page is set up as *index.html* (or whatever the default filename for your server), then just typing in the IP address or hostname of your computer will bring up your home page or main menu, the same way you did it in the server test.

Please remember that there is no need for users to be logged in to your server, or have the server drive appear as a local drive on their computer. That's one of the main reasons you are using web technology, remember? So you don't have to worry about these kinds of administrative tasks.

Of course, as always, there are ways to make things simpler and easier for the end user. If yours is the only information center on the Intranet, you can set up the browser so that it automatically opens to your home page when the user starts up the software. For instance, the Netscape dialog shown in Figure 3.18 lets you specify the opening page on startup.

### Retrieving Browser Software from the Internet

The recommended browser for any web system is Netscape Navigator, which you can retrieve from the WWW at:

http://home.netscape.com/

Netscape is not free: You are allowed to download an evaluation copy, but if you end up using it you must pay for each installed copy at a rate of about $50 each (site licenses available).

My second choice for a browser is Enhanced Mosaic, a product created by Spyglass Inc. under license from the NCSA, which originally invented Mosaic. Spyglass does not sell Mosaic directly. Instead, it licenses it to other companies for repackaging and resale. The best-known repackage job is the Microsoft Internet Explorer available free off the WWW at:

http://www.microsoft.com/

Repackaged versions of Enhanced Mosaic are also offered by companies like O'Reilly & Associates, CompuServe (Internet in a Box), and Quarterdeck.

Once a browser is set up this way, users don't have to remember *any* IP addresses, hostnames, or URLs. All they have to do is start the browser software, view your page, and start clickin'. And if desired, you can even save them that step. You can include the browser icon in the Startup window (PC) or .xinitrc file (UNIX) so that it starts automatically every time they boot the computer. Thus, the browser becomes an integral part of their everyday desktop environment.

If you plan to set up users this way—so the browser starts on bootup and automatically opens to your home page—it's best to preconfigure the software *before* it gets installed on the user machine, instead of expecting each user to set it up this way, or having to set it up that way for each individual user. Again, this is just a way to simplify users' access. So all users have to do is install the software, start it, and immediately they are connected to the Intranet.

Once the user accesses your site, all further connections to information at that site—or to other sites on the network—should be handled transparently

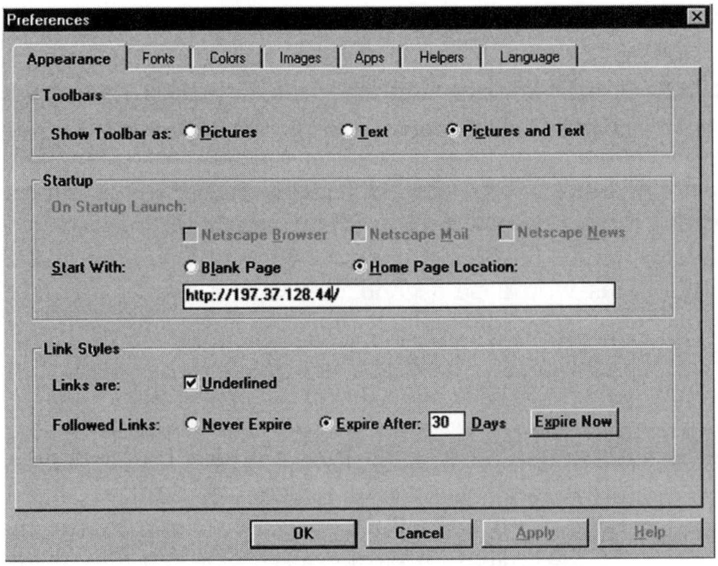

**Figure 3.18**    Netscape home page setup dialog.

through built-in hyperlinks, so that the location and content of the various servers in your company becomes a nonissue. Users should not have to worry about which machines the servers are installed on, how to connect to them, or which file to retrieve. All users should have to do is read a menu, home page, or table of contents, then just point and click to get the information they want.

### Limiting Access to Your Site

Maybe you *don't* want everyone in the company to be able to access your information. Maybe you want to tightly control the users who have access to your site. If that's the case, there's a way to do it.

Whereas most other network applications start with the assumption that everyone must log in, web servers provide open access by default—they just assume that the system should be open to the entire world. But most web servers also provide a way to restrict access to the site, an internal directory, or a set of files. Typically you can restrict user access through either of two methods:

◆ *User ID and password*. For example, you may want to set up a list of authorized user IDs and passwords for people to access the site.

When users try to access the site, the browser asks them to enter their ID/password first (Figure 3.19).

- *IP address.* The IP address method works a little differently: It can automatically limit site access to certain IP addresses (i.e., the site can be accessed only from certain machines), or it can open site access to all users *except* certain IP addresses. This method is not too useful in a corporate environment, since the person trying to gain access might be able to find a different machine that is not restricted. This would be a good method to use, however, if you were setting up a site for access by specific customers, sales reps, or departments. The user would have to be using a machine at that location to access the information on your web site.

Some server models also provide additional types of access control, such as group-level and host/domain name. Access control can typically be put into force on a server level or on a directory level. For example, you may want to restrict access to all files listed under the server. Or you may want to restrict access to just a set of files in a particular directory. Some servers may even let you restrict access to individual files, on a file-by-file basis.

The mechanics of setting up user authentication may vary depending on your server. The best way to determine what is needed is to read your server documentation. However, a generic set of procedures is included in Appendix D.

### Protecting Your Site through Encryption

Even if you do user authentication, your site is not absolutely secure because there is always a chance that an unscrupulous network administrator is mon-

**Figure 3.19** Typical user ID/password request in Netscape.

itoring the system and can capture the user ID and password as it passes through a router or other network-connected machine. This situation is of more concern on the Internet than it is on an Intranet. On the Internet, you don't know who the person might be who is intercepting the transmission. In a corporate environment, you are more likely to know which system administrators have authority to intercept and read network communications—and you may not care whether they read it or not.

Nevertheless, if your site is dispensing highly sensitive data that is subject to snooping, you should consider further protection in the form of encryption schemes. Encryption is accomplished by using a server and browsers that support the same encryption standard (such as having a Netscape Commerce Server talking to Netscape Navigator browsers). Once you have these components, encryption happens automatically. Anything that leaves the server is encrypted on the fly, travels over the network in an encrypted state, and is decrypted by the browser at the other end.

As I said before, though, encryption is normally overkill on an Intranet. Most internal webs I've seen don't even have user authentication in place, much less encryption. If you are planning to serve some of your data out across an external web, however, encryption becomes more important—especially if the data is intended for viewing only by business partners or field employees. If you plan to use encryption, expect to pay about $500 to $1,000 extra for your server.

### If There Already Is an Existing Intranet

If your network already has other web information servers on it, and you are simply adding yours to the total offering, things become a lot simpler for everyone. For one thing, you probably don't have to worry about distributing software or setting up users. By now, users probably have all the tools they need, and they are already well accustomed to using them. They may also be hooked into a central menu that appears automatically when they start their browsers.

In this case, your job is simply a matter of making sure users can get from other parts of the web to your own information center. If there is a central server for the entire company, you will want to tell the people who run it about your new server, so that they can add your information center to any menus or tables of contents they maintain for the company. To make the link, they will have to know your server's network hostname or IP address, and they may want a complete list of the content at your site. In the last chapter of this book, I will discuss ways that large webs can be managed to make the notification process easy for everyone.

## The Matter of Training

The really neat thing about having an Intranet is the way it makes information access so incredibly easy. Assuming your information center is set up right, all the user has to do is just point, click, and instantly retrieve anything on the server. But just because it's easy doesn't mean you can just put it out there and expect people to use it immediately. Some training is *always* required—and if not training, some sort of highly visible publicity about your effort. Rolling out a site on an internal web is not that much different from rolling one out on the World Wide Web. The more people who hear about it, the more hits you will get.

As an example, one day I happened to be visiting the headquarters of a major American computer manufacturer. While there, I broached the subject of the internal web with an employee I knew who worked there as a technical writer. After I tried describing it in several different ways, this person—who was obviously struggling to connect with the idea—allowed that she had *heard of* such a thing, but didn't realize it was a web. She even thought there might be some sort of software on her computer that could access it, but she certainly never had used it. Since my friend never received formal training, she had no way to connect with the concept. Obviously, here was a potentially new and quite efficient way she could use to get internal information—maybe even do research for her job—but since it was far removed from the normal information delivery channels, she had no way of understanding exactly why or how to use it.

If you want people to start receiving information through the Intranet, instead of through their normal channels, you may have to lead them the first few steps of the way. If you've already used a web browser, you understand how simple it is to use. But what people need is not so much to learn *how* to use a web browser as to learn *why* to use it. There's still a conceptual leap people have to make that they probably won't do on their own unless they've already used the World Wide Web. And even if they have used the Web, there is still a conceptual leap people have to make between the external web and the internal one. Unfailingly, someone will ask, "You mean we're on the Internet, right now?" "No," you'll reply, "this is an *in-TRA-net*." Getting people to understand the whys and wherefores of an Intranet isn't a major obstacle, but it's a hurdle nonetheless, the same way that getting people to start using a mouse and windows was a minor hurdle a few years ago.

The kind of training I'm talking about could be as simple as a brief luncheon seminar in which you sit people down, get their attention, and do a short demo. In smaller companies or workgroup situations, it may involve a brief hands-on exercise. Naturally, you may not have much success scheduling the time unless you have management backing, and that may require selling the idea upstairs first.

The success of your effort depends on what you have to show. If it's just a test page with a few pretty graphics, people may *ooh* and *ahh,* but go away shaking their heads. If it's company news, hard-to-find statistics, widely used references, online training, or data—in short, truly useful stuff people would kill to get their hands on—you may find that people buy in and start using the system a lot faster. The best way to get total buy-in, of course, is to rig it so that some part of the system is required to do their job—such as making the Intranet the place everyone must go to turn in their weekly progress reports or get employee benefit information. A good way to get people involved is to provide two-way interaction through forms and database access, so that people will be able to contribute to the system, as well as obtain information from it. Keep in mind that you may only get one shot at this: So you'd better make it good. Be sure you have all your ducks in a row and be prepared to make people go *wow.*

The main hurdle involved in explaining the Intranet to users is to avoid making it more complicated than it really is. All they have to know is (1) how to start the browser, (2) how to use it, and (3) what they can use it for—what information is available for access within the company. Under how-to-use, you should demonstrate the structure of the available web site(s), show them how to browse and navigate, and explain how to save files or print. Since the average browser has a fairly simple set of easily understood features, formal browser training itself shouldn't take any longer than an hour or two.

But there are other issues to confront, as well. One of the main issues is eliminating the preconceived notions people have about web technology, and their confusion about the relation to the Internet. If your Intranet happens to be integrated with other Internet applications, including e-mail, FTP, chat groups, and so forth, then there may be a considerable amount of additional training in how and when to use those additional tools.

Getting users acquainted with the Intranet is only the first phase of your training effort. An even more intensive period of training will likely occur from a few weeks to a few months after you first introduce the system. The second phase of training is the "publishing phase," when people decide they want to start contributing actively to the content of the Intranet. At this point, they will need to start learning many of the concepts and skills covered in Chapters 5 and 6 of this book. It's a good idea to have web publishing tools or add-ons already selected and ready for use by the time this phase occurs. You should also have a good idea of the best publishing models for your organization. It will not be readily apparent to your trainees exactly how web publishing occurs, and which are the most productive and efficient ways to go about doing it. So in addition to training on tools, you will also want to show workgroups how to organize their publishing efforts and configure both their tools and document repositories.

Once you reach the publishing phase, it is important to realize that you are already at a stage where the Intranet is poised to achieve maximum value for the organization. This is the point where you have the opportunity to achieve buy-in, empowerment, and full user participation. That's why training is especially crucial at this point: to make sure people are fully empowered instead of being angrily frustrated at their inability to mold the system to their needs. The more you help these people by "blazing the trail" and predesigning systems they can easily adopt, the simpler it will be for everyone involved and the better the chance that the Intranet will grow and blossom within your organization.

## Let One Hundred Servers Blossom

Now you have the system running and you've got everyone interested in it. So how do you keep them interested? This may be the greatest challenge of all (many a webmaster on the World Wide Web would like to know the answer to that one). The answer, dear reader, is what the used car dealer used to say: *volume, volume, volume!*

The idea is not to have merely one information center, or half a dozen. It is to have as many as it takes to empower everyone to share information across the enterprise. At pioneering Intranet sites, like SunWeb and the DEC internal web, there are hundreds or thousands of separate web servers running on the internal network (see Chapter 4 for examples). At Sun, the ratio is now nearly *one web server for every eight people.*

The more providers and users, the more valuable the overall web system is to the enterprise. Here's why: Bob Metcalfe is already down in history as the guy who invented Ethernet, the most commonly used network standard for connecting PCs. But Bob is well known for another bit of wisdom called Metcalfe's Law, which (in a loose translation) goes something like this: *The value of a network is proportional to the number of users squared.* If just one person is connected to a network, it's worthless. If two people are connected, that's better. But as you add more and more users, the network's value to the organization grows exponentially.

To Metcalfe's Law, let me add an extra fillip which I'll call *Bernard's Corollary.* My corollary is similar to the original law, but this one applies to the Intranet. The corollary goes like this: *The value of an Intranet is proportional to the number of applications, servers, and users cubed* (beat that one).

Here's what I mean. If you just have one document being served over an Intranet and one person reading it, the system has some value because (hopefully) you're already saving someone time and money. But, as you add more documents and users, the system's value increases exponentially. This is because you're saving more and more time and money for both the author and the users (since you no longer have to deliver the documents through the old, sluggish repro/mail system).

But the value really starts to expand into a third dimension when you use web to deliver different applications running on different servers. For instance, let's say one server is providing documents, another one database access, another one groupware connectivity, and another one is giving users a direct view into the mainframe. Suddenly, you are treating the web browser as a single multipurpose client in a way that makes it very simple for users to surf from one application to the next, all in a single window.

This saves a considerable amount of time because users don't have to start four different programs to use four separate applications. It also saves software costs and training costs, because you probably won't have to train users for each application. So the net cost saving shows itself in ways you may not be able to fully predict, including software, training, printing, delivery, productivity, help center support calls, systems development overhead, and many more.

The net lesson to learn from all this is simple: The more mileage you get out of a web system, and the more different applications you can serve, the better. To paraphrase another oft-heard quote: "Let a hundred servers blossom." Most of the companies that have taken full advantage of the Intranet literally have hundreds of servers operating simultaneously.

## Planting the Seeds

Before you get all caught up into a frenzy of trying to plan and create an Intranet with dozens of servers, let me pull you back from the brink and calm you down with these two words: *Don't bother.* If you carefully plant the seeds of web technology, the system will blossom on its own, just the way the World Wide Web grew to enormous proportions on the Internet.

While there are certain things we can do to control the growth and direction of an Intranet (see Chapter 9), trying to dictate content at the micro level will make the system completely unmanageable. Remember the valuable lessons we learned in previous chapters about the Internet itself—how large-scale networks can become self-replicating systems that require little or no administration? One of the greatest values of web is that it is an *empowering technology:* It grows from the bottom up and not from the top down.

So it is wisest for the people in charge of things to simply plant the seeds and let the garden grow. The best ways to do that will be covered in Chapter 9.

## Where Do We Go from Here?

Now that you understand how web technology works and how to bring a web system online, you've just gotten started. In the next chapter, I'll show you some great examples of how vanguard organizations are using internal webs to deliver information to their end users. And later chapters will show you how to create rich webs of documents, multimedia, and data. Read on for some great examples of real-life webs in operation, or skip to later chapters if you want to bone up on your web-building techniques.

## Chapter Four At a Glance

This chapter shows how four major corporations have put the Intranet into practice, including:

- ◆ Sun Microsystems, Inc.
- ◆ Nortel (formerly Northern Telecom)
- ◆ Chevron Petroleum Technology Corporation
- ◆ Digital Equipment Corporation

# The Intranet in Practice

Don't take my word for it. Look what's happening out in the real world. Creating an internal web isn't just a good idea in theory, it's already being put into practice extensively at business locations around the globe. Some companies have had their own internal Intranets with gopher and FTP services for years, but even the most forward-thinking companies didn't add web services until 1994, a year or more after Mosaic became available. Nevertheless, any company that developed full-blown, companywide web applications during 1995 was considered an "early adopter" of the technology.

This chapter profiles four different early adopters with a focus on the experiences they've had and techniques they've used to develop their own internal webs. Most early adopters have one thing in common: They are heavily represented by high-technology companies that specialize in applying technological solutions to business problems. But that doesn't mean only technology companies will be able to benefit from the Intranet. The ranks of early adopters also include companies like clothing manufacturer Levi Strauss, real estate firm Cushman Wakefield, pharmaceutical company Eli Lilly, and many more. Through their innovation and experimentation, early adopters are blazing a path with the technology that future businesses will be able to follow. Within a few years' time, the extraordinary new applications that these companies have developed will be commonplace in the business world.

Though most of the companies here are large multinational corporations, small businesses should take heart. If it's this easy to implement an internal web in companies with over 10,000 employees, imagine how easy it might be for a company with under a thousand. The only advantage that size may provide is the ability to dedicate extra resources to undertake some of the necessary experimentation that always occurs in the early days of an Intranet.

## SunWEB: From Zero to 3,000 Servers in Two Years Flat

The internal web at Sun Microsystems, Inc. had fairly humble beginnings for a system that is now probably the world's largest in terms of server count. It all started as a few pages' worth of progress reports stored on the computer of one Carl Meske in early 1994. Since Meske was the original webmaster responsible for creating the external World Wide Web site for Sun Microsystems (http://www.sun.com shown in Figure 4.1), it seemed only logical that instead of turning in his progress reports on paper, where they would get buried in someone's filing cabinet, he might instead display them online so they could be viewed by anyone who was interested in his activities.

Meske's online progress reports were mildly impressive to those who saw them, but what people really found impressive was when Meske's team created an internal mirror site for the 1994 Winter Olympics in Lillehammer,

**Figure 4.1** The Sun external home page.

Norway. Others took an interest and an informal trend began that saw people building their own internal web sites and viewing them through browsers.

Meske started thinking of other innovative ways to use the technology. One application that would eventually become a prominent feature of Sun's internal web offering was a more intelligent way to access the company's internal software distribution disk. Sun distributes about three gigabytes of commercial software which it makes available to employees through a mechanism called *SoftDist.* The software includes all the standard office applications, including programs like FrameMaker and Lotus Notes. Each network in the Sun organization has a connection to a SoftDist machine and the servers are visible as local filesystems through NFS mounting.

The problem with the SoftDist process was that there was no clean set of documents to describe what was available on the application server. If you brought up the service, you could use the UNIX "ls" command to generate a straight directory listing of the installed software (like the directory listing provided by an FTP server), but only experienced users knew what all the different directories contained. For new employees, who had a special need to get up and running with their basic work tools, there was a learning curve involved just to explore and decipher the offerings on SoftDist.

Meske developed a solution that would use both the online publishing and file retrieval capabilities of the internal web. To do this, he set up customized pages so that employees could see at a glance the list of tools they use on a daily basis, then fire up the application they needed directly from the web page. To accomplish this, he developed a set of web pages that list all the tools by category (word processing, admin tools, manager tools, IR tools) and give a one-line description of what each tool does. If there was a major support group set up to support a particular product, it would contain links to that information. For instance, for FrameMaker it tells how to take classes in FrameMaker and where to get help if you have problems.

If the user clicks a hyperlink to start the program, a CGI program checks the local environment to see if the program is available and gives the user the option to start it up or cancel. If the program is not locally available, it explains what the problem is and how to contact a network administrator for help. This system, superimposed on the traditional in-house software distribution mechanism, has significantly reduced the amount of calling around employees have to do to get up and running with key business applications.

As time passed, many of the engineers at Sun began using the web to publish their own information, and before long the internal web had 200 different servers running on it. This made it nearly impossible to keep track of all the information available. Web content was becoming increasingly difficult to use and manage. To help solve the problem, Meske created a focus group to analyze and solve the problem. Their solution: a professionally designed central menuing system where information could be listed by category. They called the result SunWEB (see Figure 4.2).

To test the new interface, they went looking for certain types of hard-core online communicators. "Anybody who would send an e-mail to the world—such as a message addressed to *all@*—we would jump on them. They're the

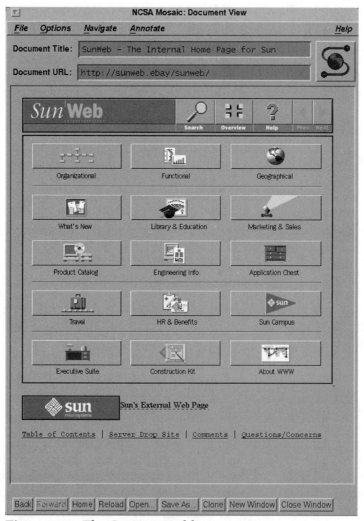

**Figure 4.2** The Sun internal home page.

perfect candidates," Meske says. Then the team worked to gain the support of IR. "They wanted to know what is the cost, to make sure we weren't going to be a hit on support costs or impact the network." To lower the support costs, Meske's team put together a basic web construction kit that included instructions on how to build a home page and how to install a web server, plus templates for personal home pages so that people could build their own pages but still look professional. To entice rank-and-file employees to the web, they added information like the company's human resources handbook. To entice company executives, they put stock quotes online. "We wanted everyone using it," says Meske, "not just engineers."

Typical of their effort was a push to get Sun product information online. "We didn't realize how big a company we were until we started looking at all the products," says Meske. "So we went to the product marketing guys and said 'We want you to build a web site so we know what you're doing. You've got all these product managers that are managing their products, why not put this stuff online?' I wanted to know what other groups were doing similar to the way they can see what I am doing on the web. Since we're now a 16,000 person company; it's nice to be able to try to figure out who is doing what. So we worked with them to build their site, we sent them e-mails explaining how we wanted them to do it. The interesting thing about it is that a lot of people are very creative and like to talk about themselves. With our templates you could put up a web site in less than 10 minutes."

Within a few months, the number of web servers online within the SunWEB exploded rapidly. "Now we have about 2,000 web sites inside the company, from personal, to project, to group sites, to functional ones," says Meske. The result has been savings in time and costs in a number of areas, not just paper publishing. "To communicate, people used to send giant e-mails with these files attached. A whole slew of costs start propagating when you're dealing with 100 K e-mail messages. Instead of all this pushing [information on people]," observes Meske, "why not do this pulling metaphor where people can go and get the information? Just send them a message with the URL in it."

At the rate the SunWEB is expanding, says Meske, the total number of servers may soon top 3,000. Since the total number of Sun employees is about 15,000, that's comes out to about *one server for every five employees in the company*. To keep up with the explosion in server population, the SunWEB managers have created a registration form that people can use to register their server with the main webmaster. The model is very much like Yahoo, where people can pick a category that they want their site to be listed under—the webmasters do the rest.

The categories originally developed by Meske's focus group, and still reflected in the SunWEB main menu (Figure 4.2), cover just about every subject imaginable, and could serve as an excellent model for any large-scale business's web system:

- *Views* are the first things the SunWEB menu provides. There are three different views of the system: an organizational view (the different companies in the Sun worldwide organization), a functional view of the company (corporate, IR, sales, marketing, etc.), and a geographical view (all the different Sun locations throughout the world, accessible by clicking on a world map).

- *What's New* is essential component of any web site also shows up prominently on the SunWEB home page, providing recent press releases for the company, online audio reports from Sun president Scott McNealy and others (called WSUN Radio), and the company's quarterly magazine *Illuminations,* which is now distributed online instead of in paper format (Figure 4.5).

- *Library & Education* is the section that is the front door for Sun's training effort (Figure 4.3). Here is where employees will find the home page for SunU, the company's catchall moniker for its internal and external training course offerings. This section also includes links to the company's libraries, where they can access research services and locate company document and electronic resources (Figure 4.4).

- *Marketing & Sales* contains all the marketing and sales databases, competitive information, marketing tools, organization information, and basic information to help sales and marketing people in the field.

- *Product Catalog* contains information on all the Sun products, for general reference by all employees.

- *Engineering Info* provides links to the engineering teams for all the different Sun products, including documentation, tools, and performance information for all the engineering organizations. "Some groups don't have their links in here," says Meske, "so it's becoming like, if you don't have it, it's not cool."

- *Application Chest* provides links to all the software tools that are available on each person's local file server, with a brief product profile, online documentation, and information on how to get training, how to get support, and how to get a standalone license.

- *Travel* explains how to prepare a travel expense authorization, provides current travel advisories for foreign countries, links to an international security home page, displays currency exchange rates,

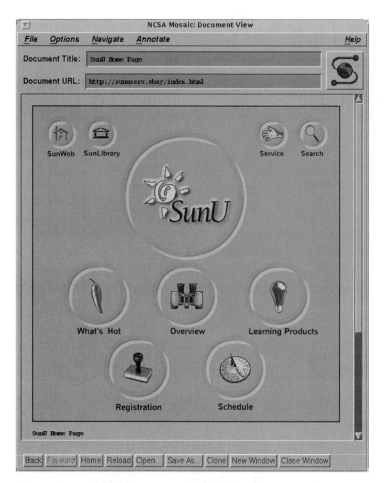

**Figure 4.3**   The Sun training home page.

and includes information about transit systems in the San Francisco Bay Area where Sun headquarters is located.

♦ *HR & Benefits* is one of the larger areas, with information about employee benefits programs, a manager's handbook, a developer's toolkit, and corporate employment information. Sun's human resources department manages the area on their own; they even have their own full-time webmaster.

♦ *Sun Campus* provides maps to all the different locations and buildings in the Bay Area, including local directories and phone numbers. This area also contains information about commuting, bus schedules, and local company-provided vans. It also shows the location of shipping and receiving areas, food services, reprographic centers, and conference rooms.

- ◆ *Executive Suite* provides links to an "executive suite of business references" on the Internet and the World Wide Web, including headline news, government sites, marketing information, and various other popular Internet sites such as GolfWeb.

- ◆ *Construction Kit* contains all the how-tos for building web sites on the Intranet, including policies and procedures, templates, graphics, clip art, and links to tools (such as a conversion tool called FtoH, which handles FrameMaker to HTML conversions). There are some HTML editors available online (such as HoTMetaL), image capture and display tools, searching tools (freeWAIS), utility tools, log statistics tools, and others.

- ◆ *About WWW* explains to new users what the web is all about and the various components of web technology such as HTML and CGI.

A search tool at the top of the screen provides a way to quickly search for specific content on the internal web. Other links at the bottom of the main menu include a "server drop site" where people can register new servers on the central directory, and a comment section that lets people post comments about the web to a newsgroup or send e-mail to the webmaster.

Meske doesn't see a problem with including materials on the internal web that are not strictly work related, such as the sports information and market quotes. "What's the difference if I'm reading my paper in the cafeteria," he says, "or taking my coffee break on the web? People at first are bitten by the browsing bug, then it becomes just another tool. We're not sending out the network police, though we do track all the packets that are going out to the Internet. We're not to the point where we're saying don't do this or that." If there are any restrictions on usage, Meske says, "most are just done at the local level. There are no mandates coming down from on top."

To help get information online, SunWEB uses a "gatekeeper" system. A gatekeeper is a person who works with the various content providers to help get their content up on the web. They also have webmasters who are responsible for the content of specific large sites such as human resources.

To make the web run, Sun carries site licenses for various Netscape products, including the Navigator browser and the Communications server, though it also makes other web server software available such as the CERN and NCSA servers for UNIX. They use CGI scripts written in the perl scripting language

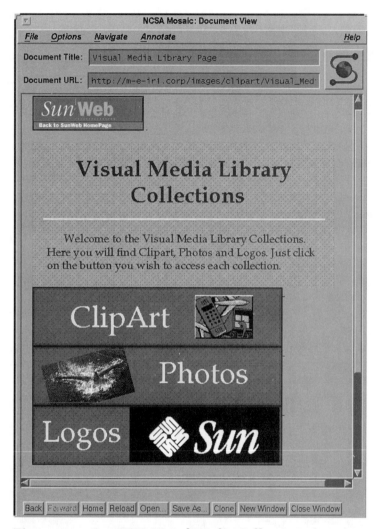

**Figure 4.4** SunWEB Visual Media Collection.

to handle access to back-end databases such as Sybase, ORACLE, Informix, and Illustra.

Some parts of the internal web are standouts, like the audio report from company president Scott McNealy. "The McNealy Report is an audio interview with people in the company or customers, or just Scott talking," Meske explains. "There are about 8 or 10 audio segments that people have done. It's a great way for people to stay in touch with the company president. He talks about his pet peeves, you know what's bothering him, it really has made him accessible to everyone."

To distribute the audio without undue performance drags on the network, Sun places mirrored copies of the files on the software distribution servers and accesses them the same way that software is accessed through the Application Chest. "Otherwise," Meske explains, "if 15,000 people go get that one-megabyte audio file, you're going to kill the network."

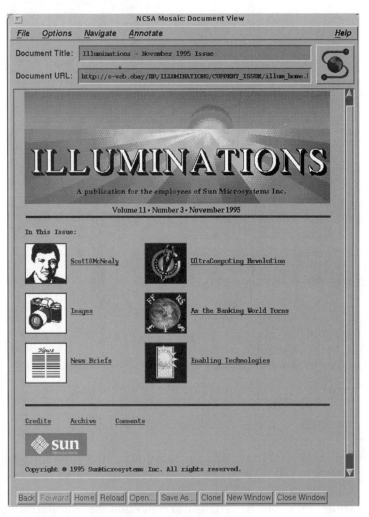

**Figure 4.5** SunWEB internal newsletter.

To integrate the internal web with the Internet, Sun uses a number of proxy servers that sit along the firewall and handle requests for outside materials. Each proxy machine handles a particular internal domain with names like *corp* (Corporate), *eng* (Engineering), *ebay* (East Bay Area), and *wbay* (West Bay Area). "We have configured the browsers so they point to the caching machines and the caching machines are the ones that do all the work," Meske explains. The arrangement minimizes traffic, so that all employees are not trying to access the Internet through the same node.

Now that the web has grown to take in all aspects of company operations, it shows the superiority of the distributed technology over other ways of serving the same information, Meske says. "Can you imagine if I tried to gather all these different web sites and tried to put them in one machine, what would happen? This way, it is distributed and owned by the owner. The network is so powerful, why not use it instead of having everything local? If I had to distribute 15,000 copies of everything, it would be prohibitive."

Typically, there is no crossover between internal and external web information, Meske says. "If it's external, then it gets pushed out onto the company's home page at www.sun.com." Sun maintains a special access site for resellers, which is accessed from the regular Sun external web server, but using a special account that requires the authorized resellers to login.

"I think that the power of the Internet is one that people have not exploited fully yet," Meske says. "People will have to have access to global information to make decisions and make them quickly. This is the kind of thing that will let us do it."

## Nortel: Opening Up Large Silos of Information

Formerly known as Northern Telecom, the company called Nortel is a global supplier of telephone and network switching equipment with 57,000 employees worldwide. It also possesses one of the largest and most sophisticated private worldwide Intranets in existence. The web serves a diverse network which incorporates over 34,000 Macs, 12,000 PCs, and 20,000 UNIX workstations, running a variety of protocols including TCP/IP, Apple Talk, and others. Nortel's backbone is a high-speed ATM network with some T1 segments that carries traffic between the various business units.

The current Nortel web is so highly integrated between internal and external components, that sometimes employees are not even aware whether they are on the internal or external legs of the network. Anyone in the world can see the external Nortel web site (Figure 4.6) at http://www.nortel.com, but only company employees can see the internal nodes. When you are browsing Nortel's internal web, sometimes the only way you can tell which segment you are on is by looking at the Location field. Most internal web servers at Nortel are referenced by IP address only (such as 47.183.5.11).

Despite the sophistication of its current web system, things weren't always so. "We are a technology company, and for some years we had links into the Internet," explains Chris Koehncke, Nortel's Director of Account Management for Global Enterprise Services. "You had to go to a gateway and telnet and ftp through a host computer to get to it."

Nortel's first efforts at linking to the World Wide Web started with a group of engineers who put together a proxy server so that they could use Mosaic to surf the Internet. Several of the engineers obtained shareware that allowed them to turn their own machines into web servers.

"Eventually," says Koehncke. "they started putting meaningful information in it, and it grew from there." Now, most Nortel employees are familiar with web technology and are using it for various aspects of their business.

One of the first groups to set up an information center was Nortel's Magellan network equipment group. They used the web to display organization

**Figure 4.6**   The Nortel external home page.

charts, competitive information, engineering plans, news releases, and a central depot of information for Magellan employees. "Because they were in the networking business," Koehncke explains, "they were the first to adopt it."

From these simple beginnings, the Nortel internal web grew to the point where it now has over 1,000 servers online representing most of the company's worldwide divisions and locations. The internal web also includes perhaps a dozen different internal newsgroups that employees can use to discuss technical or business subjects. Employees can post technical questions to a bulletin board and get back a response within 24 hours.

The web includes a central menu that comes up automatically when employees start their Netscape browsers (see Figure 4.7). There is also a spider program that goes through and indexes the content so that users can automatically search for topics by keyword.

"Our telephone directory is online and updated all day," says Koehncke. "We stopped publishing a (printed) telephone directory altogether." Nortel makes a number of its product commercials available for viewing on the internal web in Apple's QuickTime format. They're also working on a RealAudio application that will allow the chairman and other top executives to communicate directly with the company's sales force and employees in real time over the web.

"We are opening up silos," is the way people at Nortel now describe their new system: "people coming online with stored information and being able to share it." It is now common at Nortel to see http addresses of different groups and teams advertised in all the company's internal publications. "Instead of sending out a billion pages of documentation, our Human Resources department now sends out teasers," says Koehncke. "They say, here's the web address: Go here for more information."

One of the greatest challenges Nortel faced was distributing Netscape browsers to 46,000 of its internal employees, first in North America and later in Europe and Asia. The decision to use Netscape came after some deliberation. "We played with Mosaic a while," Koehncke explains, "but it didn't get commercialized fast enough." Many beta copies of Netscape were already floating around the company, so Nortel decided to standardize on the commercial release version.

According to Herschel Miller, an internal consultant who coordinated the rollout, "We realized we had to take this bull by the horns and take a serious look at the tool. We took it through reviews, and obviously it meets the needs of all three platforms [UNIX, Mac, and PC]. From there we developed a rollout process and a registration process that allowed people to get access to the external Internet."

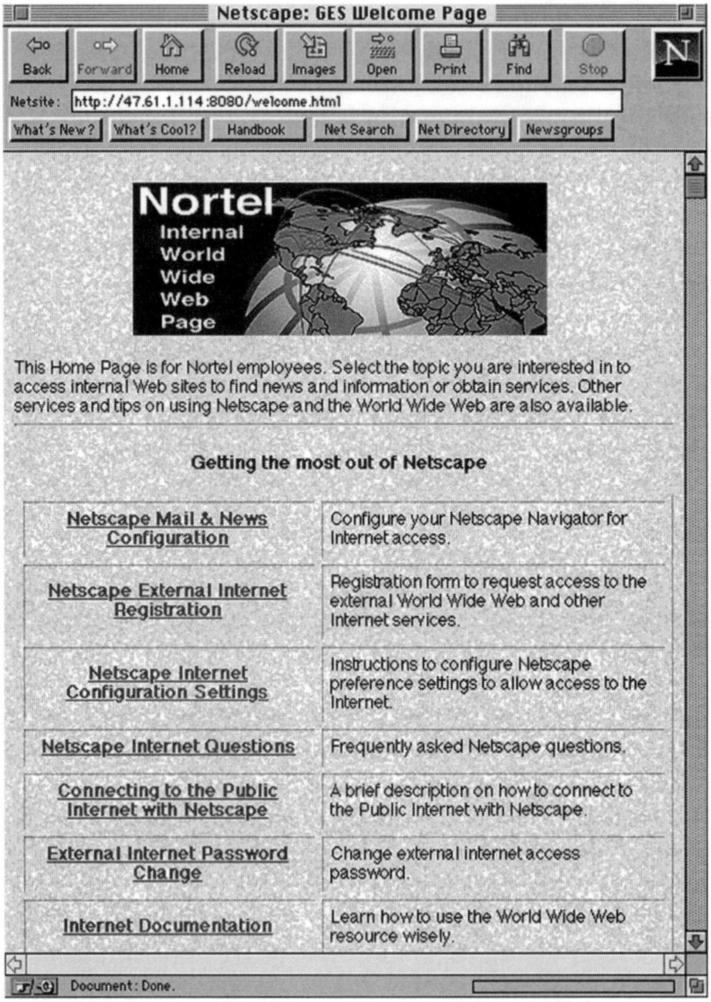

**Figure 4.7** The Nortel internal home page.

To ensure the success of the rollout, managers realized they would have to convince employees of the benefits of the new technology, For this reason, Global Enterprise Services accompanied the rollout with a massive publicity campaign coordinated by that organization's internal marketing group.

Says Miller: "Our marketing campaign explained the value of the tool to the individual and to the organization: that users could develop home pages to share information; that it would allow users to surf through and find articles or items of interest; and that it would allow access to the Internet."

The rollout team notified all senior management weeks before the general announcement, then made the announcement to employees through various routes, including e-mail and memos. Part of the publicity effort included advertisements on strategically placed multimedia kiosks that were already being used by the company as a way of providing information to employees. Stories appeared in the company's employee magazine. Rollout team members did seminars and demos for the various internal organizations.

One of the carrots that the rollout team used to entice people was the promise they could do their own home page. "We did not tell people what to put on their home page," says Miller. "Our approach to our [internal] customers is to offer them a better mouse trap, meet our customer's needs and help them meet their [external] customers' needs. We told them, you can be as creative as you want, use as many graphics as you want . . . do your own thing."

Walter L. Oldham, Senior Manager of Business Development and Process Re-engineering, is already looking at ways the company can use the technology to streamline its operations. "One of the issues we are tackling with web technology is what we call 'moves, adds and changes,' " says Oldham. "Moving folks around can cost us a lot of money. If it's a cube, the cost of the move is $1,000, and a walled office costs us $2,000. In the past year we did 11,000 moves, so that added up to a lot of money. You don't walk away with any benefits; you spent administrative dollars with nothing to show for it."

"Since I handle process re-engineering, I was able to bring together the facilities people, division representatives, and HR representatives and we put together a systematic approach using Netscape Navigator that lets people communicate their desires whether they want to hire, move or terminate. Then we put it in a graphical user interface, and arrange it so everyone is notified automatically through the Netscape Navigator when a move is needed." The backend, says Oldham, will use a CAD application to generate a map of the floor plan showing where the cubicles are with employee names or ID numbers. The resulting map will be included in the Netscape display on the fly.

Nortel is also looking at Netscape Navigator 2.x as an integrated tool that may allow them to bypass or eliminate the company's traditional internal messaging systems. For instance, the e-mail feature of Navigator 2.0 allows users to send and receive messages that include HTML elements and multimedia, giving it incredibly more power as an e-mail tool than the company's existing QuickMail and COCOS utilities.

While many companies are concerned over appropriate use of the Internet by their employees, Nortel developed a system for actually monitoring employee usage and automatically cross-charging departments for the usage of their local employees. With Nortel's Metrics system, you can type in an employee's global ID and see the exact amount of Internet access that the employee has made in terms of total megabytes of traffic. The metrics are captured each time an employee accesses the Internet through one of the company's three regional proxy servers (Figure 4.8).

According to Koehncke, "We send a monthly bill to the employee and manager indicating how much they used and it's charged against their department number. We are also doing threshold kickovers: If any one ID generates over 50 megabytes of traffic a month, the manager is automatically notified. We keep a list of every time they go to the proxy server." For Internet e-mail, however, Nortel's position is completely different. "We don't track that," says Koehncke, "you can send and receive all the mail you want."

Koehncke is not intimidated by the famous security problems of the Internet. He figures it just goes with the territory. "We have firewalls, and we have people everyday trying to break in. We see it, it happens, and people are not successful that we have been able to determine. We keep a tight rein and our

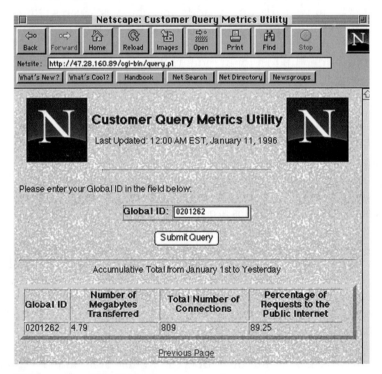

**Figure 4.8**   The Nortel user metrics page.

corporate security works hand-in-hand with us. Even our host computers have several layers of passwords and other security devices."

Now that Nortel has adopted the web, they see it as an integral part of the way they do business. "The Internet is just another tool that we use," says Oldham, "just like we let people use stamps and do memos. The difference is that it not only lets you communicate internally, but go outside and talk to customers and suppliers, and get information on your competitors."

"In the long term," says Koehncke, "we see Netscape as the program everyone starts up in the morning and everything is served from there. If you want MS Word, you start it from there. It's the universal GUI and we are on it. It gives people access to information, reduces our cost in terms of internal transactions, and allows us to do collaboration on a much larger scale."

"You've heard about Channel 1?" Koehncke asks. "People talk about cable TV having a bazillion channels, others say you will have only one channel: your channel. That's what we are working on right now for Netscape. When you come to work in the morning, you will see a Netscape page, log on, and we will generate an HTML document on-the-fly that is tailored to you, with news from management that is tailored to your particular organization or level."

Koehncke figures a system like this will help cut down on the information glut by presenting employees with only the information they need to see. "In a big company, getting the right information out to your employees is very difficult. I have a whole list of stuff people send me that I never have time to deal with. I got a videotape the other day and thanked the guy because now I have an extra blank videotape I can use in my VCR machine at home."

Like others, Koehncke foresees a massive shakeout in the software industry because of web technology—and groupware in particular. "We have 3,000 Notes users today, which is quite a lot. But Netscape is getting into the groupware market, so that will be interesting. Think about it: Netscape fits on one diskette, as opposed to Lotus Notes which comes on 30 diskettes."

"The web is like public bins that anyone can get into," adds Koehncke. "Groupware on the other hand is the way for people to collaborate in a closed society. Groupware works only when people contribute; in the web you don't have to contribute anything." Over the long term, he figures, "Microsoft and Lotus will try to figure out how to do web, and Netscape will try to do groupware, and they will work to a compromise."

Oldham compares the implementation of the internal web to recent projects he has worked on with some of the Big Six consulting firms. "There are projects I worked on where it took 3 to 4 years and $35 million dollars to design the system. With the web, however, by putting together our own virtual teams, we got this down in 3 or 4 months and knocked it right out." In fact, Nortel has been so successful at developing their own internal web that they have considered making their expertise available to other companies on a consulting basis.

## Chevron: A System in Transition

The internal web at Chevron Oil is small indeed when compared to those at Sun and Nortel. In comparison to Nortel's one-thousand-plus online web servers, Chevron—which is every bit as large as Nortel and as global in scope— still had only about 45 web servers online as of early 1996.

What makes Chevron interesting, however, is not its level of web entrepreneurship, but how closely it represents the average mix of information technologies in the business world in the last half of the last decade of the twentieth century. That is to say, it runs the entire gamut: "We have people that don't use computers at all," says one internal observer. "Then we have people who still think the mainframe is the only way to do things. We have

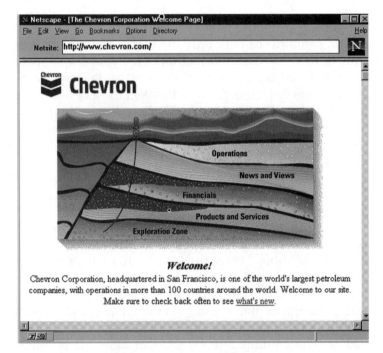

**Figure 4.9**    The Chevron external home page.

people moving out into distributive processing, and then other people moving back into large server technology on the other end."

That's not to say Chevron is a slouch in the IT department. Some of its operations are very much on the leading edge, employing the latest advanced RISC and client-server technologies to the solution of technical problems in the oil exploration and production field. But like many companies today, some business units at Chevron still harbor traditional legacy systems, the large mainframe computers still accessed through 1970s-era 3270 terminals. Chevron has already unified its business operations through a global wide area network that includes satellite links. But some links in the network are decidedly weak, with bandwidth as low as 9600 baud in some remote areas. In other cases, very small branch offices may not even have a network connection at all.

That an Intranet could grow and prosper in such an environment is testimony to its power as a communications tool. Naturally, the web has grown quickest and fullest in the areas of the company that have already moved to distributed client-server environments. Chevron technology organizations like Chevron Information Technology Company (CITC) and Chevron Petroleum Technology Company (CPTC) and their London IT group are arms of the corporation which admittedly specialize in applying computer technology to common business and scientific problems, and they are also the earliest adopters. Talking to web proponents in these organizations, you get the feeling it will be only a matter of time before the technology reaches other parts of the global organization as well, and it is these forward-looking business units that are pointing the way.

At first glance, many components of the Chevron Intranet look just as sophisticated and provide just as much value as anything at Sun, DEC, or Nortel. This provides clear proof that you don't need every business unit on board before you can start providing value to a wide range of system users.

The home page at CPTC is a great example (Figure 4.10). Starting at the CPTC home page and drilling down into the web structure, you will find an incredible amount of information about the company, its operations, and its products. Here's a summary of what you will find:

◆ *About CPTC*—a history of the company, its location, floor plans for different buildings, the business plan, strategic planning documents, flow diagrams of business models, definitions of process terminology, the funding model, financial performance, information on metrics, plus a message from the president to top it all off.

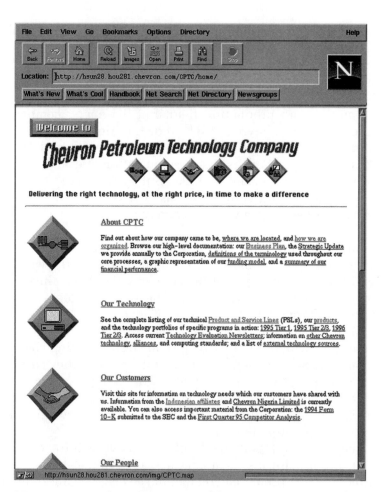

**Figure 4.10**   The CPTC internal home page.

♦ *Our Technology*—a complete portfolio of the company's technical products and service lines, detail of funding portfolios for each product and service line, information on strategic research, and links to other Chevron technology divisions on the internal web and other technology sources on the Internet. This is the largest and one of the most highly referenced sections on the CPTC web.

♦ *Our Customers*—information on CPTC's internal customers (other business units or affiliates), plus competitor analysis for companies outside of Chevron. This section is provided by people in overseas operations, as a way of aligning CPTC's operations with their business.

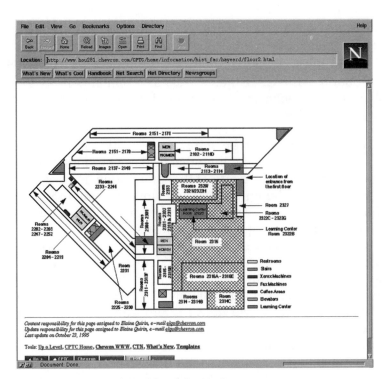

**Figure 4.11**    A CPTC building plan.

◆ *Our People*—home pages for every employee in CPTC, plus a home page for each business team, including its purpose, charter, and people on the team, with cross-links back to its product and portfolio pages.

◆ *Internal Resources*—general communications including corporate bulletins, all-employee memos, company newsletter, and a dialog box for asking questions of management. This page also provides an online library catalog where staffers can search and locate any of over a quarter million books in the Chevron libraries (Figure 4.12). There's also information on internal job openings, human resource policy information, infrastructure and all kinds of products and services that are infrastructure-related, such as business support services. This page includes monthly financial reports for every project, product and service CPTC provides.

◆ *Training*—includes course descriptions and schedules for all internal training, including the company's geological, geophysical, and reservoir management areas. This is a directory that originally was a 2,500-page document when distributed in printed form, but that now is only released on the Intranet and in Interleaf's WorldView.

♦ *Other options*—the CPTC home page also contains links to pages explaining web technology, and provides access to the corporate-wide search engine.

Naturally, these pages would be of interest not only to CPTC employees but to any Chevron customers. One thing that strikes you immediately about the CPTC pages is the impressive depth of the information and services available. The library directory and training directory alone are major resources that can provide incredible value to users without the enormous overhead of compiling, printing, and distributing paper documents.

"The web has cut down on a lot of paper, and users don't have to lug around the 2,500 page book any more," explains Sharon Sloan, leader of Chevron's publications group. Even with the old printed book, she says, "it was still hard to find out what training was being delivered, where and when. So originally we put it all together into WorldView. But probably WorldView will drop off as more people have access to the web."

The story of how the company's Intranet came together is an interesting study in experimentation, as always with new webs. One of the local players in the process was John Hanten, Strategic Planning and Communications Manager at the company's Houston office, who gets much of the credit for the depth and organization of the CPTC web site.

Chevron's ability to create a web benefited from the fact that a TCP/IP infrastructure was already in place, due to the presence of UNIX servers on the network. Before the web came along, the network was already being used for news servers, FTP servers, and file servers. In late 1994, the first components of the internal web system began with local experiments at the company's LaHabra, California facility, followed soon after by a server in London.

By February of the following year, Hanten had "tuned in" to see the offerings of the various servers already on the web. But what he saw was considerably disorganized. "On the Houston page I saw links to neat info, but no real organization at all. At the same time, some of our scientific teams were starting to learn about web technology and were looking for places to see things." At that point, says Hanten, he assembled a small group to design what the overall document structure would look like. "At nights and on our own machines, we started building pages," he said. "We wanted to pack the system with valuable information so people would use it immediately."

Instead of just organizing the information, however, Hanten and his team developed more functionality. "We tapped the resources of Roger Cutler, an experienced Chevron UNIX developer, and found a way to convert some of our legacy databases such as DB/2 to the web format. For example, we had several library card catalogs that we converted completely for access on the web. A lot of information was in obscure legacy systems that only gatekeepers had access to, and we used our programming resources to drain the databases and post the information in web pages."

Within a week, Cutler had converted the card catalogs for all the Chevron libraries and put a search engine on top of it, so that users didn't even have to contact the librarian any more to find a book or document. "If you want to check out a document, now you have forms you can use to do that," Hanten says (see Figure 4.12).

In a stroke of minor genius, Cutler also devised a way to take information from the company's human resources database and *automatically build a starter home page for every person in the company.* To get pictures of the employees, Hanten says, "we sent people around with a digital camera" and then just downloaded the images onto the web.

Surprisingly, home pages for each team were a little harder. "You wouldn't believe how difficult it was to come up with a list of all our team names," Hanten says. "At the time of the web document development, CPTC was undergoing a transition to a team-based environment. The information systems were not yet in place to automatically build team pages. Our approach was to develop a standard team page template that could be used by anyone."

"We have reined in most of the people setting up their own server—even for team pages," he adds. "If they have a team page, they maintain it on one big server. In fact, 95 percent of our pages are on two servers either in Houston or in La Habra, California. If a team wants to take on the responsibility, we create a higher level directory for them. If they don't want us to have access to it, we create a special directory. It's centralized in terms of the files being in a single place. We do that to get performance from the search engines, but the maintenance remains distributed." Though the rudimentary employee home pages couldn't be considered eye-popping by any standard, they suddenly gave each employee a stake in the web, and a definite interest in getting online and taking a look around. The pages are routinely refreshed on a weekly basis so they will stay current with the information in the employee database.

Hanten realized that what he was dealing with, in essence, was a large electronic document, so he asked the company's publications and presentations group, including Sloan and soon-to-be document manager Debbie Scott, to get involved early on as the key team for managing the web. He also realized that web technology was the culmination of a long search he had been making for just such a set of tools. "Before the web came along, we were thinking about things like Hypercard tools, where we had the capability to hyperlink from

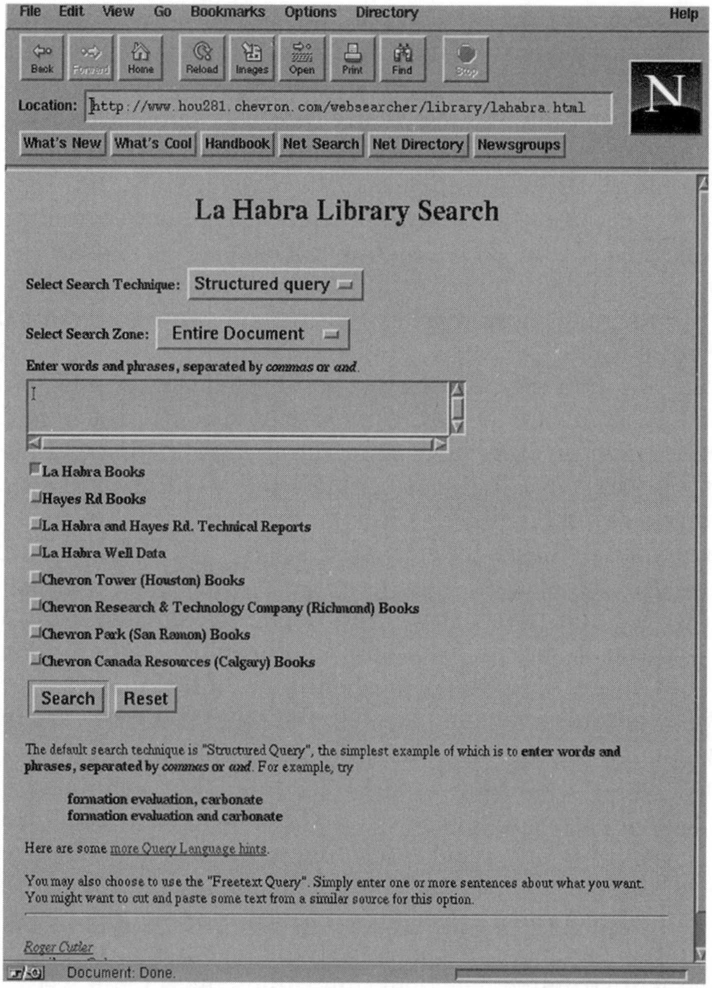

**Figure 4.12** The CPTC library search.

page to page. But we didn't have a common platform: we had people on PCs, Macs, and UNIX machines."

CPTC uses the Harvest search engine to glean information from all the other Chevron servers, so if you want to quickly search the entire population of servers on the internal web, you can do it using a Lycos-type search with keywords. In addition, the Chevron web integrates other search tools such as Verity to perform specialized searches, such as a search on technology evaluations, newsgroups, or library documents.

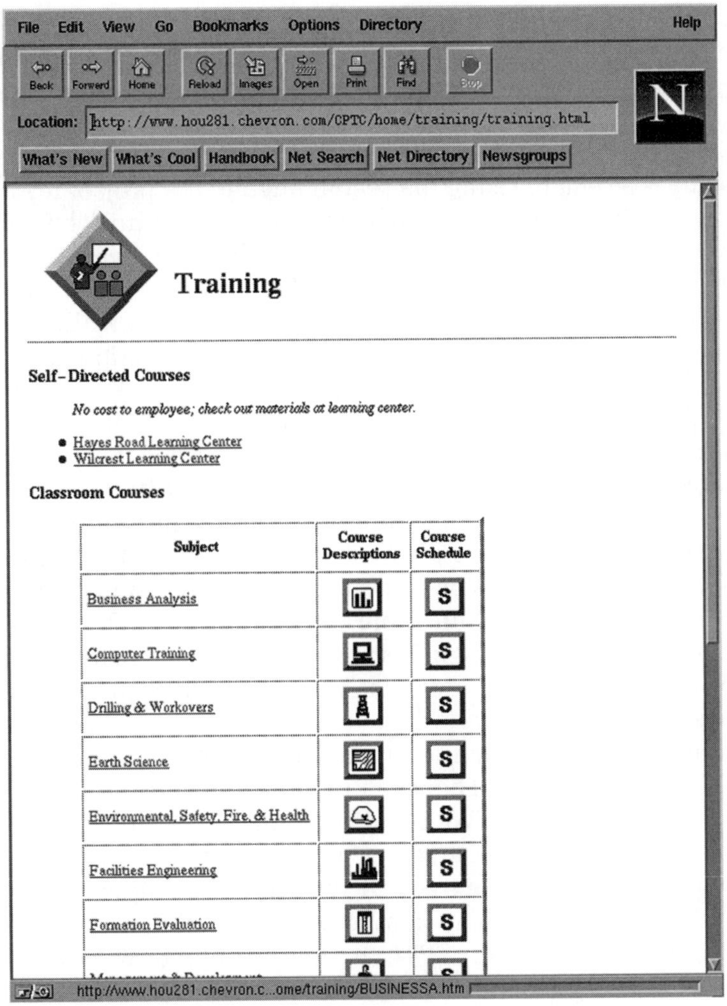

**Figure 4.13**    CPTC training page.

CPTC has added links to its webs so managers and teams can easily review financial information like the profit-and-loss statements for each project. "In the past," says Hanten, "users would have to learn a series of SQL commands to obtain the information. Now, at the end of the month, we run a batch job and create all the standard reports that the teams might use. This information was originally captured as part of our internal DB/2 billing system and Nomad project management system that most employees found difficult to use.

"The reports are generated in a flat file, automatically parsed and linked using routines developed by Cutler, and presented as preformatted text in the browser window. I monitor team activities, so I look at project financial information for each team for the month, and I also check my own. Customers can call any CPTC project leader or manager and ask how much we have spent on their project year-to-date. Using the search engine, the project leader or manager can just put in the project ID code and that pulls it up. The old way, you would have had to run a batch job in a couple of hours or overnight. You never were sure you would get the right thing." Hanten figures his company saves about $200,000 per year in mainframe costs based on avoiding all the extra batch job activity. Amazingly, producing the web applications to generate all this data didn't even require the efforts of a full-time person. It took about a week to do the programming for the financial pages, Hanten estimates.

CPTC uses Lotus Notes for those kinds of applications that require collaborative authoring, security, and the ability to provide different views of information included in the technical and internal service portfolios. Yet, there are only about 200 licenses for Notes in CPTC, and many of CPTC's customers have not adopted Notes as a standard groupware tool. To make this information available, CPTC uses the InterNotes Web Publisher. "Our main challenge with InterNotes," says Hanten and his group, is that "you really need to design your Notes database with the idea that you are going to publish on the web. Some things are very awkward unless you do that."

To manage the local web, Hanten created a group called the CPTC Web Content and Coordination Team. This team includes representatives from each of CPTC's management teams. "We identified four areas we need to look at in terms of managing the web document: (1) Is the content appropriate? (2) What kind of style guidelines do we use? (3) What browsers do we have, and how widely are they deployed? (4) Are employees aware of these things?" In terms of the actual pages themselves, CPTC assigns a content owner and an update owner for each web page. If the people responsible for content don't know how to make the change, they can communicate with someone who does. "We also have some low-key police patrollers who check for bad links," says Hanten. Since the responsible parties have their e-mail addresses included right on the page, it's quite simple for anyone spotting a problem to notify the content or update owner by e-mail.

To improve the management of the overall Chevron web, a similar coordination team was established at the corporate level to study the idea of corporate-wide standards for page content, size, navigation controls, helper applications, support for various HTML versions, and other features. One of the first decisions of the corporate-wide team was to standardize on the Netscape Navigator browser for all clients. Chevron already had a corporate license with Netscape, but that was extended to include all users.

For now, says Hanten, "Netscape is a standard part of the 'Common Operating Environment' being deployed in many Chevron organizations, which means it is installed by default on every computer in that environment." Hanten and his team are enthusiastic about the payoff from web technology so far. "In the past, our communication with Nigeria has been via e-mail, and with the time differential it was inconvenient. Now, web technology is their preferred method. We stage a lot of technical information out there, so that if they want to see what the current bug release is for a particular application, the team in charge lists it on the web. Instead of contacting a person, users can look it up. In addition, the interested customers can supply us with their thoughts, needs, desires, and problems."

The examples of savings are abundant. "We can document the cost savings we have earned by making the information centrally available. Tangible examples include the prerun financial reports and reduced hardcopy distribution of all types of documents." There are nondocumented savings as well, according to Hanten. "In the past we e-mailed information to all CPTC managers, with the result that we had all these duplicate files laying around on the network that might be current or might not be current. It's intangible things like this that we believe improve productivity and yield the greatest savings," he says.

In terms of costs for the overall environment, the incremental cost of the Netscape licenses was small compared to the added functionality web technology provided, says Hanten. "There's a cost of increased bandwidth, but that would have happened anyway with the normal growth of our network. The cost per byte of bandwidth keeps dropping."

"For a company like ours to be successful," Hanten observes, "We need to tap information sources anywhere in the world and apply the optimum technology solution. We always talk about the collective knowledge of CPTC as an organization, but before there was no way to organize or systematically access this knowledge repository." Of course, like most other Intranets covered in this chapter, the CPTC web provides seamless integration to the external world, including Chevron's own Internet home page at http://www.chevron.com (Figure 4.9). Like most other external web sites, Chevron's was designed by a Bay Area design firm. Since the business of CPTC is research, staffers have found the easy Internet connectivity incredibly useful in their daily jobs. "The real high-tech people can go out on the Internet with different searches and get answers in minutes that used to take people hours to find," says Chevron-Houston webmaster Jim O'Connor.

Other parts of Chevron are beginning to discover the marvels of the Intranet. "People in our corporate affairs group are getting very excited as they find out more about this technology and the ability to get their information out to the rest of the company," O'Connor says. "Some of the information will require sophisticated PCs or workstations. They won't be sending only text to people, but text that contains objects like video or audio."

A temporary problem, says one observer, is that some Chevron units may not budget for more sophisticated equipment right now, because it's not one of the main business needs. "It is similar to the length of time it took the company to put voice mail on all the phones in the building, not just the managers' phones. We finally got voice mail across the board two years ago, but it had been available for years."

## Digging the Internet Tunnel at Digital

Though it's mentioned last in this survey, the Intranet at Digital Equipment Corporation was probably one of the first examples of its kind in history. According to Mick Schonhut, corporate webmaster in Digital's Corporate Communications Group, work on Digital's internal web began in the company's research labs in May 1993. The external web server at www.digital.com was the first Fortune 500 server on the World Wide Web in October 1993. (See Figure 4.14.)

The Digital internal web also runs over what has to be one of the world's more massive and diverse corporate networks. The company's internal TCP/IP network encompasses over 97,000 nodes linking 377 locations around the world. The network includes VAX machines running the VMS operating system, Digital's well-known Alpha line running UNIX, VMS, and Windows NT, plus PCs running Windows and Linux. "It's a very heterogeneous environment," says Schonhut. Servers run on UNIX or NT machines, and most of the company's 400-plus web servers are Netscape Communications Servers or Purveyor servers purchased through corporate licensing agreements with the respective vendors. The remainder are mostly shareware NCSA servers.

As with other Intranets, the main application for Digital's internal web is online document delivery. Employees can also request various documents through a web page, and the documents are delivered by e-mail as plain text. The web also carries many of the company's internal newsletters, such as the *Alpha Fast Facts* and the *Quarterly Report* from the corporate research group.

According to Schonhut, the web is becoming quite popular as a way to publish internal standards, such as Digital's branding standards that tell employees, for instance, how to use the Digital logo on a piece of marketing collateral.

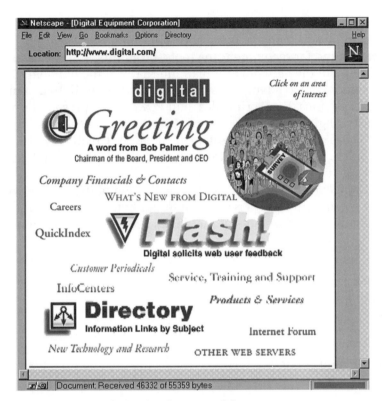

**Figure 4.14**  The Digital external home page.

Digital's marketing communications people can access the standards on a web server.

When people set up their own servers at Digital, typically they set up the software on the machine they already have. The web gives people access to a central repository of software, where they can download server kits for the various supported server types in the company.

Historically, says Schonhut, Digital has offered its employees no corporate guidelines for constructing web pages, but that is starting to change with templates available to internal users. "We are applying the [same] standards that have existed all along on the external web," he says. Digital has also created an internal organization called the Internet Program Office (IPO) which is striving to work out web issues within the company. This group brings together people from the product and services divisions, the corporate information services group, the CIO's office, and the corporate communications function.

"We have shied away from recommending authoring tools," says Schonhut, "because there are so many of them and they change so fast." But there is an increasing demand for recommending tools, he admits. "We do have standards and templates, but they are not enforced internally at the moment, though that will change too. We have templates for other kinds of online documents such as text files, PDF files, PostScript files, and PowerPoint presentations."

Apparently, Digital has no problem getting employees to participate in the Intranet. "There's so much interest in it, it doesn't really need any promotion," says Schonhut. "People want to publish on it; it can't happen fast enough. People use it on a daily basis."

Despite the fact that Digital has had some version of its internal web for five years, only recently did they create an internal home page to pull the content together (Figure 4.15). Contents of the offical internal home page include:

- What's new
- Internet program office page
- Commonly used services
- Corporate strategies
- Employee finder
- Products and services
- Directory of internal servers by category and location
- Companies and groups on the web, sorted by industry in various consortiums
- Search engine (WAIS)
- Starting points for the web
- Reference information and libraries
- Reference pointers to various kinds of tools

Anyone who places a server on the Intranet can have it added to the internal announcement directory, which is "the equivalent of Yahoo," according to Schonhut. "Someone could send a mail message and have their site listed, or a fill out a registration form." To assist its internal users in learning about the web, Digital provides special training courses "from a one-day superhighway driver's-ed course, all the way up to webmaster university," Schonhut says.

Like most other major internal webs, this one features integration between the internal and external web. But most of the public information is prepared and tested internally, first.

**Figure 4.15**  Digital's internal home page.

Digital encourages user access to the Internet, according to Schonhut. "The general thinking right now is that we have policies that cover use of company resources, and this is just another company resource. Everyone should have access to the resources—people need the Internet to do their job. E-mail is obviously crucial and web is very close second. Clearly more people use e-mail than the web right now—we send 2.4 million messages a week, and 1/3 of those go outside."

Digital is working on technology now that may radically alter the way internal webs are configured and used. The most promising technology now offered is something called the "Internet Tunnel," in which Internet-based communications can be securely piped through a company firewall. For example, says Schonhut, "you might have two companies exchange data over the Internet, encrypting and piping the commercial data so that it goes from inside one company, through the firewall at the other end. The data might include EDI, financial data, or any kind of data where you don't want someone changing it or reading it." Another application might be the ability to provide internal web pages targeted to specific customers, dealers, and external user groups that cannot be accessed by unauthorized users on the Internet.

Digital has created a variation called a "personal tunnel," where people who work at home could use a standard dialup connection on the Internet to tunnel back into a company and log on to systems inside the firewall. "If I am working at home, with my personal tunnel, I could access highly confidential information," Schonhut says. In effect, companies and individuals could use the public Internet as their own virtual private network (see http://www.digital.com:80/info/internet/).

Back at the internal web, Digital has also rolled out its own worldwide program to equip all desktop users with fully integrated web browser software. Digital's field sales reps are being equipped with web browsers on their notebook computers for referencing internal web information through dialup connections while on the road.

Digital provides all employees with help with web questions via telephone or by sending queries to a specific e-mail address. There are voice-mail menus they can call and connect to internal specialists who can help them with requests like a need for an update of web browser software. If a web server is down, there is a hotline number to call and a feedback button on the home page.

As a whole, Schonhut feels his company benefits considerably from the web, and that it has been worth the effort. "In lots of ways it's easier," he says. "People generally see it as a common access method to various applications in the company. Wherever systems are being upgraded, replaced or consolidated, web access is near the top of the list in functional requirements. In a sense it is replacing access tools we have always had, such as videotext systems and online bulletin boards. People are seeing this as a much more friendly user interface for online. It's a unifying technology, because you can convert anything to HTML. So it is the trend everyone is interested in now. When they are making investment decisions and setting their priorities, it's on the high side of everyone's priority list.

"To a certain extent there is still a concern about the hype and how does this solve business problems both for our company and our customers. But people are coming to see this is a serious phenomenon we need to take seriously."

## Where Do We Go from Here?

Now that you understand web technology and the way it is used in real business environments, it's time to take a more in-depth look at the tools and techniques used to create the typical web site. The next three chapters cover the major features and applications of the technology, including web publishing, multimedia, and interactivity.

## Chapter Five at a Glance

One of the largest applications for web technology is the online publishing of documents previously distributed using paper-based systems. This chapter explains the ins and outs of online web publishing, including:

- The basics of HTML, how to use it, what are its limits, and why it is essential for web publishing
- When and why to use HTML editors
- How to create web documents using simple add-ons to common word processing programs
- How to create web documents using WYSIWYG editing tools
- How to automatically convert large-scale document sets to web output
- How to display documents on a web without losing their original layout

# Toward the Paperless Office

Document publishing is probably what web systems do best. When you're surfing out on the World Wide Web, most of what you see is documents somebody specifically prepared for Web viewing. And most of what you do is *read those documents.* That's just the way it is: You shouldn't be using the Web at all unless you like to read things—in very large quantities.

In a corporate environment, this is good news. The fact that web systems enable enterprisewide document publishing means we can avoid the copying machine and start throwing away all those three-ring binders sitting in the closet. With the ability to instantaneously retrieve and view documents across the network, there's no reason why we should be generating tons of printed materials anymore, *just in case* someone wants to read it.

An eventual casualty of the Intranet revolution may be the CD. I have several clients now who have been using CD-ROM to distribute online documents to far-flung field locations, including remote bases in the jungles of Indonesia, offshore platforms in the North Sea, and instrumentation shacks out on the Arctic tundra. As even these remote facilities come online through satellite links, web browsers will enable them to always see the latest version of every document we publish.

Most documents you see on a web have one thing in common: They are prepared in HTML format, which makes them load quickly and display nicely inside a web browser. But the ways people prepare the documents varies all over the map. Some use common word processors like MS Word that have the ability to save documents directly in HTML format. Others edit the HTML document directly, either in a WYSIWYG or non-WYSIWYG mode. Still others take existing desktop-published documents and run them through various filtering devices or conversion programs to produce a finished web automatically. And of course there are still a lot of people (masochists for sure) who like to code their documents in raw HTML using a simple text editor.

Which method is best? The answer depends heavily on your circumstances and preferences. Some people will never be satisfied unless they personally insert every little HTML tag into their own documents. Others will never prepare a document for web consumption if they have to learn a lick of HTML. Still others have such a large volume of documents to webify that they can't think of anything but a totally automated solution. Since your needs and inclinations may vary considerably, this chapter examines the whole gamut of web publishing options, starting with basic HTML and going all the way up to sophisticated workgroup automation solutions.

## HTML: The Good, the Bad, and the Online

Let me say right off: Coding raw HTML is nasty business. If you have the luxury to do so, I say avoid it like the plague. And with the increasingly sophisticated tools available for web publishing (discussed later in this chapter), it's becoming increasingly easy to ignore this core bit of web knowledge.

Back in the early days of the Web, of course, we didn't have such luxury. There was no way to produce web documents other than to sit there and code them in raw HTML. I always compare it to the early days of PostScript, about 1985 or so. In those days, you could connect a PostScript printer to a PC, but there were no tools yet available to generate PostScript documents. PostScript tools were first available on Mac only, PageMaker hadn't been invented for the PC yet, and it would be several years before common word processors like MS Word would generate PostScript output routinely. So, sometime back in the mid-1980s I used to sit there (like a masochistic fool) and *code raw PostScript by hand* just so I could do desktop publishing on a PC. People laugh now when I tell them this, but believe me, back in the old days they would go *ooh* and *ahh*.

HTML is fast going the way of the early PostScript language. Though not a fifth as hard to use as PostScript was, it's already disappearing behind the slick façades of some quite impressive web publishing applications. In a few years or so—maybe even by the time you read this book—you'll have to examine the innards of HTML files about as often as you look at PostScript files now . . . which is practically never.

Nevertheless, at this point in history, if you want to be a web expert you're going to have to know a little something about HTML. Even if you *don't* want to be a web expert, you may find it interesting to know the good and bad points of HTML, and why it is such an essential component of web systems.

The other reason to learn HTML is because, no matter how good our tools get, there will always be some sort of tweaking you may want to do behind the scenes to get things to work *just so.* And sometimes, it's a lot quicker (if not easier) to whip out a text editor and slash away at a couple of hyperlinks that have to go through a bunch of pull-down menus and dialog boxes to achieve the same result. In other words, not everybody needs to know HTML, but *somebody* should. And if you're the person in charge, perhaps you're elected.

Appendix A contains a complete quick reference guide to the Hypertext Markup Language. But here's a few essential pointers to get you acquainted fast. (HoTMetaL jocks and Hot Dog addicts may want to skip the next few sections, but be sure to rejoin the discussion at the WYSIWYG part.)

## Plain, Ugly Text

To get started on the right foot, let me say immediately that you don't have to code a document in HTML to view it on a web. Web browsers will display plain text files directly inside the browser window. So if you just want to type a note and put it on the web, with no embellishment or further ado, then you can save it as a plain ASCII text file (with the extension *.txt*), serve it that way, and be finished with it. (While you're typing, be sure to hit the Return key at the end of each line, so the browser will know where to break your lines. Otherwise, you'll get one continuous line.)

Plain text is the simplest type of web document. It's ugly, but it works. When the text document is displayed in the web browser window, it's displayed in a monospaced Courier font, just the way it might look if you typed it on a typewriter. For example:

```
A Plain Text Document

Here's an ugly plain text document. Did I tell
you this looks ugly? Guess I did. You have to
admit, it's just plain ugly.
```

Of course, people are too proud these days to hand out ugly plain text documents. Everybody wants their documents to look sharp—whether it's desktop-published or coded in HTML. But it's really useful to think of web documents this way. To get a nice-looking web document, you can start with a plain text file, then save it with a *.html* file extension, and add HTML markup tags to it. The more markup tags you add, the fancier-looking your document will get.

## Basic Rules of HTML Coding

Don't ever join a poker game unless you know the rules, especially if your partners have been drinking heavily and everyone's packing heat. That can get you into a lot of trouble. Likewise, if you're going to get into the HTML coding game, you'd better know a few basic rules. They're not hard to learn, but they're essential. And not knowing them may cause a bit of trouble.

The first rule is structure. Every HTML document has the following basic structure:

```
<HTML>
<HEAD>
<TITLE>Title Goes Here</TITLE>
</HEAD>
<BODY>

Main heading and body goes here.

</BODY>
</HTML>
```

Notice how markup tags are used to "bracket" different parts of the document, as well as to bracket text. The entire document begins with <HTML> and ends with </HTML>. The heading begins with <HEAD> and ends with </HEAD> and the body part begins with <BODY> and ends with </BODY>. Bracketing codes like this makes it easy to remember because the end code is the same as the beginning code, except that it includes a forward slash (/). Those of you who were born at the PC keyboard, remember to stay away from that backslash key (\). These structural tags (HTML, HEAD, BODY) have little effect on the look of the document, but are important anyway, because some browsers may not display the document without them.

*Note:* To be absolutely cool and technically correct, real webmeisters (like you) include the following line at the top of the file:

```
<!DOCTYPE HTML PUBLIC "-//IETF//DTD HTML//EN">
```

This is a special tag that identifies your document as an HTML document following the document type definition (DTD) created by the Internet Engineering Task Force (IETF).

Please don't confuse the <TITLE> with the opening heading in a document window. Usually, the opening heading is done with a heading tag, such as <H1>. So for instance:

```
<HTML>
<HEAD>
<TITLE>Home Page</TITLE>
</HEAD>
<BODY>
<H1>Welcome to the Home Page</H1>
You will find a lot of information here that you really and truly
need. So start clicking...
</BODY>
</HTML>
```

when displayed in the browser, looks like Figure 5.1.

Everything inside the <BODY> part is intended for display inside the browser window. Everything in the <HEAD> part is just extra information that goes along with the document. For example, the <TITLE> part always goes

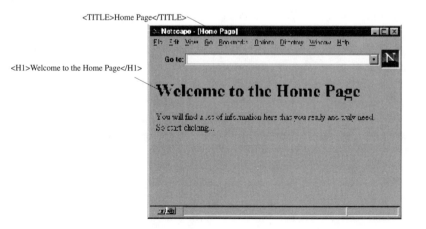

**Figure 5.1** HTML code and where it goes in the window.

inside the <HEAD> because it is not intended for display inside the browser window. Instead, it will appear at the top of the window, or inside a Title field.

The best way to understand HTML, of course, is to start coding a little of it yourself. If you have a browser and a text editor, just create a plain ugly text file and start adding HTML codes to it. You can use the server test file developed in Chapter 3 and add text and codes to it. Be sure to save your file with an *.html* extension (*.htm* in Windows 3.1) and use the browser to open it up as a local file and see how it looks.

For instance, you'll notice that even if you type plain text (with no HTML codes) into an HTML file, it already comes out looking typeset in the browser window. The only problem is that all the paragraphs run together. To separate paragraphs, you'll need to add a paragraph break like this: <P>.

Keep tweaking the file as you move along through this discussion, so you can see how different codes make text look different. While you're at it, you can create headings using the different heading codes (H1, H2, H3) and see how this affects the font size. Hey, you're learning it already!

## Look Ma, No Fonts!

One thing that strikes you right off about HTML is the lack of font specifications. In traditional publishing, the author, page designer, or typist always had to worry about whether different parts of the document used the correct font. For instance, the person who designed the document might specify major headings as 18-point Helvetica bold, minor headings as 12-point Helvetica bold, and body text as 10-point Times Roman regular.

In the earliest word processors, you had to reset the font manually each time it changed. Nowadays, we use style sheets to define all the different paragraph styles in a document, but those styles still have the fonts, indentations, and spacing set individually for major headings, bullet lists, and so forth. Style sheets make document formatting easy because you can just point to each paragraph and apply the appropriate style to it automatically. (I still run across secretaries, managers, and system engineers who still haven't figured out how to use the style sheets in their word processors, and keep resetting the font at the beginning of each paragraph . . . what a waste!)

In HTML, however, there *is* no correct font. In fact, in current versions of HTML, page designers can't specify the font at all. Don't you know this drives some of them batty? All the page designer can do is specify the level of heading, such as H1, H2, H3, and so on. The browser interprets these as different font weights, and allows *the person viewing the document* to decide which font to use and what size it should be. For example, in Netscape Navigator, the user can choose a set of base fonts for the document under the Options menu (see Figure 5.2). So if Times Roman 12 is the base font for regular body text (proportional), then the browser software scales all the other fonts as some variation of that.

Why let the user control the fonts instead of the document designer? The reason for this is because HTML files are designed to be transported across the globe to millions of viewers who have an array of different machines with different types of browsers and different monitor resolutions. This makes it next to impossible to specify an optimal font that everyone already has resident on their machine and that will match their screen resolution precisely—so why even bother? Just let the user set the fonts. In my book, this is a great thing, for several reasons:

♦ *More power to the user.* Hey, who's the best judge of what looks good, anyway? The person who writes it or the person who reads it? In my book, the customer is king. So why not let the user choose the font that looks best? After all, it's the poor user who has to sit there at the other end of the wire, squinting through bifocals at this stuff. Can you blame the person if he wants that body text a little larger, a little bolder, a little easier to read?

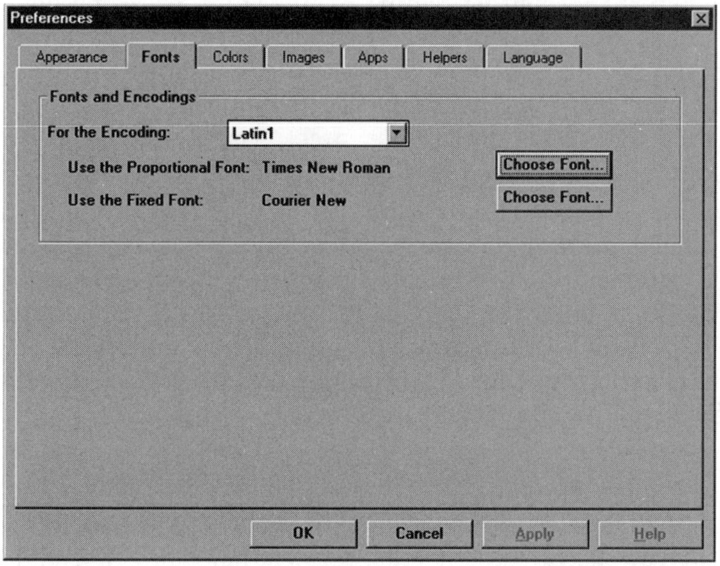

**Figure 5.2** Font-setting dialog in Netscape Navigator.

◆ *Authors can stick to authoring.* Just as the invention of movies made everyone want to be a movie star, so the invention of desktop publishing made most authors want to be graphic designers. I know some professional writing societies now where the focus has shifted away from "how to write well" to something like "how to make your words look good in print." Obviously, the cart has gotten entirely in front of the horse. Taking font decisions out of the author's hands may help set things straight again. Hopefully, authors can quit fiddling with the format and concentrate on the message. Unfortunately, companies like Netscape keep inventing all these new HTML tags that give more and more formatting control back to the author, so authors will no doubt become distracted once again.

◆ *Documents are more visually consistent.* Because fonts are controlled at the browser level, all headings tagged <H1> will always look the same way, regardless of which document the user looks at. It's the same for all the other formatting tags. From the user's standpoint, this provides marvelous consistency. Users can browse from document to document without having to adjust their eyes (or mind) to different design standards. A document published by your London office and one published in Seattle can share a kind of visual consistency that normally has to be imposed through rigorous document formatting requirements. Think of riding down the strip in Las Vegas, where every sign blares its message in different styles of type and a rainbow of neon colors. It looks great for about half an hour, but imagine if you had to confront those same lights everytime you drove down your street? Users see a nice familiar neighborhood everytime they venture onto the web.

◆ *Documents are more portable.* HTML is a variant of the Standard Generalized Markup Language (SGML), which was invented to make documents more portable between computer platforms and organizations. What works for SGML also works for HTML. Instead of using absolute formatting specifications (Palatino 14-pt. bold italic, Helvetica condensed 9.5-pt. regular), the author uses logical tags (H1, H2). It's simple and it works.

The advent of HTML led to a small revolt in the design community, where some people went into a tizzy worrying how they could preserve the carefully composed look of their paper documents once they were viewed online. Publishing tools like Adobe Acrobat came to the rescue with an online presentation format that preserves the paper-based look down to the very last dingbat.

Unfortunately, some people miss the point. They still don't understand that what looks great on a cool designer Macintosh looks like breakfast sausage on a monochrome VGA laptop. Paper documents and online documents absolutely *should not look alike,* because paper is one medium and online display is something else entirely. HTML does a lousy job of preserving the font-specific look of paper documents, but it does a great job of preserving a consistent look *across documents* and *across platforms* when viewed online.

There are exceptions to the rule, of course. You may want to put something online that *is intended* for printing, like a standard paper form that requires a signature. But importantly, we need to remember we are dealing with a new medium that has different communication requirements. The best way to do that is to discard all our old notions about what a document should look like and how it should communicate. We need a new paradigm for a new era.

## HTML at a Glance

Though it may seem a bit awkward and confusing at first, HTML is definitely not rocket science. The only complexity involved is the rapid proliferation of tags. Whereas the initial versions of HTML had only a couple of dozen tags, the total number of standard tags, nonstandard tags, and tag extensions is probably well over 100. Like everything else, however, the old 80-20 rule applies. Eighty percent of what you will do with HTML can be done with about 20 percent of the available tags. The essential tags are listed in the table on page 176. You'll see plenty more in Appendix A.

Some people will argue till they are blue in the face that many other codes are essential. But believe me, you can do plenty of damage with just these 12. Of course, there are many other HTML tags that let you do fancier stuff, not to mention all the "tag extensions" Netscape and others have created to give you precise control over borders, colors, and more. But these will get you by on 80 percent of the document material you need to publish.

## What HTML Can't Do

With every discussion of what HTML can do, there should also be a discussion of what it can't do. As anyone can tell you who's worked with it for a while, the good news about HTML is that you can do marvelous online docu-

| Text Style | Coding Used |
|---|---|
| Heading | `<H1>This is a major heading or opening heading</H1>`<br>`<H2>This is a minor heading</H2>`<br>`<H3>This is a subheading</H3>` |
| Body text | Body text may have `<B>bold</B>` and `<I>italic</I>`, but requires no special tags except the paragraph mark.`<P>` You might also use a line break`<BR>` to start a new line in mid-paragraph. |
| Ordered list (steps) | `<OL>`<br>`<LI>First numbered item.`<br>`<LI>Second numbered item.`<br>`</OL>` |
| Unordered list (bullets) | `<UL>`<br>`<LI>First item in bullet list.`<br>`<LI>Next item in bullet list.`<br>`</UL>` |
| Horizontal rule | This is used as a separator in text.<br>For example, here is text above it.<br>`<HR>`<br>Here is text below it. |
| Hyperlink | To see a file on a different server `<A HREF="http://server/filename">click here</A>`.<br><br>To retrieve a new file on the same server `<A HREF="path/filename">click here</A>`.<br><br>To go to a marker in the same file `<A HREF="#marker">click here</A>`.<br><br>To go to a marker in a different file on the same server `<A HREF="path/filename#marker">click here</A>`.<br><br>`<A NAME="marker"></A>`inserts a marker on this line. |
| Inline graphics | To insert a picture at a specific point in a document, use a markup tag like this `<IMG SRC="path/filename.ext">`. |
| Indented text | `<BLOCKQUOTE>`<br>This paragraph will be indented.<br>`</BLOCKQUOTE>` |
| Preformatted text | `<PRE>`<br>Preserves all spacing, indentation and paragraph breaks by using a fixed font. |

| Text Style | Coding Used |
|---|---|
| | `Nice for form elements, computer code, preformatted columns.`<br>`</PRE>` |
| Table* | `<TABLE>`<br>`<TR><TH>HeadCell1</TH><TH>HeadCell2</TH>`<br>`<TR><TD>Row1Cell1</TD><TD>Row1Cell2</TD>`<br>`<TR><TD>Row2Cell1</TD><TD>Row2Cell2</TD>`<br>`</TABLE>` |

*Netscape version, see Appendix A for details.

ments. The bad news is, you can't do everything. As time goes by, however, the can-do list is growing incredibly larger, while the can't-do list is growing considerably smaller.

The first thing to understand about HTML and its features is that we are dealing with a worldwide standard for marking up documents. HTML is based on agreements by international committees who spend a lot of their time arguing about arcane subjects like *document type definitions* (DTDs) and trying to come up with a set of features everyone can agree on. This shouldn't be all that hard to do, but when you're trying to please everybody in the entire world, the process does get bogged down occasionally.

The first versions of HTML (0.0 and 1.0) were notoriously low on features. Headings, body text, bullets, numbered steps, indentation—that was about the extent of it. You could do fairly simple documents, but more complex documents were elusive. The second version (HTML 2.0) added the ability to create online forms and tables, among other things. The forms feature opened up the web to interactive database access, e-mail integration, and other nifty features. But other essential document publishing features like equations, superscript, and subscript were delayed until implementation of later versions.

Due to the slowness of the standards-setting process, companies like Netscape have raced ahead with extensions to HTML that let you control any number of document-formatting features. Netscape was first to market with the ability to format tables, set background colors, control the alignment of internal graphics, and wrap text around illustrations. This all happened at a time when many of the same features were still being debated in committees. For example, Netscape added extensions to the BODY tag that allow you to specify a pattern or image that will be repeated continously in the background of the document window.

```
<BODY BACKGROUND="pattern_name.gif">
```

Netscape also created extensions to the BODY tag that let you specify a solid background color (BGCOLOR), a color for the body text (TEXT), and colors for regular links (LINK), visited links (VLINK), and active links (ALINK). Colors are specified as a hexadecimal number representing a red-green-blue (RGB) value in the format *#rrggbb*. For instance:

```
<BODY LINK="#rrggbb" VLINK="#rrggbb"
ALINK="#rrggbb">Document here</BODY>
```

*Note:* If you don't know how to calculate hexadecimal numbers for RGB colors, there are tools on the WWW that help you do it. Try http://alamak.speakeasy.org/

Of course, to view any of these features online, you have to be using a Netscape browser. Most browsers will ignore unrecognized HTML tags (i.e., anything inside open/closed angle brackets that does not follow strict spelling and formatting guidelines as published in the HTML standard). In fact, you might conclude that Netscape's oft-quoted 80 percent market share has a lot to do with its advanced lead in the HTML extensions market. If you're going to do fancy document publishing with HTML these days, you'd better have a Netscape browser sitting on the other end of the line.

## The Best Editors Around

Once you understand the nuts and bolts of HTML, you begin to realize what a bear of a coding task you have on your hands—especially if you want to do something more than just a short essay or memo. At that point you start ask-

### Where to Read About HTML Standards

There are plenty of places on the World Wide Web where you can get information about HTML standards. The best place to start is http://w3.org/

ing yourself the question, "Aren't there some software tools I can use to make this easier?"

This is the question many people were asking themselves back in late 1993 and early 1994, when web publishing was starting to catch fire as a serious pursuit for serious-minded people. Naturally, a few software companies responded with the first generation of HTML tools called *HTML editors.*

Though there are many better choices now for the serious web publisher, lots of HTML whizzes still like to use popular HTML editing programs like HTML Assistant, Hot Dog, and HoTMetal. These tools help by giving you a rough idea how the text will look when it is displayed on the page (Figure 5.3). Headings are bigger and bolder. Bullets (sometimes) look like bullets. But you still see the HTML codes sitting right there on the page. For convenience, the codes are often iconized into a single character, so that you can't accidentally delete a stray angle bracket.

HTML editor programs are actually something like web word processing programs that are still in the process of growing up. Old habits die hard, and the old first-generation HTML coding experts—the people who were doing

**Figure 5.3** Creating pages with an HTML editor (HoTMetaL).

> ### Where to Get HTML Editors
>
> If the idea of an HTML editor appeals to you, there are some sources on the World Wide Web. Try http://union.ncsa.uiuc.edu/HyperNews/get/www/html/editors.html  or http://www.stars.com/Vlib/Providers/HTML_Editors.html

web pages back when you and I were in diapers (circa 1993)—will want to see their codes until they die. That's fine, but this is a shrinking audience, and if the people who invented the first HTML editors want to continue serving that market, that's fine too. Truly advanced web word processors like Netsape Navigator Gold will make it increasingly unnecessary to see the HTML codes as you compose web pages. And that's where the future lies.

## How to Create Web Pages without Learning HTML

HTML editors are fine, as far as you can throw them. And if you're already an HTML expert and all you want to do is whip together some quick menus or edit pages, they're ideal. But what if you want to do some serious document publishing and need to speed up the process? What if you want to make web publishing as easy and simple as word processing or desktop publishing has become over the past decade?

As you can tell by now, I'm firmly against the idea of people using HTML to create web pages on a regular basis. Here's why. The value of a web system and it's worth to a company is directly proportional to the number of people who participate in it (see Bernard's Corollary in Chapter 3, under "Let One Hundred Servers Blossom"). If you plan to create a successful corporate web, many people will be involved in contributing the information that goes onto the web, and many of them will not want to use HTML.

We don't do people a favor by saying, "Oh, look at this neato web system you can use," then adding the extra statement, "Oh, by the way, you need to throw away your word processor, get yourself an HTML editor, and learn this obscure markup language called HTML." It just won't fly.

Another reason you want to avoid using HTML is that *it's incredibly unproductive and tedious.* Maybe you're a whiz at it already and can whip out those <DT> codes faster than anybody. But did you ever consider how much time you're wasting this way? Get some tools that can make you more productive.

That's not to say *nobody* has to learn HTML. In every Intranet, there must be a few knowledgeable people who can go in and troubleshoot a problem at the HTML level. We call these people *webmasters,* and we put them in charge of making sure the system keeps running smoothly day by day. If you're that kind of person, there are plenty of books on HTML, and I've even included a quick reference guide in Appendix A. But for the masses, you will want to set up the system in a way that they can contribute to the success of the Intranet without ever learning HTML.

To understand what I'm getting at, think for a second about the entire field of word processing and desktop publishing. Back in the mid-1970s, when word processing was first invented, they had departments called *word processing centers* and a job position called a *word processing specialist.* You really had to be a specialist back then to do word processing, because it involved special equipment, a lot of coding, and very complex keystrokes.

In the early 1980s, they invented word processors that ran on desktop computers, and in the late 1980s they added features like *WYSIWYG* and *style sheets.* These features made it possible to hide all the coding and quickly tag paragraphs as headings, body text, bullet lists, and the like. Now anyone can do word processing and desktop publishing—even your boss! You don't have to be an expert any more to do it, and there is no coding involved. Everyone uses these tools every day.

The same is already happening with HTML. The HTML part is not likely to go away, since it is the native document language of the web, but it will increasingly be hidden in the background. Right now, only a few years into the development of web as a technology, we already have an application called *web publishing* that is just like desktop publishing except that—instead of output to a printer—the output goes directly onto a web. (In fact, maybe we should call it *global desktop publishing.*) And the tools people use to do this are not that different from the desktop publishing tools we use now.

So, if you want to shield your authors and contributors from HTML, there are a couple of good ways to do it:

♦ *Give them WYSIWYG tools.* For instance, there are now several add-on products that give everyday word processors like MS Word and WordPerfect the ability to save files directly to HTML format. Later sections of this chapter show how these work.

♦ *Don't even ask them to change tools.* Another way to approach this subject—probably the best way—is to let people continue using the same WP/DTP tools they've always used. That way, no retraining is involved and no one has to break their stride. Instead, you just take the documents they create and convert them to HTML using one of the many conversion tools now available. Later sections in this chapter will introduce tools like *HTML Transit* that let you create entire webs from common word processing documents with only a few seconds' work.

Remember the favor I asked you way back at the beginning Chapter 3? Is your "Keep it Simple" sign still hanging there? Steering clear of HTML is one of the ways you can keep things simple for the authors in your information center.

## Using WP Add-Ons to Create Simple Web Documents

One way to create web documents without coding HTML is to use an ordinary word processor like Microsoft Word 6.0 for Windows, suitably equipped with an add-on extension like Microsoft Word Internet Assistant (Word IA). This is just an extra bit of software you can install *on top of* your existing copy of Microsoft Word that gives it the ability to create web pages. Word IA is free off the Internet or you can order it directly from Microsoft. If you don't use Microsoft Word on a PC, there are other add-on products you can use that work a lot like IA (see the sidebar on page 188).

Microsoft created Word IA in late 1994 as a way to give HTML capabilities to its widely used MS Word 6.0 publishing system. This product adds several important capabilities to MS Word, including:

◆ The ability to create new HTML documents and forms using the program's standard word processing features

◆ The ability to read existing HTML documents and edit them inside MS Word

◆ The ability to use MS Word as a web browser, like Netscape or Mosaic

Once you get a copy of it, IA installs just like any other PC program. It automatically "adds itself" to the MS Word product, so that all the functions are available from inside MS Word through the standard set of pull-down menus. You don't have to start or learn a different program, you just start MS Word and use it more or less the same way you always did (see Figure 5.4).

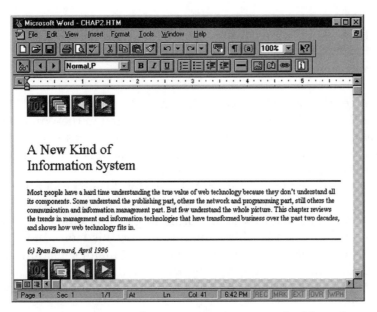

**Figure 5.4**  MS Word Internet Assistant, typical interface.

## Creating a New Document

Here's an example of how you would use MS Word (with IA already installed) to create a web-compatible document:

1. Start MS Word the same way you always do.
2. Open a *new* document using the New option on the File menu.
3. You should see "Html" as one of the choices under Templates. Select it and click OK to continue.
4. Notice that the style menu at the upper left lists the word *Normal,P.* This is your standard body text style that is used for standard body text.
5. For any line other than body text, select the appropriate style from the style menu. For example:

| Style | Text Type |
|---|---|
| Heading 1,H1 | Heading levels 1, 2, 3, etc. |
| Heading 2,H2 | |
| Heading 3,H3 | |

| | |
|---|---|
| List Number,OL | Numbered list |
| List Bullet,UL | Bullet list |
| HR | Horizontal rule (separator) |
| Preformatted,PRE | Preformatted text. |

Notice that each style on the list maps to a particular HTML tag (H1, PRE, etc.). The list of styles is quite limited in the Windows 3.1 version of Word IA, but the Windows 95 version has a more extensive style list, a wider set of features, and even lets you create tables according to the latest HTML standards.

Make your first web documents fairly simple and straightforward, with common document elements such as headings, body text, bullets, and so on. Don't try fancy formatting or font changes, because you probably won't be able to do it (more on this later). In fact, you may want to take a quick peek at the limited menu selections to see what you *can* do. If you're using IA for Windows 95, you may be able to do more advanced things like tables, but avoid doing that for now, too.

6. When you're finished creating the document, open the File menu and select HTML Document Info, then type in a title for this document and click the OK button (Figure 5.5).
7. Select the Save option from the File menu. Since this is a new file, you should see the dialog in Figure 5.6.
8. Type in a filename for the document, such as *sample.htm*. Make sure you use the extension *.htm* instead of *.doc.*
9. Select HTML as the file type under Save File as Type.
10. If you can see the server document root directory from your computer, select it as the place to store the file under Directories (e.g., C:\HTTPD\HTDOCS). Otherwise, you will need to move the file to the document root directory later for it to be visible over the web.
11. Click the OK button to save the file.

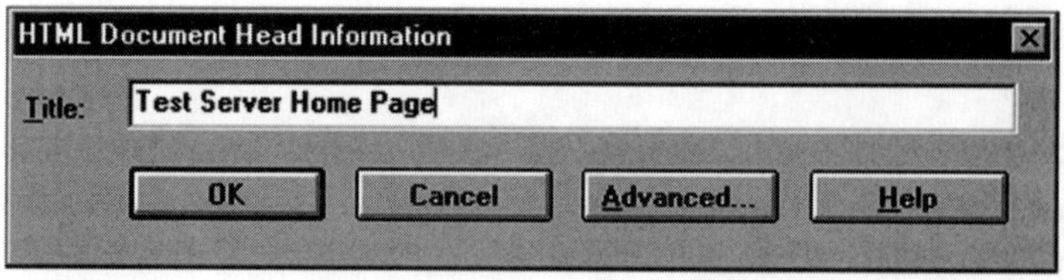

**Figure 5.5**　HTML document info dialog.

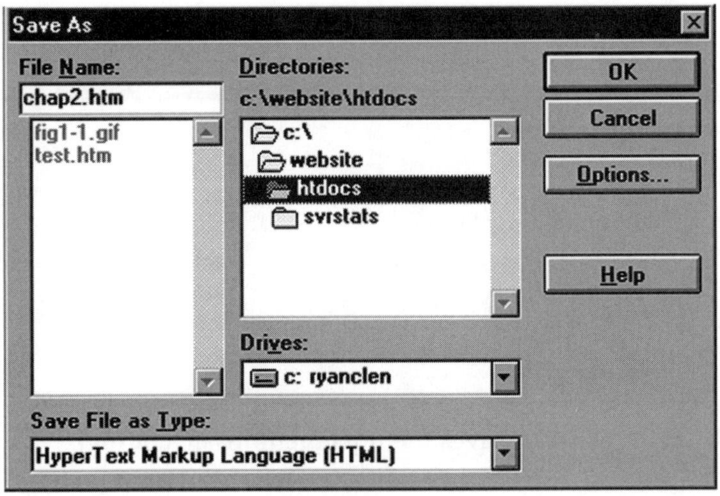

**Figure 5.6**    Save As dialog.

### How Word IA Saves the File

When you create a file and save it this way, IA doesn't save it as a normal Word file. Instead, it saves your document as a *plain text file* and uses HTML codes to mark the paragraphs you set up as headings, bullet lists, numbered lists, and such. For example, Figure 5.7 shows how your document might look in MS Word.

But when you save it as HTML in MS Word IA, the program will store it in a plain text file with HTML coding, as shown in Figure 5.8.

Notice that in the Windows 3.1 version, you'll *never* see the HTML-coded version unless you open the file using a plain text editor like Notepad. (The

---

**This Is a Major Heading**

This is some body text. And what fine body text it is, too. Just look at it.

**This Is a Minor Heading**

And here's some more body text. Pretty cool, isn't it?

---

**Figure 5.7**    How Word IA displays the file.

```
<HTML>
<HEAD>
<TITLE>IA Test Document</TITLE>
</HEAD>
<BODY>
<H1>This Is a Major Heading</H2>
This is some body text. And what fine body text it is, too. Just
  look at it.
<H2>This Is a Minor Heading</H2>
Here's some more body text. Pretty cool, isn't it?
</BODY>
</HTML>
```

**Figure 5.8**    How Word IA saves the document (basic coding).

Windows 95 version, however, gives you a way to look at the codes.) It's important to understand that the HTML-coded file is the *only version* of the document that gets saved to disk. There is no MS Word file involved at all. Furthermore, if you try to open the HTML file again in MS Word, you still won't see the codes. Instead, Word IA will hide the codes and display the information as WYSIWYG text again.

This is what I mean by a WYSIWYG authoring tool: It is relentlessly WYSIWYG in that it protects the author from seeing the actual HTML code, unlike HTML editing tools that purport to be WYSIWYG but that still show you the HTML codes while you're editing. Word IA is built on the idea that you should be able to use your word processor the same as before, but use it on HTML files.

IA is not a perfect product, of course. Out of necessity, it limits your formatting capabilities to just the kinds of things you can do in HTML. Unfortunately, it also ditches some of the other MS Word features we have come to know and love—and that would be very helpful in web publishing—such as the ability to generate automatic tables of contents and indexes, or the ability to group multiple documents together into a master document.

As you will see in the next section, Word IA is not even *true WYSIWYG,* or what I would call web-WYSIWYG. But the initial versions of Word IA were a nice start and a needed addition to the HTML arsenal. And with new products being rolled out by Microsoft, the Word-compatible options will certainly improve over the years. Microsoft plans to incorporate HTML features into its entire line of products in the near future. Of course, you will never use tools like Word IA if you're a webmaster or an advanced web programmer. But it's not a bad tool to hand people who regularly create standalone, isolated documents for use on the Intranet.

## Editing Existing HTML Documents

A nice feature of Word IA is the ability to both read and write HTML files. That means you can use it to edit existing web pages, even if they were created using a tool other than Word IA. In fact, IA was one of the first tools to provide two-way HTML capability and it is still (at this writing) one of the few word processing tools around that can pull off this feat.

Another nice part of Word IA is that it gives you the ability to take any regular MS Word file, open it, then save it in HTML format using the Save As option. If you start with a Word document and try to convert it to HTML, however, be sure to check whether the original document was styled properly with tags like Heading 1, Heading 2, and Bullet. If not, the entire document may come out as body text in HTML. Also, you may also lose any illustrations that were in the document (in early versions of the product, you have to go in and reinsert the pictures *after* the document is converted to HTML). Later in this chapter, we'll look at more advanced tools that can convert MS Word and other files to HTML format without losing illustrations and other features.

Remember, since IA is a WYSIWYG tool, when you read in an HTML file it won't let you see the HTML codes. But that's good because it limits you to the task at hand: editing the document. To see how this works, try it on the test.htm file you created in Chapter 3 (see the "Hello World" Server Test, page 83).

1. Make sure you have access to the server root directory from your local computer. If not, copy the test file over to your computer.
2. Select the Open option from the File menu. This displays the File Open dialog, as illustrated in Figure 5.9.
3. Select the server document root from the Directories list (e.g., C:\SERVER\HTDOCS). At this point, you should be able to see the test file in the File Name column. If not, change the List Files of Type option to All Files.
4. Select the test file, then click the OK button.

Notice that the file opens in a WYSYWIG format inside MS Word, even though it was originally saved as a plain text file with HTML codes. The major headings (marked by <H1>) are automatically styled in a large bold font, and

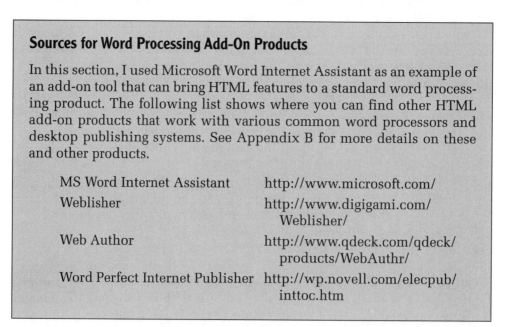

**Figure 5.9** MS Word File open dialog.

the bullet list appears as bullets. Not an HTML code in sight. You should be able to use IA to open and edit any other HTML file this way. When you're finished, make sure it gets saved back to disk as an HTML file.

## Sources for Word Processing Add-On Products

In this section, I used Microsoft Word Internet Assistant as an example of an add-on tool that can bring HTML features to a standard word processing product. The following list shows where you can find other HTML add-on products that work with various common word processors and desktop publishing systems. See Appendix B for more details on these and other products.

| | |
|---|---|
| MS Word Internet Assistant | http://www.microsoft.com/ |
| Weblisher | http://www.digigami.com/ Weblisher/ |
| Web Author | http://www.qdeck.com/qdeck/ products/WebAuthr/ |
| Word Perfect Internet Publisher | http://wp.novell.com/elecpub/ inttoc.htm |

## Web-based WYSIWYG Editors

Products like Word IA are great for people who don't want to change tools, because it lets them keep their existing word processor or DPT tool, but just use it in a slightly different way. I wouldn't recommend it for large-scale web publishing applications, but it works fine for what it does—creating standalone web documents that can easily be plugged into an information center.

The main problem with products like the early version of Word IA is that the WYSIWYG is still imperfect. Word IA 1.0 gave you a good idea of what the document will look like on the Web, but if you open the same document in a web browser, you'll notice it looks slightly different (Figures 5.10 and 5.11).

The problem of true web-WYSIWYG was solved by a new crop of tools that provide an editing environment that exactly mimics the major browsers. These new tools work just like the big word processors, but the display you're editing is almost dead-on what you will see on a web.

One of the most impressive tools in this category is the FrontPage Editor by Microsoft Corporation. The FrontPage Editor is part of an integrated suite of web development tools for PCs that includes a built-in web server and various web site administration tools. You can obtain an evaluation copy of

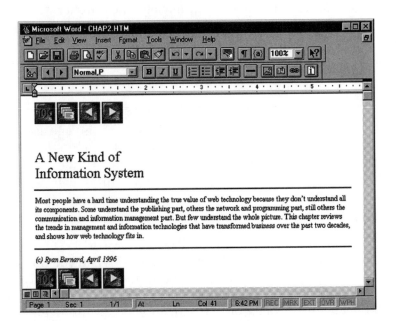

**Figure 5.10**  Document in Word IA.

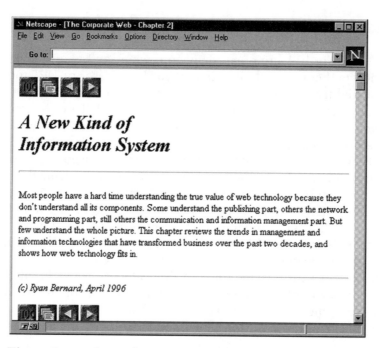

**Figure 5.11**    Same document in Netscape browser.

this software by going to the Microsoft site on the World Wide Web (http://www.microsoft.com/msoffice/frontpage/) and downloading it directly.

> *Note:* Please keep in mind that I'm just using FrontPage as an example of an entire generation of tools that will make web publishing easier. It's impossible to cover every tool on every platform, but there are already similar tools for the Mac and UNIX environments, as you will see in the sidebar on page 195.

The best way to understand how FrontPage Editor works is to install it, then open up a web page using the File/Open command. When you do, the display looks just like the page as you might view it in the Netscape browser (Figure 5.12).

Once the document is open on the screen, you can insert the cursor and start editing. While you're at it, notice how similar the FrontPage document editing interface is to Microsoft Word or many of the other popular word pro-

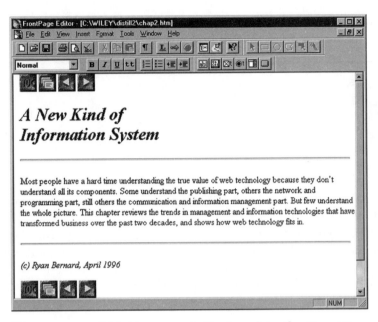

**Figure 5.12**   Web Document displayed in the FrontPage Editor.

cessors. You can see many of the same buttons on the toolbar, including those that let you do boldfacing and italics, plus the buttons that do numbered steps, bullets, and paragraph indents. There are all the same buttons for Cut/Copy/Paste and File New/Open/Save, plus the same kind of style tag list you see in the toolbar of Word and Word IA. But notice that—unlike Word IA—FrontPage *doesn't even bother* to put the HTML equivalent in the style list. In Word IA, for example, the style list reads:

```
Heading 1,H1
Heading 2,H2
Heading 3,H3
Normal,P
etc.
```

FrontPage, instead, says simply "Hey! Who needs to be reminded about HTML?" In other words, just let people edit the document the way they always did before, and let the *software* take care of all that nerdy HTML stuff. So the tag list in FrontPage Editor just says:

> Heading 1
> Heading 2
> Heading 3
> Normal
> etc.

the way people always used to see it in a normal word processor, before we got confused by the HTML issue.

Of course, if you want to create a new document using FrontPage, all you have to do is use File/New and you get a clean blank page to start with. Front-Page is web-author friendly in that it offers a number of standard templates and wizards for various types of web page design, as you can see from the list in Figure 5.13.

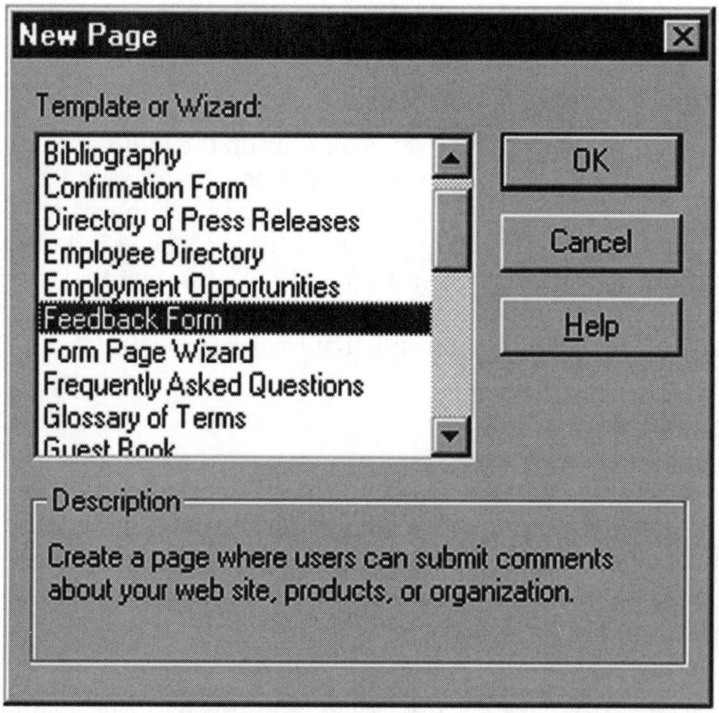

**Figure 5.13**    FrontPage's new page dialog.

Again, this exactly mimics the way other common desktop applications work. For example, MS Word gives you document templates (memo, fax, report, etc.) and PowerPoint gives you presentation templates (text and graph, table, etc.). Nothing new there—and that's the good thing about it.

But notice that FrontPage automates many of the special web creation functions. For example, if you are creating a form to be used online, FrontPage has toolbar icons that let you easily insert a pushbutton, radio button, text field, or pull-down menu directly on your web page (see Figure 5.14 below and see the detailed discussion of forms in Chapter 7).

Then, if you want to create a hyperlink, all you have to do is shade the text you want users to click, then click on the Create/Edit Link button in the toolbar (or select Link from the Edit menu). When you do, you get a menu like the one displayed in Figure 5.15.

Notice how you can easily choose other pages at your site to link to, or select links on the local web or the World Wide Web. If you want to link to a document that doesn't even exist yet, you can do that too by selecting the New Page tab, typing in a page name, then going off to create that document.

Best of all FrontPage includes a new type of feature called a WebBot (short for *web robot*) that works a lot like the field codes in MS Word or the variables in FrameMaker. For instance, you can insert a *timestamp bot* anywhere on the current page and FrontPage will automatically insert the current date at that spot when you save it to the web. That's fairly common in web page design, as well as in published documents. However, there are more advanced bots like the *scheduled image bot* that lets you specify an image to be displayed only during a scheduled period of time, or a *scheduled include bot* that inserts the contents of a separate text file during a specified time period. There's also a *substitution bot* to automatically indicate who last edited or created the document, an *annotation bot* that lets you write notes to yourself on the web page, and several others. To round off the list of features, FrontPage Editor even includes that hoary (but indispensible) old word processing standby, the spell checker.

**Figure 5.14**    Form widget toolbar.

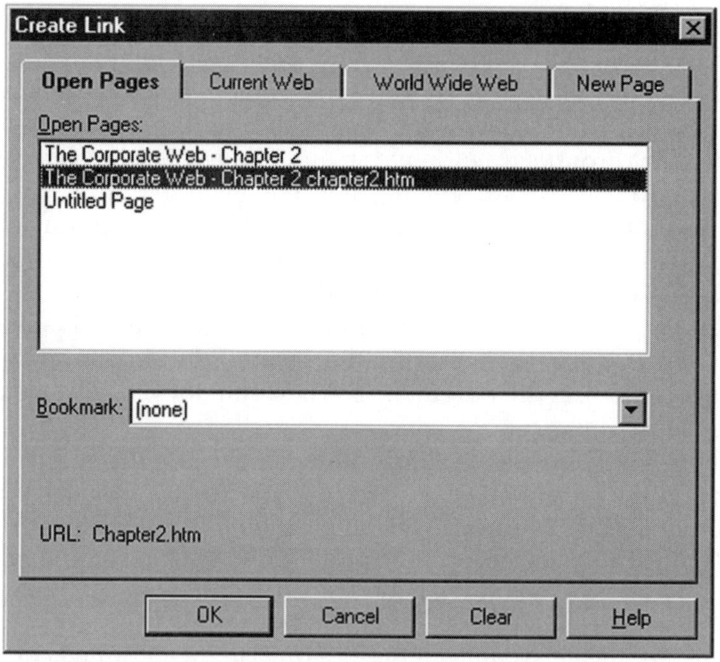

**Figure 5.15**　FrontPage create link dialog.

Netscape offers a nearly identical tool with its Navigator Gold product. With Gold, however, you get both a web browser and editor in one tool. When you go to open a URL on a web, the product asks if you want to open it in a browser or editor window. If you select "editor window" as the option, it automatically lets you save the entire web page to your local hard drive, including the images that are included on the page. Once you have the page saved, you can start editing it using the standard editing features of any word processor, including style tags, cut and paste, paragraph formatting, font emphasis, and other HTML-compatible features (see Figure 5.16). The nice thing about Navigator Gold is that the HTML features supported by it will more likely match the full complement of official Netscape tags and extensions.

## Automated Web Publishing Systems

Tools like Word IA and FrontPage are fine for creating small webs where the authors actually control the look and feel of the web pages. But what about large sets of documents being used, created, or updated by a staff of authors

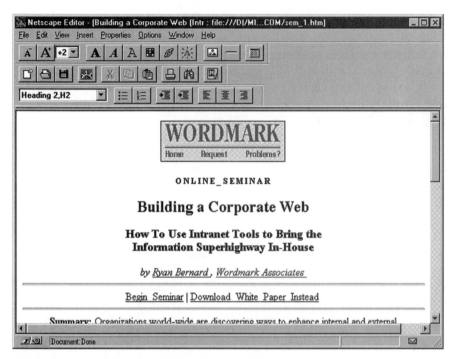

**Figure 5.16**    Netscape Navigator Gold.

---

**True WYSIWYG Web Editors**

In this section, I used FrontPage Editor and Navigator Gold as examples of WYSIWYG web publishing tools. Here's where to find information on these and other similar tools on the WWW:

| | |
|---|---|
| FrontPage Editor | http://www.microsoft.com/msoffice/frontpage/ |
| Navigator Gold | http://home.netscape.com/ |
| Adobe PageMill | http://www.adobe.com/ |
| InContext Spider | http://www.incontext.com/products/spider1.html |

who don't want to learn about web pages and HTML? Fortunately, the next category of web tools lets you create extensive sets of interlinked web documents automatically, and completely "in the background," which means you don't actually see the documents as they are being processed.

The main benefit of this arrangement is that your authors can keep using their existing tools—programs like FrameMaker, Interleaf, MS Word, Word-Perfect, and others—without missing a beat. Your staff can continue producing documents just the way that they always have done, and you only need one person to take a little time to transfer the documents for delivery on the web. The transfer of documents from paper to web can be automated in a such way that it can become as simple as the click of a button or a quick batch command. Figure 5.17 shows how that might look in a workflow diagram.

There are several major tools available for automated web publishing (see the sidebar on page 202). To show how they typically work, I'll use as an example *HTML Transit,* a PC-based web document publishing system from InfoAccess, Inc. HTML Transit can handle documents prepared in Interleaf, FrameMaker (MIF), MS Word, WordPerfect, Ami Pro, Write, ASCII, or Rich Text Format (RTF). It automatically converts the source documents, with all embedded illustrations, into a web-compatible format, storing the text as HTML files and the graphics in separate GIF or JPEG files. But it preserves the relationship between text and graphics so that the illustrations will still display properly within the documents when they're viewed in a web browser.

While the conversion is underway, HTML Transit can also split long documents into a series of smaller files that are more easily readable in a web envi-

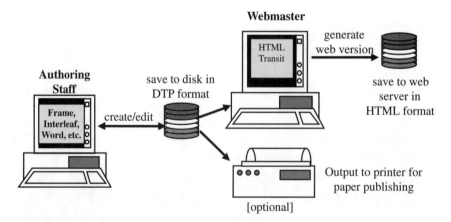

**Figure 5.17**   Automated web publishing.

ronment. For example, you may want it to split a document at every major heading and save each individual section as a separate "web page" (HTML file). HTML Transit can automatically build a hyperlinked table of contents for the entire set of documents or an individual table of contents for each separate web page. A hyperlinked index is possible, too. Special graphics, navigation buttons, and customized headers and footers can be inserted automatically on every page, along with a time stamp and an address or signature. All of this happens on-the-fly as the web documents are being built. The complete processing time for a moderate-size group of documents might be a few minutes to half an hour. What's more, you can save the customized conversion template for each set of documents, so the next time the authors edit or update the documents, conversion becomes as easy as the click of a button.

The person viewing the result of an HTML Transit conversion on the web might first see a table of contents that is completely hyperlinked to various heading levels as desired. The user could click on any title in the table of contents and immediately go to that page. Once on the page, the user would see navigation buttons that allow the reader to progress forward or backward from page to page or section to section in the documents.

To understand how the conversion works, let's walk through key parts of the process. HTML Transit 1.0 opens with a series of pushbuttons you can use to set up standard mapping templates for converting document sets to the web (Figure 5.18).

The pushbuttons are arranged in sequence to show the logical workflow. For example, the first thing you must do with HTML Transit is define the location of the files to be used for input and output. In effect, all you are doing is pointing to the source and then pointing to the destination. This is important, since it allows HTML Transit to draw information out of a document repository and automatically deposit the finished web into a server folder. That way, you won't have to hunt down individual files and worry about copying them to the right place. And in all future conversions, HTML will automatically know where the source and destination files reside and handle the conversion automatically (Figure 5.19).

As you specify input files, HTML Transit automatically reads the style sheets of those files to find out which styles need to be converted. The next step is to Assign Elements—create a one-to-one mapping template for assigning HTML markup tags to various style sheet elements. HTML Transit helps out a little if it sees tags it recognizes (like the Heading 1 tags that are common to MS Word style sheets). Otherwise, you will need to assign HTML tags to be used in converting each different paragraph style in the source document (Figure 5.20).

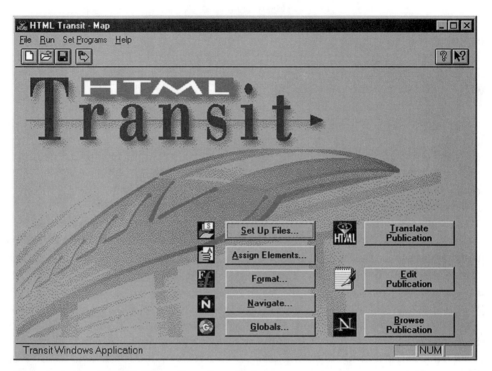

**Figure 5.18**    HTML Transit main window.

The nice part of HTML is that it doesn't require the original document authors to use style sheets at all. You can identify certain text patterns or font changes to be mapped to specific HTML tags. For example, suppose a document's major headings are numbered 1.1, 1.2, and so on, and always use 18-point Helvetica Bold. You could ask HTML Transit to recognize every instance

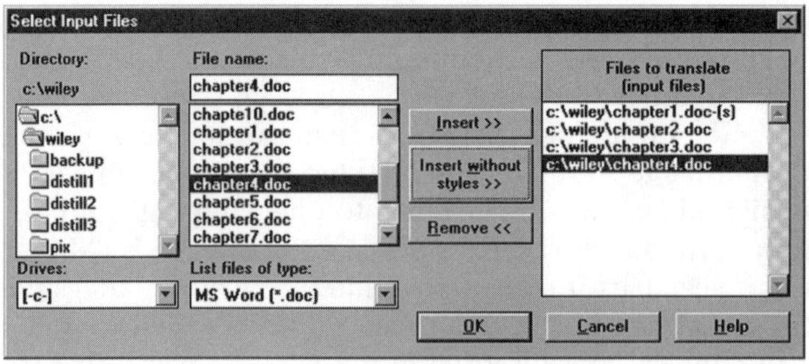

**Figure 5.19**    HTML Transit input files selection dialog.

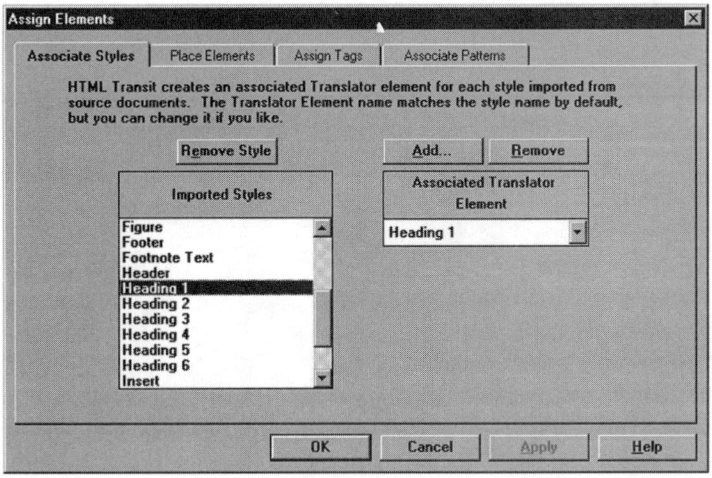

**Figure 5.20**   HTML Transit's associate styles dialog.

of number-dot-number (such as 1.1) as a major heading style (<H1>). Or you could ask it to recognize every instance of 18-point Helvetica Bold, and map it to <H1>. (See Figure 5.21).

Once you have all your HTML tags associated with document styles, it's time to define the look and feel of the final web document. Popping open the

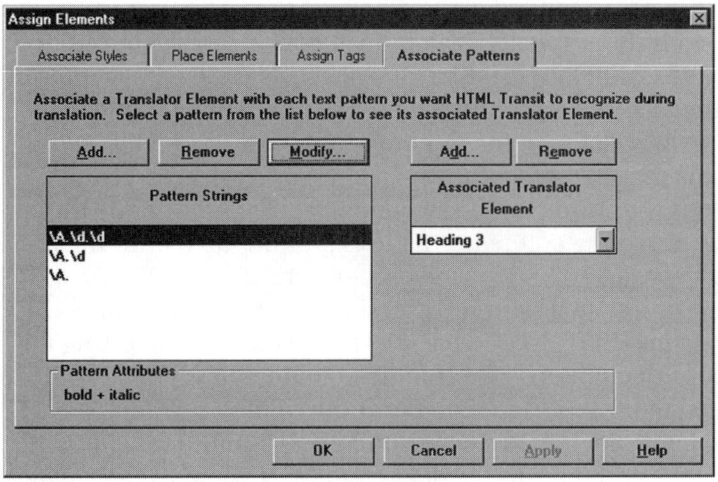

**Figure 5.21**   HTML Transit's pattern mapping dialog.

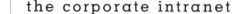

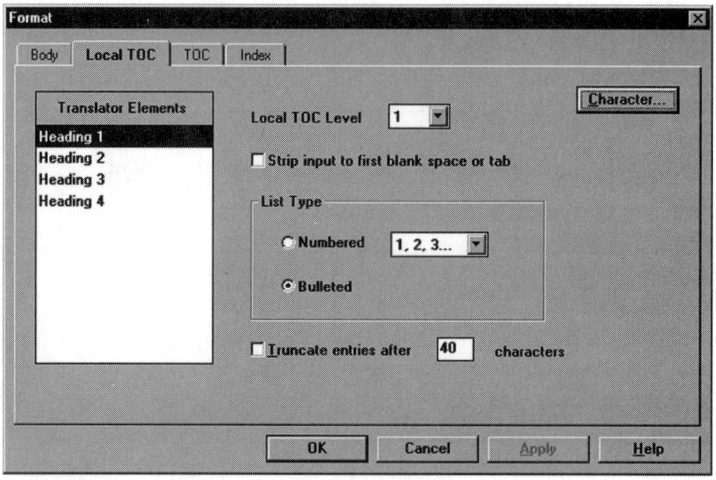

**Figure 5.22** HTML Transit's format dialog.

Format dialog lets you define the look and handling of body text, tables of contents, and indexes (Figure 5.22). Tables of contents can be defined for the entire document set or each individual HTML page (Local TOC).

Popping open the Navigate dialog lets you define the style and positions of navigation buttons that will appear on each page (Figure 5.23). You can have buttons that will help users navigate easily to the previous page, next page, table of contents, index, or a specific page. The links can be placed at the bottom or top of each page, or even at every occurrence of a particular style (such as H2). All you do is specify which ones you want, select the desired button style from the Gallery, and HTML Transit does the rest. As it builds the web, it will automatically determine the proper link that goes with each navigation button on each page. Imagine the work that would be involved if you had to figure all this out on your own!

The last step in setting up a conversion process is to define the Globals. This includes selecting the colors for the background, text, and links, the handling of titles and addresses, and various other options. (See Figure 5.24.)

Once you're finished setting up the conversion, you can save all of your choices as a "map file" to be used any time you are converting the same (or a similar) set of documents. The last three buttons in the main window let you run the conversion and then either edit the final converted files (if desired) or browse them online (to make sure you approve of the results).

Next time the authors edit the documents and you need to generate a new set of web files, all you have to do is open the old map file and run the translation.

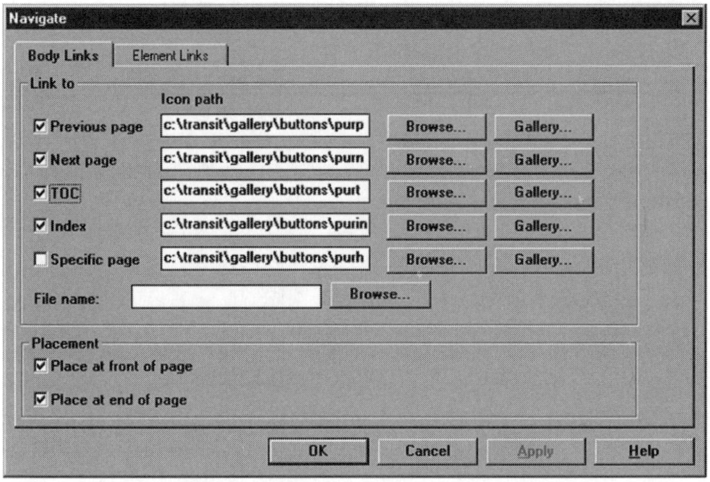

**Figure 5.23**    HTML Transit's navigate dialog.

The program remembers how the conversion was set up the last time, and it even remembers where the source and destination files are located. As long as the document files keep the same names and the same source location, you should never have to set up the conversion again—just run it when you need it.

Furthermore, if your authoring group is organized enough so that everyone uses the same style sheet consistently in their documents, then the same map

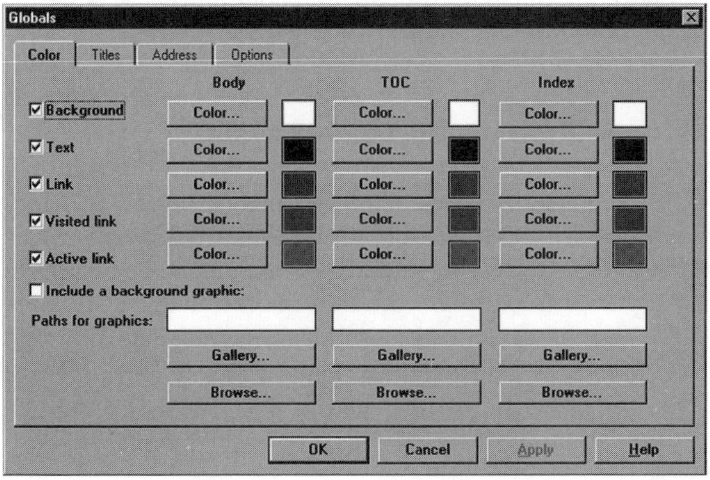

**Figure 5.24**    HTML Transit's globals dialog.

---

**Tools for Automated Web Publishing**

In this section, I used HTML Transit as an example of an automated web publishing tool. However, there are several other major tools available on the market now. Here's where to find information on HTML Transit and other similar tools.

HTML Transit       http://www.infoaccess.com/
> PC-based tool for conversion of MS Word, WordPerfect, Lotus AmiPro, Interleaf, FrameMaker, others.

WebMaker       http://www.harlequin.com/
> UNIX, Mac, or PC tool for conversion of FrameMaker documents.

Cyberleaf       http://www.ileaf.com/
> UNIX tool for conversion of Interleaf, FrameMaker, Word, WordPerfect, and RTF.

Other Tools
> http://www.stars.com/Vlib/Providers/Translators.html

---

file can be applied to any set of documents produced by the same group. This is a great argument for setting up word processing templates and document authoring standards in your work group, and organizing your authors to work this way. You will only need to run one conversion process any time you want to publish information on the web.

## Why and When to Preserve Document Layout

Up to this point, we've only talked about ways to create HTML documents for delivery over a web. If you read Chapter 2 closely, you realize you can serve any kind of file over the web—even native word processing files. But if you've followed my arguments closely, you also realize that HTML files are absolutely the best way to present any web document since they are designed exactly for that purpose. It's like using a spoon to eat soup. HTML files work better than anything else for display inside web browser windows, and they also happen to be ideal for network delivery because they involve very compact file sizes.

What happens with HTML delivery, however, is that it permanently changes the look of your documents. As we mentioned before, users will be able to choose whether they want to see your documents in Helvetica, Times Roman, or dozens of other fonts. Multicolumn documents will typically revert to a single-column format. Page headers and footers designed for 8½ × 11 printing will disappear. Tables will have a different look to them. Navigation buttons may be inserted that didn't clutter the print version of the document, but that are essential for online viewing. The net effect is that the carefully designed structure of your print document will be thrown out the window (so to speak) to be replaced by something tangibly different.

As you should know by now, this is a good thing. Documents *should* look and work differently online than they do in print. The end user *should* have control over font styles and weights. Web presentation is a new medium—in the future it will be the *primary* medium for information delivery—so it's best to throw away all those preconceived notions and paper-based paradigms that tell us how a document should or shouldn't look.

Having said all that, there may be many cases where it's actually desirable to serve people documents over the web in the same format as the print version—right down to the last *dingbat,* as it were. There are a number of foreseeable situations where this may apply:

- *Business forms.* Every company has plenty of forms that employees, customers, suppliers, and dealers use to conduct business with the organization. Chapter 7 will explain how you can put many of these forms online, getting rid of the paper-shuffling aspects of your job. However, if management still requires the paper forms, if the layout or design of the form is important, or if the form absolutely requires an employee signature, you may want to distribute the form online in a print-ready format so that it can be easily printed and used.

- *Printable documents.* There may be documents you want to serve over a web that that are *meant to be printed* and distributed by hand. This might include white papers, product literature, price sheets, training materials, handbooks, newsletters, and other small documents. Providing printable documents on the Intranet is a matter of convenience, especially if not everyone in your company has web access. It's easy enough to print any document from the Intranet by simply using the Print option in your browser. But when you print a document from the web browser, all you get is the information that's on the current "page" (i.e., the file that's currently loaded in the browser window). If a web document extends over several "pages," the user may have to print each section separately, and for large documents this can be quite tedious. If you have any large documents being distributed exclusively online, you may want to supply a printable version for the convenience of users who prefer to read it in print. On my own World Wide Web site (http://wordmark.com) I make several printable white papers available so that web users can download them, print them, and hand them out to people who are just learning about the Intranet. People from companies all over the world come to my site every day and get copies of these white papers—you may have even seen them making the rounds where you work.

Notice, in most cases above, that these are forms or documents that are meant to be printed. This usually isn't a problem, because most documents begin life in print and are then converted to the web. But if the document began life on the web, you may have to reverse the workflow and go backward from a web model to a paper-based model. In other words, the printable version should look like a print document—with headers and footers and nice-looking margins—and not like a web document.

## How to Preserve the Original Layout

The main question then becomes: How do you get a document online on the web *without* losing the formatting? There are several ways to handle this.

### Use the Original Application

The easiest way—for the webmaster anyway—is to leave the document in its original format and serve it across the Intranet that way. Don't even worry about converting it to HTML, just ship the original document files over the network to anyone who wants them. It's not hard to do—just place a link on your web page that references the file directly. For instance:

```
<A HREF="http://server/path/docname.doc">Click here</A>.
```

might be an MS Word file stored on your web server. When the user clicks on such a link, the browser will ask whether it should save the file to disk. The user can then save the file to any desired directory and filename on the local system. (See Figure 5.25.)

This assumes, however, that all of your users have the appropriate software to use the file in its original format. For example, if it's an MS Word

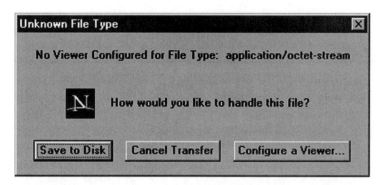

**Figure 5.25** Netscape Save Messages for served file.

file, you assume your users have MS Word or MS Word Viewer, which they can use to view or print the file. If it's a PowerPoint file, you assume they have PowerPoint or PowerPoint Viewer installed locally. Users can even configure their browsers to automatically recognize certain document extensions and fire off the appropriate viewing application. For instance, it might recognize any file with the extension *.ppt* as a PowerPoint file, so that when the browser receives a file with that extension it will automatically start PowerPoint Viewer and display the file. The same might be done with the extension .doc and the MS Word Viewer. In Netscape, the Helper Applications dialog lets users associate file extensions with the applications used to view them. (See Figure 5.26.)

### Use an Intermediate Application Like Adobe Acrobat or Common Ground

The other way to present documents in their original format is to use an *intermediate application* that was designed especially for the purpose. Two major applications that come to mind are Adobe Acrobat and Common Ground. Both allow you to convert the document to an intermediate format that preserves the original document format (more or less) and allows you to view the document online or print it.

Adobe Acrobat uses a proprietary file format called PDF (Portable Document Format) that is like a compressed version of PostScript. The difference between PDF and PostScript is more than just file size, however. PDF provides the ability to add hyperlinks to a file, including not only embedded hyperlinks that work in the Acrobat environment, but HTML hyperlinks that access web URLs as well. Acrobat was originally designed as a product that would allow people to view any kind of word-processing document online. But start-

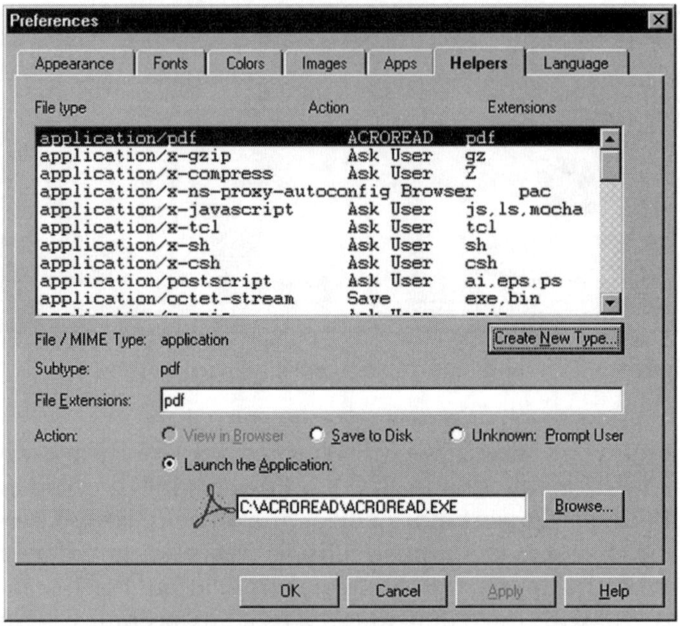

**Figure 5.26**  Netscape Helper Applications dialog.

ing in 1995 the inventors of Acrobat have been working to integrate the product with the web, to the point where a PDF file can now be made to display directly inside a web browser using a plug-in application.

Remember how you can produce PostScript output from just about any word processor by simply printing to a PostScript file? Well Acrobat gives any word processor the ability to produce PDF output by printing to a PDF file. To do this, you need to purchase either the Acrobat Exchange or Acrobat Distiller program. Exchange provides a module called PDF Writer that is like an extra printer driver for your computer's operating system. When you go to print, you can select PDF Writer as the "print device." But instead of printing, the output goes to a PDF file (such as *mydoc.pdf*). Exchange also lets you edit the resulting PDF file by adding hyperlinks or notes to it. Distiller goes a step further by letting you read in and edit raw PostScript files, then output them to PDF. There are other products in Adobe's repertoire of Acrobat tricks, including Acrobat Capture, which helps you convert scanned documents to PDF, and Acrobat Catalog, which creates a searchable database for online documents.

Once you have a document saved in PDF format, you need a way that users can access it, view it, and print it. For this purpose, Adobe provides free software called the Acrobat Reader that you can distribute freely to all your users. In early 1996, Adobe also made available a free plug-in module for Netscape called *Amber,* which lets you view Acrobat documents directly inside the Netscape browser window. But users must have the Acrobat Reader or Amber already installed on their computer before they can use the PDF document you provide.

Once you've taken a word processing document and saved it to PDF format, you can serve it over the web by attaching it to a hyperlink like the following:

```
<A HREF="http://server/path/docname.pdf">Click here</A>.
```

When the user clicks on the hyperlink, the server automatically retrieves it and sends it across the network to the user. What happens next depends on what kind of software the user has.

- ◆ If the user has Acrobat Amber, then the document will display directly inside the browser window.
- ◆ If the user has Acrobat Reader defined as a helper application, the browser will start the Acrobat Reader software and display the document inside the Acrobat Reader window.
- ◆ If the user does not have a plug-in or a helper application defined, the browser will prompt the user to save the file to disk, where it can then be opened, viewed, and printed using Acrobat Reader.

Regardless of the method, the document that the user sees should look almost exactly like the original printed document produced in MS Word, FrameMaker, or any other WP/DTP application. And when the user prints it— whether from the web browser or the Acrobat Reader window—the resulting printed copy should look just like the original document.

Common Ground, by Common Ground Software, provides many of the same capabilities as Acrobat in the sense that it has a portable document format called DigitalPaper that can be viewed online through a special viewer called the MiniViewer. Common Ground uses the Bitstream TrueDoc standard for reproducing fonts, which allows it to reproduce any TrueType or Type 1 font without substitution (unlike Adobe, which uses its own substitute fonts). According to Common Ground, this apparently results in smaller file sizes and quicker loading than Acrobat files. The product also uses an enhanced display technology that it claims provides sharper images on the screen. Finally, Common Ground touts its ability to download a page on demand. With most online document systems, the viewing program opens or downloads all the pages in a particular file. Common Ground's page-on-demand

**Where to Get More Information**

You can use the following World Wide Web locations to get more information about Acrobat, Common Ground, and Envoy:

Common Ground

http://www.commonground.com/miniviewer/

Download free MiniViewer for Mac or Windows

http://www.commonground.com/

Adobe Acrobat Overview

http://www.adobe.com/Acrobat/Acrobat0.html

Download Acrobat Reader for Windows, Mac, DOS, or Unix

http://www.adobe.com/Software/Acrobat/

Envoy

http://www.twcorp.com/

feature speeds up downloading by only retrieving the page you desire. Another tool called Envoy provides similar features.

## Where Do We Go from Here?

Anyone who's used web systems for a while can tell you that web publishing is great, but it's just the beginning of what you can do with a web system. The next two chapters will explain other applications, from the simple display of graphics and multimedia files to some of the more advanced database applications.

**Chapter Six at a Glance**

Multimedia is one of the most eye-catching and most rewarding aspects of web publishing. With web technology, you can easily incorporate still images, sound, and moving images into your document. To help you do it, this chapter explains:

- The most common image formats used in web systems, and how to create them
- How to insert static or dynamic (clickable) images into web documents
- How to create image libraries for use by everyone in your company
- How to insert sound and video into documents
- How to use various plug-in applications to blend multimedia right into the text of the web page

# chapter six

# Harnessing the New Media

I have this amazing image in my head—maybe we all do—that someday sitting down at the computer will be like walking into a giant bazaar. Signs will glare at us, horns will blare at us. Enticing creatures will beckon from the shadows. Old friends will pop up, flash a wide grin, and whisper secrets in our ears. A robot elf will sprout from the corners of the screen and ask, in plain English (or French, or whatever the local language), exactly what it is we're looking for today. After a short dialog, the elf will disappear and return seconds later with that elusive item we've been seeking.

A bit overblown, no doubt, but not entirely out of the realm of possibility. There are already "agents" out there to locate things for us—there just aren't any with an elf's crinkly face and squeaky voice. We already know it's possible to put sound and video online—every kid with a CD-ROM drive and a personal computer has their own animated encyclopedia where they can listen to frogs croak and geese honk, and watch math problems get solved by themselves.

What's more, we all know a picture is worth a thousand words, and that— when the world is ready and the tools are right—our own online documents will come alive with photos, animation, spoken solutions to knotty problems, or all of the above. We can all look forward to the day when the Grand Unification Theory applies not only to particle physics, but to data, documents, sound, and video all blended into a nice colorful interactive stew.

Web technology brings all of it a step closer by making it easy to add images, sounds, and moving pictures to documents. Thanks to HTML, instead of using expensive software you can now cobble together multimedia presentations with something as simple as a text editor. Of course, if you're the one *creating* the sounds and images, your computer may need sound, video, and image-processing capabilities. But these are increasingly available as built-in options with most computer systems sold today.

Thanks to the flexibility of web systems to serve any kind of file, hypertext can become something more than just hypertext. You can click on a picture of the world to see a country or region. You can see a person's face and click his mouth to hear a sound, or press a button inside a document and see a talking head materialize on the screen. The old silent-era web page with the real-time camera shot of someone's empty coffee pot is old hat by now, replaced by pages that come alive with embedded animation and sound. New tools like RealAudio, StreamWorks, QuickTime, Shockwave, and media.splash, are making the things you can do with web pages mighty impressive.

In the business world, however, we don't do things just because they're impressive. We do them because they make sense or because they make people more productive. In the typical business network, for instance, many of the technical problems with delivering enhanced media are solved. At speeds of 10 Mbps or higher, you're no longer limited by the lowest common denominator of 9600 baud or 14.4 Kbps, the way you are on the World Wide Web. Online pictures load much faster; even sound and video become more practical. So we know we can serve enhanced media over a network. But the question now becomes—do we want to? Will these new forms of communication really make us more productive and contribute to the bottom line?

In many cases, they already do. Nortel publishes commercials for its products over the company's internal web, and the president of Sun Microsystems issues audio reports delivered companywide. If you remember the example from Chapter 4, those reports are one of the main ways rank-and-file employees stay in touch with the thinking of their president. It has truly opened up a new method of communication within the enterprise.

But even advanced Intranet sites like those at Sun and Digital don't use multimedia extensively over their internal networks. Despite the faster network speeds available on Ethernet (as compared to WWW), rich media still takes up so much bandwidth that it can create a serious drag on network performance. Thus, until companies start threading fiber-optic cable between their desktop computers, any use of video or sound on an internal network will have to be closely scrutinized for its overall value to users. In this environment, a taped message from the president may be fine, but other forms of rich media may have to wait for more powerful networks.

Having said all that, there are many simple ways you can jazz up the information at your internal web site, starting with fancier pictures, built-in pushbuttons, and clickable maps, and progressing all the way up to full-motion video and streaming real-time sound. This chapter is designed to provide you with the extra information you need to incorporate these elements into your web sites if the mood or ability strikes you.

## Of GIFs and JPEGs

The nicest part of a web publishing is the ability to incorporate fully illustrated information into your online documents, including color photos, charts, and drawings. With the web, the graphics are *inline,* which means they can be mingled with text in such a way that the text wraps around the graphic. (See Figure 6.1.)

To display correctly inside the web browser window, the image must be stored and served in an appropriate graphics format that the browser will recognize and display. Currently, the most widely used image format is the Graphics Interchange Format, better known as GIF. This a trademarked graphics file format developed by CompuServe for delivering high-quality images in an online networked environment. Since CompuServe was one of the first commercial information delivery services to go online, they needed to create

**Figure 6.1**   Typical inline graphic in a Web browser window.

a picture format that was platform independent and highly compact and would take less time to transmit over network lines.

Once created, GIF was adopted by the people who invented the first web browsers for the same reasons. Notice that the developers specifically chose the GIF format and programmed their browsers to display it. Theoretically, a browser should be able to display multiple types of images, and some already do. But the only other web-compatible image file format even remotely competitive with GIF is the format known as JPEG (pronounced *jay-peg*).

The JPEG format got its name from the Joint Photographic Experts Group, which is part of the International Standards Organization (ISO). One reason it is becoming a popular standard for web images is because it is supported by Netscape, the most popular web browser on the market.

Netscape made a wise selection in adopting JPEG as an alternative graphics format, mainly because it's possible to compress some JPEG files up to four times smaller than comparable GIFs. When compared to full-color data, the actual compression ratio may be as small as 20 to 1. The reason JPEG can do this is because it lets you actually *get rid of* extra data in the file that isn't essential to the quality of the image. As it turns out, the perception of the human eye is such that you can drop large amounts of data in some types of graphics files without significantly affecting the way it looks to the average viewer (this is why JPEG is called a *lossy* format, because it actually loses part of the data). When compared side by side with the original image, you might notice a little bit of degradation. But for that little bit of degradation you may have reduced the actual file size by 75 percent or more. (See Figure 6.2.)

The nice part about JPEG is that you can control the amount of loss that occurs, squeezing the image to get the optimum trade-off between file size and image quality. If you just want to do a rough thumbnail—say for the table of contents in an image catalog—you can distill the image down to its barest essentials and end up with an incredibly small, fast-loading file in the process.

GIF file
(38K)

JPEG file
75% compression
(20K)

JPEG file
20% compression
(8K)

**Figure 6.2**   Image comparison (GIF versus JPEG).

Another powerful aspect of JPEG is that it supports both 8- and 24-bit color, whereas GIF handles only 8-bit. *Bit* refers to the amount of color information stored *per pixel* in the image display. Storing 8 bits per pixel provides a palette of up to 256 colors, while storing 24 bits per pixel provides a potential palette of 16 million colors. Most average desktop monitors today support 256 colors (8 bits). By contrast, you'll only find 24-bit color on high-end graphic workstations like Silicon Graphics and some Macs. The important point about JPEG, however, is that it doesn't matter whether the original color was 8- or 24-bit; it will display properly on nearly any monitor. And 24-bit JPEGs still look better, even when displayed on 8-bit machines.

Despite these features, GIF and JPEG both have their respective advantages:

◆ GIF is better if image quality is the top priority. It is also better for simple illustrations, like organizational charts and stick diagrams, because it is better at compressing large fields of uniform color.

◆ JPEG is better than GIF for compressing color or grayscale images that have complex, continuous color variations (such as photos of people or natural scenes), simply because GIF is not as good at compressing such images.

◆ JPEG should never be used for straight black-and-white images, or images with uniform color fields, because it is not as good as GIF at this type of compression, and it tends to "fuzz" any objects with sharp edges—such as embedded text.

Notice how the advantages and disadvantages mentioned above are all somehow related to the image's final file size. In today's computers—even with our massive hard drives and high-speed networks—storage space and bandwidth are *always* at a premium. The name of the game is getting large files into the most compressed and easily deliverable format available, while preserving acceptable levels of quality. (See Figure 6.3.)

So what does this all mean to you, the person who is just trying to get information from Point A to Point B across a corporate network? If you regularly create images and save them as BMP, PICT, PCX, TIFF, or XWD, maybe it's time to start saving everything you do as GIF or JPEG. Due to the influence of the World Wide Web, most popular word processors and desktop publishing tools are now almost universally adopting GIF and JPEG as acceptable image formats. So GIF or JPEG will be useful no matter what you do. And they are absolutely essential for use on the web.

If you're using Netscape, or some other browser that recognizes both formats, it's not necessary to choose one or the other as the standard way of saving images. You can mix and match image formats freely in the same doc-

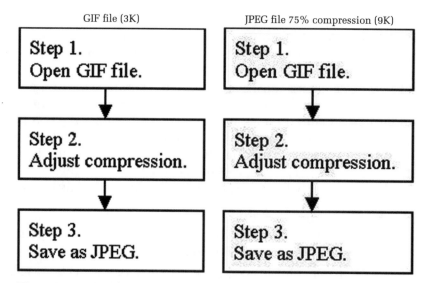

GIF file (3K)                    JPEG file 75% compression (9K)

**Figure 6.3**   Diagram comparison (GIF vs. JPEG).

ument, so that some images might be presented in GIF format and others in JPEG. Netscape even gives you a way to reference two alternate image formats at the same time (as explained later in this chapter).

**Where to Read More About GIF and JPEG**

Check these WWW locations for more reading on the GIF and JPEG formats.

http://home.netscape.com/assist/net_sites/impact_docs/

http://www.cis.ohio-state.edu/hypertext/faq/usenet/
    jpeq-faq/part1/

## How to Create GIF or JPEG Images

Though GIF and JPEG were virtually unknown a few years ago, they are now carried as a standard export format in common graphics programs such as Corel Draw, Freehand, Adobe Illustrator, and many others. That means you can use any of these tools to create your image and then simply save the image as a GIF or JPEG file. Once the file is saved, you can link it into your documents using the HTML codes explained in the next section, or by using the Insert/Image feature in many common WYSIWYG web editors.

What happens if you have illustrations already embedded in your documents? For instance, many WP/DTP apps these days—like FrameMaker, Interleaf, and MS Word—have their own suite of drawing tools that let you create graphics right on the page. Typically there isn't an easy way to export these kinds of graphics to separate files unless you have the right tools. A conversion tool like WebMaker or HTML Transit is designed to automatically extract the graphic illustrations from the DOC file and save them as separate GIF or JPEG files.

What happens if your illustrations are already saved as separate files, but they're in the wrong format? If you're on UNIX, the PBM utilities will do nicely to convert from one format to the other. If you're on PC, look at a tool like Hot Shot. Graphics manipulation tools like Photo Shop, Image Magick and LView Pro are handy too, because they let you see the image while it is being converted, so you can use different interactive filtering or size-adjustment techniques and instantly see the result.

No matter which format you use, it's important to always make graphics as small as possible. No image should be larger than about $600 \times 400$ pixels, so it will be fully visible inside the browser on any screen resolution from VGA on up (otherwise, the user will have to scroll to see it all). Most graphics, unless they contain text, are still quite readable even at thumbnail size. Remember:

---

### Where to Find Graphics Manipulation Tools

You can find the tools mentioned in this section at the following locations on the Internet:

| | |
|---|---|
| Image Magick (UNIX) | http://www.povray.org/povcdrom/cd/programs/util/imagick/index.html |
| LView Pro (PC) | http://www.jumbo.com/graph/win/graphics |
| Image Alchemy (Mac, PC, UNIX) | http://www.handmadesw.com/hsi/products.html |
| xv (UNIX) | ftp://ftp.cis/upenn.edu/pub/xv/ |
| PhotoShop | http://www.adobe.com/ |
| General reference | http://www.atmel.com/atmel/products/gif_viewers.html |

The smaller the image the smaller the file size, the faster it loads, and the less of a drag it will be on network performance.

## How to Create Interlaced GIFs

When using GIF images, there are some popular tricks for image manipulation you can use that are widely used on the World Wide Web. The main technique for improving the performance of your web page is the idea of using *interlaced GIFs.*

Normally, when a picture displays in the web browser, it unfolds from top to bottom, like a window shade coming down. With an interlaced GIF, however, the picture unloads in layers so that it seems to fade in. At first you see a fuzzy rendition of the picture as the first layer loads, then you see progressively sharper resolution appear as the additional layers kick in. Normally, an effect like this would not be a mere curiosity. But, due to enhancements in browser technology, the net effect is to make things much easier and faster for the user.

To understand why the interlaced GIF is faster than a regular GIF, you have to know a little about the history of the World Wide Web. In the earliest versions of Mosaic, you had to wait for the entire document to load before you could see any of it. This included not only the HTML file itself, but every GIF referenced inside the file. If the file was very large and contained multiple large graphics, the user might have to sit there for several minutes, staring at a blank screen and waiting for the document to completely download.

When Netscape was invented, they adopted the interlaced GIF format almost immediately, because it allowed them to deliver information to the end user much faster. Instead of waiting to load every image before displaying the page, Netscape did a quick first pass on the GIFs, then immediately went on to display the text. That way, the user could start reading immediately, even while the remaining layers of the GIFs continued to slowly fade in. (See Figure 6.4.)

Despite the obvious convenience factor, interlaced GIFs may not be appropriate for every use. For instance, I never use an interlaced GIF for the human face, because the effect is decidedly weird. It's always distracting, because I sit there waiting for the entire picture to finish loading so I can tell whether the person is really *that ugly* or not. Human faces aside, interlaced GIF is a great format for large images, especially if the file size is more than 5 to 10 K.

Preparing an interlaced GIF requires the right tools. Some drawing programs and conversion tools give you a choice between GIF 87 and GIF 89 when you are saving (or exporting) the file. GIF 89 is the interlaced format. Others provide a clearly marked option for "interlaced GIF." Of course, that's the one to select. If your only export or saving option is just "GIF," then it's

**Figure 6.4a**    First pass of an interlaced GIF.

probably just a straight unlaced GIF. In that case, you'll need a new set of tools to produce the desired effect (see the sidebar on page 221).

## How to Create Transparent GIFs

Normally, when you create a picture and insert it into a web document, it occupies a rectangular space even if the image shape is irregular. For example, if you draw a picture of a target, then display it as a GIF in a web document, you may see the target inside a white box (assuming the HTML document's background color isn't white, too). The white box isn't an element you created when you were drawing the target. It's just the internal background color of the GIF itself.

A nice feature of the GIF format is that you can make the background color transparent, so that you see right through the GIF background to the back-

**Figure 6.4b**    Final image of an interlaced GIF.

ground color of the web document. This means that the "apparent" shape of the GIF can be as irregular as the image itself. (See Figure 6.5.)

As you can tell, this is not an option that increases user convenience, but it does result in a nicer-looking picture because the image seems to float against the document background. For this reason, you may not want to use trans-

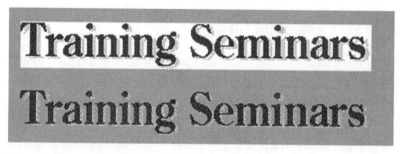

**Figure 6.5**    Nontransparent vs. transparent GIF.

parency widely, but it is nice to use for key images such as logos or opening page graphics.

Again, the key to preparing a transparent GIF image is having the right tools. Some drawing programs like LView Pro and Image Magick now come with the ability to create transparent images—or "mask" background colors (as LView labels it). There are even shareware programs like *giftrans* that do nothing but convert regular GIFs to transparent ones.

## How Images Fit into Documents and Web Pages

Once you have GIF or JPEG images created, inserting them into your web documents is a fairly simple process. If you are using software that does it automatically for you, like any of the WYSIWYG web editors mentioned in Chapter 5, you can simply use the Insert/Image or Insert/Picture menu option in the program. If you really want to optimize the way your images work, however, this is one of those cases where it helps to understand a little about the way HTML works. When inserting images into a web document, it's important to understand that you can't copy an image into an HTML file and store it there the way you can with most word processors. Instead, the image must be saved as an external file (GIF or JPEG) and referenced by an IMG tag within the document. For example, this little snippet of HTML code references a file named *computer.gif:*

```
Here's a photo of my computer:
<IMG SRC="computer.gif" ALT="My Computer">
```

### GIF Tools on the WWW

If you're looking for GIF tools to make your image backgrounds interlaced or transparent, look no further than the WWW. Here are some sites where you can find many:

| | |
|---|---|
| WinGIF (PC) | http://www.jumbo.com/graph/win/ graphics |
| Giftrans (Unix) | ftp://sunsite.unc.edu/pub/packages/ infosystems/WWW/tools/giftrans |
| GIF Converter and Transparency 1.0 (Mac) | ftp://ftp.uwtc.washington.edu/pub/ Mac/Graphics |

When the browser sees the IMG tag, it retrieves the SRC image file (such as *computer.gif*) from the server and inserts it into the displayed document at the location of the IMG tag (Figure 6.6).

Notice the ALT extension tells the browser what to display in case—for some reason—the browser can't find the image or fails to load it properly. (See Figure 6.7.)

Netscape has added some very useful extensions that make image handling more flexible. For instance, regardless of the original size of an image you can automatically rescale the picture on-the-fly so that it fits into a defined area. For example:

```
<IMG SRC="big.gif" WIDTH=420 HEIGHT=100>
```

where both the height and width are specified in pixels. Remember that VGA is 640 × 480 pixels, SVGA is 800 × 600, and high-resolution screens are 1024 × 768 or better. So 300 pixels is roughly half the width of a VGA screen or less than one-third the width of a high-resolution screen.

Interestingly, the HEIGHT and WIDTH extensions also help speed up the velocity at which web pages load into the browser. This is because they clue the browser how large the final image will be, so that the browser can reserve the space for the image without having to poll the server an extra time to get the information. This results in a faster and more efficient document loading process, without frequent back-and-forth communication between the client and server.

Normally, when an image is placed in the text it appears in the exact spot where the <IMG> tag occurs in the text. Text does not wrap around the image; instead the image is treated as though it were just another character in the line of text. The IMG tag gives a way to vertically adjust the position of the image

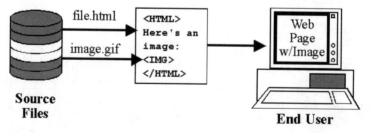

**Figure 6.6**   How images are inserted into web pages.

**Figure 6.7**    Example of image error and alternate description.

relative to the accompanying line of text, if any. This is the ALIGN option, which can have a value of BOTTOM, MIDDLE, or TOP. For instance:

```
<IMG SRC="big.gif" ALIGN=BOTTOM>
```

means that the bottom of the illustration will be even with the baseline of the current line of text. Most web browsers support these options. However, Netscape added horizontal alignment options to its browser that you can also add to your document markups. In particular, the ALIGN=LEFT and ALIGN= RIGHT extensions allow you to float the image at the left or right margin in such a way that text wraps around it. Other Netscape variations on the ALIGN tag can be seen at http://home.netscape.com/assist/net_sites/html_ extensions.html.

Netscape even gives a way to load two different images at the same spot. This provides a way to accommodate very-high-resolution images without slowing down the user too much. For example, a very compact low-resolution JPEG image could be loaded first, and then (assuming the user stays on the page for a while) it can be slowly replaced by a much bulkier high-resolution GIF. The tag syntax for this would be:

```
<IMG SRC="highres.gif" LOWSRC="lowres.jpeg">
```

Inserting images works much the same way whether you're coding HTML by hand or using a WYSIWYG tool such as Word IA or FrontPage. In a WYSIWYG program, you might place the cursor where you want the image to go, select Insert/Picture from the pull-down menu, then specify the external file that already contains the image. (See Figure 6.8.)

The selected image is inserted into the document by reference and is displayed at the point of insertion while you are editing. But this doesn't mean

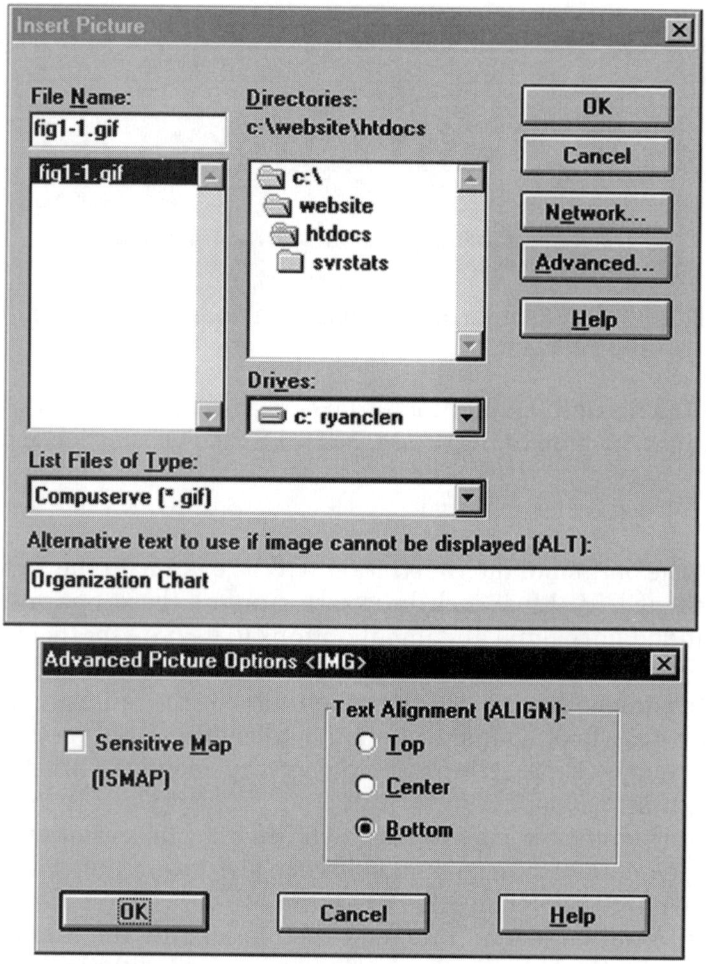

**Insert Picture**

File **N**ame:
fig1-1.gif

fig1-1.gif

**Directories:**
c:\website\htdocs

📁 c:\
📁 website
📁 htdocs
📁 svrstats

OK

Cancel

N**e**twork...

**A**dvanced...

**H**elp

List Files of **T**ype:
Compuserve (*.gif)

Dri**v**es:
💾 c: ryanclen

**A**lternative text to use if image cannot be displayed (ALT):
Organization Chart

**Advanced Picture Options <IMG>**

☐ Sensitive **M**ap
(ISMAP)

Text Alignment (ALIGN):
○ **T**op
○ **C**enter
◉ **B**ottom

OK   Cancel   **H**elp

**Figure 6.8**   Insert Image dialog in Word IA.

that the image has been inserted into the file permanently. When you save the HTML file to disk, the referenced image remains in a separate file.

## Serving Other Kinds of Image Files

Earlier, I made the point that GIF and JPEG images are the only kind of image you can display in a web browser. This is technically correct if we are talking about *inside the browser window*. Actually, you can serve any kind of image (or any other kind of file) over the web if you really want to. The only difference with other image types is that they cannot display inside the browser window.

For example, suppose you have a PCX file that you want to serve over the web without converting it to GIF. You would not use the IMG tag for this purpose, because the IMG tag would try to insert the illustration directly into the web document (and cause an image load error). Instead, you would put a *hyperlink* into your document that references the image file. For instance, if the PCX filename is *schema9.pcx,* the HTML code might say:

```
Click <A HREF="schema9.pcx">here</A> to see the exploded schematic drawing.
```

When the user clicks the word *here,* the web browser retrieves the PCX file and brings it to the browser where it can be viewed or saved to disk. To view it, the user must have a local helper application (such as Windows Paintbrush) already installed and associated with the PCX file extension inside the web browser. So when the browser receives the file, it opens the helper application and displays the image. As special plug-ins are created for Netscape Navigator, there will likely come a day when any graphics format can be displayed inside the browser window. However, as always, plug-ins will require the same kind of special installation that helper applications do.

Naturally, this would be quite an inconvenient way to serve random images, because users would have to either save the image to disk, then open it up in a separate application, or go in and configure helper applications on-the-fly the first time they download any particular type of image. However, if you already have the system set up that way from the beginning—so that Paintbrush (or Autocad, or whatever) is already configured as a helper application on every user platform, then it's easier to handle.

The advantage of a corporate Intranet is that we can do these kinds of things if it saves time and money, since (theoretically) we have more control over the end-user configuration. Something like this would be a lot less practical on the World Wide Web.

## How to Create Random Pushbuttons

Occasionally, when scrolling through a web document, you may encounter a pushbutton sitting right there on the page—even right in the middle of a sentence. When you click the pushbutton, it brings up something completely different. This kind of effect is just a variation of the old text-based hyperlink. Remember that a text-based hyperlink looks like this:

```
Click <A HREF="newfile.html">here</A> to see something completely different.
```

Instead of having the word *here* hyperlinked, you might draw a picture of a button, save it as a GIF file, and insert the image of the button into the middle of the hyperlink instead:

```
Click
<A HREF="newfile.html"><IMG SRC="button2.gif"></A> to see something completely
    different.
```

Many varieties of server software already have sample buttons available that you can use for purposes like this. Notice the button picture is stored as a separate GIF file and referenced using the IMG tag. Programs like WebMaker and HTML Transit also come with infinite varieties of navigation buttons that can be inserted into documents. If you want to save time and avoid having to draw your own buttons, look around in the web software installation directory for these kinds of GIFs. Otherwise, you may want to develop your own generic (or specialized) pushbuttons that you can seed into your documents on a regular basis, whenever the mood strikes you.

## How to Create Clickable Image Maps

If you've used the World Wide Web much, chances are you've seen many clickable imagemaps. For instance, the Virtual Tourist (http://wings.buffalo. edu/world/) presents you with a map of the world, and you can click on any country, region, or locality to visit that place. Imagine the many ways you could use something like this in your organization.

Imagine, for instance, that your company manufactures airplane engines and you want to be able to take the engine apart piece by piece, simply by clicking on it. So a click on the manifold assembly might show an exploded diagram of that component, and a second click might bring up a list of parts in the component assembly. On a more general level, you may want to present employees with a map of your company's main campus or headquarters building, then have them click a building (or floor) to see what's in there (a floor plan, an employee directory for that location, pictures of the people who work there, etc.).

The idea behind a clickable imagemap is that each part of the graphic image can be defined as a separate *hot zone* so that when the user clicks on it, the browser retrieves something from the web server. The hot zone area—and the something it retrieves—is usually defined in a table stored inside a map file that looks like the one in Figure 6.9.

What to display if user clicks
*outside* a defined hot zone

```
default   http://server_name/error.html

rect   0,0    25,45    http://server_name/doc1.html
rect   0,45   25,90    http://server_name/doc2.html
rect   0,90   25,135   http://server_name/doc3.html
```

Hot zone      Hot zone        What to display when user clicks
shape         coordinates     inside hot zone

**Figure 6.9**   Typical map file.

This is a fairly simple file to create. The *rect* entry, for example, defines each hot zone as a rectangle that lies within the specified pixel coordinates. When the user clicks inside these coordinates, the web server delivers the specified file. Hot zones don't have to be rectangular. They might also be circles, triangles, polygons, or points. The shapes allowed and the map file format may vary, depending on the server you're using. So it's best to check your specific server installation for examples.

Another way to specify map images is to place them directly into the HTML file. Netscape, for instance, provides tags you can use for client-side imagemaps, but these maps will not work for all browsers. They can also become ponderous if you use the same imagemap repeatedly, such as a toolbar.

The main problem with creating imagemaps, of course, is identifying the correct pixel coordinates for each hot zone. To do this, you may need a special tool like xv or LView Pro (see the sidebar on page 217). With these tools, you can display the image, place the cursor at any point in the image, and read the coordinates from the screen. Some server software packages like Website come equipped with special tools that do nothing but create map files. For example, Website's Imagemap Editor lets you actually draw the hot zones right on the image and identify the URLs to reference for each hot zone, and the software creates the map file automatically. (Figure 6.10.)

You must create a separate map file for each different clickable illustration in your documents, unless for some reason all your illustrations are the same size and all hot zones map the same way. This is not as unusual as it sounds. For example, you might have a navigation bar at the top of every page that looks like a row of buttons. And when the user clicks one of the "buttons" (i.e., a specific hot zone on the navigation bar) it always maps to the same locations (home page, table of contents, index, etc.). If the bar links to a different location every time (for example, if some buttons always take the user

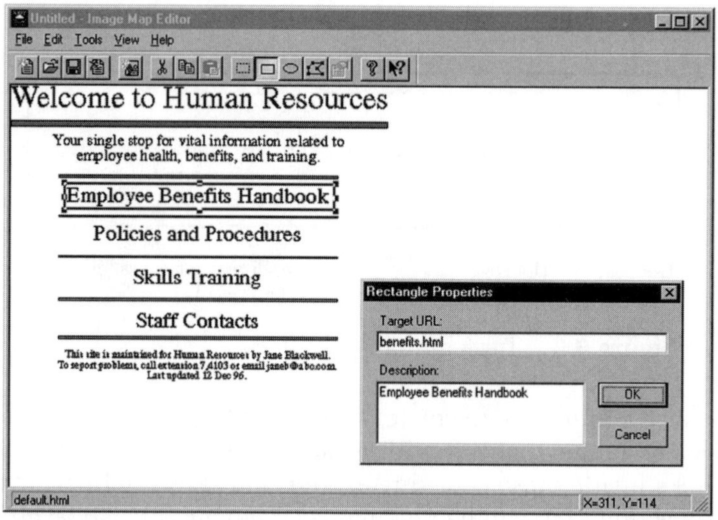

**Figure 6.10**    Imagemap Editor with hot zones identified.

to the "next page" or "previous page") a clickable imagemap may be the wrong way to go. Instead, you may find it easier to have separate navigation buttons that are controlled individually through hyperlinks directly inside the document's HTML file (instead of in a separate map file).

The finished map file may need to be stored in a special directory your server uses for this purpose. The file may also require a specific filename extension, such as .map. Again, this is a function of your individual server, and you should check the server documentation for details.

Once you have the map file created and stored on disk, you can make it work only by using the correct hyperlinking syntax in your document. For instance, if the clickable image is named *homehead.gif* and the map file is called *homepage.map* the correct syntax should be:

```
<A HREF="homepage.map">
<IMG SRC="homehead.gif" ISMAP>
</A>
```

Notice how the hyperlink tag (A) wraps completely around the image tag (IMG), in effect making the image the hyperlink. Don't forget the ISMAP part, or else the image mapping feature won't work at all. Of course, you should always check your server documentation for examples, and look around in your server installation directory for demo map files that may be sitting around.

**The New Client-Side Image Maps**

Version 2.x of Netscape Navigator also supports the concept of "client-side imagemaps." Instead of creating a map file and storing it in a special server map directory, you can place all the mapping information directly inside the document at the location of the image. The benefits of doing this are several. First, it gives users more control over image mapping, since they don't have to ask the server administrator for permission to write a separate map file into protected server areas. Second, it simplifies file management because there isn't an extra map file to keep track of. Finally, it actually makes the imagemaps work faster. With a server-side imagemap, each click on the image requires a special "hit" on the server to reference the map file and look up the coordinates of the hyperlink. Naturally, this slows the turnaround speed on the hyperlink. With a client-side imagemap, the image coordinates are referenced and interpreted locally, so that the URL can be fetched in a single hit. For more information on client-side image maps, see http://home.netscape.com/assist/net_sites/html_extensions_3.html

## The Power of Referenced Images and Image Libraries

One powerful feature of HTML is the ability to pull your images from any source on the Intranet. Thus, for example, if the image is stored on a different server somewhere within your organization (or on the World Wide Web), you can reference it directly from any HTML document, without having to copy it to your own local disk. To do this, just insert a complete URL as the SRC extension in the <IMG> tag, such as:

```
<IMG SRC="http://server_name/file.gif">
```

This may be a little harder to do if you're using a WYSIWYG web editor. The more sophisticated ones actually let you specify a URL-based file rather than a local directory-based file when inserting a picture on the page. (See Figure 6.11.) Otherwise, you may have to do a special code insert into the document, or failing that, edit the HTML file by hand.

The power of referenced images can be seen if your company keeps a centralized image library. Thus, someone in your company might keep a single set

**Where to Find Imagemap Editors**

Most servers I've seen now come with their own imagemap editors. So do many of the new web publishing packages. However, if your software doesn't include these handy tools, you can still find easy-to-use imagemap editors out on the WWW at the following locations:

| | |
|---|---|
| MapEdit for UNIX and Windows | http://sunsite.unc.edu/pub/packages/infosystems/WWW/tools/mapedit/ |
| WebMap for Mac | http://www.city.net/cnx/software/webmap.html |
| Various tools and platforms | http://www.stars.com/Vlib/Providers/Imagemaps.html |

of common images like logos, building photos, or executive photos that everyone can access across the web by referencing the image in their documents.

But the same power applies whether the images are centralized or widely dispersed. For instance, human resources might store on its web server a copy of the most current organization chart for your department. Instead of copying the organization chart to your local disk drive, you can just insert an IMG tag into your local document that retrieves the organization chart directly from the human resources server.

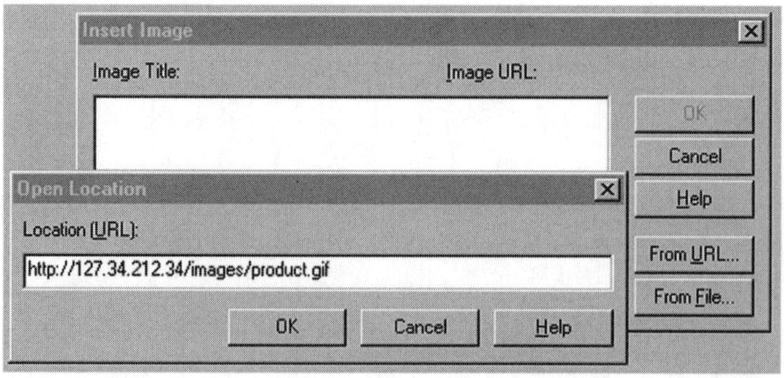

**Figure 6.11**   FrontPage Editor's Insert Image dialog.

Think about that for a while. If you copied the organization chart to your local disk drive, it would go out of date as soon as human resources revises the chart (for example, as soon as your boss is fired). But if you reference it instead through a web URL, then your document *always has the latest version of the organization chart,* automatically delivered direct from the source to your document. In other words, if someone views your document on the web, they will actually see the very latest organization chart as it is currently stored on the computer in human resources, even though the document they're viewing it through is one you created. And if human resources updates the chart five minutes from now and someone opens that document again, *it will automatically contain the new chart,* even though the document itself did not change.

The same can be done for engineering drawings, product photos, schematic diagrams, or any kind of image that is widely used or referenced by people in your company. In fact, you could even use the web as an excellent way to catalogue all these illustrations: Let everyone keep their own web-based repository of images for public use, and then have a central web menu where people can go to access all the different image libraries. Thus, the care and maintenance of images can be distributed out to all the departments in your company, but the *access to the images* can be centralized through hyperlinking.

Arranging things this way could produce all kinds of unseen benefits. Instead of having 5,000 copies of the company logo floating around on everyone's disk drives and servers, you could have just one copy—the official one from the web server in corporate communications. Instead of doing the old file-chase routine everytime you need that image, you can check the image library, find the correct URL, and insert it in your document. You've not only saved the company a great deal of disk space, but saved everyone a great deal of time.

So, if you're creating an information center for your local department or work group, why not throw away all those outdated organization charts, logos, product photos, and drawings? Get other departments to bring their images online on the web, then start using fresh stuff, direct from the source.

## Inserting Sound and Video into Documents

Like oddball image types, you can also serve sound, audio, and video from a web document. But you cannot display these or embed them directly inside the document. Instead, you can have a hyperlink that points to a file, and when the user clicks the hyperlink it will retrieve the file. For example, the following snippet of HTML code references a file called *toot.au,* and serves it to the browser when the user clicks the words *hear the horn:*

```
Click here to <A HREF="toot.au">hear the horn.</A>
```

Likewise, the following line of HTML might serve up a video file in MPEG format called *film.mpg:*

```
Click here to <A HREF="film.mpg">see the film.</A>
```

Clicking either type of hyperlink retrieves the file from the web server and sends it to the browser. What happens next depends on whether the user has appropriate software called a *playback device* on their local computer, as well as an appropriate sound card.

## Multimedia Playback Devices

The first requirement for playing back a multimedia file is a helper application or playback device that is installed on the user's local computer. There are also multimedia plug-ins that do the same thing. For example, to hear the contents of a sound file, the user must have a *sound player* (or plug-in) that can read and play back the digitized sound stored in the file. To play back a video file, the user must have a *video player* (or plug-in) that can read and play back the digitized motion picture it contains.

If such a playback device or plug-in is already installed as a helper application on the user's computer, the file will download and play back automatically. If not, the browser may ask the user whether to save the file to disk or configure a helper application to play it.

Let's assume the former case applies—that the playback device is a recognized helper application. As soon as the user clicks the hyperlink, the web server begins sending the file over to the browser. However, in even the fastest networks, there will be a noticeable pause while the file downloads. Because sound and video are so data intensive, they are typically quite large files. A few minutes of sound or a half-minute of video may involve several megabytes of data. So the system pauses while the entire file loads. Then, once the file is finished loading, the helper application opens and plays back the sound.

> *Note:* Notice here and in the rest of this section that I have intentionally limited the discussion to traditional sound and video formats. In the next section, I'll cover a new type of technology called *streaming audio* and *streaming video* that can be delivered across networks *without* the characteristic pause between the time the user requests it and the time the file begins to play.

What happens if the user doesn't have a helper application or plug-in for sound or video? Actually, this is quite unlikely unless the user is working on an extremely old system. Most computers sold these days have built-in media players that can handle both sound and video. However, since each major type of computer system is developed in an isolated environment, each uses a format that could be considered native to that environment. The table shows a number of popular media formats and the computer environments where they are usually found.

| Media | File Format | Primary Environment |
|-------|-------------|---------------------|
| Sound | AU | Sun, NeXT |
| | AIFF | Macintosh, SGI |
| | WAV | PC |
| Video | MPEG | All |
| | QuickTime (MOV) | Macintosh |
| | AVI | PC |

Which format to use? Well, of course, there are several considerations. If you plan to deliver sound or video over a corporate network, the first question you might ask is: What kind of equipment are people using? For instance, if everyone has a PC, the AVI video format may be fine, but not if you have Macs or UNIX machines on your network. In a mixed environment, MPEG is most commonly used for video, but QuickTime is fast becoming a popular standard. Most versions of Mac, and any PC with Windows 95, have a built-in video player that can handle either MPEG or QuickTime. For older UNIX machines, you may need to hunt down video players for either format (see the sidebar on page 235).

The situation is a little different for sound, but not much. Just as GIF and JPEG have become the standards for displaying images, AU and AIFF are considered unofficial standards for audio on the World Wide Web—and thus, by association, for any web system. If PC users don't already have AU and AIFF players installed, Netscape provides a built-in solution. Every copy of Netscape for Windows comes bundled with a built-in companion utility called the Netscape Audio Player (NAPLAYER), which is automatically configured as Netscape's helper application for sound. NAPLAYER recognizes and plays back sound encoded in the AU and AIFF format, including 8- or 16-bit sound. (See Figure 6.12.)

So, assuming that all your users are using Netscape, AU and AIFF may be good formats to standardize on.

**Figure 6.12**    Netscape's NA Player.

## Sound Cards

The ability for the user to play back common multimedia formats relies on more than just the playback software. Users will not be able to hear the audio component of a sound or video file unless they also have an appropriate sound card installed on their machines. What's more, the sound card will probably need to support 16-bit sound, since that is currently the most widely used standard.

Older machines may not have a sound card at all, or if they do have a sound card it may be an 8-bit card. If you send a 16-bit sound file to a machine equipped with an 8-bit card, the sound file will try to play back, but no sound will be produced. So if you plan to use video and audio widely within the Intranet, it may be a good idea to check around and make sure all your users have the proper equipment.

In this sense, the sound card is the truly crucial component in a multimedia web system. If your users don't have sound cards, it's a major problem because equipping every user would mean purchasing all those cards and then taking every computer apart to install them. Compared to the absence of a sound card, it's a minor problem if your users don't have the correct playback software. You can easily make a shareware playback program available for downloading from your site (or point your users to an Internet/Intranet location where they can download it).

## How to Create Sound and Video for Web Consumption

It's beyond the scope of this book to delve into all the details of audio and video production. If you want to do it and become good at it, there are plenty of books on the subject. Suffice it to say that you can produce sound and video files rather easily if your system is equipped with a sound card, a video card, or similar multimedia hardware. Many systems being sold today already have sound and video built in; on others it may be an add-on option. Assuming you're not working with older equipment, you should be able to plug microphones, tape recorders, video cameras, or VCRs directly into the back of your computer (or directly into the sound card) and transfer sounds or images directly to the hard drive. In most cases, the multimedia hardware also comes with software and instructions on how to capture the sound and video from external devices and save it in various digital formats on disk.

The only problem may be that the available storage formats are not the exact ones you need. For example, the sound board on a PC may be able to save sounds in the WAV format used by standard PC applications, but not in the AU or AIFF format used by the Netscape Audio Player. If you wanted to convert the sound from WAV to AU or AIFF, you might need special conversion software to do it.

However, once you are able to capture the sound, save it to disk, and store it in the appropriate format, you can easily serve it over the web. Just make sure the file has been stored in the appropriate server directory using the appropriate file extension (such as .au, .aiff or .aif). Then be sure to make the hyperlinks on your web page point to the file.

## Streaming Audio and Video

Most common multimedia formats—like MPEG, AU, AIFF, and even Quick-Time—were developed well before the World Wide Web became so explosively popular. Just a few years ago, the idea of serving multimedia over a network was not even a consideration. For this reason, the traditional multimedia formats work best on standalone computers or on computers connected to a network file server, where they can be read directly from disk and played back to the local machine. If you try to serve such files across a network, you get that characteristic pause as the browser waits for the entire file to download and then starts up the application to play it in.

Responding to the growing popularity of the WWW, several companies are rushing to the forefront with new audio and video formats that are specifically designed to be delivered across a TCP/IP network. These new formats

### Where to Find Shareware Video and Audio Players

Netscape gives you access to many of the helper applications and plug-ins you can use for video and audio. For details, see http://home.netscape.com/assist/helper_apps/index.html.

are called *streaming audio* and *streaming video* because they are designed to be received and played back in a stream, rather than all at once. If you think of network-delivered multimedia as a stream of packets being shipped to the user in a specific sequence, the web browser in effect is opening each packet as soon as it comes through the door, rather than waiting for the entire shipment to arrive. Thus, playback can occur almost immediately, as soon as the first packets in the stream begin to reach the browser.

## Understanding the RealAudio Format

One of the most promising such formats is RealAudio (RA) created by Progressive Networks. RealAudio is exemplary not only because it was one of the first streaming formats to emerge, but also because it was one of the first plugins to be developed for the Netscape browser.

At its core, RealAudio is just another way to store sound on a disk. Instead of using WAV, AU, or AIFF to store your audio files, you can use the RA format. Unfortunately, since RA is not (yet) a widely used standard, traditional sound playback devices do not recognize it. There is also the problem of getting sounds into the RA format: Many widely available software tools let you create WAV, AU, or AIFF, but don't (yet) let you store sounds as RA. To counter these problems, Progressive Networks developed several tools:

- ◆ *RealAudio Player.* This free device can play back RA sounds stored in local files or delivered across a network via web. This is equivalent to the Netscape Audio Player or any of the other common playback devices that you may already have installed on your local computer. And like the others, it must be installed as a helper application with the browser before the user can retrieve and play back RA sounds automatically.

- ◆ *The RealAudio Plug-In.* Starting with version 2.0 of RealAudio, the RA Player software was available as a plug-in application to Netscape Navigator 2.0 and higher versions. This means that—instead of appearing *alongside* the browser as a separate helper application— elements of the RA Player might actually appear *inside the browser window,* as explained later in this section.

- ◆ *The RealAudio Encoder.* If you want to convert sounds to RA from other formats like WAV and AU, this free utility program will do it. Just load the old format into the encoder and it automatically creates the new RA file for you. It even lets you add a title and description to the file that will be visible in the RA Player window when you play back the sound.

◆ *The RealAudio Server.* Unlike the previous RealAudio components, the RA Server costs money, and is required if you want to serve streaming audio RA files. As explained below, you can serve individual files by simply hyperlinking them into documents. Even though the server can be quite expensive, or you could probably use a single server for all the audio needs of an Intranet.

## How to Serve RealAudio to Users

If your users have a RealAudio Player installed as a helper application, you can serve RA sound files (*.RA or *.RAM) by simply embedding them in a hyperlink, such as the following:

```
<A HREF="http://server/toot.ram">Click here for sound.</A>
```

When the user clicks on the hyperlink, the browser will immediately fire up the RA Player as a helper application and begin playing back the RA sound. Assuming you are using a RealAudio server, the sound plays *as it comes through the network* rather than waiting until the entire stream of data has arrived. The RA Player appears in a separate window outside the browser window, which contains all the controls the user might need to pause and restart the sound stream, increase or decrease the volume, and see what is being played (title, description). (See Figure 6.13.)

If your users have Netscape 2.0 or greater, and you have installed RealAudio 2.0 or greater as a plug-in, then you can code your web documents so that the RA Player controls are actually embedded right inside the browser window. Thus, you might have a start button and a volume control inserted directly

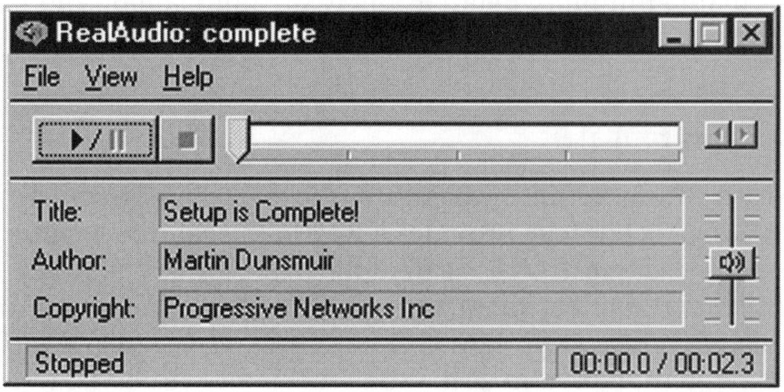

**Figure 6.13**    The RA Player.

between paragraphs in a document, or appearing alongside a photograph, so that an extra window does not have to be opened for the helper application.

This is done by using Netscape's special EMBED tag to embed the RA sound file and RA Player components directly into the web page. Just go to the point in the web page where you want the controls to appear, and specify the sound file and controls as follows:

```
<EMBED SRC="http://server1/toot.rpm" WIDTH=100 HEIGHT=50>
```

Notice that the EMBED tag is like the regular IMG tag in HTML, except that instead of specifying an image, you are specifying a multimedia file that will be played back by the plug-in device. Also notice that the file extension is now RPM instead of RAM or RA, to indicate that the file is designed for use in plug-in mode. The default configuration of the plug-in controls is for *all* the controls to appear at the inserted location on the web page. If you want to display only individual controls such as the volume slider, you would specify the exact control(s) to be displayed. For instance:

```
<EMBED SRC="http://server1/toot.rpm" WIDTH=100 HEIGHT=50
CONTROLS="VolumeSlider">
```

You can also specify that the file start playing automatically when the page is loaded (instead of asking the user to start the sound by clicking the controls). To do this, you would use the AUTOSTART attribute. For instance:

```
<EMBED SRC="http://server1/toot.rpm" WIDTH=100 HEIGHT=50
CONTROLS="VolumeSlider" AUTOSTART=True>
```

There are many other attributes you can control for RealAudio plug-ins. These are explained in more detail at the RealAudio site on the World-Wide Web (http://www.realaudio.com/products/ra2.0/plug_ins/).

### The Stream Works Format

Whereas RealAudio only encompasses audio files, the StreamWorks format provided by Xing Technology provides a way to stream information from both video and audio sources. Like RealAudio, Xing offers a media server, an encoder utility, and a client that can be installed as a helper application for use alongside the browser window. Unlike RealAudio, StreamWorks was not available as a Netscape plug-in at the time this book was being written.

There are several major differences in design and operation between RealAudio and StreamWorks technology. The main difference is that Stream-Works is not a new multimedia format. Instead, it is a way of taking existing MPEG data, serving it across the network as a stream, and playing it back on-the-fly as the stream reaches the client end. To accomplish this task requires both a special server and a special client, both of which cost money. The nice thing about StreamWorks is that its transmission modes can accommodate different client speeds from the very high-end to the very low-end. If the client is attached to a 14.4 Kbps modem, StreamWorks scales the data flow down to one frame per second (or every other second) and AM sound quality. At much higher speeds (say 3 Mbps or more), StreamWorks can deliver full-screen full-motion video and better than FM-quality sound.

Due to cost, complexity, and the special client-server requirements, a tool like StreamWorks is not a practical component for widespread use on internal webs. However, if a single department or division needs to serve high-end video or audio to selected audiences over fast network connections, this may be just the technology you need. In that case, a single StreamWorks server installed within the department's LAN may be sufficient.

## Shockwave and Other Multimedia Plug-Ins

One of the most promising recent trends in web browser technology is the development of a raft of new plug-ins for Netscape Navigator 2.x. We've already looked at the RealAudio plug-in, but it is just one of many new multimedia tools available for integration with the web browser.

The idea of a plug-in is to get all the action to happen "inside the browser window." If you recall the discussion of web browsers in the first few chapters of this book, you'll remember that the most promising aspect of web technology is the idea that it might provide users with a single, universal interface for *any type of information* or computer resource. The main thing keeping the web browser from being a universal GUI, however, is the fact that it can deal directly with only a handful of file types, like HTML, GIF, JPEG, and TXT. All other files served to the browser require some type of helper application that plays alongside it in a separate window.

Plug-ins reduce the need for helper applications and extend the capability of the web browser to display more file types inside the window. The plug-in concept is becoming a major entree for software companies that might otherwise be left behind in the mad scramble onto the web.

A good example is Shockwave. This plug-in was invented by Macromedia, the same people who invented the popular multimedia development tool called Director. Shockwave gives you the ability not only to play back movies, animations, and presentations created using Director, but to play them back directly inside the Netscape browser window. Instead of having a web page with a static image of a product like a car, you might have a web page that contains a video or animation of the car actually moving down a highway. The moving picture would appear in a certain area of the web page, the same way an image does. The only difference is that the image area would be animated.

To deliver such a web page to the end user, you would first use Macromedia Director to create the moving image and save it in a Director file (.DIR). Then you would use another Macromedia product called Afterburner to compress the image down into a special file format called DCR. Finally, you would use the Netscape EMBED tag to embed the image directly into a specific location on the web page. For instance:

```
<EMBED SRC="http://server3/movie.dcr" WIDTH=240 HEIGHT=100>
```

This tag would create an image area 240 pixels wide and 100 pixels high within the web document at the exact spot where the EMBED tag occurs. When the user loads the page, the moving animation would run automatically inside the specified image area. Since the image position is fixed inside the document, if the user scrolls the document, the moving image scrolls with it. You could even embed multiple Shockwave images in the page so that different parts of the page contain moving images as the user reads through them. Any movie can also contain interactive buttons and text fields that accept keyboard input from the user. You can also program the movie using Macromedia's Lingo programming language to actually access information from the network and open other URLs on the web based in different user interactions.

Naturally, to make these effects available to your users, you will need to make sure each user has the Shockwave plug-in installed on his or her local machine. As always, this should be a lot easier to do on an Intranet than on the World Wide Web, since you probably are dealing with a known group of employees, customers, or suppliers.

As mentioned earlier, RealAudio and Shockwave are two of the more interesting Netscape plug-ins. But there are a whole slew of others available, including:

- *Acrobat Amber,* a plug-in that lets you view and use Adobe Acrobat files (.PDF) directly inside the browser window. Normally, you would use Acrobat Reader to view PDF files, but the Amber plug-in eliminates the need for an extra window.

- *Corel CMX Viewer,* a way to view vector graphics saved to Corel's special CMX format. Vector graphics are sharp-edged images produced by tracing objects, instead of converting them to a bitmap or *raster* format as is done in GIF or JPEG.

- *Envoy,* a plug-in that works like Acrobat Amber to let users see published pages inside the browser.

- *VDOLive,* a way of compressing and viewing video images in real-time over low bandwidth connections.

- *WebFX,* a plug-in tool that lets you view three-dimensional effects created using the World Wide Web's esoteric Virtual Reality Modeling Language (VRML).

- *QuickTime* plug-in lets you view QuickTime movies in the browser window.

For more details on all the available Netscape plug-ins, see the Netscape site on the World Wide Web at http://home.netscape.com/comprod/version_2.0/plugins/.

---

### Where to Find Multimedia Apps and Plug-Ins

You can use the Internet to download evaluation copies of various multimedia software and plug-ins. You can see a complete list of all current Netscape plug-ins at http://www.netscape.com/comprod/products/navigator/version_2.0/plugins/ You can also reference some of the major plug-ins and other multimedia applications at the following locations:

| | |
|---|---|
| RealAudio | http://www.realaudio.com/ |
| Shockwave | http://www.macromedia.com/ |
| Streamworks | http://www.xingtech.com/ |
| VDOLive Plug-in | http://www.vdolive.com/ |
| media.splash | http://www.sybase.com/ |
| QuickTime | http://quicktime.apple.com/ |
| ViewMovie QuickTime Plug-in | http://www.well.com/~wanski/ viewmovie |
| Acrobat Amber | http://www.adobe.com/ |

## Where Do We Go from Here?

Now that you understand the power of the web to deliver published documents and multimedia, that leaves only one more uncharted area: data and applications. The next chapter will explain how you can use web technology to create interactive forms that help users tap into databases, run remote client-server applications, and perform other astounding feats.

## Chapter Seven at a Glance

The most powerful aspect of web technology is its ability to provide users with interactive access to data and online applications across a computer network. This chapter introduces the various technologies and how they fit into corporate Intranets, including:

- How HTML forms work, and how they can be used to communicate with users over a web
- How CGI programs work, and why they're often needed for interactive communication
- How to create virtual documents through on-the-fly web publishing
- How to set up forms and CGI without programming
- Some common database access tools and how they work
- How to set up search applications for your web sites
- Why Java will change the nature of software as we know it

# Serving Data and Applications

Web technology has evolved quite a bit since the day the idea first popped into Tim Berners-Lee's head. In the beginning, HTML was primarily a way to deliver documents. Somewhere along the way, back when Marc Andreessen worked at the NCSA, somebody decided that HTTP should do something more than just serve files. So they wrote an extension to the web protocol called CGI—the *Common Gateway Interface.* And they invented extra HTML tags that allowed a web page to act like a regular form or dialog box, with pull-down menus, radio buttons, check boxes, scrollable lists, and text fields.

Suddenly, the web became a two-way street (or an information superhighway, depending on your metaphorical preferences). Sure, you can ship all the information to users that you want. But at the same time, users can talk back to you. You can send users data, and they can send data right back. It's nifty, it's neat, but it's something more than that. It represents a whole new way that data and applications can be delivered.

CGI was only the beginning. After CGI came various *application programming standards* (APIs) developed by the people who brought you Mosaic and Netscape. Then came the Java programming language with its flashy name and flashier concept. Then JavaScript and more—each development bursting onto the scene before the surprise over the last one had faded. If there are any conclusions to be drawn from all this gunfire and smoke, it is that the web is becoming something exponentially greater than what it was before. It's becoming a programming environment and very much like an operating system—but a virtual one that operates through networks rather than through the local synapses of the desktop computer.

The most stunning example of how quickly and completely this will change the software industry came in early 1996, when Microsoft Corporation abruptly announced a massive business reorganization around the concept of supporting the Internet and the Intranet. It's not hard to see what caused Bill Gates to reshuffle his entire organization and development strategy. When Netscape and Java came blazing into the business world in 1995, people began to predict the death of desktop operating systems like Microsoft Windows. With these new tools, and the promise of virtually unlimited network bandwidth capacity just over the horizon, we may soon come to a state of affairs where all computer resources and applications can be delivered directly into the web browser—so that this simple tool does indeed become a universal GUI (graphical user interface).

This is not great news for Microsoft, no matter how vaunted its current position in the world of business applications. As the business markets began to sit up and take notice of developments on the Web, Gates had to emerge with his own show-stoppers: new Internet and Intranet technologies will be built into all future Microsoft desktop applications.

So, while online publishing and multimedia are two of the neatest things webs can do, programming and interactivity are where the real action is these days. And, more than anything else, this is where the promise of the web lies. Software developers and IT managers should sit up and take notice that the time is drawing near when their standard programming tools and system models will likely be replaced by what is coming down the Intranet turnpike. And everyone else should rejoice, because the new developments in web technology will make it easy for many of us to create our own network-delivered desktop applications.

## Web Forms: The Source of All True Power

In fact, things are already easier. New HTML tags introduced in the 2.0 standard, and new tools that work alongside web servers, already make it possible for anyone to create their own web applications. You want interactivity? You got it.

To show just how easy it is, I want you to do something that used to take programmers a long time to accomplish. I want you to create a key element of a computer program called a *dialog*. You know what a dialog is: You use them all the time in all of your windows-based programs, whether on a PC, Mac, or UNIX workstation. These are the windows where you type in information, click buttons, and select from pull-down menus.

Using HTML, you can create a dialog box in a few minutes with a plain old text editor and a few simple codes. Start your text editor now, open a new file, and type in the code as shown in Figure 7.1.

Notice the <FORM> tags. On a web, we call a dialog a *form*. But make no mistake—it's still a dialog just like the dialog boxes you see in myriad other

```
<FORM>
<PRE>

My name is <INPUT NAME="name">

My room number is <INPUT NAME="room">

This is what I want for lunch:

<SELECT NAME="lunch">
<OPTION>Pizza
<OPTION>Burger
<OPTION>Chicken
</SELECT>

Here's some other things I need:
<TEXTAREA NAME="extras" ROWS=4 COLS=60>
</TEXTAREA>

<INPUT TYPE="SUBMIT" VALUE="Place the Order">

</PRE>
</FORM>
```

**Figure 7.1**   Example of form coded in HTML.

programs. Now let's save the form as a text file using the name *myform.htm* and open it up as a local file in your browser (Open File option in Netscape). If you did your typing correctly, you should see the Form dialog displayed in a WYSIWYG format as shown in Figure 7.2.

Notice I already filled in some words for you. Go ahead and fill in the same words, then click the button labeled "Place the Order." If you're using Netscape 2.0 or greater (results not guaranteed in other browsers), you should see the form get spit right back at you like it is in Figure 7.3.

This isn't what usually happens when you fill in a form on the World Wide Web. Normally, your browser sends the form data off to the server for processing. It didn't happen because this impromptu form isn't connected to a server or being accessed over a web. We're accessing it as a local file. So why bother with this example? Well, take another look. Don't look at the jumble of form fields on the screen. Instead, check out the line of codes in the Location field

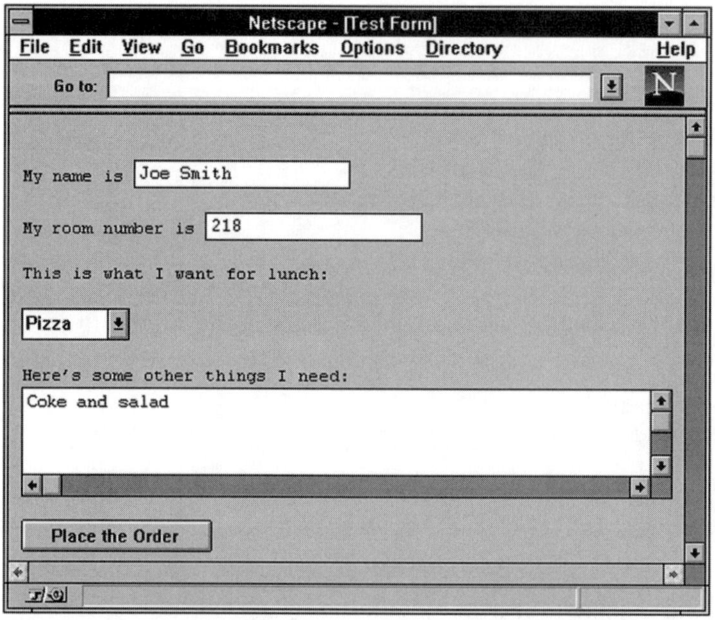

**Figure 7.2**    Form resulting from HTML codes.

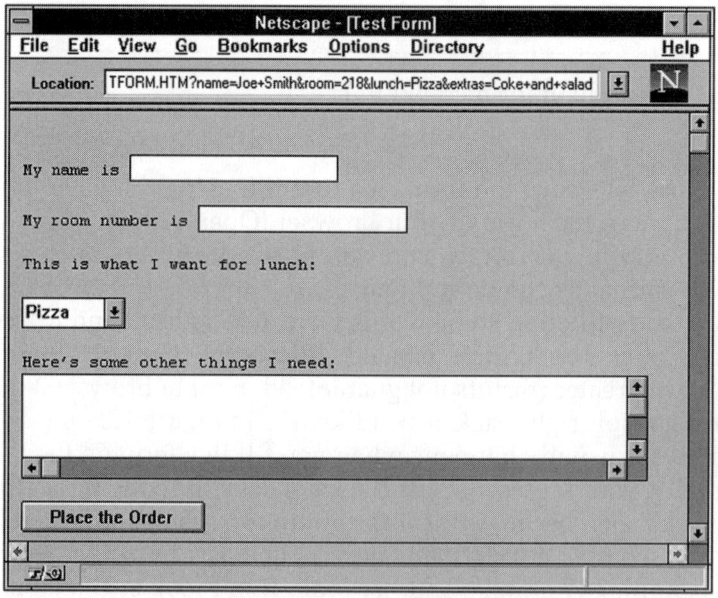

**Figure 7.3**    Netscape result of clicking button.

at the top of the screen. In Netscape, you should see something like this (if your own browser doesn't do this, don't worry, just look at the example here):

```
name=Joe+Smith&room=218&lunch=Pizza&extras=Coke+and+salad
```

This is how data looks when it is extracted from a form and passed back to the server. In a sense, the browser has taken what you typed in on the form and packaged it into a single string of communication that—translated into broken English—means something like this:

```
"the name is Joe-Smith & the room is 218 & the lunch is Pizza & the
extras are Coke-and-salad."
```

If you were dealing with a real form on a real web server, this is the kind of message your browser would send to the server for processing. And the server, in turn, might read the message, process it, and send an e-mail to the cafeteria (assuming they do deliveries, of course), saying:

```
"Joe Smith in Room 218 wants a pizza with a Coke and a salad."
```

Then it might turn around and add a record to a database like this:

```
Date: 12/31/96
Employee Name: Smith, Joe
Lunch Selection: Pizza
Extras wanted: Coke, salad
Cost: $7.95
```

It might also do a few calculations, put two-and-two together, and send an urgent fax to the company nurse with the following startling news:

---

**FAX**

**To: Company Nurse**
**From: Web Server, Food Services Dept.**
**Total Pages: 1**
**Subject: Cholesterol Alert!**
**Please be aware that the following employees ordered pizza five days in a row:**

- Harris, John T.
- Landry, Vera
- Smith, Joe
- Taylor, Barney

**Please schedule them *immediately* for a complete physical, including lab work and a treadmill test.**

**Signed,**
  **Your Friendly (But Concerned) Local Web Server**
  **in the Food Services Department**

Of course, let's not forget about the poor guy who ordered the food. The web server might send a custom-generated HTML form back to the browser that looks like this:

**Thanks For Your Order**

We just received your order for a Pizza plus a Coke and salad. A total of $7.95 will be added to your employee account and deducted from your next paycheck. Or, if you would like, we can charge that to your Visa card. Just enter the card number below:

  _Yes, charge it to my Visa card.

  _No, charge it to my employee account.

Visa No:

Send Visa   Return to Food Services Main Menu

Notice that this could go on indefinitely. The user fills in a form, the server replies with a request for more information. The user supplies extra information, the server responds again until the transaction is complete. If you spend any time at all on the World Wide Web, you know this kind of give-and-take is old hat by now. Many companies are already selling their own products this way.

My intent *is not* to prove you can sell products on the World Wide Web (though there are many people who do). Instead, I want you to understand exactly how and why web servers can extract information from users. If you

**So, You Want to Be a Form-Coding Expert . . .**

If you want to learn more about coding web forms in HTML, there are plenty of places to learn about it on the World Wide Web. A great place to start is:

> http://union.ncsa.uiuc.edu/HyperNews/get/www/html/
> guides.html

California-based Web Communications also has a good introduction to forms and many other aspects of web development in its Comprehensive Guide to Web Publishing at:

> http://www.webcom.com/webcom/html/

A somewhat technical and laborious discussion of forms is offered by the people who originally brought you Mosaic:

> http://www.ncsa.uiuc.edu/SDG/Software/Mosaic/Docs/fill-out-
> forms/overview.html

think about it, *all* computer programs that exist in the world today are based on this kind of interaction. Whether you are using a word processor, a spreadsheet, or a database, the main purpose of any program is to capture information, process it, and store it.

So what's new about that? The difference is that the web browsers and servers are universal tools for developing client-server applications that can be delivered across the network, that we might actually use to *substitute* for other programs, or even *replace* them. At the very least, it's a cool way to get information to and from users.

## The Advantages of Web-Delivered Applications

Web is not the first technology to capture information from users over a network. That's what all client-server programs are designed to do, including widely used applications such as Oracle and Lotus Notes. But when you add a web component to a traditional client-server application, you gain a couple of things that traditional client-server programs *can't* provide on their own:

◆ *Instant cross-platform compatibility.* Web browsers have been designed to run on practically every computing platform available. And since HTML and Java are a totally machine-independent uncompiled languages, interpreted on-the-fly by the browser, applications can be delivered instantaneously to any platform in a network, without having to develop or compile special-purpose clients for each application and platform. This takes a lot of the work out of the traditional application development process.

◆ *Universal access and scalability.* Web forms can be accessed from *any node* in a network through a simple hyperlink, creating an application that requires no user setup or login. If you create a form on your local server, theoretically anyone who has a web browser can open it by simply clicking the appropriate hyperlink inside their local browser. The form can look like any other document— you can even insert it right into the middle of existing documents ("You like my newsletter? Tell me about it . . ."). Since they can access the form like a document, users don't have to call you and say, "I want to use your application. Can you come and install it on my local computer?" Installation is not a consideration, and the problem of *scalability* is not even an issue: the application is instantly scaled to the entire enterprise.

◆ *Universal GUI.* Web forms allow you to deliver client-server applications through a single, universal graphic user interface—the web browser—which can be reused for hundreds of other applications. Of course, other client-server and database applications let you set up forms, too. Anyone who's used Lotus Notes or Microsoft Access can tell you that. But not all of them let you embed a form within a document, so that the dialog can become "chatty" and colorful, filled with multimedia if necessary, and totally self-explanatory. And, since all forms can be viewed throughout the network using the same web-browser tool, there is no need to set up and train users on a separate tool for each individual application. Once they install a web browser, that is the only client-server tool they may need to learn about for some time to come. Each new application is installed through a simple hyperlink, and each new application can be *embedded inside its own documentation.*

What's more, creating forms for the web is a breeze, especially if you have a WYSIWYG web publishing tool like Word IA or the FrontPage Editor discussed in Chapter 3. With these programs, you can use toolbar icons to build all the components of a dialog, including text boxes, radio buttons, pull-down menus, pushbuttons—you name it. Just place your cursor in the document where you want a pull-down menu to be inserted, then click the appropriate icon on the toolbar (Figure 7.4).

Now you understand how web forms are put together and why they're useful. So let's delve a bit deeper into the workings of the web. The mechanics of the form itself are just a part of the total picture you need to understand how the web works.

## CGI: The Other Half of the Puzzle

Notice in the previous examples that the web server did some fairly fancy stuff. First, Joe Smith ordered a pizza, Coke, and a salad. No surprise there: That's probably what Joe orders every day. The surprising part is all the different things the web server did with it. In particular, the server:

◆ Sent an e-mail message to the cafeteria

◆ Sent a fax to the nurse

◆ Created a database record

◆ Sent Joe a thank-you note and asked for more information

◆ Took a Visa card number from Joe and charged the order to Joe's Visa account

Of course, the web server is not a superhuman organism that automatically knows how to do all this stuff. These things are typically programmed using a standard called the *Common Gateway Interface* (CGI). CGI is just a method the web server uses to communicate with other "back-end" applications such as databases, e-mail systems, and so forth.

Since CGI implies the creation of a special-purpose program, the main question becomes: Who's going to do the programming? In the old days, if you built the form, you were elected by default to handle the programming, too. Not only did you have to know how to code a web form, you also had to know

**Figure 7.4**    Word IA toolbar icons for creating forms.

how to program the CGI to do all the fancy stuff—or hire a programmer who could do it. Increasingly, however, web servers are coming with built-in programs or tools that do a lot of the fancy stuff for you. So all you have to do is create the form (naturally, since you want to be able to control how it looks), then tell the web server what to do with the form output. Given the fact that you may never have to do CGI programming, it's still nice to understand what CGI is, so that you can understand exactly what I'm talking about, and so you can know what it takes to make a web form interactive.

Keep in mind that the CGI component isn't the powerhouse it seems to be. The real fancy footwork is actually handled behind the scenes by some fairly ordinary applications: the database tools, the e-mail tools, and the client-server applications we have all come to know and love (Figure 7.5). In effect, we haven't abandoned all our old tools so that the web can take over. All we've done is just pasted a new "front-end" on all those old client-server applications, the same way you might paste a smiley-face on the front of your computer monitor. The old applications are still doing all the work, but we're just repackaging the results into a shiny new format called a *web page* that frees us from the old boundaries of having to install each separate application on each individual user's machine. Now everyone can access the application throughout the enterprise, at the click of the button. And if we want to bring another application online tomorrow, well guess what? A little hyperlink here, a little hyperlink there, and *voila, there it is . . . .*

The CGI component of a web system, therefore, is just a humble servant that sits between the web server and back-end application and does all the work of passing information back and forth between them. Actually, let's say this is a humble *multilingual* servant. Any CGI program must speak two or more languages: the language of the web server, and the language of any back-end applications, so that it can take information from the web server and explain it to the back-end application, and it can take information from the back-end application and explain it to the web server.

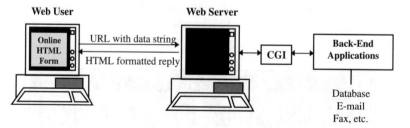

**Figure 7.5**   Where CGI fits in the puzzle.

For instance, in our previous example, Joe Smith placed an order for pizza that was sent to the web server as a message looking something like this:

```
name=Joe+Smith&room=218&lunch=Pizza&extras=Coke+and+salad
```

The web server takes the message pretty much as is and passes it along to the CGI program. The CGI program has to take the message apart piece by piece (*parse it* in programmer lingo), and do something with it. If it's communicating with an e-mail system, it might cram the information into an e-mail message and ship it out using the command-line interface for the local e-mail program (notice form data in bold):

```
To: Inez@Cafeteria
From: Web Server No. 253
Subject: HUNGRY GUY
Joe Smith in Room 218 wants Pizza for lunch with a Coke and salad.
```

Notice that the CGI program has taken information originally communicated in web server language and translated it into e-mail language. In fact, you could say that it "repackaged" the data—took it apart and wrapped it inside an e-mail message. If the back-end application is a database, the CGI program can communicate using Standard Query Language (SQL).

CGI is not rocket science. It's just a way of taking standard input from a web server, extracting the data, then passing it along to the back-end applications. This is so simple that in the early days people didn't even use compiled programs to do this—they just used simple scripts written in uncompiled languages like *perl*. Now that the vendors of back-end applications have caught on—people like Lotus and Oracle—they've developed their own data interfaces to handle communication between the web server and their databases. Third-party software developers have jumped into the breach as well, and they're selling multipurpose CGI programs that can talk to a variety of back-end applications. People are even selling web servers that already have databases integrated with them. Likely, these types of integrated packages will become increasingly prevalent until they merge into single products: databases that do e-mail, speak webese, and publish online documents.

## How CGI Talks Back to the User

The nice part about CGI is not only that it can receive data from the user and transfer it to the back-end, it can also take data from the back-end and send it to the user. This process is as simple in reverse as it is in fast-forward. For instance, a CGI program might get a request from a manager who wants to know the names of all employees who ate pizza today. The CGI program might take that request, turn around and query a database for the information, then take the output from the database and send it back to the manager.

How to send it back? Well, if the CGI program is lazy, it might just take the raw output from the database and transmit it back as a simple stream of text. But that wouldn't be too friendly. More likely, any CGI program with a little self-respect will take the data and make it look nice, wrapping it in HTML codes so it displays magnificently on the screen. Figure 7.6 shows how that might look when diagrammed.

Notice how the data is extracted from the database and inserted into the middle of an HTML document. In the example above, the HTML document would always look the same, but the *variables* (bold words in the middle panel) would change. Of course, there's more to it than that. The CGI program itself, when you look at the raw source, contains a lot more than just this swatch of HTML. But somewhere in there, there's a place where it spits out this kind of HTML code with variables inserted in the middle.

Does this look familiar? In effect, the CGI program is sending users something like a form letter with key data variables inserted into the appropriate slots. The CGI program passes the finished form letter to the web server, which passes it back to the web client, which displays it on screen as a nice-looking, helpful reply to the users—pretty much the same way a traditional form letter gets delivered on paper through snail mail.

In web lingo, we call this kind of action "HTML coding on-the-fly." In a single motion, the CGI program extracted data from the database, wrapped HTML codes around it, and delivered it back to the browser the same way the web

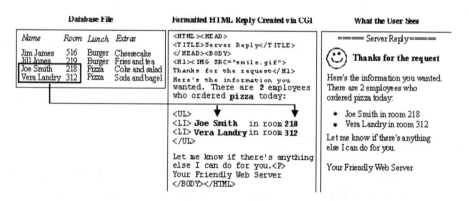

**Figure 7.6**   How data gets from the back-end to the user.

server delivers any preformatted HTML document. Users, sitting there on the other end of the line, may not even realize they're viewing web documents that were generated on the fly. They may not realize that *the document didn't even exist until the actual moment it was requested.* They just see a document that happens to contain exactly the information they're looking for.

Think about that for a moment. Something's going on here that's truly awesome. We have finally reached a point in the development of business systems where it's no longer even necessary to publish documents anymore—whether for print, for web, or whatever. Instead, we can just keep our information handy in a table or a database somewhere, then let the web server and the CGI program do all the work of formatting it, publishing it, and delivering it to the end-user. The document does not get published until the end-user asks for it. When you think about it, why should it be any other way?

This is what I mean when I talk about *documents-as-data* and *data-as-documents.* In the web systems of the future—indeed in the web systems of today—data and documents will come apart, recombine in different ways, and sometimes fuse into a single entity.

## How to Do Simple Database Publishing Without CGI

You can see from the previous example that the essential workings of a CGI program is a lot like creating a form letter. In fact, if you want to have some fun sometime (you can see how I spend *my* spare time), why not take Microsoft Word, or any other word processing program, and create an HTML form letter of your own? Remember the mail-merge feature in your word processor? You can use it to do database publishing on the web, without even owning a database or CGI program. You don't even need an add-on application like Microsoft Word's Internet Assistant.

Here's how you do it. Set up a table in your word processor with all the information you want to publish. This could be anything from product catalog specifications to the list of employees in your department. I use a table like the one shown here to keep track of the names and addresses of all the people in my local professional organization. For example:

| Name | DBA | Address | CSZ | Phone | Fax | Email |
|------|-----|---------|-----|-------|-----|-------|
| Joe Smith | The Smith Company | 1234 Main Street | Mytown, ST 12345 | 987-6543 | 123-4567 | jsmith@smith.com |
| Jill Jones | Jones and Associates | 4321 Main Street | Mytown, ST 12345 | 987-1234 | 123-7654 | jill@jones.com |
| etc. | . . . | . . . | . . . | . . . | . . . | . . . |

Then I set up a form letter that is basically an HTML document with all the codes and variables inserted the way you might do a mail-merge. For instance, here's the kind of form letter I use to generate a simple web-based directory for my professional group:

```
<HR>
<H2>«Name»</H2>
«DBA»<BR>
«Address»<BR>
«CSZ»<P>
Telephone: «Phone»<BR>
Fax: «Fax»<BR>
E-mail: <A HREF="mailto:«Email»">«Email»</A>
```

Notice that this form letter contains three different types of information: HTML codes (such as <HR>), mail-merge variables (such as «Email»), and plain-English words (such as "Telephone:"). When I run a mail merge operation on this form letter, the resulting output looks like this:

```
<HR>
<H2>Joe Smith</H2>
The Smith Company<BR>
1234 Main Street<BR>
Mytown, ST 12345<P>
Telephone: 987-6543<BR>
Fax: 123-4567<BR>
Email: <A HREF="mailto:jsmith@smith.com">jsmith@smith.com</A>
<HR>
<H2>Jill Jones</H2>
Jones and Associates<BR>
4321 Main Street<BR>
Mytown, ST 12345<P>
Telephone: 987-1234<BR>
Fax: 123-7654<BR>
Email: <A HREF="mailto:jill@jones.com">jill@jones.com</A>
```

In effect, all the data from the table was inserted in place of the mail-merge variables, and now I'm left with a raw HTML document. So, if I take this document, save it as a text file called *members.html,* and then use my web browser to open it, the information looks more like this:

**Joe Smith**

The Smith Company
1234 Main Street
Mytown, ST 12345

Telephone: 987-6543
Fax: 123-4567
Email: jsmith@smith.com

**Jill Jones**

Jones and Associates
4321 Main Street
Mytown, ST 12345

Telephone: 987-1234
Fax: 123-7654
Email: jill@jones.com

Notice (way cool) that the e-mail addresses are completely hyperlinked, so they're immediately clickable. This is a little trick I did back in the mail-merge file, wrapping hyperlink tags (A HREF) around mail-merge variables. When users see the web page with these addresses on them and click on a highlighted e-mail address, it will pop up the e-mail window with the address already inserted—so they can dash off quick e-mails to society members.

Of course, I add standard stuff at the top and bottom of the directory, such as a title, an introduction, the date, the HEAD and BODY tags, and so forth. These are just separate HTML-coded files I keep handy (one for the top, one for the bottom), and which I insert into the final mail-merge document before saving it out as a text file.

But now look what's happened: Whenever somebody changes his or her address or phone number, or if a new member joins, I don't change the HTML document. I just update the original table. Then, whenever there are enough database changes to justify a new web directory, I just run the mail-merge on the file and there it is: a new HTML file with all the information in it. I save the new file onto my web server (overwriting the old file) and suddenly I have an updated web directory online—generated automatically with no real HTML coding involved.

Of course, this process requires a little work to open the form letter and run the mail-merge, but it's so easy it's almost funny. If I wanted to get more sophisticated, I could use an actual database program like Microsoft Access or even Oracle or SQL Server. And I could even configure output reports that create the same kind of automatic output as my mail-merge application (wrapping HTML around data). The ultimate step, of course, would be to use a CGI program that automatically handles the work of extracting the data and delivering it to end-users on-the-fly. That way, users wouldn't have to wait for me to generate a new directory every few weeks. They could always get the latest information directly from the database (assuming I keep the database updated).

But for such a small directory, I don't think I'll bother. Remember: The sophistication of the tool you choose depends on the sophistication of the application. You can start doing database publishing with something as simple as a word processor, or end up with massively scalable database architectures if that's what you need. But it's no use killing a flea with an elephant gun.

## How Forms and CGI Work Together

Now that you understand forms and you understand CGI, it's time to understand the simple mechanics of how they connect. Remember the form example I showed you way back in the beginning of this chapter? (Figure 7.7.) I used a simple <FORM> tag with no embellishments, because I wanted to make things as simple as possible. In real life, however, you would never create a form with just a simple FORM tag like that. Instead, the FORM tag is coded in such a way that it tells the server which CGI program to run and how to run it. For instance:

```
<FORM METHOD=POST ACTION="http://server3/cgi-bin/getdata.exe">
My name is: <INPUT NAME="name">
My room is: <INPUT NAME="room">
(etc.)
 .
 .
 .
</FORM>
```

Notice that the form content is bracketed by opening and closing FORM tags. All form-based tags (INPUT, TEXTAREA, etc.) inside these brackets will be treated as live fields in the form. Any form-based tags that lie outside these brackets will be ignored.

```
<FORM>
<PRE>

My name is <INPUT NAME="name">

My room number is <INPUT NAME="room">

This is what I want for lunch:

<SELECT NAME="lunch">
<OPTION>Pizza
<OPTION>Burger
<OPTION>Chicken
</SELECT>

Here's some other things I need:
<TEXTAREA NAME="extras" ROWS=4 COLS=60>
</TEXTAREA>

<INPUT TYPE="SUBMIT" VALUE="Place the Order">

</PRE>
</FORM>
```

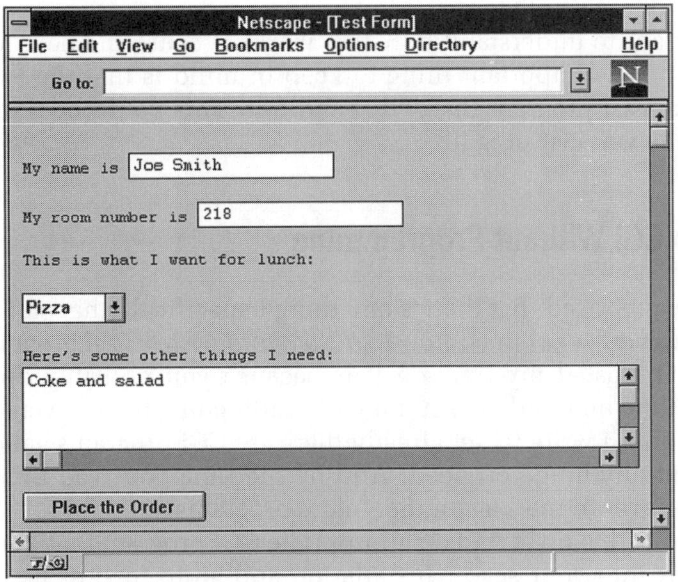

**Figure 7.7**   Previous form code and display.

Also notice in this example that the opening FORM tag references a CGI program called *getdata.exe,* which is located in the *cgi-bin* directory on *server3.* This is the program that knows how to handle the data coming out of this particular form—obviously, it's already installed and available on the web server for this specific purpose. (For every form, there *must* be a corresponding CGI program to deal with the output.)

Finally, the FORM tag specifies the method used to communicate with the CGI program. For most forms, the method is *POST.* (There are other methods, but let's not worry about those right now.)

When a user fills out the form and clicks the Submit button, the user's entries are passed back to the server in the format we saw before:

```
name=Joe+Smith&room=218&lunch=Pizza&extras=Coke+and+salad
```

The server reads this string, and it fires up the program called *getdata.exe* in the *cgi-bin* directory and passes the data to it. At this point, the form itself expires in memory. The data has already been captured and sent to the back-end for processing, so the form no longer serves a purpose. The next thing that happens at the browser end is a response from the CGI program: usually a thank-you note, or a document containing the user's requested data, or another form for more interaction. If it's another form, the second form might point to a different CGI program (or to the same one, if the program is designed to handle the output from multiple forms).

It's important to understand how this works because the next few sections depend on it. The important thing to keep in mind is that the form actually points to the CGI program that will handle it. This could be a program you design, or one you just plug in.

## How to Do CGI Without Programming

You may have noticed that there's one thing I specifically haven't done yet in this book: I haven't explained *how to design and write* a CGI program. The reason I haven't wasted my time on it is because you probably don't need to waste your time on it either. You may be reading this book several months or even a year after I write it, yet already there are CGI programs galore that will do just about anything you need. And by the time you read this, there will probably be several times again that many programs.

All you'll need to do is find an appropriate CGI program that does what you want, plug it into your server installation and go to town. The only reason you'd ever want to write your own CGI program is if you're doing something so weird—or so new—that no one ever thought of it before. The chances of that are getting increasingly slim, because CGI tools are coming out of the woodwork.

Here's a little story to illustrate what I'm talking about. One day I was hard at work, pretty well minding my own business, when I got a call from a graphic artist whose business associate had installed a web server on her Mac computer just before he flew the coop. She liked her web server, and it was working just fine, but she wanted to do some new things with it. She wanted to set up a way that people could automatically set up classified ads on her web site to buy and sell items. The problem she was having was quite simple and common to the web neophyte: She didn't understand how to put a form together or make it work.

I showed up at her office a few days later all ready to explain how the web works in the simplest language I could muster. She seemed a bit puzzled as I rambled on about forms and CGI and databases. I told her we might have a few technical problems putting it together, but nothing we couldn't fix with a little research and careful selection of our tools. The first thing we would have to do is design the form. . . .

"Oh, well. I've already done that," she said. And sure enough, there was the form she'd designed, up on the screen, all ready for people to fill out. "Wow," I thought to myself, "this lady is a fast-learner. She's already mastered the form codes in HTML 2.0."

"That form looks great," I told her (and it did—it looked just as good as any form *I'd* ever designed). "But it still won't work. You've got to have something to connect it to. People will fill out the form, push the Submit button and nothing will happen. There's no way to capture and store that data." I started to explain to her about how we would have to get up a CGI program, or find one that could do what we needed.

"What do you mean it doesn't work?" she interrupted. "Here, look at this." Then she filled out the form, clicked the Submit button, and in a twinkle of an eye there was a "thank you" message up on the screen. I jumped out of my chair and lunged toward the screen. "Let me see that form," I said. Grabbing the mouse from her hands, I popped open the View Source dialog and scanned the HTML code. This is what the FORM tag said:

```
<FORM METHOD=POST ACTION="/NetForms.acgi$/classified/adentry.fdml">
```

"*Aha,*" I shrieked. "This form uses a CGI program already! The FORM tag shows it's being handled by something called *NetForms.acgi.*"

The bit about the FORM tag meant practically nothing to my friend. But, at this point, she admitted that yes indeed she had found a tool called NetForms lurking around on her computer. And, after a few fits and starts, she'd used it to create the form we saw. And somehow the form was connected to something automatically, so that when you filled it out, it added your classified ad to a list that anyone could browse.

Problem solved, case closed—I had made the trip for nothing. Here was someone who actually knew *nothing* about HTML form codes or about CGI, who was already creating interactive web applications without knowing it— and furthermore without help from any experts. And she was doing it all with

---

### Examples of Simple Form Processing Programs

There are scores of CGI programs available that you can easily plug in to your server. You can read about these tools and even download them into your computer at sites on the World Wide Web. Here are just a few examples of common tools on various platforms.

NetForms (Mac): Takes output from a form and adds it to a set of web docouments that can be accessed from a central list.

http://www.maxum.com/NetForms/

PolyForms (PC): Takes output from a form and uses it in the body of an e-mail or saves it to file in HTML, comma-delimited, or flat text format.

http://wgg.com/files/PolyForm/

W3 Toolbox (UNIX): Interfaces with flat files, formats in HTML, sends e-mail.

http://w3.com/

Other CGI programs are available on the Web. Here's where to look:

Mac only—http://www.comvista.com/net/www/cgi.html

Windows NT/95—http://www.primenet.com/~buyensj/ntwebsrv.html

All platforms—http://WWW.Stars.com/Vlib/Providers/Database.html

this new generation of CGI tools, of which NetForms is just a single, simple example. Actually, that's the way it *should* be. If we're going to make our webs as easy to use as desktop publishing and accessible to everyone, we need CGI tools like this that even novices can use.

## Database Solutions for Web Access

Mail-merge, NetForms, PolyForms, and other similar tools are fine as far as they go. But at some point, keeping a simple list or a separate file for each record becomes too unwieldy, and you need a more powerful way to process information. That's where database tools come in. A database can help organize and manage very complex sets of information in ways you can't do using other tools. Relational databases like Oracle, Sybase, Microsoft Access, SQL Server, dBase, and others are designed especially for the purpose.

If you don't already use database tools, there are plenty to choose from. Chances are, however, that your company already uses database tools for a number of information processing applications. If you aren't using one yourself, maybe there are other people with experience or expertise in a particular package who can help you get started. Or maybe you have information already stored in a database that you want to make available over the web. In either case, if there are already database solutions in-house, it's probably better to stick with what you know, or with what other people have found useful in your organization.

### Creating and Maintaining the Database

Most of the work in a web database application concerns creating and maintaining the database itself, not serving it over the Intranet. If you are creating a new database, you will have to choose the software, design the database, populate it with data, and maintain the data. If you already have a database installed and populated, then your job is mainly just keeping it updated.

At this point, however, it pays to consider the type of model you want to follow for administering the database and for providing web access.

◆ *Closed Administrative Model.* In some cases, you may want people to freely access data over the web, but you may want only one person or a small group to have control over actually changing the data, adding new records, and deleting old records. This is called the *closed administrative model* because database administration is not open to the whole world—it's limited to an authorized person or group (Figure 7.8).

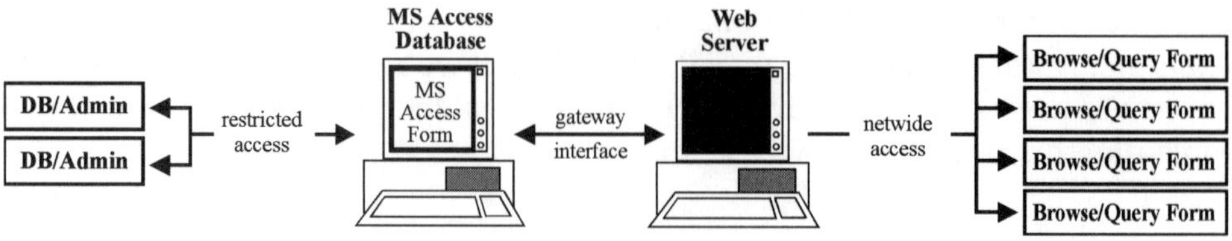

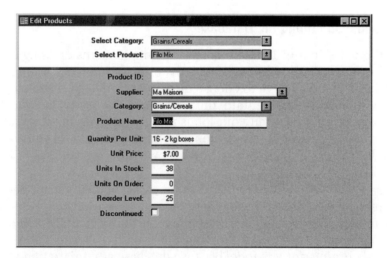

**Figure 7.8**  Closed model of database administration.

In a closed model, you would typically provide two interfaces: one for the users and one for administrators. The administrative interface would be through the standard database management structure. For instance, in Microsoft Access, the administrator might have a special form used to edit, update, and maintain the database (Figure 7.9). That form might be accessed and used on the same internal network loop (i.e., on the same file server) where the database resides.

Users, on the other hand, would access the database through the web. You would create a special form (as explained in the next section) that allows them to run queries against the database and to view the information online no matter where they are in the company. This kind of access could even be limited to a select group of users if necessary, through various user authentication schemes (see discussion of security later in this chapter).

**Figure 7.9**  Database administration form in Microsoft Access.

◆ *Open Administrative Model.* In other situations, you may want to make the administration of the database open so that it can be updated from any location on the network. For instance, you might want to have a database that anyone can use to sign up for company seminars. As another example, you may want to restrict database access to certain users or groups, but still make it possible to access the database from any location in the network. For example, you might have a restricted database that only sales reps can use to enter daily sales reports from the field, for use by the marketing department (Figure 7.10).

In either case, you could set up the database so that people can access it, view it, and update it entirely through the web browser interface. You might create a single web form for the purpose or multiple web forms. You might still have a centralized database access form for your own convenience, or for large-scale data population or maintenance projects, but most people with casual usage would access and edit the database through the web.

## Connecting the Database to a Web Server

Once you have a database online and ready to roll, the second part of the task is connecting it to a web server. Compared to the task of setting up and maintaining the database, this is the easy part.

Regardless of whether you follow the open or closed administrative model, you're going to want to set up one or more forms that people can use to access the data. Typically, your forms will allow people to enter data for insertion in the database, to edit the database, or to run simple queries against the database. A web server CGI program would then be used to process the form entries and interface them to the database.

For instance, suppose you want to have a database that people can use to register for company-sponsored training programs, and also use to see who

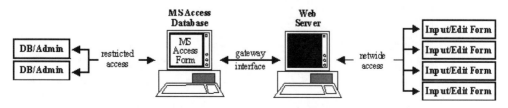

**Figure 7.10**   Open model of database administration.

has signed up for seminars. This would require two forms: one that people use to sign up, another they use to query.

In the first form, people might enter their name, department, building number, the course they want to sign up for, and the date they want to take it on. The *name* field would be a plain text box, of course. The *department* and *building number* could be text fields, or preformatted selection lists. The *course* and *date* fields would definitely be preformatted selection lists reflecting the available choices. If users can sign up for multiple seminars, the form should be designed to support multiple seminar/date selections (Figure 7.11).

When the user fills out the form and presses the Submit button, the form gets sent to a CGI program, which takes the user's entries and selections and inserts them into the database using SQL commands or other access methods such as *open database connectivity* (ODBC). The web form field entries would be keyed directly to fields that already exist in the database, so that all the CGI has to do is create a new record and populate it with the existing data.

A second form would be used to let anyone (or a restricted list of authorized users) go in and see who has signed up for the training courses (Figure 7.12). Users could search the database by name, department, course, or date—or any combination of these. For example, if the user selects a seminar name, it might return a list of all the people who have signed up for that seminar. If the user

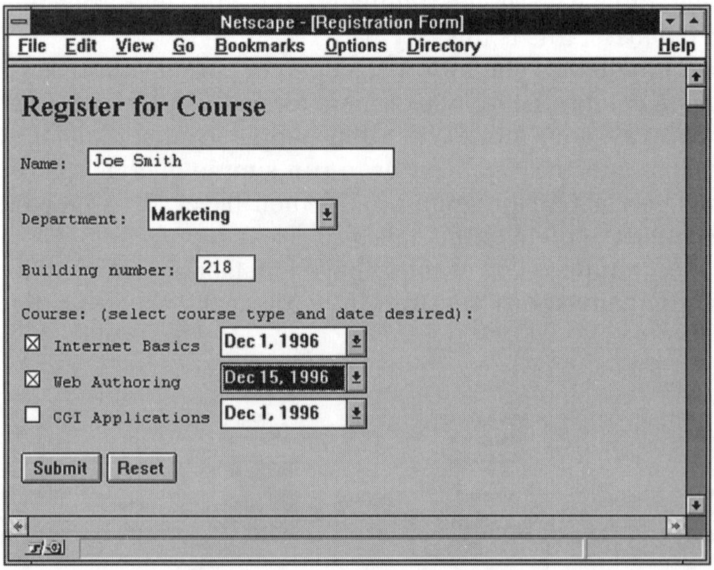

**Figure 7.11**    Web form used to sign up for company seminars.

selects both a seminar name and date, it might show just the people who have signed up for that seminar on that date. If the user selects a department name, it might show all the people in that department who have signed up for training.

To retrieve the data, user selections would be passed from the form to the CGI program, which would then submit a query to the database. The results of the query would then be received by the CGI and formatted for final display in the web browser window.

Notice that, regardless of the types of forms you set up, you will need a CGI program to pass new records or queries to the database. The key question is what type of CGI program to use. If you have a lot of programmers sitting around twiddling their thumbs, you might give them this as a project and let them develop a CGI program from scratch. It's probably easier, however, to just find an existing CGI program that can handle the database access automatically. There are plenty of tools already out there, as you will see in the next section.

## Using Cold Fusion and Other Data Access Tools

There was a time in the history of the web when CGI programming was an absolute requirement for anyone who wanted to create database interfaces on

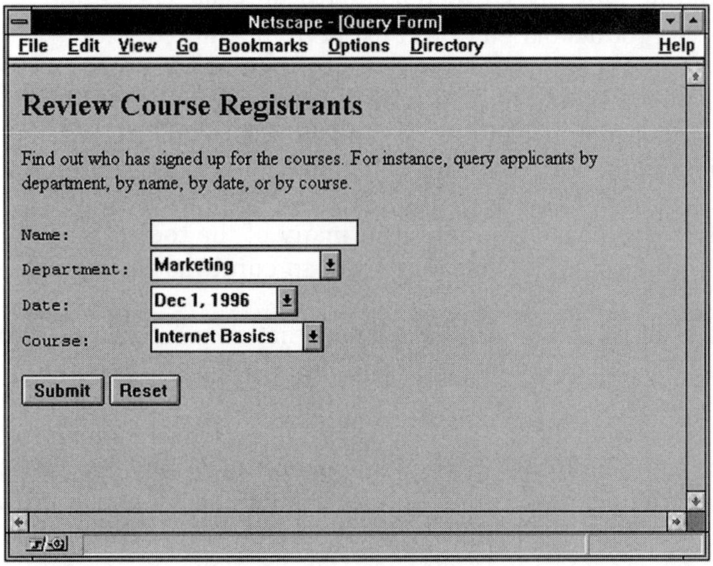

**Figure 7.12**   Web form for querying the database.

## Advent of the Universal Server

One of the most interesting new developments in the database field is the advent of the universal server, a concept obviously inspired by the new possibilities of the Intranet. Oracle's universal server, for instance, touts itself as combining all the features of a relational database with with full web support, text management, messaging, and multimedia object management. The universal server rolled out by Informix results from its merger with Illustra—the combined product merging Informix's strong transaction processing and relational capabilities with Illustra's ability to process documents, photos, web pages, sound, video, and other objects. Watch for other major database vendors to take the same approach.

> Oracle Universal Server     http://www.oracle.com/
> Informix Universal Server     http://www.informix.com/

the web. As the technology continues to develop, however, it's clear that this is no longer a foregone conclusion. One of the best ways to connect web servers to databases may be the new crop of database interface tools that are coming onto the market. There are several major products that have gotten attention in the trade press (see the sidebar on page 273). But one of the best examples is a product called Cold Fusion from Allaire L.L.C.

Cold Fusion is a general-purpose CGI program for Windows NT or Windows 95 that is designed to let you easily create interfaces to several types of back-end database applications, including Microsoft Access, FoxPro, SQL Server, Paradox, Excel, dBase III or IV, and flat files. If you're not using one of these types of databases, or the Microsoft Windows platform, check the accompanying sidebar for others. But many of the tools you find will work a lot like Cold Fusion, so you may want to continue through the following examples.

The power of tools like Cold Fusion is that they let you do sophisticated database access and query by simply adding more markup tags to your HTML documents. Cold Fusion recognizes the extra markup tags as instructions on how to process the data. This works because HTML allows any kind of markup tag to be included in your documents. The browser and server will ignore any markup tags they don't understand, but back-end applications may be able to recognize the additional markup and use it. The special tags Cold Fusion recognizes are called *Database Markup Language* (DBML).

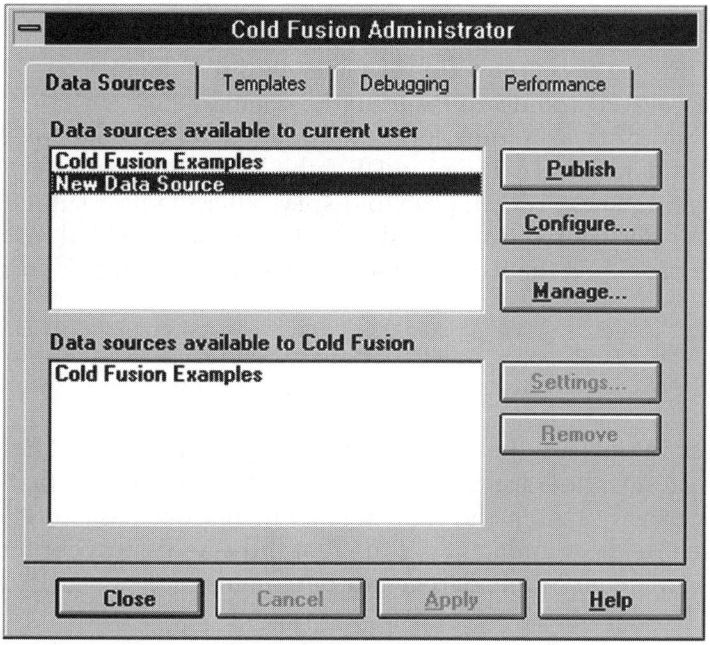

**Figure 7.13**   Cold Fusion data source setup dialog.

To use Cold Fusion, you must first install it like any other software. When you do, the program adds itself to the appropriate web server installation directories and includes other resources like documentation and test files.

Once installed, the first step is to use the administrator panel supplied with the software to identify your data source(s). Cold Fusion takes advantage of the ODBC feature of Windows. The idea behind ODBC is a lot like the idea behind printer drivers: There's a specific driver for each database installed in your computer that other applications can use to drive the database engine. All you have to do is point the application to the data source, and the driver handles the actual operation of the database (Figure 7.13).

Once Cold Fusion understands the location of your data sources, the next step is to link your forms to the database through simple markup tags. Suppose you've created a form that people can use to register for company seminars. The results of the form are to be inserted into a table called "Signees" in the data source called "SeminarDB." To do this, you would set up the FORM tag at the top of the form so that it calls the Cold Fusion CGI program (dbml.exe) and tells it to insert the results of the form into the database. This is how it would look:

```
<FORM ACTION="/cgi-shl/dbml.exe?Action=Insert" METHOD=POST>
```

In effect, this tag says "the following form will run the program *dbml.exe* in the directory *cgi-shl* and do an *insert* to the database."

The next set of tags in your form are "hidden input" tags to identify the name of the data source (SeminarDB), the table to insert new data into (Signees), and the next HTML page to display after the user submits the form (thanks.html). Of course, this implies that you have created an additional HTML page providing the user with a message such as a thank-you note.

```
<INPUT TYPE="hidden" NAME="DataSource" VALUE="SeminarDB">
<INPUT TYPE="hidden" NAME="TableName" VALUE="Signees">
<INPUT TYPE="hidden" NAME="NextPage" VALUE="thanks.html">
```

After these initial tags, the rest of the form is just the standard fields used in any form to collect data from the user. The only difference is that each field name must exactly match the field names in the database so Cold Fusion knows which fields to update. So if the first three fields on your form are text boxes that map to the *Name, Room,* and *Dept* fields in the database, your form tags would look like this:

```
Your Name: <INPUT TYPE="text" NAME="Name"><P>
Room Number: <INPUT TYPE="text" NAME="Room"><P>
Department: <INPUT TYPE="text" NAME="Dept"><P>
(etc.)
```

Of course, you would finish out the form with the Submit button and the closing FORM tag, like so:

```
<INPUT TYPE="submit" VALUE="Register Me">
</FORM>
```

But that's all you need. When a user opens the form, fills it out, and clicks the Submit button, Cold Fusion will take the action specified in the FORM tag (Action=Insert) and will insert a new record into the database table specified in the hidden INPUT tags. If you wanted to update an existing record, the action would be "Update" instead.

This is just a simple example. But it gives you an idea how easy it is to set up a database application for a web form, not only in Cold Fusion but in many other web database tools. Of course, insert and update are not the extent of it: Cold Fusion provides a lot more markup tags that let you do more advanced things like full SQL queries, data validation, and on-the-fly formatting of query results.

**Other Database Web Tools**

In this section, I used Cold Fusion as an example of a program that lets you do database access without programming. But there are many other tools available. Here's where you can find more information about Cold Fusion and other tools.

> For Windows NT/95:
> Cold Fusion—http://www.allaire.com/cfusion
> dbWeb—http://www.aspectse.com
> DataRamp—http://dataramp.com
> WebBase—http://www.webbase.com

> For UNIX:
> Htmlscript—http://htmlscript.volant.com/
> Web Genera—http://gdbdoc.gdb.org/letovsky/genera/genera.
>    html
> GSQL—http://www.ncsa.uiuc.edu/SDG/People/jason/pub/
>    gsql/starthere.html

> For more Windows NT Web Server Tools, check Appendix B or look at these WWW sites:
> http://www.primenet.com/~buyensj/ntwebsrv.html
> http://webcom.com/wordmark/cooltool.html

## Creating Search Operations at Your Site

In my mind, the perfect web site would be the one that greets you with nothing but a question and a Search Field.

## What are you looking for? [                    ] **Search**

   All you would have to do is type in words to describe what you're looking for, then hit the Search button to find what you need. If you've ever been to the Yahoo site on the World Wide Web (http://www.yahoo.com/), or any of the other major web directories, this is exactly how they work. You type in one or more keywords, and get back a clickable list of results. For instance, on an Intranet, you might type in the words *employee benefits* and get back a list of clickable entries such as:

◆ Employee Benefits Handbook
◆ Company 401K Plan Cancelled
◆ Newsletter: HR Quarterly
◆ News Release: Exercise Room Benefits Local Employees
◆ Features and Benefits of New HR Tracking System

There are some problems with such an approach. The first problem is, unless the search tool has access to every bit of content on the Intranet, the user may have to guess what kind of content is located at your site. This is easily remedied by a short introduction explaining the general type of information at your site.

The other problem, as anyone who has done a search knows, is that the results can be decidedly mixed. Searches for specific topics often have a way of turning up a ton of extra information you may not be looking for. Or they may turn up nothing, even though there really is something there. (Great example: I defy you to find information about client-side imagemaps at the Netscape WWW site. The information is there, all right, but the search tool won't find it.)

Despite the problems inherent in web site searches, a search tool is a definite convenience for your users—especially if your web site contains a large variety of information. You could do like Yahoo on the WWW (http://www.yahoo. com/) and place the Search field prominently at the top of your home page. Or, like many web sites, you could provide a search form as a secondary page accessible from your home page or other pages in your web site.

Web searches implemented using search tools are basically just another type of CGI application. In some cases, the search engine itself was not originally designed for use on a web, and for this reason a special CGI program is used to communicate with it the same way CGI communicates with other back-end applications. In other cases, the search tool may have been designed specifically for use on a web and thus the CGI program itself may be a self-contained search tool.

Most high-powered search tools use an indexing method in which the content files are searched offline and an index file is built. The index file is never seen by the user, it only exists for use by the search engine. When the search is conducted, the search is done not on the content files, but on the index file. At first this might seem to be an inefficient way to do things, but actually it is more efficient and much faster to search a tightly formatted index than it is to search a loose collection of documents. In fact, the tighter the index format, the faster the search. This is no small consideration, since most users are not going to like it if they have to wait more than a few seconds for the results of their search. You can see the beauty of a really powerful search engine when you use one of the major web search tools like Infoseek (http://www2.info-seek.com) or Alta Vista (http://altavista.digital.com/). After typing in a keyword, you get dozens of matching hits in a flash.

If you have an information center on an internal web, chances are you don't need a search engine as powerful as Alta Vista; you may be able to get by with something a lot simpler. Regardless, if you're going to provide a search option for your users, you may need several elements:

- A search application that may include both a search engine and an indexing tool.
- A CGI program designed to communicate with the search application. Chances are, this will be supplied as part of the search application. In some cases, the CGI program *is* the entire search application.
- A form that allows users to enter keywords for the search. This part you will create yourself. Or you can insert a search field using the <ISINDEX> tag in Appendix A.

You will install the search application and CGI in your server's CGI program directories. Then you will set up the search form so that it is accessible through your home page or through other hyperlinks. The form must be set up to reference the CGI program correctly as shown in the following example.

## A Simple Search Example

To show you how the form and the search application connect, I will use the example of a shareware product called Web Server Search for Windows. WSS is a very small and simple Visual Basic search program for the Microsoft Windows environment that operates without benefit of a separate indexing scheme (see sidebar on page 278). Instead, it searches the entire content of listed directories each time a search is performed—a feature that may make it more thorough, but certainly slower to operate on large file collections than other types of search engines.

WSS comes off the Internet as a zip file that you must unzip and install in the server's CGI area (cgi-win). To set it up, you simply edit the program resource file (search.ini) and specify the server document root and other directories you want to make available for searching. For instance:

```
[Search]
DefaultDir=c:\website\content
AltDir1=c:\website\content\newsletr
AltDir2=c:\website\content\archive
AltDir3=c:\website\content\docs
```

Once you have the resource file set up, you connect the search tool to the form through the FORM tag and a series of hidden INPUT tags (much the way we did in the Cold Fusion example earlier in this chapter). For example:

```
<FORM METHOD="POST" ACTION="/cgi-win/search.exe">
<INPUT TYPE="hidden" NAME="numdir" VALUE="2">
<INPUT TYPE="hidden" NAME="psearch1" VALUE="AltDir1">
<INPUT TYPE="hidden" NAME="psearch2" VALUE="AltDir2">
```

In the ACTION part of the FORM tag, */cgi-win/search.exe* is the path and name of the WSS search tool. The first INPUT tag identifies the number of directories being searched. The next two tags identify the specific directories to be searched (based on the entries in the .ini file). These are all the tags needed to connect the form to the search tool and identify the scope of the search. The rest of the form would include at the very least a Search input field, a Submit button, and the closing FORM tag. For instance:

```
Search String: <INPUT SIZE=30 NAME="fsearch">
<INPUT TYPE="submit" VALUE="Perform Search">
</FORM>
```

When the user fills in the form and clicks the Submit button, the *search.exe* program would perform a search on all the files in the listed directories and return to the browser a page containing the titles, headings, or filenames of the HTML documents containing words that match the specified search keywords. Each of the returned titles is hyperlinked so that if the user clicks the title, it opens the referenced document.

### Other Common Search Engines

Perhaps the most commonly used search engine on the Web, at least in the early years of its existence, is the *Wide Area Information Search* (WAIS) tool originally developed as a joint project of Apple Computer, Thinking Machines Corporation, and Dow Jones. WAIS includes an indexing program that can index many different file formats including HTML, text, and images. WAIS exists in both a shareware format (freeWAIS) and a commercial version distributed by WAIS Inc. The shareware version provides an indexer, server software, and search engines for local or remote index databases.

A problem with WAIS is that it runs only on UNIX machines, which makes it unusable if your web server is a PC or Mac. It also creates an index file that is somewhat larger than ideal (about 40 percent of the size of the original files). A similar UNIX-based shareware program called Glimpse creates a tighter index file (about 10 percent of original content size) and thus can do a somewhat quicker search.

Though WAIS and Glimpse are primarily shareware, some commercial companies have marched into the breach with their own search engines:

- Topic Internet Server by Verity, Inc. is a UNIX- and NT-based set of tools (indexer, engine, CGI) based on the powerful Topic search engine used in many document management applications.
- PLWeb by Personal Library Software is a powerful and sophisticated UNIX-only search tool used at some of the WWW's most popular sites including the Electronic Newsstand and the AT&T 1-800 Directory, Magellan, and Pathfinder.
- Excite by Architext Software is a index-based search engine that does concept-based searches of document repositories stored on UNIX or NT machines. Excite was being offered free in its first version (UNIX only).
- For the Macintosh, you may want to consider Apple WebSearch by Apple Computer, which works with the WebStar and Mac-HTTP servers to provide searching of multiple information sites (including WAIS databases).

## How Java Will Change the Software World

One of the most incredible developments in the ongoing saga of web technology is the way webs are serving as a platform for new varieties of software and programming tools. One of the most notorious is Java, a programming language developed by Sun Microsystems.

Java is the first programming language created primarily for the web. Instead of including just text and graphics, a web page might also contain a tiny program or *Java applet* that is designed to produce an effect.

**Where to Find Search Tools**

Here's where you can find many of the search tools discussed in this section, along with other search tools not discussed here.

Commercial WAIS—http://wais.com

FreeWAIS—http://cnidr.org

Glimpse—http://glimpse.cs.arizona.edu:1994/

Web Search for Windows—http://wgg.com/wgg/best/search.htm

Topic Internet Server—http://www.verity.com/products/tis.html

excite—http://excite.com/navigate

Harvest—http://harvest.cs.colorado.edu/

Apple WebSearch—http://kamaaina.apple.com/

For instance, when you display a web page with an embedded image, the IMG tag retrieves the image from the server and displays it at that spot in the text. With Java, however, there may be an APPLET tag embedded in the page that retrieves a small bit of executable Java code stored on the web server. When this code is retrieved, it runs automatically as soon as it hits the browser. Any display produced by the code displays right there in the text, at the location of the APPLET tag (Figure 7.14).

The most interesting uses of this technology are probably yet to be imagined. But to understand how this might work, think again about the concept of helper applications. If you click on a hyperlink to retrieve a sound file, for example, typically there must be a helper application installed on your end that can work with the browser to play back the sound. The problem is that there isn't always a way to guarantee that every user will have that helper application installed.

Imagine if, instead of being programmed in C or Visual Basic, someone had programmed the helper application as an applet using the Java language. Now, instead of being installed at the client end, the program can sit on the web server end waiting for someone to retrieve the page it is embedded in. If you retrieve that page, the Java-encoded playback software is retrieved with it. When the Java software reaches the browser, it automatically plays back the sound. In a manner of speaking, the sound now comes "wrapped in its own playback device." The playback device at this point becomes nearly as evanescent as the sound itself. The software, in effect, is being used without

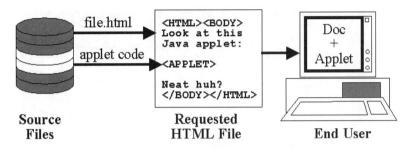

file.html

applet code

```
<HTML><BODY>
Look at this
Java applet:

<APPLET>

Neat huh?
</BODY></HTML>
```

Doc
+
Applet

**Source
Files**

**Requested
HTML File**

**End User**

**Figure 7.14**   Diagram of Java applet retrieval.

even being installed. It takes up no long-term space on your hard drive because it is used only as needed. And the program itself, even though it plays back locally, is totally network delivered.

Some of the other applications for Java show how flexible the applets can become. For instance, you might have a form used to calculate loan rates for the user. Instead of being sent back to the server for calculation, the loan parameters could be calculated right in the browser like a spreadsheet. Java applets might be used to animate a web page with multimedia or ticker-tape displays. It might also be used, for instance, to embed live graphs or a working clock directly inside a web page (Figure 7.15).

The most incredible aspect of Java is the way it threatens to turn the entire established order of the computer world on its ear. Java is already being hailed by analysts as the "magic bullet" that might someday kill off industry giants like Microsoft Corporation. The reason is not obvious, but it's quite simple. Theoretically, in future, when networks have all the bandwidth in the world to deliver large files instantaneously, programs like Java will make it possible to serve entire applications across a network to anyone with a browser. That means that the software will no longer have to be purchased and installed on the client side. All applications could potentially be delivered on the fly to any computer with a web browser whether it is UNIX, Mac, PC, or some platform that hasn't even been invented yet.

This is possible because Java differs significantly from other programming languages that must be compiled individually on different machines. If you write a program in C, it must be compiled separately for UNIX, Mac, or PC. You cannot run the UNIX version on a PC or the Mac version on a UNIX machine. Java, on the other hand, is an "interpreted" language that is read and interpreted by the browser as it comes across the network. The only requirement is a browser that contains the Java interpreter, which at first included

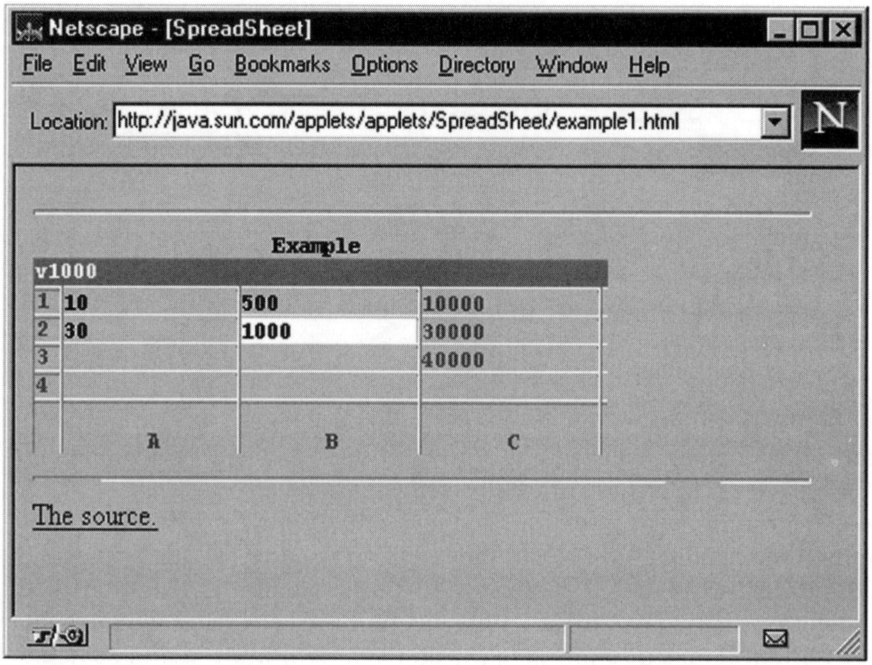

**Figure 7.15** Example of Java applet (spreadsheet).

only Sun's HotJava browser and Netscape's Navigator 2.0 browser, but which will certainly expand to many other browser tools.

In effect, Java will be able to bypass computer operating systems and could conceivably make operating systems like Microsoft Windows obsolete (or certainly less important). Likewise, if predictions are to be believed, software that was designed primarily for desktopcentric applications will be less important in a world of networkcentric applications. What Java will make possible with software is a lot like what HTML makes possible with documents: Instead of installing software on every computer *just in case* people need it, we will be able to store a *single copy of the software* at the web server and then deliver it to users on demand or *just in time.* This new way of delivering software should practically eliminate the kind of installation and maintenance costs organizations now endure.

Naturally, since Java is a programming language as detailed as C, there is no way you're going to be able to create applets unless you are a programmer or hire someone who has Java experience. At some point, however, it will be possible to acquire Java applets that do just what we need done, and embed them in our web documents. At that point, we'll just have to know how to use the APPLET tag to retrieve and initialize the applet.

The markup language below is an example from the Java web page (http://java.sun.com) that retrieves a spreadsheet applet as part of the web page. Notice that the APPLET tag works like an IMG tag, right down to the WIDTH and HEIGHT specifications. The PARAM tags are used to pass initial parameters to the application. The result is shown in Figure 7.15.

```
<APPLET CODE="SpreadSheet.class" WIDTH=320 HEIGHT=120>
<PARAM NAME=rows VALUE="4">
<PARAM NAME=c3 VALUE="fC1+C2">
<PARAM NAME=c2 VALUE="fA2*B2">
<PARAM NAME=c1 VALUE="fA1*B2">
<PARAM NAME itle VALUE="Example">
<PARAM NAME=b2 VALUE="v1000">
<PARAM NAME=b1 VALUE="v500">
<PARAM NAME=cols VALUE="3">
<PARAM NAME=a2 VALUE="v30">
<PARAM NAME=a1 VALUE="v10">
</APPLET>
```

Sun has also created an applet scripting language called JavaScript that conceivably *could* be used by nonprogrammers. JavaScript is a language like Visual Basic that could be used to dynamically script the behavior of Java objects. Sun uses the example of a Java multimedia weather forecast applet that could be scripted to display certain images and sounds in response to local weather conditions. Netscape is designing its own web management tools—specifically LiveWire—to include Java Script. Conceivably, in the near future, you will be able to buy Java applets off the shelf and then script them any way you need them.

## Exploring APIs

Another important area of investigation for anyone building a serious corporate web is the new *application programming interfaces* (APIs) for web browsers and servers. An API is a standard tool used in the programming world that allows applications to control each other. The control occurs at the program code level, where programs issue each other commands like "get data," "delete file," and "register progress."

APIs are useful if you want to make the software do something more than its standard bag of tricks. For example, I maintain an avid interest in using

Netscape as a replacement for traditional online help tools like WinHelp in the PC environment, or FrameViewer in the UNIX environment. The reason we use WinHelp and FrameViewer for online help is because they both give software developers "hooks" they can use to control the help windows from inside another application.

For example, if you write a program, you can rig it so that when the user clicks the Help button, it starts up either WinHelp (PC) or FrameViewer (UNIX/Mac) and displays a specific page in the online help. Now imagine, instead, that you could do this with Netscape and pull the online help documents right off the Intranet. To do that you have to not only open the browser from inside the other application, but actually open it with a specific file displayed and even a specific heading in a file.

In the early days of the Web, this was not possible. But Netscape and other companies have steadily added API functionality on both the client and server side so that it is indeed possible to control both the Netscape client and server from other applications. The Netscape APIs are called NCAPI (client side) and NSAPI (server side).

In the PC environment, NCAPI lets you use both *dynamic data exchange* (DDE) and *object linking and embedding* (OLE) to control the browser window(s). The DDE controls let you do things like open and close a Netscape window, load a specific URL into the Netscape window, issue alerts and progress messages, query and list the open windows, resize and reposition windows dynamically, and do other interesting things. The OLE controls provide support for applications like *streaming viewers* (such as the RealAudio player).

On the Mac platform, communication occurs through Apple Events. In UNIX, Netscape lets you control the viewer through X properties and a command line interface. For example, issuing the command:

```
netscape -remote 'openURL(http://server1/doc.html)'
```

would open a Netscape window with a certain document displayed in it, as specified by the openURL function.

Netscape's server-side interface (NSAPI) gives developers a way to control and extend the functionality of the server. Normally, web servers are controlled indirectly through the CGI. With a Netscape server, however, it is possible to write even more powerful server-side applications that actually reach inside the server and tinker with its internal mechanisms. Studies have shown these types of server-side applications not only extend the core functionality of the server, but provide a significant performance advantage over plain CGI. NSAPI is supported mainly on UNIX and NT platforms.

NCSA Mosaic has an API feature similar to the Netscape NCAPI called the *Common Client Interface* (CCI). The CCI does many of the same things as NCAPI, including opening a Mosaic window at a specific URL. Although the available call functions are extensive, the CCI API is available only on UNIX platforms.

Spyglass Mosaic, on the other hand, provides an extensive set of client and server-side APIs that is competitive with Netscape's developer interfaces. Unlike NCSA Mosaic, from which it is derived, the Spyglass product supports not only UNIX API activity, but also PC and Mac through DDE and Apple Events. Many of the commercial Mosaic browsers and Internet packages currently on the market incorporate the Spyglass technnology, including the Microsoft Internet Explorer, Internet Anywhere, Internet in a Box, Quarterdeck Mosaic, DEC PathWorks, Oracle Websystem, and many others. Spyglass Mosaic is actually a licensed and improved version of the original NCSA Mosaic browser, which is the granddaddy of them all.

If you want to do API programming, of course, you will need a programmer who understands not only web client-server technology, but the data exchange and control issues associated with the specific environments where the activity is occurring. If your network supports several different platforms, this may

---

### Where to Read About APIs

If you want to delve more deeply into the application programming interfaces for Netscape and Mosaic, check out the following WWW sites:

Netscape API—http://home.netscape.com/newsref/std/server_api.html

http://home.netscape.com/newsref/std/ddeapi.html

http://home.netscape.com/newsref/std/oleapi.html

http://home.netscape.com/newsref/std/x-remote.html

http://home.netscape.com/newsref/std/mac-remote-control.html

NCSA Mosaic CCI—http://www.ncsa.uiuc.edu/SDG/Software/XMosaic/CCI/cci-spec.html

Spyglass Developer Interface and APIs—http://www.spyglass.com/techspec/specs.html

make the idea of API programming a little more difficult. But the results may be well worth the effort.

## Groupware and the Rumored Death of Lotus Notes

*Groupware* is a nebulous term that has come to encompass everything from e-mail applications to databases. It is also one of the hottest buzzwords in business software today. If you followed my discussion of computing history in Chapter 2, or if you've just had your ears glued to the rail for a while, you understand that the immense popularity of groupware is the culmination of many trends in the business world over the past decade, particularly the trend toward empowering teams and workgroups to take responsibility for business processes. For this reason, the groupware tag could probably be applied to any software that helps workgroups communicate better, including e-mail, online forms, online databases, and common document repositories.

Many people see Lotus Notes as the quintessential groupware application. Notes combines a document database, a messaging system, and configuration tools that let users create their own custom business applications. Like web systems, it supports the custom design of fill-out forms that can be used across the network to capture user input to a database.

Probably the neatest trick that Notes performs, however—and apparently the hardest feature for others to duplicate—is a feat called *replication*. This means that users should be able to work on multiple copies of the same document or database, and have all of their changes automatically reconciled across the network. Thus, for instance, you might take a copy of a group-authored document on a business trip with you, work on it on the airplane, then bring it back to the network and your changes would automatically be reconciled in all other copies of the document in the network.

One of the hot debates raging in the press and on the WWW is whether internal webs will make tools like Lotus Notes obsolete. Writers in InfoWorld were quoted as saying, "Eight months ago, there were 10 things that Notes could do that the Web couldn't do, now that is down to two." Even IBM, which purchased Lotus just three months earlier, hosted its own networking forum in late October 1995 in which one panelist asked out loud: "Is the Web going to be the death of Lotus Notes?" (http://www.raleigh.ibm.com/for/forum5.html).

Naturally, like anything else, both web and Notes solutions have their own strengths and weaknesses. One problem with Lotus Notes is its scalability. In Notes R4, the maximum limit of users per Notes server is 1,000. With web technology, a single web server can accommodate the entire organization. Another issue is cost. A U.S. company with 1,000 employees found it could create an Intranet system to share information companywide for a total cost of about $50,000. A similar system using Lotus Notes would have cost $500,000.

The big problem with web, of course, is that—when it comes to documents—it's still basically one-way. Though schemes are being developed to deliver documents back to the server, there's more to it than that. You can use an Intranet to retrieve a document off the network and display it inside a helper application like MS Word, but you can't save it back at its original location on the web server unless you have local read-write access to the server directories. If you save it somewhere else, however, the web loses track of it. And of course, there is no such thing as replication in the web—at least not yet. By the time you read this book, who knows? At the current pace of development in web technology, new products are introduced every day.

Nevertheless, the groupware issue was obviously involved when Netscape Communications purchased Collabra Software, Inc. The flagship product of Collabra is something called Collabra Share, a groupware product that supports collaboration and group conferencing among workgroups. Collabra Share can use your company's existing e-mail system to provide communication between workgroup members, but instead of going to individual mailboxes, the messages are kept in a central repository where they can be viewed and managed by anyone in the group.

Interestingly, Collabra Share supports hypertext linking to internal documents and to the WWW. It also provides additional functionality in powerful agents that can do file replication across a network, pull mail off a mainframe e-mail system, and pull information off of Internet newsgroups. The most fascinating feature is the way that Collabra interfaces with Lotus Notes database—providing complete bidirectional connectivity (Figure 7.16).

### Groupware on the Web

If you're interested in looking into groupware solutions for your web system, check out these Internet/WWW sites:

Lotus InterNotes Web Publisher—http://www.lotus.com/inotes/

Collabra Share—http://www.collabra.com/

TILE—http://www.tile.net/tile/info/viewlist.html

**Figure 7.16**   Collabra Share.

## Where Do We Go from Here?

Now you've done it. You've finished an extensive survey of the three most important applications of web technology that exist. It began in Chapter 5 with online publishing, continued in Chapter 6 with multimedia, and concluded in this chapter with database access, online interactivity, and web applications. Do you still have a nagging question in the back of your mind? Are you still wondering what the heck the Internet might possibly have to do with all of this? You may have noticed (other than for the occasional sidebar on WWW sources) that I have largely ignored the role of the Internet in the development of an Intranet. But the question still remains: What relationship, if any, should there be between the internal Intranet and the external Internet? The next chapter tells all.

## Chapter Eight at a Glance

What is the relationship between the internal and external web? This chapter explores the subject by discussing:

- How and what to communicate over the external web (Internet/WWW)
- How companies connect to the Internet
- The difference in server models and design approach between the internal and external web
- How companies use proxy servers and firewalls to achieve integration between internal and external webs
- Special ways you can communicate with external customers, dealers, and suppliers

# Interfacing with the Internet

The Internet has become so pervasive in our thinking about web technology, it may be hard for some people to understand that it's not even a required component of any of the systems or applications discussed so far in this book. You don't need an Internet connection to make your Intranet work. You don't need permission from the Internet authorities, or any kind of an "Internet license." There is no magic elixir that seeps through the wires from the Internet to fire up your internal network. The Intranet works on its own simply because you have a TCP/IP network—the same way the World Wide Web works on the global TCP/IP network called the Internet. You could operate your Intranet from now until the year 3000 without *ever* being connected to the Internet.

Having said this, it's equally important to make a point that is almost diametrically opposed. To have the best Intranet, you really *should* be connected to the Internet. Not for technical reasons, but because it makes good business sense. People on your network should be able to access sites on the Internet as easily as they access sites in the next room. And you should be looking at ways to start communicating routinely across the firewall with business partners, suppliers, customers, and dealers. Not just with e-mail (as many businesses already do) but with data, published documents, and multimedia.

Why make both points? Because business leaders fall into two categories: those who grudgingly embrace the Internet and those who flail against it. There's still a lot of paranoia about the security problems of the Internet— some of it justified. There's also a concern that if you give employees a direct connection to the World Wide Web, they'll abuse it. Some business managers have a well-developed fear of new technology, or an irrational fear of the unknown. Many just avoid it because they don't understand it. For all these reasons and more, many companies can quote you a dozen reasons why they *shouldn't* be connected to the Internet. If your company fits that description, fine: You can still use an Intranet quite productively within the closed environment of your private LAN or WAN.

Others realize the obvious. Increasingly now and in the near future, the Internet will be a vital and indispensible component of any long-term business communications strategy. No business exists in a vacuum; there are customers, dealers, and suppliers out there in the real world with whom you have to communicate. And that's what the Internet will increasingly help us do—communicate with the rest of the world outside our own private networks in ways we never imagined before.

## The Paranoia, the Puffery . . . and the Possibilities

Actually, there's a good chance your business *already uses* the Internet to communicate with external customers and suppliers. Most businesses have e-mail systems that connect to the public data networks either directly or indirectly, so that it's possible to transfer messages from J.P. Morgan to Federal Express, from Microsoft Corporation to Compaq Computer, or from Your Company Ltd. to My Company Unlimited. This e-mail traffic hops a ride on the Internet to make the journey between Company A and Company B in the world of private enterprise.

It does so—by the way—entirely without the kind of paranoia you see attached to every other use of the Internet, even though most of that traffic flows unsecured and unencrypted through wide-open public channels. Chances are, your confidential message to your key dealers about the pending release of your top-secret product goes cruising out onto the Internet, right past all that pornography and Beatles traffic, past all the WebLouvre GIFs and all the Cool Sites *du jour*—without your even realizing it. And any unscrupulous network administrator in a position to do so can watch your message scurry by and take all the notes he wants. (I'm sorry I have to bring this to your attention, but if you want to be paranoid and morally indignant, you might as well know all the facts. I doubt, however, that you will disconnect your e-mail system tommorrow.)

Most businesses also use the World Wide Web in a limited sort of way. Any self-respecting company now has its own external WWW site to provide an "Internet presence" to the rest of the world. But most often the external site is a static set piece: a fancy bit of puffery developed by some creative design agency to make your company look like a billion dollars to the rest of the world. Many WWW sites are totally one-dimensional and unidirectional. They spew out marketing information to customers—which is certainly a vital task for any business to accomplish—but ignore many of the other ways that a web system could be used to enhance business opportunities, productivity, and customer service.

What's missing from the current WWW equation is a fluid two-way stream of communication that mimics the normal flow of information and commerce in the business world. Instead, that two-way flow is still being handled through all the traditional methods: a sales rep cruising the back roads with a trunkful of product catalogs, a ream of invoices flipping out of a high-speed printer, a sack of bulk mail hefted onto the loading dock, an express mail delivery person striding down the hall, or a room full of customer service reps chattering over the phone.

Though e-mail systems are already used for two-way communication, traditional text-based e-mail systems are really like the electronic equivalent of the Post-It note. Only occasionally are they used to send something more substantive, like an attached PowerPoint file. A method called *Electronic Data Interchange* (EDI) is another way that businesses exchange data, but EDI is a complex technology that is limited in scope and not easily accessible to the average user. The best way to handle that bidirectional stream may be through web technology, because that's the only technology that gives us instantaneous point-and-click access to the full range of rich data types on any computing platform, regardless of where that platform is located, whether it's on a private network or a public one like the Internet.

Assuming that web will be the communications method of choice for the next generation of systems, the challenge becomes to integrate the internal and external webs in such a way that they enhance this bidirectional flow and provide seamless access across the firewall. This brings several questions to mind:

- Is there any crossover between an internal and external web? What are the things they have in common and what are the differences?
- How are the servers for internal and external webs set up and configured?
- Who are the external users for your business; what and how should you communicate with them?
- Can people on the outside access the inside; can people on the inside access the outside? How does that work?
- What are the security issues related to the external web? Will it ever be safe to have an Internet connection?

These are all good questions, which will be answered one by one on the following pages.

## The External Side of the Corporate Web

In previous chapters, I've spent a lot of time talking about the internal web (Intranet), but not much time talking about the *external web* (Internet). Before going any further, let me clarify what I mean by the external web, because it's an important concept to understand. The external web includes the kind of corporate and promotional sites you see regularly on the World Wide Web. For instance, anyone with a web browser and an Internet connection can view the public web sites of Microsoft Corporation, Ford, Merrill Lynch, Chevron, Netscape, Bank of America, Miller Brewing, and thousands of others.

But the external web doesn't have to be limited to the kind of high-profile sites regularly seen on the WWW. The external web can include *any* web service delivered to external users: not just customers, but also suppliers, dealers, business partners, and outside sales reps. This may include components that are public (such as your company's regular WWW site), components that are private (such as a service protected by password and ID), or components that are semiprivate (such as a "shadow" WWW service that is only publicized to dealers or business partners).

Just because web services are external doesn't mean the *servers* are physically located outside your network—though they might be. They might also be located at various places inside your physical network, with links to the outside.

The important thing to understand about the external web is that it can be used to serve a lot more than just the traditional types of information you see on today's commercial WWW sites. Here are some examples of the different types of data you might consider serving.

### Sales and Marketing Data

Of course, your external web can, should, and probably already does serve a lot of traditional marketing data, including:

- Product brochures
- Online electronic catalogs
- Product specs and manuals
- Product promotions and discounts
- Real-time product pricing
- Frequently asked questions and answers about products

- Ordering information, or online ordering and billing
- Interactive registration
- List of dealers or sales contacts
- Multimedia demos

Parallel sets of information could be provided for each product, so that a customer interested in the XYZ Widget could get a sales brochure, a complete set of specifications, FAQs, manual, and so forth. Typically, sites containing sales and marketing information are open to the general public over the Internet. In some instances, however, your business may serve the general public or end user, and you may want to limit its exposure to specific customer audiences. (See Figure 8.1.)

## Customer Support

Customer support will increasingly play an important role in an external web. Here is a short checklist of options:

- Contact information
- Release notes and upgrade notices

**Figure 8.1** Typical marketing-oriented web page.

- Online warranty registration and information
- Online literature request forms
- Troubleshooting and maintenance procedures
- Frequently asked questions
- Viewable/printable product manuals
- Online problem-reporting and evaluation forms
- Customer forums and chat groups
- Accessory catalogs and online ordering forms

Typically, customer support might be provided as a public service. In special cases, however, you may want to limit access to registered customers only, depending on the type of products you sell and your market requirements. (See Figure 8.2.)

### Supplier/Dealer/Sales Support

An external web site can help suppliers, dealers, or field reps stay in touch with company operations. It also can provide an excellent way to link customers and

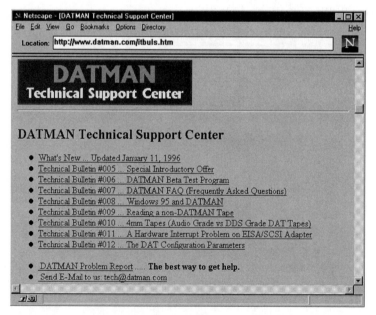

**Figure 8.2**   Typical technical support page.

sales reps "downstream" directly to supplier information "upstream." The following list shows the types of information you may include:

- Contact information
- Details on VAR/dealer programs, special promotions, discounts, etc.
- Passthrough links to supplier web pages, industry web pages, conferences or other sites
- Product release notes and upgrade notices
- Market surveys and focus group studies
- Competitive cross-referencing
- Links to competitor pages
- Wholesale pricing
- Downloadable and printable product literature
- Downloadable canned presentations
- Product troubleshooting and maintenance procedures
- Interactive problem-report forms or request for service
- Complaint and feedback forms
- Sales report forms
- EDI or business-to-business data transfers

The creative part of the external web comes in designing and implementing ways that this kind of data can be served to exclusive audiences. For instance, such information could be served from internal or external machines, with or without password protection, and with or without IP address filtering. The service could be provided over the Internet or through dialup networking or other private network connections.

## Employee Recruiting

Many companies are using the World Wide Web for employee recruiting as a way to save money on classified advertising and other recruiting expenses. Employee recruiting ads or notices may be posted on your own company's web pages or on third-party pages provided by headhunters or employment listing services such as CareerMosaic (http://www.careermosaic.com/). (See Figure 8.3.)

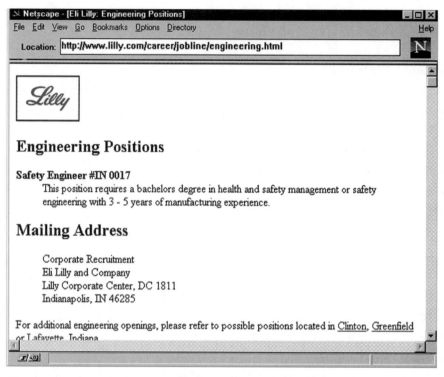

**Figure 8.3** Typical employment listing.

## Doing Business on the Internet

Assuming you need to do business with the general public on the Internet, the question is how to set up shop. The most common way to do business on the Internet is through a public WWW site that is freely accessible to anyone. The way you set up shop depends largely on your organization's internal expertise, capabilities, and goals.

### Renting Space: The Simplest Option

Just as many businesses rent their retail space from shopping malls, so many business open shop on the WWW through "Internet malls" or third-party hosting services. In this case, your company simply rents space on an existing web server that is already connected to the Internet and maintained by a pro-

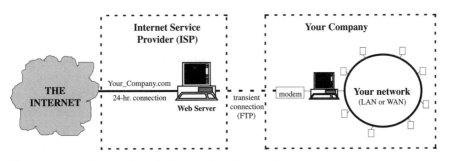

**Figure 8.4**   Example of a hosted web service.

fessional organization that is in the business of providing Internet and web services. The organization you will typically rent such a server from is called an *Internet Service Provider* (ISP). (See Figure 8.4.)

The service itself is physically located at the ISP's site. There is a computer connected to the Internet and monitored 24 hours a day, with your web pages and other content stored on its physical hard drives. To get your content files to your provider's computer, you might use a dial-up Internet connection and the file transfer protocol (FTP). The connection you make is temporary—it's made just long enough to upload the files—so there is no serious concern about security.

The host computer could be located anywhere in the world. Your company could be in Miami, for instance, and use a third-party service in Seattle. So, when selecting a third-party host, especially for dedicated web service, it pays to shop around because rates vary considerably. And of course, the best place to shop is on the Internet.

---

### How to Locate a Web Hosting Service

If you want to shop around for third-party ISPs that provide web hosting services, look no further than your nearest Internet web browser. One of the best places to look is on a list of providers called simply "The List" at:

`http://thelist.com/`

## Dedicated Service with Unique Domain Names

When you use a hosted third-party service, you may be one of dozens or even hundreds of other businesses that the ISP hosts. This raises the question of how users will be able to contact the web server in such a way that they access your files uniquely, without interference from all the other traffic at the ISP hosted server. There are several ways to do this, but the typical way is through dedicated service with a unique domain name.

For instance, you may have a machine set up at the ISP site that is purchased especially for your company and dedicated to your own use. The machine is connected to an Internet port that is assigned a dedicated IP address. If you have a large audience accessing a large site filled with lots of multimedia and graphics, this is the best way to go. You're not sharing drive access or CPU cycles with other hosted sites—the full power of the machine is at your disposal. Naturally, this is more expensive than other options, but compared to other types of business communication expenses it may still be rather small—from several hundred dollars to over $1,000 per month.

So how do users reach your dedicated machine? Typically the ISP registers a domain name for you (in the format *your_company.com* or *your_group.org*) through the Internet registration authority (InterNIC) in Herndon, Virginia. At this point, you may want to consider how the domain name will read. This is a lot like choosing a logo, since Internet users will always think of your company using this name. It should be easy to guess, too, since many Internet users may not know it, but may try to guess it based on your company name. For instance, consider the domain names for Microsoft Corporation (*microsoft.com*) or John Wiley & Sons (*wiley.com*).

A problem may arise if you want a domain name that is already taken. One of the main functions of the InterNIC is to guarantee that all domain names are unique, just the way all trademarks are unique. Without unique domain names, conflicts may arise in resolving a request for service, and a request sent to one company may end up at another. If your domain name is already taken, you have little choice other than to select another one.

When registering the domain name, the InterNIC wants to know the name and address of your company, the name and phone number of administrative contacts, and the IP addresses for your primary and secondary name servers (DNS). The name server is an Internet-connected computer that stores a special *host table.* The host table does little more than simply map specific domain names to IP addresses. For example:

```
www.abc.com    173.28.2.14
ftp.abc.com    173.28.2.15
```

```
def.com         173.28.2.16
www.ghi.com     173.28.2.17
www.jkl.com     173.28.2.18
```

Thus any Internet request sent to *www.abc.com* will be routed automatically to the IP address listed in the host table. When your service is set up this way, a user can enter your domain name in a URL:

```
http://www.abc.com/
```

and hit your server directly.

## Shared Service

Most ISPs can provide cheaper service if you agree to share the server with other companies. A site on some shared servers can be as low as $50 a month or less. You can still have your domain name point to the server, but—since all the different sites on the server can't share the same server document root— your material may be placed in a subfolder off the document root. That's not so bad, except it makes your URL look like this:

```
http://www.abc.com/abc/
```

or even like this:

```
http://www.abc.com/~abc/
```

Smaller companies may not mind this, since the service is cheap, but for larger companies, this clearly does not have the prestige of a clean and simple URL like:

```
http://www.abc.com/
```

## Advantages and Disadvantages of Hosted Web Services

Regardless of the hosting method used, the idea of letting an ISP host your web service has many intrinsic advantages and disadvantages. Among the advantages are:

   ◆ Smaller learning curve; ability to get a site up faster.

- No worries about security. All security problems are placed in the lap of the ISP.

- No need for special on-site equipment, technical talent, or other resources.

In fact, if you want, most ISPs are glad to prepare all your web content and services for you, as well as providing a place to store and serve them. Thus, your own staff would not have to learn HTML, database applications, or web publishing. All that could be outsourced to the ISP.

The disadvantages of using an ISP are not all that great if you plan to have a static service that doesn't change much. The main disadvantage in that case is that you have to manually transfer the data to the remote server.

But suppose you want to have a more dynamic service, such as an online catalog where products can be added and subtracted daily, or where catalog pages are assembled from a dynamically changing database on the fly? Suppose you want customers, dealers, or sales reps to be able to access up-to-the-minute information on product pricing or discounts, or connect to other internal corporate data services? Such applications become much more complicated when you have a web hosting service acting as liaison, mainly because there is an open synapse in the data stream between you and the customer. In fact, if you want to provide an advanced, dynamic, and powerful web service, you almost certainly will have to consider bringing your server in-house.

## Setting Up Your Own WWW Service

Third-party hosted services are ideal for companies that don't want the hassle of setting up their own web site. However, it may be that you don't like the idea of putting your WWW service in the hands of another company, that you already do have the resources on-site, or that you want more control over your web service—including the ability to dynamically stream data out to external users. In that case, you should set up your own WWW service (Figure 8.5).

To set up your own service, you need an Internet connection, a registered domain name, a valid Internet IP address, a web server, and web content that is prepared in a web-compatible format. Since the Internet is a global environment, your server and its informational content should be available 24 hours a day. If you serve a local or regional market, 24-hour access may not be as important, but you should correctly assume that your users may want to visit the site "after-hours and on weekends." Thus, a full-time server is always recommended. To get a better idea of what's involved, let's look at each of the required components individually.

### The Internet Connection

When you want to connect to the phone system, you don't just run your own wire out to the nearest telephone pole. You call the phone company, which makes the connection for you, then charges you monthly for the service. Likewise, if you want to connect to the Internet, you'll need to do it through a local ISP, which will provide the physical link and bill you monthly for it.

The actual connection can be achieved in many different ways. It can be made through ordinary phone lines using analog equipment such as a *modem* or digital equipment such as *ISDN*. The technology you use depends on your needs. A modem provides exceedingly narrow bandwidth—about 36 Kbps maximum, which is enough to serve only a few customers at a time. ISDN is a bit faster (56 to 128 Kbps) and can serve two to four times more information than a plain modem. But if you're serving a large market using rich media— including graphics, video, and audio—even dual-channel ISDN may be too slow.

A common way to connect businesses to the Internet is through a partial or full T1 connection, which provides up to 1.5 Mbps service through a leased line. Instead of a modem, this type of service usually requires a special high-speed digital converter called a CSU/DSU. Costs may range from under $100 per month for dedicated modem service to several hundred dollars a month for full T1 access.

### Optional LAN Connections

The diagram in Figure 8.5 shows an example of how an on-site Internet connection and web server might work. Notice in this case that the Internet connection reaches all the way into your physical plant, but that *the link to your LAN or WAN is optional*. Naturally, you will make the connection all the way into your LAN if:

♦ You want to access the web server hard drives over the LAN, without having to physically carry files to the web server on a floppy disk or tape.

♦ You want your internal users to be able to access the Internet and the WWW.

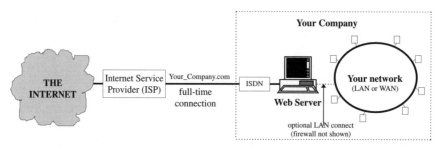

**Figure 8.5**  Example of an on-site Internet web server.

◆ You want to provide Internet services from points *inside* your network or on the fringes of your network.

If you're truly paranoid about Internet security (and perhaps you should be, as I'll explain later), you can have your cake and eat it too. You can place a web server in-house with a full-time Internet connection, but without connecting it to your LAN. That way, the web server itself is exposed to a security threat, but the LAN isn't.

### Registered Domain Name and IP Address

For users to reach your on-site web server, you would still have to register an Internet domain name as before (see p. 298 earlier in this chapter). And the ISP would probably help you do this, as before. Any requests addressed to your company's domain name, such as:

```
http://www.abc.com/
```

would be forwarded through the Internet to the port on your ISP's router where the leased line is connected, and thence onward to your web server.

The question arises: If you have your LAN connected to the Internet, do you need to register a separate domain name and IP address for each internally connected computer? The short answer is no. As the later discussion on security will show, you want to limit direct Internet connections to as few nodes as possible. Ideally, there should be only one or two nodes on your network that connect to the Internet, so you can concentrate all your security efforts at that one spot.

Regardless of whether your connection point is at a single node or at several nodes, only the Internet-connected nodes need to be directly addressable from the Internet and registered with a domain name and a reserved IP address. All communication with these nodes on the Internet side is subject to the rules of the Internet, but all communications on the internal side are subject to the rules of your internal network.

Each node on your internal network will have its own IP address—it must for TCP/IP to work—but these do not correspond to reserved IP addresses on the Internet. They look just the same, and in some cases your local machines may actually be using IP address numbers that are already assigned to computers out on the Internet. But since these internal nodes are not directly addressable from the Internet, it doesn't matter.

### The Web Server and Content

A web server for external access will typically be installed on the gateway computer where the Internet connection first enters the LAN. The web content to be served out on the Internet will be placed on this server, including the HTML files, image files, and other components that form the core of your offering.

## Why Security Is Important

Notice I return again and again to the idea of security. This is because security on the Internet is a constant and serious concern. No matter what kind of private network you operate, you will definitely not want to have it connected to the Internet without at least installing some basic security options.

You can be assured that there are plenty of unemployed and technically proficient people out there (employed ones, too) who have nothing better to do with their spare time than sit around and try to break into private computer networks. We call them *crackers,* because they try to crack your system the same way a burglar cracks a safe. Some of these people are quite benign (some might even be your own employees, trying to see if they can get in from home). Some may be simply bored or looking for a technical challenge. A few may be malicious vandals or thieves.

Companies that have LANs connected to the Internet will tell you that attempted break-ins are quite common. "We do have firewalls," says Chris Koehncke of Nortel, "and we have people every day trying to break in. We see that it happens, but it hasn't been successful that we've been able to determine." But just because there are guaranteed security problems doesn't mean you should reject the Internet as a way of doing business, or turn away and hide your head in the sand. When you're doing business on the Internet, you might want to accept the fact that security threats are just part of the territory, then plan for them and manage against them. The best way to deal with them is to set up rigid defenses and monitor them on a daily basis.

The idea of controlling Internet security is remarkably similar to the idea of controlling security in the real world. Thieves tend to strike at night or whenever there's no one around. And there's never been a security device invented that could keep them out, if they're truly determined. You can install every kind of security device on your house or office building—including burglar bars, padlocks, deadbolts, and alarms—and the thief can break through all of them given enough time, inclination, and lack of vigilance on the owners' part.

Installing Internet security, therefore, is much like installing locks on your doors. The thief might be able to break through all of them, but the more you've installed, the longer it takes. If you install enough security measures, the thief may make a quick mental calculation, weigh his options, and decide it may be easier to break in somewhere else.

Even if a break-in occurs that's not to say anything bad will happen to your system. The person may have proved his point, gotten his jollies, and logged out. Sometimes, however, crackers do illegal and devastating things. They may steal passwords, tap into confidential employee data, insert viruses, and even erase files or entire hard drives. These are the cases you want to protect against.

It's certainly beyond the scope of this text to serve as a complete guidebook to the installation and use of Internet security devices. There are plenty of other books devoted exclusively to the subject at your local bookstore. But it's fair to give you a basic idea of what's involved—not so you can install your own firewalls, but so that you might understand how you can set up a system to "communicate around them."

## Communicating Around a Firewall

Generally speaking, a firewall is a mechanism designed to prevent unauthorized access to a private network area. The firewall activity typically occurs right at the *gateway,* the computer on your internal network that is first touched by the Internet connection. Since all the defensive activity is concentrated at the gateway, this machine is also called the *bastion host* after the bastions that formed the most critical points of defense in medieval castles.

Naturally, because the firewall is designed to limit communications, that's exactly what it does. If you have people on your internal network who want to access the Internet, or people on the outside who want to access internal services, the firewall tends to get in their way. However, there are methods you can use to get around the restrictions of the firewall without unduly compromising security. Let's look at a few typical firewall setups and the ways that Intranet developers can work with them and around them. Keep in mind, however, that you should never try to work your way around a network firewall without the full consent, cooperation, and assistance of the network firewall administrator.

## Dual-Homed Gateway

Imagine if you took the machine housing the web server (Figure 8.5) and installed two network cards in it: one connected to the internal network and one to the external network (i.e., the Internet). All routing between the two networks is turned off so that any communications from outside or inside terminate at this machine. This is called a *dual-homed gateway* (Figure 8.6).

The problem, of course, is directly related to the structure of the firewall: IP network communications stop dead at the first network card and are unable to proceed onto the second network. This is an inconvenience mainly for people on the inside who want to use the Internet—they would have to log onto the firewall machine and use it from there. This setup also eliminates the possibility that any services might be provided to the outside from inside the network.

A dual-homed gateway works fine, however, if the company's external web server is installed directly on the firewall machine. This way, both internal and external users can access it without restriction. Passing network communications across the gap may require the installation of a proxy server, as described later in this section. Some administrators feel that dual-homed gateways may be insecure, because a cracker could potentially exploit a weakness in the web server software to gain access to the bastion host, and thus to the entire network served by the internal card.

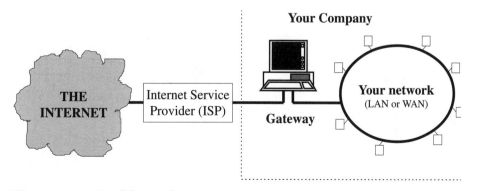

**Figure 8.6**   Dual-homed gateway.

## Screened Host Gateway

Another security mechanism takes advantage of a service performed by certain types of network routers called *packet filtering.* The router can examine each packet of data that comes through the network and determine where it came from and where it's going to (this is what routers do anyway), then reject various packets based on their target service. For example, a router could reject all requests for access to your network except the ones specifically destined for the WWW server (port 80). This eliminates other services that a cracker might use to gain entry to your system, such as telnet, rlogin, and so forth.

To create a more secure firewall, the administrator can program the router to screen out all communications that are not specifically targeted to the bastion host (Figure 8.7). Anything targeted to an internal machine may be rejected, or the administrator may allow selective communication with certain closely monitored and controlled internal machines. At the same time, the router can be configured so that any requests for Internet service coming from within the network will be passed through without filtering. Thus, internal employees can potentially access Internet services without the use of a proxy server.

## Screened Subnet

This configuration is similar to the screened bastion host, except the host might be part of a subnetwork that lies between the Internet and the main enterprise network (Figure 8.8). This subnetwork might contain other services that you need to provide external users, such as FTP or even other specialized web applications. Screening routers on both sides of the subnetwork filter out unwanted traffic in both directions.

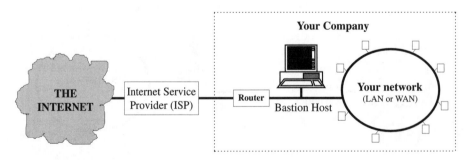

**Figure 8.7**   Screened host gateway.

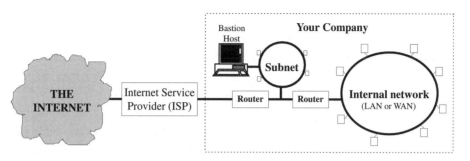

**Figure 8.8** Screen subnet configuration.

## Proxy Servers

A proxy server is not a firewall; it is a special-purpose server that helps people communicate around and through firewalls and that otherwise helps the internal network operate more efficiently. For instance, Netscape offers a proxy server as one of its commercial applications, and the old CERN server has a feature that lets it operate in *proxy mode.*

Proxy servers actually help improve the network operations on your internal web, because they allow internal users to easily funnel their requests through a central caching device that limits the number of repeat accesses to the same site. For instance, if two users request the home page of the *Wall Street Journal* in the same day, the proxy server processes the first request and delivers the requested page back to the first requesting user—meanwhile storing a copy of it in the server cache. Then, if a second user requests *WSJ* on the same day, the proxy server simply retrieves a copy from the cache. To use the proxy server for Internet access, each browser on the internal network must have its proxy options set to the correct server.

## Setting Up Firewalls

Hardware and software configuration is only a small part of network firewall administration. There are other steps that a trained administrator can take to make the bastion host more secure, including disabling some of its internal functions, laying traps for potential crackers, and monitoring certain key processes on a regular basis.

If your organization wants to connect its internal LAN to the Internet, you should hire a qualified network administrator who has thorough training in firewall setup and maintenance, who will be involved in the daily operations of the firewall and monitoring of the site. This kind of network security requires constant vigilance by someone who knows the signs of trouble and who can respond quickly when a problem arises. Never attempt to install or modify a firewall configuration on your own.

## Back-Door Access for Special Users

So far, all the discussion has been about giving external users access to the *public entrance* of your web service. If the Internet is like a public highway and your company's domain name is the knob on the front door, then any member of the public can find out where you do business, turn the knob, and walk in the front door. This is fine if you are providing information to the general public. But what about other external users who may require more targeted or even protected information—the field reps, commercial partners, dealers, and suppliers who help make your business a success? This section explores some of the ways you can provide more targeted or limited access for these types of users.

### Hidden Entryways

A simple way to provide limited access to special audiences is to include additional audience-specific material on your external web site but set it up in such a way that it is accessed through a different home page. The material would not be visible to the general public because there would be no links on the main home page that lead to the special pages (though there might be links in the other direction). For instance, you might create a folder off the main server root called *dealers* that can be accessed through your normal domain name.

Thus, any member of the general public who wants to access your web site would do it like this:

```
http://www.abc.com/
```

and they would instantly see the main home page with links to all the information available to the general public. Dealers, on the other hand, might be told that they can access special dealer information by entering the following URL:

```
http://www.abc.com/dealers/
```

and they would be served a special dealer home page that is not accessible any other way. In fact, if you are in a position to supply your dealers (or other special audiences) with web browsers, you could preconfigure their browsers to open automatically to the special home page for their particular group upon starting. Members of the general public would be unaware that your site contained any other material, and thus would bypass the dealer information entirely.

## Pass Keys

Of course, the previous scenario is not a secure one. Any member of the general public could also access the dealer pages if someone told them about the special URL. If you really object to the public seeing the dealer page—especially if you want to keep your competitors out—you could put password protection on the *dealer* folder so that only registered dealers could access it. Appendix D of this book explains how to password-protect a specific folder so that all the files in that folder require user login.

Of course, this will require some maintenance on your part. You will have to authorize each individual user the way you do with more traditional password-protected computer applications. You may be able to automate this process somewhat by creating a user registration form in which a CGI script takes the user information and checks it against a database or e-mails the specific user with confirmation.

Once password protection is installed, you could easily add links to password-protected material from the main public home pages (with appropriate forewarnings that a password will be required). The user would click the link and automatically see a login dialog that would accept a user ID and password.

## Exclusive Access

If you had some way of capturing the specific IP addresses of the machines used by people in a special audience, you could potentially restrict a specific site to only people using those machines. In this case, the password file mentioned in Appendix D would say:

```
<Limit GET>
order deny,allow
deny from all
allow from dealerpro.com
allow from natsales.com
</Limit>
```

By the same token, you could make it hard for known competitors to access protected information from their own machines by filtering out their company domain names. For instance:

```
<Limit GET>
order allow,deny
allow from all
deny from voracious.com
deny from megawidgets.com
</Limit>
```

Admittedly, this isn't a particularly secure method of allowing or denying access, since it isn't specific to individuals. Competitors that you shut out by domain name could still potentially access your site through independent accounts purchased from local service providers. And machines that you have authorized for access could be used by anyone, such as a competitor who happens to be doing business with the same dealer.

## Special Services

Instead of burying hidden material in your existing web sites, you may want to create special web sites or services that are dedicated to a specific function. This is especially useful for high-traffic, high-volume applications that you don't want bogging down your regular server. Netscape, for instance, maintains a special server for its general store (merchant.netscape.com) that is separate from its main home page server (home.netscape.com), though both are equally accessible to the public. Sun Corporation maintains a site for its Java group (java.sun.com) that is separate from its regular home page server (www.sun.com).

You could conceivably apply all of the restrictions mentioned so far to the special server site, including hidden access, password protection, and IP filtering.

## Private Entries

Again, all the solutions so far assume access through the Internet to public web servers that would normally be open to the public, but that are controlled in some way. But there is one other solution that you may find useful that many companies use to provide guaranteed secure access to the inner network. That solution is called *dialup networking.*

If you've ever taken out your own account with a local Internet service provider, you're already experienced with dialup networking. Your computer dials the provider's number, connects automatically, and logs in to the remote computer using a preprogrammed script. At the end of the login process, a SLIP or PPP application is started and suddenly your computer becomes a TCP/IP node on the Internet. This allows you to easily run any TCP/IP client application such as e-mail, FTP, or WWW and access any available servers on the Internet.

Now imagine that the same thing happened, but with your own company. You might dial in and be logged automatically as a node on the Intranet. Then you could start up your Netscape browser and cruise the Intranet, just like anyone in the corporation. Some companies like Nortel and Sun are already providing their external sales reps with this kind of dial-in access, connecting to pages filled with information that is vital to their mission out in the field.

## Special Assistance

When you're trying to reach out to external audiences, part of the problem is that many of your customers, dealers, sales reps, or suppliers may not yet have web access or networking tools installed on their local computers. Many people remain far behind the curve in the online world, and it will be years before they catch up. Without standard internetworking tools, however, there's no way you'll be able to convert an entire class of users to the benefits of online web-based communications.

In some situations, you may find it feasible to actually provide financial or technical assistance in getting your customers, dealers, or other user audiences online. For instance, one client of mine paid millions of dollars every few years to print full-color catalogs for distribution to customers. Imagine how many copies of Netscape you can buy with the first million dollars (something like 41,000). And imagine the number of user accounts you could pay for with the next million dollars (about 100,000 basic CompuServe account-months). Wouldn't it make sense to put the catalog online, then pay to connect your technolaggard users to it? And if they don't have computers, perhaps you could work a deal to subsidize their purchases through volume-buying discounts and help pay to bring them into the modern world? Then you might pocket a good chunk of that last million and buy pizza for everyone.

## Inside Looking Out: Integrating the Two Sides of the Web

If you ever visit a company with a highly developed Intranet, you may notice the almost seamless ease with which links from internal pages cross over into the external web. The experience can be totally transparent, even though the user is crossing rather rigid network boundaries between the private and public worlds in the process.

For instance, while researching this book, I had a chance to visit with a local salesperson for Nortel, who was showing me how he used the company's web system in his daily work. The man knew his way around the web quite well, but he still didn't understand quite how it all fit together. I watched him move from some of the company's internal web pages, out to the company's external web page, and then effortlessly into the web pages of some of his company's competitors.

All the while, the salesman was under the impression he had never left the Nortel Intranet. He actually thought that the competitor pages had been created by Nortel for the benefit of the company's sales staff so he could easily see the people and products he would be competing against. At that point, I felt obliged to explain that much of his web surfing was happening out on the external Internet. I took a little time to expose the Location field on his browser and showed how he could roughly tell from the Location field *when* he was on the Internet and *when he was not.*

Not everyone in your company will need external access to the Internet, but for many of them it will be a priceless addition to their productivity. Most companies I know provide external access indiscriminately to internal users, but some of them are cracking down. Digital says it will institute new controls to warn users when they are crossing into the public sphere, so they will be more conscious of their use of external bandwidth. Nortel has developed a tracking system that automatically logs and bills all external web time to individual departments. The time is not that expensive, it averages a few dollars a month per employee. But the system helps discourage nonjustifiable joy riding on the external web.

The employees who really need access to the Internet are the ones who are already outward-looking in their jobs. Research staff are at the top of the list, since questions that once took days to research can now be resolved in minutes on the Internet. Sales and marketing staff are a fast second, since they need to keep up with the activities of both customers and competitors. As soon as employees are empowered to access the Internet from their desks, they quickly and invariably find it an indispensible part of their job. With Internet access, information on any topic is just a few keystrokes away; whether it is government regulations, scientific research, stock or commodity prices, competitive data, market studies, proceedings of professional organizations—you name it and it's there. This kind of global reach and instant access to information can do much to boost productivity within your organization and give your company a solid jump on the competition. If you hesitate—and many companies have—then your competition has an ideal opportunity to get the jump on *you.*

## Where Do We Go from Here?

This chapter has covered all you need to know about the different issues regarding access and integration of internal webs and external ones. Other than the issues covered here, there is no significant difference in the technologies and techniques that you use to build one or the other—the internal or the external. Now we move on to the last chapter of the book, in which I explain the different management and control issues related to the development of an internal web.

## Chapter Nine at a Glance

This final chapter explains the management issues related to corporate Intranets. Most specifically:

- Control issues and control models related to internal webs
- The importance of using the web as an enabling technology
- How structure and centralized access can be imposed on the web after the fact
- How various methods can be used to turn the web into an ad-hoc corporatewide knowledge base
- How standards, templates, and workflow designs can be used to minimize disruption to the organization and increase productivity
- How to achieve buy-in from employees and management
- Budgeting, licensing, and support issues for internal webs

# Managing the Web Explosion

"How odd," you may think. Here we are, at the last chapter of the book, and it's only now that the author starts talking about management issues. Aren't we supposed to do our planning up front? Isn't management supposed to lead, rather than follow? If we're going to implement such a potentially massive new information system, don't we first have to whip out our graph paper and our spreadsheets and do feasibility studies and have committee meetings and plan and put together project teams and hire squadrons of programmers and computer network wizards?

In fact, shouldn't we just turn this over to some bigtime consulting firm like Anderson or Deloitte & Touche and let them figure it all out? Don't we know from experience that every new wave of computer technology is massively more complex than the previous one, and that it will require massive new layers of infrastructure and massive amounts of expertise to pull it off? Isn't this, after all, what the client-server revolution has taught us?

Welcome to the Web Era. You are now in an era where many of your employees—by and large—may be able to set up servers by themselves, thank you very much; an era when employees have the power to help themselves and management may sometimes happen a little bit after the fact.

Remember in Chapter 2 where I explained that most internal webs are developed from the bottom up, rather than the top down? Remember how it tends to start with technologically savvy individuals, then spreads out from there as other people see the models and witness the technology in action?

In most companies that were early web adopters it has been with the tolerance of management, rather than at their urging, that the Intranet was formed. Lucky is the manager who fully understands what's going on. Executives are getting little help with this from their IS staffs. Some corporate IS departments are still mired in the mainframe world and are only starting to explore client-server. Those that are heavily committed to client-server have jumped into some very expensive proprietary technologies and big-bang projects that require a lot of administration and maintenance, and it will be some time before they get their heads unstuck enough to see what is happening around them. When they do, they may find that their original assumptions about client-server technology have to be completely rethought. "IS people were asleep when personal computers happened," says Chris Koehncke of Nortel, "and I think they are asleep now on the World Wide Web."

In companies where employees are truly empowered, people tend to take this technology and run with it in all kinds of unexpected ways. In fact, you might gauge the intellectual health and level of entrepreneurship within your own organization by the speed at which web systems are adopted and grow. In companies where employees are functionally empowered, technologically enabled, and intellectually challenged, web technology may spread very fast. In companies that ration technology and where initiative is stifled by layers of bureaucratic control, you may see some signs of life on the webfront, but the general rate of adoption may be incredibly slow. The quickest adoption often occurs at companies like Chevron and Nortel, where savvy managers catch on and help lead the charge.

Web systems will work best when people are given the same freedom to use them that they now have with ordinary business applications like desktop publishing and spreadsheets. It's important to recognize that web technology—at its core—is not rocket science. It's just another business communications medium, like desktop publishing is now, but one in which the network substitutes for paper. But it's also important to realize that web will exponentially increase the speed and immediacy of business communications and that it will eventually suck in all the other information streams—not just words and pictures, but data, multimedia, messaging, conferencing, and applications.

When this happens, watch for a further flattening of organizational structures and drastic changes in the management of information systems. In the Web Era, midlevel managers will have an even smaller role as the intermediaries who interpret and transfer information between the bottom and top rungs of the corporate ladder. Grunt-level workers and executives will have a common platform for communication where they can silently (or even audibly) audit each others' web pages, hear each others' concerns, and add their voices to corporatewide discussion groups focused on special topics. The new technology will enhance the communication of corporate goals, performance targets, and employee feedback across the organizational nexus.

IS managers may find their entire world shifting around them once again, as the internal web becomes the dominant environment for delivering data and applications. The entire method of application design and delivery may require a new phase of reengineering with a focus on more modular, applet-based information systems, and a more serious look at ways of integrating the entire information stream, including data, documents, multimedia, and applications. IS will certainly continue to be the guardian of back-end legacy data, but will find more and more of their information being served out directly onto the Intranet. Many application programming functions may devolve out to individual departments or information centers, as people create their own form-based interfaces to data sources.

None of this should suggest that an internal web is unmanageable, or that there aren't concrete steps that should be taken to manage it. In fact, there are many management issues that must and should be addressed to ensure that people can use the new technologies in efficient and productive ways. This chapter will discuss the key management concepts, and suggest ways that management can cope with the coming web explosion.

## The Matter of Control

When you work with the Fortune 500, you find yourself being ushered through the halls and back alleys of some of the world's most massively structured organizations. Miles of mazelike corridors opening onto warrens of cubicles, with doors that you need secret codes to pass through. Large organizations love control, and the larger the organization, the more effort they spend controlling things. It's no wonder, then, that one of the biggest impediments to adoption of a web may be the control issue.

This is not a subtle thing at all. In fact, people make no bones about it. I recently met with a potential client (at a research arm of one of the Fortune 10) who was thinking about setting up an internal web, but with only a few servers that could be controlled by the company's computer services group. "Our company likes control," he and others told me. "We might not want just anyone going out and setting up a web server, or using one of these things."

This is a typical argument I hear all the time. But think about it. If the company likes controls so much, where are the controls on the telephone and e-mail systems? Who controls the desktop publishing and interoffice mail systems? Anyone can use a word processing program to prepare a document, print as many copies as they want and drop all those copies into interoffice mail to be distributed throughout the company with *no questions asked!* Where's the control there?

"We can't control every word processor or copying machine," these people may argue. "That would be impossible. Everybody needs those tools to do their job."

That's my point exactly! You don't mind employees wasting money to print all this paper and hand-deliver it to locations worldwide. They can do *that* without restriction. But if someone wants to use the network to bypass these archaic information distribution systems, they have to ask for permission first. Does that really make sense?

Of course, at this point in the book, we all understand that the control issue is a vestigial part of the old information systems models. In traditional computing environments, you start with the idea that *everything is prohibited* unless someone in power enables it. Thus, people who want access to computer resources are typically given access only if they request it. With web systems, on the other hand, access is automatically granted *unless it is specifically restricted.* In other words, everyone starts with full access to the system, and they are restricted from key applications only where that type of control is absolutely necessary (such as with highly confidential product designs, personnel records—that sort of thing). The new paradigm is that you should let the system grow free at the grassroots, then you take a little time to manicure the lawn.

## Understanding the Web Control Model

That's not to say that control is not a legitimate issue. There must always be some amount of access control, even in an open system like a web. It's just that the control model has changed; almost inverted. On its face, a web server is the epitome of control. With web, however, the controls are totally nonintrusive, built in, and decentralized.

Think about it: If I install a web server on my computer today and create documents and data to be accessed through that web server, then—by default—any user on the same network can see that information instantly without logging in or without even knocking on the door. A simple click is all it takes to whisk the information away to the user's machine. In a system like this, you might think there's no control at all.

But look what's really happening. Can anyone access just *any* information on my computer? No. . . . The people who are looking at my web site are seeing *only the information I want them to see.* In other words, I—the individual, the author and provider of the information—can exercise control over who sees what by moving it into the web server document folders. No one (unless they are a somewhat bored and very talented hacker) can see any other information on my computer unless I physically move it to the server folders. So I exercise control by choosing what I want to publish.

The bottom line is this: If I want people to see certain information on my computer, *I am the one who makes that decision—little old decentralized me.* Furthermore, I have the ability to let people view my information without the help of a network administrator. And, if I don't want people to see certain *other* information on my computer, again I am the person in control.

In either case, it's a win–win situation both for me *and* the network administrator. I don't need the administrator's help authorizing each individual user of my personal client-server system. And the administrator doesn't have to be constantly managing user access to every server in the network. To put it in computer industry terms, you might say that after all the hype about open systems, client-server is finally moving to a truly open, distributed, and decentralized model, because in a web the old models of network administration have suddenly evaporated.

In a web system, the control model is split the same way that the viewer-author model was split in online publishing (as previously discussed in Chapter 2). There are now two levels of control involved, which could be called *author* versus *viewer control,* or *server-side* versus *client-side control.*

The diagram in Figure 9.1 shows what I mean. Think of the web server as sort of neutral territory being visited from both sides by two opposing camps. On one side are the authors of the information, who are mainly responsible for publishing it and keeping it up-to-date. On the other side are the users of the information, who are mainly responsible for browsing through it, learning from it, and occasionally interacting with it. Here's how the control systems work on both sides of the equation.

## Author/Server Control

On the author/server side, we have the issue of who will be able to create new information and deposit it inside the web server directories, who will be able

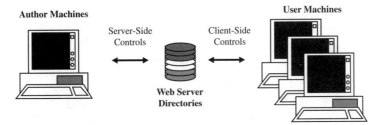

**Figure 9.1**   Web access control model.

to update the information, and who will be able to tamper with the configuration of the file systems or other aspects of the server host computer.

If I have a personal web server installed on my local machine (See Figure 9.2), this issue is totally up to me. The nice thing about an Intranet is that anyone can set up a server and be responsible for their own content and server configuration. The entire approach of this book is that individuals would actually do this on their own—use the network as an information dissemination tool for their own purposes, the same way they currently have unlimited use of the phone and interoffice mail system. Though unlimited and unregulated growth of "personal servers" would have been unthinkable, impermissible, and undesirable in older networks with limited bandwidth and centralized administration models, they will be increasingly desirable in the high-speed mass-audience wide-area networks of the future where the network is suddenly too far-flung to treat as an empire and too high-speed for anyone to quibble about individual traffic burdens.

In many cases, however, the server may be set up and maintained by a team, workgroup, department, or business unit, where many people are contributing documents or data. In these situations, the traditional control models are more likely to apply: The server could be installed on a network file server, with the server directories mounted as a local file system on each contributor's machine. That way, each author could directly access and edit the information just as though it were stored on a local hard drive.

In this case, permissions would be set on the server side to make sure that only members of the group could access the directories to change their content. Or an automated process could be used to transfer and convert web content in a shared workgroup directory to a set of production server directories controlled by a webmaster (Figure 9.3).

On a wide area network with built-in Internet software, access to the server directories could be provided in other ways: including FTP and telnet either through the network or through dialup SLIP or PPP connections. Thus, for

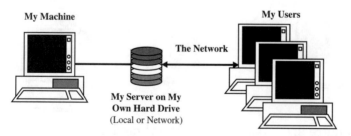

**Figure 9.2**   The personal server model.

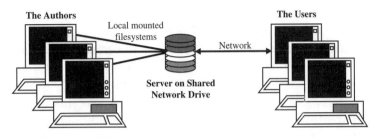

**Figure 9.3**   Workgroup server model.

example, authors might create and manage the content on their own local computers, then use FTP to transfer the completed files over to the web server. A time-triggered "cron" job could be set up as an batch process to automatically do this on a regular schedule.

In fact, the FTP transfer method is used widely on the Internet, in cases where web sites are maintained on third-party-hosted computers. For instance, many third-party services like Internet Direct or Webcom Communications maintain Internet-connected web servers where users can deposit their content. Users then use FTP to transfer content updates to the site. In general, FTP access is not as desirable as direct access, but provides an alternative when direct server mounts would be difficult or inappropriate.

## Viewer/Client Control

Access control issues are entirely different on the viewer or client side of the web model (Figure 9.1). Here we start with the idea that there is no control at all, other than the fact that the access is read-only. In other words, anyone on the network can hit the web site and extract the contents, but no one can edit or change the contents at the site. That's for starters.

Beginning with this open model of universal read-only user access, we then have other levels of access control:

◆ *Read-write access to selected materials.* The authors or developers of the web site can selectively provide users with both read access and write access to certain materials. For instance, the authors might include interactive forms that can insert or update records in a database at the author's site. Though rarer, its not hard to imagine that future server-side applications will be used to pass edited documents back and forth from authors on the server side to collaborators on the client side. Chapter 7 discusses how two-way interactivity can be enabled on a web site.

- *IP address filtering.* The authors or developers of a web site can selectively allow or deny access from specified IP addresses. Most likely, this would be used to limit access to certain audiences, such as people in the same department or work group, or to certain classes of users such as dealers or sales reps. See Appendix D for details.

- *User authentication.* If desired, web authors and developers can take their sites all the way back to the old login model where everyone who accesses the site must have a user ID and password. Naturally, this increases the administrative burden considerably, since each user ID and password must be set up individually at the web server (see Appendix D for details). But some web authors and developers may want to use this feature interactively to "register" people for their sites. A form could be provided so people can register their own user ID and password the first time they enter the site. A CGI program could be used to append the user ID and passwords automatically to the site's password authorization file, so they don't have to be maintained manually. Using this method, the site authors have a way to capture a real snapshot of their potential user audience. Furthermore, user names and e-mail addresses captured on the registration form could be used as mailing list to notify registered users of changes to the site.

Though access issues may seem a somewhat arcane subject, they are really at the core of the entire management issue. Though the web comes with certain access controls built in by default (read-write on author/server side, read-only on user/client side), much of the creative work in developing web systems revolves around how access is manipulated to provide different kinds of services and functionality.

## Virtual Centralization and Planning after the Fact

How's that for two interesting new buzzwords? *Virtual centralization . . . Planning after-the-fact.* Sit back while I explain what they mean.

As you're probably thinking by now, the fact that we let people go off and do their own thing on a web leads only to chaos. Web pages and information centers proliferate haphazardly out on the network, without any plan or structure. *With so much information being generated at so many sites,* you begin to wonder, *how does the user find anything at all?*

As it happens, that's exactly the kind of question people ask themselves all the time on the World Wide Web. Anyone who's used the WWW understands what a chaotic place it can be, with hundreds of thousands of different web sites scattered throughout the world, and no central menu connecting them all. To cope with this random proliferation of web sites, certain individuals, entrepreneurs, and companies leapt into the fray and developed search tools and directories like Lycos, InfoSeek, and Yahoo.

This is a lot like what happened a century ago when the first telephone systems were developed—only later to be followed by comprehensive white pages and yellow pages listings. Nowadays, its quite easy to find the number of any private or business telephone anywhere in the world. Just look it up in the phone book. The same will eventually happen on the WWW.

Yahoo (at http://www.yahoo.com/) is about as close as the WWW comes right now to a full-fledged yellow pages. Its directories cover just about every topic, and the listings are quite extensive and impressive. But the early Yahoo model was limited because it depended on voluntary registration for much of its information. A better model could be found in the Excite and InfoSeek approaches (http://www.excite.com/ and http://www2.infoseek.com/), which use robots to automatically scan the WWW for content, then build their own reference indexes that users can quickly search. The superiority of these methods became apparent when Netscape switched its Internet directory services from Yahoo to Excite, and Yahoo quickly changed its method to follow the Excite model.

So what does all this have to do with virtual centralization and planning after the fact? Exactly this: If the Internet had been planned, it would never have happened. At least not in the wildly successful format that it has evolved into today. If everyone had been waiting for their marching orders to come from some central authority, we would all still be waiting. There is simply no way to plan anything of the size and scope of the Internet, then execute a plan in any reasonable time frame that could keep up with the rapid advance of technology. A system like the Internet can evolve only on its own, like a biological organism that has been given the freedom to grow and mutate according to natural laws that we still don't fully understand.

The beauty of the Internet model—especially the hypertext features of the WWW—lies in the fact that you can impose a structure on all this chaos *after the fact*. Using hypertext, you can build a centralized directory or provide search tools that automatically connect users to the information they need, and do it in such a way that it *appears to have been planned that way all along*.

In the days before HTML and the WWW, it would have been impossible to build an extensive system like this without planning it up front. You would have had to set up the structure of all the different departments, decide the types of information and applications each one would serve, set up the access paths and the user authorizations, specify the tools and protocols that would be used to prepare and transfer data between systems, roll the system out a division at a time, correct your errors, train and retrain, and eventually wind up with a functioning system that is already obsolete. To a certain extent, this is the way all computer systems are currently designed and implemented.

With web technology, however, it's possible to just give users the tools and let them create information centers at will, then come back after the fact and impose a structure on all the chaos. The structure is in the form of a centralized menu or directory service that contains hyperlinks to all the content. This could be done using either of two models already used on the WWW:

- *The Yahoo model.* Your web could have a central registration page that all information centers could use to register their services on a voluntary basis. The registration information could then be automatically appended to a central menu by a CGI program, or it could be manually added by the webmaster in charge.
- *The Excite/Infoseek model.* You could set up a robot or search engine to automatically search the internal web and index all of its content. Users could enter a set of keywords and automatically find all sites on the web that match the entered keywords.

Once you create a centralized directory service for your web, the web now gives *the appearance* of being centralized, when in fact it is completely decentralized (thus the term *virtual* centralization.) And it gives *the appearance* of having been planned, when in fact nothing of the sort occurred (thus the idea of planning *after the fact.*)

So you really have the best of both worlds: employee empowerment, people doing their own thing, yet with a management technique that captures what they're doing and makes it accessible to the average user. You get to sit back and let people put the technology to its best uses, then come behind them and paste a big smiley-face on the whole mess. It's kind of like the ultimate manager's dream, isn't it?

## The 80-20 Rule, in Spades

Once you understand the concept of virtual centralization, you find yourself once more staring at one of those awesome revelations you get from time to time with web technology. This one has to do with the 80-20 rule.

You've heard about the 80-20 rule. It applies to many things: 80 percent of the money is earned by 20 percent of the population, 80 percent of the pizza is eaten by 20 percent of the gluttons, 80 percent of the complaints received by your company are made by 20 percent of the customers—that sort of thing. In this case, the 80-20 rule applies to information systems.

One of the key moments in computing history was probably the day—sometime back in the 1970s or early1980s—when they changed the name of most corporate computer departments from "data processing" (or DP) to "information systems" (or IS). This change recognized that computers could be used to deliver something more than just raw data in the form of mind-deadening numbers; instead they could be used to provide people with useful *information.*

The job of computer departments, then, was to capture information, process it, and present it to users in an automated way. And they've done an admirable job, considering what they've had to work with. Back in the days of *data processing,* the computer room was like a scene out of Dr. Frankenstein's lab. The old CRT displays were covered with gibberish. Today your very own "personal" computer is more likely to greet you with a smile, a catchy tune, or even visions of flying toasters romping in outer space.

But the job of automating information systems is far from complete. Even today, with all their growth and technical sophistication, corporate information systems only handle about 20 percent of the total information available in the enterprise. The other 80 percent falls under the category of *miscellaneous.* Information systems are great at handling all the mission-critical data, including customer information and accounting records, but not all the other stuff, such as reports, memos, catalogs, specifications, manuals, budgets, project schedules—you name it.

Nowadays, these various bits of information are *prepared* on computers, of course. But then they often get transferred straight into the *old* information system: the copier, mail room, and filing cabinet systems that handle tons of paper every day. Normally, you can't see these documents online unless you're the one who authored them. Or if they are online, they're online in an inaccessible way: in certain people's in-boxes, on certain network file servers that can only be accessed by certain groups at certain times, locked in PC Win-Help systems, and so forth. There hasn't been a way to take all of this information and catalog it the same way you can catalog information in a database. Raw information is a messy business that doesn't easily submit to neat solutions the way raw data does.

The problem of automating the other 80 percent of corporate information, therefore, has been partly due to a lack of suitable technology. That's no longer true with the web. First, people put their information online using web publishing tools, conferencing tools, and messaging tools—instead of going onto paper with the old desktop publishing tools. Then a search engine comes behind and makes it all accessible enterprisewide within seconds.

The feat you accomplish with virtual centralization is a little like what might have happened if you had deliberately set out to bring online the other 80 percent of data that remains untouched by the corporate IS function. But instead of years of dogged efforts by squadrons of bleary-eyed IS people and contract programmers, it all happens automatically within seconds.

Imagine being able to catalog and have at your fingertips every message, memo, report, or other document produced by any person in the company. Sounds incredible doesn't it? If you don't believe it can be done, go to Lycos on the WWW (http://www.lycos.com/) and enter a query for "Ryan Bernard." You'll instantly see a list of most of the places on the World Wide Web where my name is mentioned (about 70 at last count), including many of my own pages and messages I posted to random Internet newsgroups as far back as fall 1994. How embarrassing; but also, how incredibly amazing. If you can do this kind of search for any subject or name across a global network with hundreds of thousands of servers, imagine what you can do in a more limited corporate network environment.

Of course, the fact that it happens magically on Lycos doesn't mean it will happen magically on your Intranet. It won't happen until the web is fully populated with information from all segments of your organization. So the trick will be how to get the ball rolling, how to gain wide acceptance of web technology in your organization, and how to be "smart" in your use of the technology so that everyone remains productive during the transition.

## The Role of the Vanguard Team

Assuming that we finally have an information technology that can be organic, self-generating, self-cataloguing, and self-sustaining, what kind of role can management play, anyway? Glad you asked, because there are plenty of ways a system like this can and should be managed.

Probably the best way to manage an Intranet may be to have an internal vanguard team that functions as consultants and advisors to the rest of the organization on web technology. It may be that your company already has such a group that has charged ahead with its own internal web site and that is full of people who already salivate over the technology. If not, it's likely that such a team might be assembled from the ranks of IS, network services, or other groups that have an IT orientation. Or you may want to pick individuals from various disciplines, such as technical communications, marketing communications, database services, corporate communications, and IS.

The responsibilities of an internal vanguard team could be quite diverse, but would probably include:

- Promoting the use of web technology within the organization
- Helping train employees in how to use the technology
- Developing standards and templates for web page design to promote a more consistent interface and level of quality
- Developing standards and templates for offline tools that feed content into the web
- Researching and recommending productivity tools that will help automate web publishing and programming functions
- Dealing with software licensing and distribution for various common web tools, such as browser and servers
- Evaluating and critiquing the contribution of different departments to the overall Web
- Answering questions and providing support functions such as a 24-hour help center or online discussion groups where people can get their questions answered
- Advising departments on innovative ways to apply web technology to specific applications
- Providing the technical expertise where needed to develop more advanced applications such as interactive forms, CGI programs, and database integration
- Keeping track of changes in the Web, possibly by certifying Web sites or providing a registration form
- Creating and maintaining high-level menus or search tools that provide a centralized path for accessing all Web resources
- Assisting in managing the overall Web, including broken link analysis and usage reporting

An internal consulting group set up to perform these tasks can help promote organization goals without creating a centralized bureaucracy. At first it may be that such a group exists independently of IS, since in many cases an Intranet is considered a foreign concern to IS. It may be that someday this evolves into a department that actually swallows the IS function completely.

## The Importance of Standards

Another area where management can make a difference in the development of an Intranet is by promoting standards for development, design, and production of the new systems. There are basically two ways your company can deal with an internal web: (1) Everybody reinvent the wheel every day and do things in the hardest possible way, or (2) everybody benefit from a set of standards, guidelines, and tools that will help people work smart and be as productive as possible. Admittedly, these are two opposite extremes of the spectrum. There are gray areas in the middle, somewhere. But it pays to examine both the worst case and the best case to make a point.

### Worst Case: No Guidance, No Standards

Let's look at the worst case first. Assume that everyone is on their own without any standards, guidelines, or training to help them. First, everyone will have to go off and learn about web technology on their own. They'll have to read books like this one (actually, not a bad idea) or do about a year's worth of thinking and study on the subject before they realize how web-based communications can benefit the entire organization. Then they'll have to find it in their heart to put the organization's best interests ahead of their own lethargy, and start using the web. Not too likely, right?

Next, they'll have to locate some tools, or accept the tools selected by others in their group. Assuming the worst case—that someone in their group is already an HTML whiz and *just adores* using HTML editors—then they'll probably start with an HTML editor, too. This will triple or quadruple the time they have to spend learning how to publish on a web, and each document they produce will be hacked together with about five times the effort it would have taken otherwise. The documents will be full of coding mistakes, may look rather like something the cat coughed up, will be difficult to navigate, and may have broken icons every place an illustration was supposed to occur. Instead of making things easier, the web suddenly made them harder.

To do database publishing, web authors will have to take the same path: learning what it is, finding the tools, and so forth on their own. With multimedia it will be the same. Instead of helping people in their jobs, the web will hinder people and make their jobs harder. Instead of using the web to carry important communications, they will turn back furtively to the old methods, frustrating your goal of bringing the entire organization online.

## The Ideal Scenario

Now let's look at how a well-designed set of standards, guidelines, tools, and workflows can help an organization. The first step is: *Everyone freeze!* Hands off the HTML editors. Let's get the following straight right from the beginning:

◆ Nobody changes tools.
◆ Nobody learns a stitch of HTML.
◆ Nobody does anything different, with a few key exceptions.

Here are the exceptions:

◆ If you already use Microsoft Word, here's a set of templates you can use for various types of documents: memos, manuals, reports, newsletters.
◆ If you already use FrameMaker, here's a set of templates you can use to do the same thing.
◆ If you already use "whatever," here's a set of templates for that.

Now everybody can go on about their business, but just use these templates whenever you want to create documents. When you're finished, save your work in *this set of directories.*

The templates would contain a set of *style tags* (also called a *style sheet*) that everyone should use to format their documents: Heading 1 for major headings, Heading 2 for subheadings, Bullet for bullets, Body for body text, and so on. To use the style tags, just point at the paragraph you're typing and select the correct tag from the style menu. It's a little disorienting the first few times, particularly for the class of people I call "creative formatters"—but you get used to it. You can distribute the templates as hyperlinked directly from a web page, and include online instructions on how to use them or a full-fledged online style guide. (See Figure 9.4.)

Some people quibble about this. You talk to companies that have never used templates, and they say it can't be done. Then you talk to companies that use them all the time and they say it's no big deal. The fact of the matter is this: When it comes to web publishing, you can either (1) ask people to change their habits slightly by adopting templates, or (2) ask everyone to learn new tools, or (3) have someone who reformats and styles every paragraph of every document that needs to go onto the web.

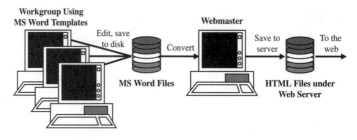

**Figure 9.4** Workgroup model using standard templates.

Personally, I think it's easier to distribute the workload in such a way that everyone cooperates in maintaining a publishing standard. This helps us avoid the retraining that would be involved in a move to new tools, or the rework and doubling of effort required if we have to reformat everything that everyone writes. Style sheets are not hard to use: in fact, they will make everyone more productive even if you *aren't* doing web publishing. (In fact, I know some companies that win regular annual awards for their technical manuals based in part on the fact that the template design and documentation models almost guarantee an award-winning result.)

The nice thing about style sheets is that, if you can get everyone using them correctly (and that's not really such a big *if,* assuming they're well-designed and people understand why they're important), documents will go up on the web in seconds. For each set of templates, there will be a set of map files and a tool like HTML Transit, WebMaker, or Cyberleaf that can suck the documents right out of their source directories and turn them into published web documents on the fly (see Chapter 5 for an extensive description of the tools). The important thing is that the templates and the map files be designed to work together by someone who understands style sheets, HTML conversions, the tools involved, and the formatting requirements of the web.

Once all the elements in a template-based workflow are set up and meshed properly, the conversion process is so easy that a single administrative assistant (or webmaster) could easily handle all the conversions required by a workgroup—or even a set of workgroups—without seriously breaking stride. The only steps required for each set of documents would be to open the conversion program, specify the files to be converted, specify the conversion map file to use, and let the conversion run itself (see HTML Transit conversion examples in Chapter 5). If any given set of documents change often, you may want to find ways to set up the conversion as a time-triggered batch process that runs automatically either nightly or weekly (depending on frequency of updates)—converting the same set of files regularly on a fixed schedule.

## The Alternatives

If you feel that workgroups shouldn't be required to use templates, it's still not a major problem. However, for each new document that comes down the pike, the person designated as webmaster will have to create an entirely new conversion map, or may have to go in and edit the documents manually. If you have an extra person to spare, this may be an acceptable way to go. But keep in mind it may be a full-time job for someone to handle all the editing and conversion needs for an active workgroup.

If you are strictly opposed to the idea of templates and style guides, and you don't want to dedicate a full-time webmaster to edit the documents, the next option is to have your workgroup members drop all their current tools and retrain on web publishing tools. In that case, I recommend WYSIWYG editing tools like Netscape Navigator Gold, Adobe Pagemill, FrontPage Editor, or MS Word Internet Assistant.

The idea of serving data and multimedia is a little more tricky, but easily dealt with. If you set up a web advisory group in your company, it should be the job of that group to locate tools that are compatible with the database platforms most commonly used on your network (see discussion of database access in Chapter 7). Once these tools are selected, a person trained as a webmaster could create the forms and database hooks needed to set up interactivity. Compared to ongoing document publishing efforts, the need to create new database access applications is relatively rare. Someone who is good at this might spend a day or two a week filling the needs of several workgroups.

Multimedia is not a problem if the workgroup is already familiar with illustration and multimedia tools. Typically, if you're going to do sound or video on a web, it will typically be done by some group in your organization that was already using these anyway. The web advisory group can choose the appropriate multimedia conversion tools and give the workgroup the appropriate training needed to use them and to embed multimedia into web documents (see Chapter 6 for a discussion of multimedia).

## Achieving Buy-in from Employees and Management

Letting people take the technology and run with it is one thing. But if you're going to create a truly companywide Intranet, you're going to need participation from everyone. That means not only identifying mission-critical applications and creating teams to develop them, but getting everyone to use the Intranet as a standard conduit for their own critical information.

One of your greatest challenges in doing this will be helping people understand the benefits of the new communications model. Just because you find this technology powerful and productive, you shouldn't assume everyone will share your feelings automatically. To get everyone working on the same channel, it's going to be necessary to achieve buy-in from both the executive level and the grunt level. To bring benefits to the entire enterprise, the web must achieve a certain level of saturation within the organization.

Preliminary reports back from the front say that it's not easy to impress rank-and-file employees in the benefits of this technology unless several things happen:

- Upper management makes it clear that it supports the effort, and that it considers a companywide Intranet to be an important strategic tool of the organization.
- The web contains a critical mass of important applications that people need in their daily work and that are essential time-savers. That means not just documents but crucial up-to-the-minute data, like the profit-and-loss statements Chevron maintains for each team (see Chapter 4).
- Rank-and-file employees get the tools and training they need to make web publishing easy—and even fun.

Never underestimate the enthusiasm of empowered employees. In places where employees have been given the right tools, the right models, the right emphasis on benefits, and the right training, the Intranet has achieved critical mass and taken off. In some places, the Intranet is so popular that other problems arise: the problems of keeping people from doing *too much* with it and using it for inappropriate purposes, such as putting up pictures of their children and dogs.

In places where employees don't get the proper tools and training, where management imprimatur is absent, or where the web is still in an experimental or stripped-down stage, the task will be harder. People may applaud the new technologies, then turn around and go right back to doing things the old way.

Of course, no matter how much you try to train and promote the Intranet, there will always be some people who just won't "get it." I always think of the comments David Letterman gave to Microsoft chairman Bill Gates, during the promo tour for Gates' book *The Road Ahead*. Gates sat there on "Late Night," enthusing about how the new Internet technologies would improve the way people communicate with each other, while Letterman, a self-admitted computer Neanderthal, developed this massively quizzical expression on his face. "Why would people *do that?*" shuddered Letterman, referring to the fact that people communicate using e-mail and web pages. "Haven't these people ever heard of . . . *fax?* Didn't anyone ever tell them about . . . *the telephone?*" For people like this, who fail to see the shortcomings of the old technologies, there's probably little point in trying to explain new communications models like the Intranet.

There's also something to be said for a laissez-faire attitude. After all, you shouldn't have to force people to use web publishing tools, any more than you have to force them to use desktop publishing. People already use desktop publishing as a matter of convenience, to help rapidly develop the standard written communications required in every job. They should use web publishing the same way, but also for its added benefit of allowing document distribution without the hassle of printing and distributing paper documents. When people see the benefits of the Intranet fairly presented—that it can speed up their communications and take the drudgery out of distribution, it should be sufficient to turn them on. But that doesn't mean it necessarily will.

## Budgeting the Web

As I continue writing this chapter, I keep hearing the subliminal murmurs from all you bottom-line managers out there: "Yeah, sure. So how much will it cost?" A few more paragraphs go by, and again I hear that insistent muttering in the background: "Yeah, yeah. So what's it going to cost me?"

Naturally, any time you adopt new methods and tools, there are going to be new costs. But change is now a constant in the business world, and the cost of change is always with us. Changing tools to keep up with the technology curve is good business, because it increases productivity, which lowers costs. If new tools don't do this for us, we should reject them.

The costs of developing new web systems will show up in two main areas: the cost of retooling and the learning curve. Let's look at these one at a time.

### The Cost of Retooling

The cost of new tools arises mainly from the fact that everyone in your company will now have to be equipped with a web browser to use the Intranet. Many companies with Intranets are buying site licenses for Netscape Navigator, which run well below the $49 per seat normally quoted as the purchase price. Nortel, for instance, spent several hundred thousand dollars to purchase a company-wide site license. As new versions of Netscape arise, they will likely keep paying to upgrade. Obviously, the hundreds of thousands Nortel spent is no small change, but the net cost per employee is tiny compared to the cost for most other types of software.

If you don't want to spend money on a tool like Netscape, there are shareware and freeware options that may be less expensive. For instance, Microsoft is distributing free over the Internet its excellent Internet Explorer software for Windows, which is based on the Enhanced Mosaic product developed by Spyglass under license from the NCSA. In the near future, Microsoft plans to include the Internet Explorer as a standard part of its Windows software, and most other popular desktop operating systems for UNIX and Mac will probably include comparable tools. When that happens, it will be interesting to see how many companies continue to shell out money for Netscape and how many just take advantage of the free browsers built into their desktop systems. It's likely that Netscape will continue to be the most advanced browser in the pack, but there's a related question: How long can Netscape keep adding features before the browser itself becomes overly complicated and hard-to-use?

Besides the cost of browsers, there will also be a cost for new servers and authoring tools. Naturally, the number of servers required to support a web might be quite low—in the dozens, depending on your company size—but the costs of each server may be anywhere from $500 to $1,500. Again, this is not major investment money for any sizable company. Still, if cost is a consideration, you may find shareware and freeware servers on the Internet that cost less than the standard commercial server products.

On the authoring side, there's an opportunity to save money by making sure that people aren't retooling unnecessarily. This is one area where a good set of standards, templates, and workflow models can save people from retooling, by making sure that web content can be generated from standard office documents, and by making sure that only a few specialists will be needed to handle the technical requirements of HTML coding or CGI programming.

As part of the cost of retooling, consider the efforts required to roll out the new tools. As part of its push to standardize the entire company on a single browser, Nortel developed standard toolset configurations for its Mac, PC, and UNIX platforms, then enlisted the help of its marketing and PR department in spreading the word among internal employees. To save time, confusion, and support costs, the Netscape software was configured in such a way that—upon installation—it automatically referenced the proper proxy servers for Internet access and also opened automatically to the standard internal home page that centralized access to all the top-level resources, as well as most lower-level servers.

### The Learning Curve

The main cost of retraining should be in the areas of:

◆ Introducing rank-and-file employees to the web and the web browser tool

◆ Showing key development groups how to set up and maintain servers

◆ Training in web publishing techniques, where required.

The steepness of the learning curve—and the training costs involved—will be directly related to how sophisticated your Intranet is and how well you were able to avoid certain key stumbling blocks. For instance, the web browser itself requires practically no training, since all you have to do is point and click. Extra training may be required, however, in the concept and benefits of a web—why it works the way it does and why it is better than some of the old tools used for publishing and data delivery.

If the web includes newsgroup-style discussion threads, your training may need to include the newsreader features of the browser. If it includes Internet integration, your training may need to expand to include Internet concepts in general and a tour of key WWW sites and directory services.

More training will be needed on the authoring and development side for key groups of content providers. If your organization already uses style guides and templates for document publishing, or if you plan to use them, there may be very little training required, since most people can continue using their standard publishing tools. The training burden will increase as you move away from that ideal to the idea of people learning new WYSIWYG editing tools or even raw HTML coding.

## Software Licensing and Support Issues

A key point to remember, of course, is that many of the tools you may need to build or maintain an internal web are available over the Internet as freeware or shareware. When using these types of tools obtained from the Internet, it's important to understand the difference between the various types of software licensing options, as well as the quality and support issues involved. First a definition:

◆ *Freeware* is just that: programs offered for free in the public domain without licensing restrictions.

◆ *Shareware* is trademarked and copyrighted software that is initially offered for free during an evaluation period but that requires a registration or licensing fee if used in an ongoing basis.

Freeware often includes programs created by universities or nonprofit organizations that may be offered for free to other similar institutions but that may not be free to commercial for-profit organizations. For instance, the original NCSA Mosaic product was issued with such stipulations. However, the freeware category includes sophisticated commercial products offered by highly respected software vendors, including Microsoft's Internet Explorer, Internet Assistant, and Word Viewer products, or Adobe Corporation's Acrobat Reader product. Often the big software vendors offer freeware as an extension to their regular line of products. For example, Word Viewer makes Microsoft Word files available to a wider audience by allowing anyone to view Word files online. Similarly, Acrobat Reader allows anyone to view PDF files created using Acrobat Exchange or Acrobat Distiller.

Shareware includes programs offered by individual programmers, small programming shops, small companies, or even respected commercial vendors. Many software developers turn to shareware as a method for distributing software because, although it increases the risk of piracy or abuse, it also lowers marketing costs to almost nil. Increasingly, companies are offering beta versions of their products over the Internet as shareware or evaluation versions that have built-in time limits.

Netscape, for instance, regularly offers the latest beta version of its Navigator browser for free downloading over the Internet, but builds in a time lock that disables the program after a certain date. Commercial versions without a time lock can be purchased from Netscape on a per-copy basis, or as a site license. Most of the other popular web tools are offered for downloading from the WWW on a free-trial basis for a limited period of time.

Freeware and shareware often suffer from the perception that they are inferior products simply because they are inexpensive or easily obtained. While this may be true for certain isolated products, this is not necessarily true as a rule of thumb. If there is any inferior aspect to freeware and shareware, it is the fact that they often tend to be unsupported products, in the sense that you are not likely to receive human assistance in case you have trouble. Increasingly, the only support offered are documentation and troubleshooting tips, lists of frequently asked questions, and the occasional product-related newsgroup where you can ask other users questions, or e-mail support where you can mail in questions and receive mailed answers.

If you plan to offer shareware or even freeware as standard equipment to users on your network, you should consider both the licensing and support issues involved. Licensing is especially important in a commercial environment because you may expose your company to liability if you fail to live up to the terms of the licensing agreement and fail to pay the registration fees associated with a product.

Always read and be prepared to comply with the fine print in the README files that come with the product before authorizing it for widespread use on your network. A careful virus scan on the original copy of the product is also a good idea. You should adopt freeware and shareware only with eyes wide open to the potential support issues involved. If documentation and technical support are *not* offered with the product, these are things that your organization may have to provide to users that may add to your cost. In that sense, shareware may not always be the deal it is cracked up to be, and it may actually be cheaper overall to invest in a more expensive commercial product that *does* offer actual support and documentation.

## Where Do We Go from Here?

This concludes the main body of the book, and the survey of the tools, technologies, and techniques used in developing and building an Intranet. I hope you are able to put these all to good use within the context of your own organization, to bring a new level of immediacy and functionality to your networked environment, and to improve communications across your organization.

Several appendices included in the back of the book will help you cope with additional issues. In particular, there is a summary of some of the more interesting tools available for use on the Intranet, a procedure for adding security measures to your site, a quick reference guide to HTML, and a glossary. Good luck in your web-building chores, and watch for future editions of this book that will track the ongoing development of new technologies within the Intranet environment.

For information on seminars or training materials for The Corporate Intranet, see the Wordmark Associates home page at http://www.wordmark.com/.

# HTML Quick Reference

WYSIWYG editors like Netscape's Navigator Gold and Microsoft's FrontPage Editor are making it easier to create web documents without coding raw HTML. Yet there may still be times when you want to inspect an HTML document, construct one from scratch, or fiddle with one.

This appendix provides an easy-to-use reference to the most commonly used tags in HTML. This list is not meant to be all-inclusive, since many HTML tags attributes are quite obscure, some are more trouble than they're worth, and other new ones are being dreamed up every day. Rather than confuse you with mind-numbing detail, I want to provide the most useful tags in an easily referenced format, then point you to places where you can go for more detail or more comprehensive lists.

Please notice that all of these tags are optional, in the sense that you can potentially leave any of them out of the document without causing irreparable harm. A lot depends on the individual browser being employed by the user. Some browsers are more persnickety about what kind of coding errors they will forgive, and the buggier the browser the more chance for problems.

What's truly important when coding HTML is to avoid incomplete tagging (such as an <H1> without a corresponding </H1>) or random characters that may be misinterpreted—especially an open angle bracket (<) that doesn't have a corresponding close bracket (>) and that doesn't enclose valid HTML code. Also watch for missed closing quotation marks, such as:

```
<A HREF="file.html>
```

HTML interpretation may vary from browser to browser. However, most browsers are quite forgiving, and will simply ignore any unrecognized or misspelled tags inside open/closed angle brackets. Tags can be spelled in upper- or lowercase—though uppercase tags are easier to spot when you're visually scanning a file. The general rule of thumb is this: Never use a tag in a way it wasn't designed to be used. You may be able to fool your own browser into setting up the fonts or table layouts a certain way, but other browsers may interpret your unusual tagging sequence quite differently.

Another common rule is to avoid randomly overlapping tags such as:

```
<CENTER><A HREF="file.htm"><H1>Text</CENTER></A></H1>
```

Instead, try to nest your tags more symmetrically:

```
<CENTER>
<H1><A HREF="file.htm">Text</A></H1>
</CENTER>
```

Be careful about spacing when coding lists and hyperlinks. The angle brackets should be snug against the accompanying text. For instance, if you code a hyperlink with an extra space before the closing tag, such as:

```
Click <A HREF="file.html">here </A>for more.
```

you may get an underlined hyperlink with an unsightly hanging shirttail, such as this:

```
Click here for more.
```

Finally, remember that web browsers will ignore any carriage returns and extra spacing you include in your documents, except on lines that are preceded by the <PRE> tag and ended with </PRE>, such as:

```
<PRE>
Spacing    and      carriage
returns    are      both
honored    here     .
</PRE>
```

Outside a <PRE> area, all carriage returns are treated as extra spaces, and all extra spaces after the first one that occur between words or tags are ignored. This means you can arrange the tagging and text in just about any visual format that makes it easier for you to visually scan. Everything will be wrapped and interpreted correctly in the final document. Of course, some experimentation may be required, and rigorous inspection of the result is always a good idea.

The rest of this appendix contains the HTML tag quick reference. Tags are arranged in major categories by function, for easier reference. For each type of tag, I show the format and provide a short description. Multiple equivalent options are separated by vertical bars, such as left | right | center.

---

**Want More Information?**

If this HTML sampler is not filling, you can find much larger feasts on the World Wide Web. The W3 Consortium maintains complete HTML specifications at http://www.w3.org/pub/WWW/MarkUp/. In particular, look for both the HTML 2.0 and HTML 3.0 spec. For Netscape-specific HTML extensions, see http://home.netscape.com/assist/net_sites/index.html. As of this writing, the HTML 3.0 spec had expired, but is likely to still be used as a model for future HTML enhancements. When in doubt, always test the feature in your Intranet's supported browsers.

---

## Document Structure

```
<HTML>
<HEAD>Header Components</HEAD>
<BODY>Body of Document</BODY>
</HTML>
```

These tags delineate major sections of the document, including the beginning/end, header area, and body area.

## Header Components

### Title

```
<TITLE>Document Title</TITLE>
```

Defines the title to appear on top level of the browser window.

### Base URL

```
<BASE HREF="url">
```

The document base URL, if you want to set the base URL to something other than the default used to reference this document. All subsequent partial A HREFs in this document will be relative to the BASE HREF.

### Search Field

```
<ISINDEX HREF="URL" PROMPT="user_prompt">
```

Inserts a keyword search field automatically at the top of the document. Also can specify the server-side resource to use the results of the search field, and the prompt that the user sees. Often used in server-generated documents. Not sufficient on its own to cause a search. More often, you will see search fields treated as a simple INPUT field inside a form (see *Forms* later in this appendix).

### Descriptive Meta-Fields

```
<META NAME=Field_Label CONTENT="Field Contents"> or
<META HTTP-EQUIV=Identifier CONTENT="Information">
```

Defines additional fields (metadata) used to describe document contents or properties that can be used by other applications for document indexing, reference, or retrieval. For instance:

```
<META NAME=Author CONTENT="John Smith">
```

indicates that the author of the document is John Smith.

## Background and Foreground Colors

The BODY tag can occur only once at the beginning of the document. However, several extensions to the BODY tag are available that control the appearance of background and foreground elements in the document. These can be used in any combination, but all must be included inside the BODY tag.

### Background Pattern

```
<BODY BACKGROUND="file.gif">
```

Specifies the file containing the pattern to be tiled in the background. *HTML 3.0 and Netscape.*

### Background Color

```
<BODY BGCOLOR="#rrggbb">
```

Specifies a red-green-blue (RGB) value to be used as solid background color. RGB numbers are expressed as hexadecimal values. ***Netscape.***

### Body Text Color

```
<BODY TEXT="#rrggbb">
```

Specifies a RGB value to be used as text color. RGB numbers must be expressed as hexadecimal values. ***Netscape.***

### Link Colors

```
<BODY LINK="#rrggbb" ALINK="#rrggbb" VLINK="#rrggbb">
```

Specifies a set of RGB values to be used as the color for regular links, the currently active link (ALINK), and any previously visited links (VLINK). RGB numbers must be expressed as hexadecimal values. ***Netscape.***

## Headings and Body Text

### Headings 1 Through 6

```
<H#>Heading Text</H#>
<H# ALIGN=left|right|center|justify">Heading Text</H#>
<H# NOWRAP>Heading Text</H#>
```

Specifies up to six levels of headings, where # indicates heading level (1, 2, 3, etc.). Optionally you may include alignment or suppress automatic word wrap. Opening and closing tags must have same number (<H1>, </H1>).

### Paragraph Break

```
<P>
<P ALIGN=left|right|center|justify>
<P NOWRAP>
```

Inserts a paragraph break in body or heading text. Optionally, you can specify paragraph alignment and suppress line wrapping.

### Line Break

```
<BR>
```

Inserts a line break in body or heading text.

**Suppress Word Wrap**

```
<NOBR>text to keep together</NOBR>
```

Protects enclosed text from arbitrary line breaks. ***HTML 3.0 and Netscape.***

# Lists

**Unordered List (Bullets)**

```
<UL>
<LI>First item
<LI>Second item
<LI>etc.
</UL>
```

Defines a bulleted list. Each list item must be preceded by <LI>, which starts a new line with bullet inserted automatically. Nesting allows for multiple levels in a bullet list. Netscape provides an additional TYPE attribute that changes the shape of the bullet (TYPE=disc | circle | square). TYPE can be used inside <LI> to change bullet type in midstream.

**Ordered List (Steps, Outline)**

```
<OL>
<LI>First item
<LI>Second item
<LI>etc.
</OL>
```

Defines a numbered list. Each list item must be preceded by <LI>. Each <LI> starts a new line with next sequence number automatically inserted. Nesting allows for multiple levels in numbered list (1., 2., 3., a., b., c., etc.). In HTML 3.0, the opening OL tag may include attributes:

<OL CONTINUE>          Continue numbering where previous list stopped.

<OL SEQNUM=number>     Start numbering at specified *number.*

Netscape provides an additional TYPE attribute that lets you specify the type of numbering by example (TYPE=A | a | I | i | 1) and a START extension that lets you specify the actual starting character for the first number in the list (START=E | e | V | v | 5). TYPE can be used inside <LI>

to change numbering type in midstream, and VALUE can be used to set the number.

### Definition List

```
<DL>
<DT>Term<DL>Definition
<DT>Term<DL>Definition
</DL>
```

Creates a glossary-like definition list with terms (DT) and associated definitions (DD). The definitions are typically indented below the terms.

## Miscellaneous Layout Elements

### Horizontal Rules

```
<HR>
<HR SRC="URL">
```

Inserts a horizontal divider into the text with a paragraph break before and after. The second option uses an actual image in place of the default rule. ***HTML 3.0 only.***

```
<HR SIZE=pixels WIDTH=pixels|percent ALIGN=left|right|center NOSHADE>
```

This format diagram shows the special Netscape extensions that allow you to specify thickness, width, and alignment. Horizontal rules thicker than 1 pixel are giving an embossed look unless you specify NOSHADE. ***Netscape only.***

### Preformatted Text

```
<PRE>
Text with preserved spacing and line breaks.
</PRE>
```

Delimits an area of the document where the browser should honor carriage returns and spacing between words. Normally, extra spaces are discarded and carriage returns are treated as extra spaces. Preformatted treatment is useful especially where text is aligned in columns without benefit of table formatting, or where the exact layout of a text area should be preserved.

### Notes

```
<NOTE SRC="URL" CLASS=NOTE|CAUTION|WARNING>
Text of note.
</NOTE>
```

Treats a section of text as a note box, caution box, or warning. Optional SRC attribute inserts an image or icon to appear before the note.

### Footnote

```
<A HREF="#fn1">referenced text in main body</A>
<FN ID=fn1>footnote text</FN>
```

Hyperlinks a section of text to a footnote. Depending on the browser, the footnote text might be displayed in a pop-up window that appears when the user clicks the referenced text. The reference must be to a variable footnote ID, and must be preceded by a # sign.

### Block Quote

```
<BQ>
Text of quotation.
</BQ>

<BLOCKQUOTE>
Text of quotation.
</BLOCKQUOTE>
```

Marks an extended passage that must be treated as a quotation, such as by indenting left and right. Treatment depends on browser. HTML versions prior to 3.0 support only the full tag spelling: BLOCKQUOTE.

### Address

```
<ADDRESS>Text of address.</ADDRESS>
```

Marks a group of words intended as an address, signature, or author's name, typically placed at the bottom or top of the page. May get special font treatment, depending on browser.

## Hyperlinks

### Go To URL/File/Bookmark

```
<A HREF="URL|file|#bookmark">hyperlinked text</A>
```

Creates a hyperlink to a specific URL, file, and/or bookmark within a document. Any bookmark name must be preceded by # sign and must link to a defined bookmark name (below).

### Bookmark

`<A NAME="bookmark_name">bookmarked text</A>`

Defines a bookmark for hyperlinking to a specific location in a document. In HTML 3.0, you can use the ID attribute to include a bookmark name inside of any tag, such as:

`<H1 ID=bookmark_name>`

## Images

### Regular Images

`<IMG SRC="URL" ALT="alternate text" ALIGN=top|middle|bottom>`

Inserts an inline image stored in the specified *URL*. The SRC tag is required. Optionally you may specify alternate text to be displayed in case the image fails to display properly. Alignment can be top, middle, or bottom in relation to text baseline.

```
<IMG SRC="URL" ALT="alternate text" WIDTH=pixels HEIGHT=pixels
ALIGN=top|middle|bottom|left|right>
```

HTML 3.0 adds the ability to float the image at the left or right of the text column and wrap text around it (ALIGN=left|right). HTML 3.0 and Netscape both allow you to specify image size in pixels (HEIGHT=*pixels* WIDTH=*pixels*) for faster loading and on-the-fly autorescaling.

```
<IMG SRC="URL" ALT="alternate text"
WIDTH=pixels HEIGHT=pixels ALIGN=top|middle|bottom|
left|right|texttop|absmiddle|absbottom|baseline
BORDER=pixels VSPACE=pixels HSPACE=pixels>
```

Netscape adds the extra alignment options *texttop* (align with top of highest text in current line), *absmiddle* (align with middle of current line), *baseline* (align bottom with current baseline), and *absbottom* (align with bottom of text on current line). You can also specify the width of the border in pixels (including BORDER=0). Finally, you can specify extra space around the image in the horizontal (HSPACE) or vertical (VSPACE) direction.

### Imagemaps

```
<A HREF="mapfile_URL">
<IMG SRC="URL" ISMAP>
</A>
```

Same as regular images, except IMG tag must include additional attribute ISMAP. Entire IMG tag is wrapped inside a hyperlink that points to the imagemap coordinates file. All attribute extensions for alignment, borders, spacing, and size in HTML 3.0 and Netscape apply the same way here.

### Client-Side Imagemaps

Netscape supports a way of setting up imagemap coordinates directly inside the HTML document. This avoids the use of separate imagemap coordinate files and makes the imagemap connections to server files more efficient. For full details, see http://home.netscape.com/assist/net_sites/html_extensions_3.html.

### Captioned Figures

```
<FIG SRC="URL" WIDTH=pixels HEIGHT=pixels
ALIGN=right|left|bleedright|bleedleft|center|justify>
<CAPTION ALIGN=bottom|top|left|right>Caption text</CAPTION>
<CREDIT>Credit text</CREDIT>
</FIG>
```

Defines a figure with optional associated caption and credit. SRC is required to show image. ALIGN attribute is optional and may specify "bleeds" (start at left or right edge of window). WIDTH/HEIGHT options work the same as in IMG tag. Caption is aligned relative to figure.

## Tables

### HTML 3.0 Tables

```
<TABLE BORDER NOFLOW WIDTH="spec"
ALIGN=right|left|bleedright|bleedleft|center|justify COLSPEC="specs"
UNITS=en|relative|pixels DP="symbol">
   <CAPTION>Table caption text</CAPTION>
```

```
<TR><TH>Header text cell1<TH>Header text cell2<TH>...
<TR><TD>Body text r1c1<TD>Body text r1c2<TD> ...
<TR><TD>Body text r2c1<TD>Body text r2c2<TD> ...
    .
    .
    .
</TABLE>
```

Defines a table with optional borders, alignment, column specifications, caption, and content. BORDER causes borders to appear around all cells. NOFLOW disables text flow around the table. WIDTH specification is in units specified by the UNITS attribute. Each table row begins with <TR>. Cell types are indicated by <TH> for header and <TD> for body (data). Header cells are centered by default; data cells are flush left. These can be changed by inserting an ALIGN attribute into the tag at the row level (inside TR) or at the cell level (inside TH or TD). Cell alignment options are left|right|center|justify|decimal with any special decimal alignment symbol specified using DP. Vertical alignment in a cell can be specified using

```
VALIGN=top|middle|bottom|baseline
```

Column or row spanning is done with the COLSPEC or ROWSPAN attribute (for instance, COLSPEC=2 causes the cell to span two columns). Default column sizing and alignment can be overridden using the COLSPEC and UNITS attributes inside the TABLE tag. For instance:

```
<TABLE COLSPEC="L10 C60 C30" UNITS=relative>
```

indicates that the first column should be left-justified and the next two columns centered, with relative size of 10, 60, and 30—so that, for instance, the center column takes up 60 percent of the available horizontal space. Decimal alignment is also allowed by using D and specifying a separate DP attribute to define the alignment character (such as DP="."). ***HTML 3.0 only.***

**Netscape Tables**

Table tagging in Netscape is quite similar to the HTML 3.0 specification, except that Netscape uses closing tags on cells. For instance, table header cells begin with <TH> and end with </TH>. Netscape provides other extensions that allow you control cell spacing, padding, border thickness, and more. See http://home.netscape.com/assist/net_sites/tables.html.

## Fill-Out Forms

### General Layout

```
<FORM METHOD=POST|GET ACTION="URL">
Content of form.
</FORM>
```

Defines a section of the current document to be treated as a form, with input fields, pushbuttons, and other widgets that users can employ to enter data or select options, then submit to the server for processing. METHOD controls the format that will be used to ship form results from the browser to the server (GET is default, but normal method is POST). The ACTION specifies the server-side program that will process the results of the form. All other fields below fit inside the form (that is, between the opening and closing form tags). Form submission returns the NAME and VALUE of each field to the server when the user clicks the Submit button.

### Single-Line Text Field

```
<INPUT
NAME="field_ID"
SIZE="width_in_characters"
MAXLENGTH="max_no_characters_allowed"
VALUE="default_value">
```

Inserts a single-line text field of a defined size with optional maximum length and optional preinserted value that the user can change.

### Password Field

```
<INPUT TYPE=PASSWORD
NAME="field_ID"
SIZE="width_in_characters"
MAXLENGTH="max_no_characters_allowed"
VALUE="default_value">
```

Same as single-line text field, except that user entry is hidden so that others cannot see it on the screen.

### Integer Field

```
<INPUT TYPE=INT
NAME="field_ID"
SIZE="width_in_characters"
```

```
MAXLENGTH="max_no_characters_allowed"
VALUE="default_value">
```

Same as single-line text field, except that entered value must be a whole number.

### Hidden Field

```
<INPUT TYPE=HIDDEN
NAME="field_ID"
VALUE="field_value">
```

Inserts a hidden field that is not visible on the form, but that is sent to the server as part of the form result. For instance, you could use these fields to tell a server-side CGI program which database source and table to update with the form results. However, these fields will have no effect unless the server-side application is already programmed to recognize them. Normally included directly after the opening FORM tag.

### Check Box

```
<INPUT NAME="field_ID" TYPE=CHECKBOX
CHECKED> Text of option
```

Inserts a check box that can be turned on or off. External text shows the user what is being selected. CHECKED attribute causes the check box to appear as checked initially.

### Radio Buttons

```
<INPUT TYPE=RADIO NAME="field_ID">Text of option 1
<INPUT TYPE=RADIO NAME="field_ID">Text of option 2
(etc.)
```

Inserts a series of radio buttons that can be turned on or off, and that are mutually exclusive (only one can be on at a time). All buttons should have the same NAME. If you want one to be turned on by default, indicate using CHECKED attribute. External text shows the user what is being selected at each button position.

### Range Field

```
<INPUT TYPE=RANGE
NAME="field_ID"
MIN=min_value
MAX=max_value
VALUE=initial_value>
```

Inserts a slider (or other widget depending on browser) that can be set between a specified minimum and maximum value. Slider can be positioned initially at a specific value (default is middle of range). ***HTML 3.0 only.***

### Scrollable Text Area (Comment Box)

```
<TEXTAREA NAME="field_ID" ROWS=## COLS=##>
Optional text to be initially displayed in area.
</TE A>
```

Inserts an open text field of variable width and height, with a scroll bar in some cases. COLS defines width in characters. ROWS defines number of visible text rows.

### Pull-Down Menu

```
<SELECT NAME="field_ID">
   <OPTION>Text of option 1
   <OPTION>Text of option 2
   <OPTION>Text of option 3
   (etc.)
</SELECT>
```

Inserts a pull-down or pop-up menu that contains multiple options. Only one option may be selected, unless you include the MULTIPLE attribute. Normally the first option is selected by default, unless you include SELECTED as an attribute in the OPTION tag.

### Submit Button

```
<INPUT TYPE=SUBMIT
VALUE="Button Label"
SRC="URL">
```

Inserts a Submit button that is used to submit the content of the form to the server. Button label and SRC image are optional. Default button label is "Submit."

### Reset Button

```
<INPUT TYPE=RESET
VALUE="Button Label"
SRC="URL">
```

Inserts a Reset button that is used to reset the form to its original values (for instance, if the user wants to start over). Button label and SRC image are optional. Default button label is "Reset."

# Mathematical Equations

`<MATH>expression</MATH>`

Inserts a mathematical expression into text. Supports a full range of math expressions. For a complete discussion, see the HTML 3.0 specification at http://w3.org/.

# Character Formatting

### Boldface
`<B>bold text</B>`

Defines beginning and ending of boldfaced text.

### Italics
`<I>italicized text</I>`

Defines beginning and ending of italicized text.

### Underline
`<U>underlined text</U>`

Defines beginning and ending of underlined text. Not available in some browsers.

### Monospaced font
`<CODE>monospaced text</CODE>`

Defines beginning and ending of text shown in monospaced font, such as computer code.

`<TT>monospaced text</TT>`

Defines beginning and ending of text shown in monospaced font, such as computer code.

### Emphasis
`<EM>emphasized text</EM>`

Defines beginning and ending of emphasized text (usually italics, depending on user preference).

```
<STRONG>emphasized text</STRONG>
```

Defines beginning and ending of strongly emphasized text (usually rendered in bold, depending on user preference).

### Strikethrough

```
<S>deleted text</S>
```

Defines beginning and ending of text with strikethrough line. *HTML 3.0 only.*

### Citation

```
<CITE>citation text</CITE>
```

Defines beginning and ending of a citation (usually rendered in italics, depending on user preference).

### Literal Characters

```
<SAMP>literal characters</SAMP>
```

Defines beginning and ending of a string of literal characters.

### Keyboard Response

```
<KBD>keyboard response</KBD>
```

Defines beginning and ending of the text of a keyboard response, such as in a computer manual.

### Variable Text

```
<VAR>variable name</VAR>
```

Defines beginning and ending of a variable name in the text.

### Super/Subscript

```
<SUB>subscript text</SUB>
```

Defines beginning and ending of subscript text. *HTML 3.0 only.*

```
<SUP>superscript text</SUP>
```

Defines beginning and ending of superscript text. *HTML 3.0 only.*

## Special Characters

The official HTML specifications on the WWW include many codes for special characters, such as *&eacute;* to produce the character é, and &169; to produce the copyright symbol (©). In fact, most of these special symbols aren't even supported by popular browsers like Netscape Navigator.

Netscape recognizes and renders practically any special character you can type into a plain text file using the standard Latin-1 character set, including a standalone "less-than" sign (<), which would normally herald the beginning of an HTML coding sequence. The main exception is if you want HTML code to actually show up on a web page. Instead of typing in the HTML code literally, you will have to use &lt; and &gt; in place of the normal angle brackets. Thus, for something like:

```
<H1>A Major Heading<H1>
```

to appear literally on the web page, it would have to be coded into your HTML document as:

```
&lt;H1&gt;A Major Heading&lt;H1&gt;
```

### Infinite Flexbility with Style Sheets

If you think you ever might want to create your own HTML style, the newest versions of HTML will offer infinite flexibility through the use of user-defined style sheets. Check out the technical paper on style sheets at:

http://www.w3.org/pub/WWW/TR/WD-style.html

Keep an eye on this topic, because this is destined to become a hot new issue in future web publishing systems based on HTML 3.0 and later versions of the HTML specification.

All other characters can be typed in literally. Your main problem may be getting your word processor to provide you with a way to type these in (for instance, in MS Word 6.0, you would use the Insert/Symbol option).

Other browsers may not be so sophisticated, adroit, or forgiving as Netscape Navigator, however. If you ever think you might need to use the special set of HTML symbol codes, you can look them up in several places on the WWW, including the HTML 3.0 specification at http://w3.org.

# appendix b

# Cool Tools for the Intranet

Here's a summary of most of the web tools mentioned in this book, plus a few others thrown in for good measure, that should add pizzazz and productivity to any Intranet site. For regular updates to this list, see the Cool Tools site on the WWW at http://wordmark.com/.

## Authoring/Publishing

*Netscape Navigator Gold* by Netscape (http://home.netscape.com/) now lets you edit web content from directly inside the Netscape browser, in a completely WYSIWYG fashion.

*Microsoft Word Internet Assistant* by Microsoft (http://www.microsoft.com/). Free add-on extension to Word 6.0 lets you easily create documents and forms, then just "save as" in HTML format. Real easy to do hyperlinks and forms. Problem with early versions is it will not let you use document management features of Word, like "master document" and automatic TOC and index generation.

*FrontPage Editor* by Microsoft (http://www.microsoft.com) allows completely WYSIWYG editing and includes a raft of templates and wizards to make page construction easier. Helpful "bots" do special jobs, like add the current date to each edited page.

*PageMill* by Adobe (http://www.adobe.com/) provides full WYSIWYG web editing on a Mac, very much like Navigator Gold and FrontPage Editor.

*Internet Studio* by Microsoft (http://www.microsoft.com) is that company's long-promised high-end web authoring, design, and management suite of tools. No sign of it at press time. Previously code-named *Blackbird.*

*Weblisher* by Digigami (http://www.digigami.com/Weblisher/) integrates with several Windows word processor programs including MS Word, Ami Pro,

Lotus WordPro, and WordPerfect. Impressive list of multimedia and HTML conversion features, including ability to select the level of HTML you prefer (1.0, 2.0, etc.).

*Webmaker* by CERN and Harlequin (http://www.harlequin.com/) converts FrameMaker files to HTML webs, automatically extracting and rebuilding graphics and tables in GIF formats and generating hyperlinked navigation buttons, headers/footers, TOCs, and indexes. Now available on both UNIX and PC platforms.

*Cyberleaf* by Interleaf (http://www.ileaf.com/ip.html) converts many of the most popular word processing and DTP formats to Web, including MS Word, WordPerfect, FrameMaker, Interleaf, and others.

*WebAuthor* by Quarterdeck (http://www.qdeck.com/qdeck/products/Web-Authr/) works with Word 6.0 but also includes an Author Manager and Image Manager for managing links to other documents or images. Recognizes nonstandard HTML tags. PC only.

*HTML Transit* by InfoAccess (http://www.infoaccess.com/) imports native formats of all major word processors and autogenerates documents, tables of contents, indexes, etc. Supports multiple versions of HTML. This is the kind of tool that should make it possible to generate webs without asking people to change their authoring tools. By the same people that gave us Guide Passport. PC only.

*InterNotes Web Publisher* by Lotus Development Corp. (http://www.lotus.com/inotes/) automates the process of publishing information to the World Wide Web by converting Lotus Notes documents into HTML. INWP uses Lotus Notes to coordinate and collect Web information from network sources, then translates the documents and views into a series of HTML pages.

*Collabra Share* by Collabra (http://www.collabra.com/) includes the ability to embed web links in the documents, so that someone using a document can hyperlink to other documents. Chosen by Netscape to provide the groupware component of its product suite.

*AnchorPage,* by Iconovex (http://www.iconovex.com) is a syntactical document analyzer and markup language inserter. Reads text documents, converts to HTML, and creates clickable index.

*CatMake* hypermedia catalog and presentation maker, from HyperAct, Inc. (http://www.hyperact.com/hyperact.html).

*Word Perfect Internet Publisher,* by Novell (http://www.novell.com/) works with WP 6.1, free add-on. WP IP Pro is $49, lets you use WP as a browser, WP 6.1 SGML edition $595 lets you edit HTML documents online.

*Internet with an Accent* by LanguageWare (http://www.accentsoft.com/) lets you publish and view multilingual e-mail messages and web pages.

*InContext Spider* by InContext Corporation (http://www.incontext.com/) provides an easy browsing and editing tool for web pages, with templates.

## Multimedia/Graphics

*StreamWorks* from Xing Technology Corp (http://www.xingtech.com), provides real-time streaming video and audio reproduction over a web system.

*RealAudio* from Progressive Networks (http://www.realaudio.com/) is a client-server application that lets you hear audio files in real time.

*VDOLive by* VDONet Corporation (http://www.vdolive.com/) is a streaming video application that provides up to 15 frames/sec of full-motion video over standard dialup connections. Server and viewing tools available. For NT or UNIX.

*LViewPro* distributed by MMedia Research (mmedia@world.std.com) is an image file editor for Windows. It loads/saves image files in many common formats, including JPEG and GIF. Also does transparent backgrounds.

*Image Alchemy* by Handmade Software Inc. (http://www.handmadesw.com/) converts over 70 image file formats and is available on all major platforms.

*Adobe Acrobat* by Adobe (http://www.adobe.com/) is a great way to preserve paper-based layout in an online environment for documents that require it, such as fill-in forms requiring a signature. Now available as a Netscape plug-in called Acrobat Amber.

*Shockwave* by Macromedia (http://www.macromedia.com/) is being integrated into Netscape Navigator as a standard plug-in device that lets you view multimedia created using Macromedia Director through the web browser.

*media.splash* by Powersoft (http://www.powersoft.com) is a low-cost object-based tool that helps you add animation and interactivity to a web site with no programming.

*WebAnimator* by DeltaPoint (http://www.deltapoint.com/) is an animation tool for web sites that works on the Mac and PC.

*SmartSketch Animator* by FutureWave (http://www.futurewave.com/) is a similar animation tool that works on the same platforms.

*Insoft* products by nSoft Inc. (http://www.insoft.com/) include CoolTalk and CoolView, which use networks to carry phone service and video conferencing, respectively.

*CU-SeeMe* by White Pine Software (http://www.wpine.com/) provides video-conferencing over the Internet or any TCP/IP network, including white-board for document collaboration.

## CGI/Gateways/Database Access

*Oracle Websystem* by Oracle Corporation (http://www.oracle.com/) includes a WebServer and PowerBrowser that integrate with Oracle 7 databases. Provides a powerful development environment for web applications. Oracle also offers a Universal Server combining the functions of a rela-tional database with web support, text management, messaging, and multi-media.

*Informix/Illustra* by Informix (http://www.informix.com/ and http://www.illustra.com) are recently merged examples of database engines that have been repositioned for the Intranet, merging the mission-critical transaction processing of Informix with Illustra's ability to handle documents, photos, web pages, geospatial data, sound, and video objects.

*Java* by Sun Microsystems (http://java.sun.com/) is a new-generation object-oriented programming language like C++ that is being touted as one of sev-eral replacements for CGI. Scripting tools like JavaScript promise to put Java functionality into the hands of nonprogrammers.

*web.sql* by Sybase (http://www.sybase.com/) helps make the connection between web servers and Sybase databases.

*Cold Fusion* by Allaire (http://www.allaire.com/cfusion) is software that links databases with web sites using CGI and OBDC gateways. Has drivers for SQL Server, Access, Excel, FoxPro, and many others.

*Htmlscript* by Volant (http://htmlscript.volant.com/) lets you do CGI-scripting using new HTML tags that support variables, operands, and IF statements. According to its creators, this new feature allows anyone to create interac-tive web sites. UNIX only (future NT).

*Web/Genera* is a software toolset that makes it easier to integrate Sybase databases into the WWW. It can be used to develop a web front-end to an existing Sybase database, or create a new one. The toolset lets you write a specification for the database and the desired appearance on the Web, then autogenerate SQL commands and formatting instructions that extract data and present them in HTML. Offered by Stan Letovsky through an NSF grant (see http://gdbdoc.gdb.org/letovsky/genera/genera.html).

*GSQL* is a gateway program offered through NSCA (http://www.ncsa.uiuc. edu/) that provides a web-based forms interface to SQL databases. GSQL creates forms based on commands found in proc files and creates an SQL query that can be used to access a database.

*Polyform* by Willow Glen Graphics (http://wgg.com/files/PolyForm/) is a simple CGI tool for Windows platform. All you do is provide a script name, output type, and return page filename, Polyform does the rest. Outputs to flat file and/or e-mail. Built-in SMTP mailer.

*WebSpin, WebScan,* and *WebForm* from W3.COM (http://w3.com) provide several CGI/interactive functions. WebSpin will generate HTML pages automatically from a flat file database. WebScan is a search engine for web sites that returns customized HTML pages of matched records. WebForm generates custom responses to standard HTML fill-out forms without CGI scripting. Results are automatically saved to a text file or mailed to users.

*MindWire,* by DCN, Inc. (http://www.durand.com) lets you create a dynamic multimedia online service offering simultaneous modem, network, and Internet connectivity options. It includes applications for e-mail, messaging, chat, and classified ads plus it also provides a development platform for third-party interactive applications including a database API.

*dbWeb* by Aspect (http://www.aspectse.com/) provides multiplatform access to databases on the Web or on a LAN via OBDC without HTML or CGI programming, although interface is exclusively through Windows NT servers like Website, EMWAC, and Purveyor. Provides full insert/update/delete capabilities as well as query-by-example record selection for dynamic SQL and stored procedures. $695 (evaluation available).

*Templar* by Premonos Corp (http://www.premenos.com) sits between e-mail and EDI apps and allows you to transfer electronic information over an Internet or Intranet.

*BestWeb* by Best-Seller Inc. (http://www.bestseller.com/) is an intelligent interface builder for connecting to dBAase, Access, Foxpro, Paradox, and other databases.

*Sapphire/Web* by Bluestone (http://www.bluestone.com/) provides a visual development tool for building web-based client-server apps that connect to Oracle, Sybase, or Informix.

*Topic Internet Server* by Verity (http://www.verity.com/) is a search engine that works in conjunction with web servers to locate information stored in a wide range of document types. Features enterprisewide search, full-text indexing, and scalability. Supports search queries through standard HTML forms and CGI interface. Available on UNIX or PC platforms.

*IBM CICS Gateway* by IBM (http://www.hursley.ibm.com/cics/saints/main. html) translates CICS 3270 data streams to HTML on the fly, giving instant access to mainframe data through a web browser interface.

## Servers/Site Administration

*Netscape Web Servers* by Netscape Communications (http://home.netscape. com/) comes in several flavors, including a regular Communications Server, a secure Commerce Server, a News Server, and a Proxy Server. UNIX or NT versions.

*Netscape Livewire* by Netscape Communications (http://home.netscape.com) is that company's full suite of site editing and management tools, including the Navigator Gold editor, a site manager, server extensions (NSAPI plug-ins), JavaScript, a relational database with SQL interface, and server "front panel."

*Microsoft Internet Server* by Microsoft (http://www.microsoft.com/) is a web server being bundled free with Windows NT.

*Website* by O'Reilly & Associates (http://website.ora.com/) is the commercial version of the original win-httpd server by Robert Denny; now runs on Windows NT platform.

*Webstar* by Quarterdeck (http://www.qdeck.com/) is the commercial version of the original MacHTTP server for Macintosh platforms.

*NaviPress/NaviServer* by Navisoft (http://www.navisoft.com) is a web client-server combination that simplifies the building and administration of sophisticated web sites. The NaviPress lets you browse and edit web sites remotely. NaviServer has its own built-in database (Illustra) that can be accessed and updated through simple HTML form commands. Supports online real-time user and group administration, automatic full-text search capability, page archiving and version control, and more. NaviSoft is a division of AOL. NT UNIX.

*FrontPage* by Microsoft (http://www.microsoft.com) provides an integrated authoring and serving environment like NaviSoft's that provides a server, site administrator, editor and server extensions.

*SiteMill* (http://www.adobe.com/) is Adobe's entry into the web site management market, with some of the same automatic web configuration and link-repairing features as competing tools like FrontPage and Livewire. For Mac.

*Purveyor* by Process Software Corp. (http://www.process.com) is a web server for Windows NT that includes a graphic user interface, sample home pages and forms, online support, report generators, and security features.

*IwareConnect* by Quarterdeck (http://www.quarterdeck.com/) turns a NetWare server into an Internet firewall and allows it to communicate Internet stuff to PCs without having a TCP/IP stack at each client. IWare InternetSuite (same site) is a set of products to run on clients to access Internet applications, without TCP/IP. The suite can interface to internal web hosts and other TCP/IP apps on an internal network.

*Worldgroup* by GALACTICOMM (http://www.gcomm.com/) is a web server apparently built atop a previous BBS product called Major BBS Version 6. As such, it allows access from web clients or non-web clients. Ads for the product in the likes of *BYTE* magazine position it as a way of doing workgroup applications through a web interface.

*Netware Web Server* by Novell Corporation (http://corp.novell.com/announce/webserve/) is a web server designed to run on top of Novell's popular Netware 4.1 network operating system.

*OpenMarket Web Server* by OpenMarket Corp. (http://www.openmarket.com) is a high-performance UNIX web server that is rated at 1,200 concurrent connections.

*EMWAC* by the European Microsoft Windows NT Academic Centre (EMWAC), at Edinburgh University (http://emwac.ed.ac.uk/) is a freeware web server for Windows NT. The commercial version of this software is now marketed as Purveyor.

*BASIS WEBserver* by Information Dimensions (http://www.idi.oclc.org). Built on the BASISplus document database engine. Full text retrieval with extended relational database management.

*InfoBase Web Server* by Folio (http://www.folio.com) lets you serve information on the Web, CD-ROM, or in-house network. Includes firewall software.

*BorderWare* firewall server by Border Network Technologies (http://www.border.com/) integrates packet filtering and gateway technology with application servers into a single highly secure self-contained system. Features *Network Address Translation* that finesses the difference between internal and external IP addresses. Runs on 486 or Pentium.

*DynaWeb* by Electronic Book Technologies (http://www.ebt.com) provides a way to produce and serve HTML output from EBT's SGML databases. The server uses a mapping file that specifies HTML-equivalent tags for their existing SGML document element types. Available initially as an add-on module to existing DynaText publishers.

*PLWeb* by Personal Library Software (http://www.pls.com) lets you do searches and retrievals from multiple distributed databases to a web. Supports many of the most advanced database retrieval/update features. A powerful tool for consolidating the information content from widely distributed data sources. UNIX only.

*SurfWatch* (http://www.surfwatch.com/) monitors and blocks access to sites on the Internet. Helps keep your employees from dabbling in forbidden newsgroups and other time-wasters.

*WebMapper* by NetCarta (http://www.netcarta.com/) checks links at a web site and creates a map of the site. PC and UNIX.

*BSDI Internet Server* by Berkeley Software Design (http://www.bsdi.com/) provides an all-in-one server that handles web, e-mail, FTP, news, and others. The BSDI Internet Gateway also provides the same features on Novell networks, even if network nodes are not TCP/IP enabled.

## Browsers (Web Clients)

*Netscape Navigator* by Netscape Communications (http://home.netscape.com/) is the most advanced and full-featured browser available. Supports not only the most advanced HTML features, but includes many of its own. Now supports plug-ins for other applications such as Acrobat, Java, etc.

*HotJava* by Sun Microsystems (http://java.sun.com) is a browser that can download special-purpose applets on the fly. Thus, instead of requiring a local helper application, the file being downloaded might include its own program code that self-executes as it downloads to the browser.

*Microsoft Internet Explorer* by Microsoft (http://www.microsoft.com/) is Microsoft's version of Enhanced Mosaic and Bill Gates's attempt at a Mozilla killer.

*Enhanced Mosaic* from Spyglass (http://www.spyglass.com/) is the technological scion of the original NCSA Mosaic and the source platform for many other web browsers including Microsoft Internet Explorer. Spyglass licenses the browser for resale by other companies, but you can use this site to find the other companies who sell or give away web browsers.

*Emissary* by Wollengong (http://www.twg.com/) incorporates advanced e-mail, Usenet, FTP, telnet, and WWW features into a single tool.

## Search Tools

*excite* by Architext Software (http://www.excite.com/navigate/) is a search engine that works under UNIX servers. Soon for Windows NT.

*Web Server Search* by Willow Glen Graphics (http://wgg.com/) is a CGI-based search engine for the PC platform that searches up to 100 directories and outputs a clickable list. Supports "and/or" queries; some security features.

*Webcompass* by Quarterdeck (http://www.quarterdeck.com/) is an agent-based search tool you can use to search multiple servers over a network.

*SrchD* by Microsoft (http://www.microsoft.com/) is a simple text search engine for Windows that does keyword searching of HTML directory trees.

*WAIS* is one of the oldest search engines available for web site indexing. Available in a free version (http://cnidr.org/) and a commercial version (http://wais.com/). UNIX only.

*Glimpse* is a freeware product (http://glimpse.cs.arizona.edu:1994/) that provides index and searching facilities for UNIX systems only.

*Harvest* (http://harvest.cs.colorado.edu/) is a set of tools that let you retrieve, organize, search, cache, and replicate information gathered from across an Internet or Intranet. Based on Glimpse.

*AppleSearch* by Apple (http://kamaaina.apple.com/) is a web-compatible search engine for use with web servers installed on the Mac platform.

# Glossary

**Anonymous FTP.** A way of connecting to an FTP server without a user ID and password. If an FTP server is set up for public use, you can log in with the user ID of *anonymous* and use your mail address as the password. People who log in this way are usually limited to a fixed set of public directories. Most web browsers can perform anonymous FTP automatically.

**API (application programming interface).** A set of routines or function calls that allow an application to control, or be controlled by, other applications.

**Applet.** A small program usually written in the Java programming language which is intended for delivery over a network to be interpreted on the fly at a Java-enabled client.

**Application.** Any computer program designed to accomplish a specific task or related set of tasks.

**Backbone.** The main trunkline of a network, which supports all the branches and subnetworks. Usually higher-speed than the other parts of the network, so that it can easily handle communications between all the outlying parts of the network.

**Back end.** Processes or applications that run behind the web server, from the point of view of the user or client. For example, a web server might use Oracle as a back-end database for serving data to users.

**Bandwidth.** The data transmission capacity of a network connection, usually expressed in kilobits per second (Kbps) or megabits per second (Mbps). For instance, the bandwidth of a typical consumer modem is about 14.4 Kbps. The Internet backbone, on the other hand, has a bandwidth of 45 Mbps. Data transfer volumes and speeds increase as the bandwidth increases.

**Browser.** See *web browser*.

**CERN.**   The European Particle Physics Laboratory in Geneva, Switzerland, where the original protocols for the World Wide Web were first developed and implemented.

**CGI (Common Gateway Interface).**   A standard communications interface that allows web servers to communicate with back-end processes, such as databases or other server-based applications.

**CGI script.**   A short, uncompiled computer program written using a scripting language (typically Perl) that handles the communication between web servers and other applications. For instance, when a user fills out an online form, a CGI script might be used to take the output from the form, extract the key data, and insert it into a database using SQL commands. Or the script might similarly be used to take a user-defined keyword, insert it into a SQL query, use the query to extract data from the database, wrap HTML markups around the data, and send it back to the user as a document containing the information the user requested.

**Client.**   The part of a client-server application that runs on the user's local machine and interacts with remote servers located on other parts of the network. For example, Netscape Navigator and Enhanced Mosaic are client programs designed to obtain data and files from remote web servers.

**Client-server.**   A way of designing computer applications that divides the work between two separate but linked applications. The client application typically runs on the user's local workstation, helps the user request data from the server, and displays the requested data appropriately on the user's screen. The server application typically runs on a remote computer located elsewhere on the network, handles requests from multiple clients, processes the data as requested, and returns the results to the client. See also *server* and *client*.

**Database.**   Any file or set of files containing data stored in an organized format.

**DBML (Database Markup Language).**   A language used to embed hidden database access commands inside of plain text documents, the same way HTML is used to embed hidden document publishing and hyperlinking commands inside of plain text documents.

**Directory.**   The term used in UNIX and PC environments to describe a location on a hard drive where files are stored. This is equivalent to the term *folder* in Mac and Windows 95 systems.

**Domain.**   A way of organizing the Internet, characterized by the suffix of the domain name. For example, *com* is the commercial domain which includes organizations like *microsoft.com* and *fedex.com,* whereas *edu* is the educational domain which includes entities such as *rutgers.edu* and *harvard.edu.* Other domains include *org* (nonprofit organizations), *mil* (U.S. military organizations), *gov* (U.S. government organizations), and *net* (network providers and service centers). Special geographical domain suffixes are provided for Internet services originated in countries outside the United States, such as *ca* for Canada, *fr* for France, or *de* for Germany.

**Domain name.** An easy-to-remember name that can be used to address a specific computer over the Internet. Typically, the domain name is associated with a specific IP address and can be used interchangeably with its assigned address. For example, if the domain name *abc.com* is assigned to the computer at network address 192.2.123.45, you can use either *abc.com* or 192.2.123.45 to address the computer. See also *host name* and *IP address.*

**Download.** To transfer a file from a host computer to your local computer. See also *upload.*

**Dumb terminal.** A type of computer display used with mainframe systems that has no computing power of its own. All the work is done by the mainframe computer. The dumb terminal displays data locally and captures the user's keyboard response.

**Environment.** A set of conditions or components that control the operating requirements of a computer system. For example, the "Mac environment" includes the operating system components, applications, utilities, and hardware components that are built into the Apple Macintosh computer system. See also *platform.*

**Ethernet.** A bus-based network technology used to connect computers. Ethernet networks traditionally used coax cable, though other cabling formats have been developed. The typical bandwidth of Ethernet is about 10 Mbps. A new technology called Fast Ethernet is 100 Mbps.

**External web.** A set of web servers installed on your Intranet or on the Internet that can display data and information for anyone who is *not* directly connected to your network.

**Firewall.** A control mechanism placed on a private network to prevent unauthorized entry from the public sphere.

**Folder.** A term used in Mac and Windows 95 environments to describe a location on a hard drive where files are stored. This is equivalent to the term *directory* or *subdirectory* in UNIX and PC systems.

**Form.**   A hypertext document containing various GUI-style fields and devices, including text boxes, pull-down menus, pushbuttons, radio buttons, and check boxes.

**Freeware.**   Software that is distributed free-of-charge, usually through the Internet or through more traditional computer bulletin boards.

**Front end.**   The client interface. In other words, the "front" side of a client-server application that directly communicates with the user. Compare *back end.*

**FTP (File Transfer Protocol).**   An Internet-based client-server application that lets you exchange files with other computers. You can log in to a remote FTP server and display lists of files, just the way you do it on your local computer. Then you can *get* files, transferring them from the host computer to your computer from your own computer. In some cases, you can also *put* files, transferring them from your computer to the host computer. The first web browsers included the ability to download files from FTP servers. See also *anonymous FTP.*

**Gateway.**   An interface between different types of networks or applications, which may control access to the network and automatically convert the data from one format or protocol to another.

**Gopher.**   An Internet-based client-server application that became popular several years before web technology hit its stride. You can use a gopher client to log onto a gopher server and view a plain-English menu of the information available there. The menu may include graphics icons, and lets users retrieve files at the click of a button.

**Groupware.**   Software that allows multiple users to work as a group on the same set of data or documents. Groupware often includes integrated e-mail and other group-oriented communication features.

**Helper application.**   A program used to play back special file types.

**Home page.**   The opening page or main menu of any web site. Normally, this page appears by default if you fail to request a specific file.

**Hostname.**   An easy-to-remember name that can be used to address a specific computer on an internal network. Typically, the hostname is associated with a specific IP address and can be used interchangeably with its assigned address. For example, if the hostname *hrweb* is assigned to the computer at network address 192.2.123.45, you can use either *hrweb* or 192.2.123.45 to address the computer. See also *domain name* and *IP address.*

**HTML (Hypertext Markup Language).** A standard way of marking up text so it can be displayed online in a web browser. HTML includes not only style tags for headings, bullet lists, and the like, but also provides ways of creating *hyperlinks,* online forms, multimedia, and embedded applications.

**HTTP (Hypertext Transfer Protocol).** The standard protocol used to communicate between web clients and web servers.

**Hyperlink.** A coded link in hypertext that causes new information to be retrieved.

**Hypertext.** Any text that contains links to other sources of information.

**Information center.** Any division, department, business unit, group, or individual in a company that has information to share with others. Also, the web service used to publish that information.

**Internet.** A global collection of private networks that are interconnected through public links.

**InterNIC.** The Virginia-based organization responsible for registering Internet IP addresses and domain names.

**Intranet.** A set of web servers installed on your internal network that can display data and documents for anyone who is directly connected to your network.

**IP address.** A string of numbers, such as 192.2.123.45, that identifies a specific computer on a network using the TCP/IP protocol. See also *TCP/IP* and *domain name.*

**IP filtering.** The ability to limit server access to certain IP addresses, or to exclude certain IP addresses from server access.

**ISDN (Integrated Services Digital Network).** A communication technology used to transmit relatively high-speed digital data over ordinary telephone lines. ISDN speeds range from 56 to 128 Kbps, depending on the number of channels used.

**Java.** A programming language created specifically for the web environment. As opposed to traditional programming languages like C, which must be compiled into versions that can only run on specific platforms, Java is designed to be delivered in an uncompiled format and "interpreted" at the web client end. This makes it completely platform independent. Compilers are also available as an option.

**JavaScript.** A scripting language that can be used by nonprogrammers to orchestrate and run Java applications.

**Kbps.**  Kilobits per second, a common unit of measure for bandwidth. For instance, 14.4 Kbps is the typical data transfer rate of most consumer modems. These modems transfer data at the rate of about 14,400 bits/second.

**Legacy data.**  Data stored on older computer systems or in older file or database formats that often remains behind as the *legacy* of out-dated technologies. Often, this data presents a formidable challenge to client-server developers because it is still useful, but not always easy to integrate into more current systems.

**Mainframe.**  A large computer typically kept in a separate room that serves as the core processing unit in most large corporations.

**Mbps.**  Megabits per second, a common unit of measure for data transfer rates.

**Modem** (modulator-demodulator).  A device used to transfer data between computers by converting the data stream into a burst of sound that can be transmitted over a phone line and then returned to its original state at the other end.

**Mosaic.**  The first full-featured windows-based graphical browser for web applications. Mosaic was originally developed (and is still available from) the National Center for Supercomputing Applications (NCSA). An enhanced version was developed by Spyglass Inc. under license to NCSA, and the enhanced Mosaic browser now provides the underlying technology for many other popular web browsers, including Microsoft Internet Explorer.

**NCSA.**  Usually refers to the National Center for Supercomputing Applications in Urbana, Illinois. Also refers to the National Computer Security Association.

**Network.**  A set of wires or wireless channels that connect computers and allow them to exchange data.

**ODBC (Open Database Connectivity).**  A method of communicating with databases through a "driver" interface that works on the same principle as a printer driver. This way, if you want an application to control a certain type of database, you select the ODBC driver for the database and the control mechanisms are handled automatically.

**Online publishing.**  Publishing information in such a way that it can be viewed online. Also see *web publishing*.

**PDF (Portable Document Format).**  A platform-independent file format used to deliver published documents online. PDF supports hyperlinking to other

PDF documents or to web URLs. PDF was developed by Adobe Corporation for use with its Acrobat line of products.

**Perl.**   A scripting language commonly used to program CGI scripts in early web systems.

**Platform.**   A specific combination of operating system and hardware that dictates the operating requirements of a computer application.

**Plug-in.**   A program designed to play back special file types directly inside the browser window.

**PPP (Point-to-Point Protocol).**   A communications protocol commonly used to connect computers across a serial line on a TCP/IP network.

**Protocol.**   A standard way of packaging and transmitting data across a network. There are many network protocols available that work with different types of hardware and computing systems. There are also many levels or layers of protocols that may operate simultaneously as part of the same network application.

**Provider.**   In Internet terminology, the person, group, or organization that provides information or services to end users. For example, a *content provider* is someone who provides formatted information or data to end users. A *service provider* is someone who provides network connectivity.

**Router.**   A hardware device used to route traffic through a network.

**Server.**   A term used in various ways to describe different aspects of network computing. From a hardware standpoint, it may refer to a specific hard drive or dedicated workstation that is used to store common data and applications shared by multiple users. From a software standpoint, it is typically the half of the client-server application that handles the processing and storage of data. A "web server" is the software that transfers files to web browsers on request, or the machine it is installed on. See also *client-server* and *web server.*

**Shareware.**   Software that is distributed free-of-charge for evaluation purposes, but which usually requires a registration fee after a trial period.

**SLIP (Serial Line Interface Protocol).**   A communications protocol used to connect computers across a serial line on a TCP/IP network.

**SMTP (Simple Mail Transfer Protocol).**   A common protocol for handling e-mail messages over TCP/IP networks.

**Streaming audio/video.**   A method of delivering multimedia data so that it can be read or played back in near real time, or as it soon as it is received.

**Subdirectory.**    A term used in UNIX and PC environments to describe a location on a hard drive where files are stored. This is equivalent to the term *folder* in Mac and Windows 95 systems.

**T1, T3.**    Network connections that range from 1.5 Mbps to 45 Mbps.

**TCP/IP.**    A dual-purpose network protocol that serves as the conveyor belt for Internet services. TCP is the Transmission Control Protocol which handles the packaging and sequencing of data. IP is the Internet Protocol which handles the addressing and routing of data to specific computers on a network.

**Upload.**    To transfer a file from your local computer to a host computer. See also *download*.

**URL (Universal Resource Locator).**    A string of information used to send a request to a web server. The most common URL format for web use is http:// server_name/path/filename.ext. However, a URL can also be used to send queries or data in the format http://server_name/cgi-bin/query_ string. URLs can also be used to communicate with other types of servers. For instance, to load a file from an FTP server, you could use the URL ftp://server_name/file.

**User authentication.**    The process of protecting a web site by requiring a user to enter an authorized ID and password before entering the site.

**WAIS (Wide Area Information Service).**    A client-server application used to provide quick searchable access to online databases. WAIS can operate on its own as a client-server application, but is often used as a search utility for web applications because some web clients support direct access to WAIS servers.

**Web.**    Any collection of online documents or forms that are hyperlinked to each other, especially through HTML and HTTP. The term "web" comes from the fact that the documents are connected through hyperlinks, forming a sort of weblike document network.

**Web browser (client).**    A software program designed to help users request information from web servers and display the information once it is returned. The term *browser* is a popular way to refer to a web client, since it lets users easily browse through large sets of information stored on any number of web servers worldwide.

**Web publishing.**    A form of publishing akin to desktop publishing, but where the finished document is displayed on the web instead of on paper.

**Web server.**    A software program designed to serve files and data to web clients (browsers) such as Netscape or Mosaic. Also may refer to the complete installation of server software, server content, and server hardware.

**Web site.**   A set of information accessed through a web server, which is available to any user with a web browser, no matter where they are located on a network. This is a generic term, and could apply to sites on an internal or external web. The term *WWW site* refers specifically to sites people access on the World Wide Web.

**Web system.**   A set of web servers and clients that are configured to work together as a system.

**World Wide Web (WWW).**   The worldwide public network of web sites available on the Internet.

**WYSIWYG (What You See Is What You Get).**   A common term used to describe the way information looks when it is finally published, usually applied to online displays that have a final published look. Compared to a non-WYSIWYG display, which might show embedded codes or a rough approximation of the final look, WYSIWYG looks *just like* the final document or display that the user will see.

**WYSIWYG web editor.**   An HTML editor such as Netscape Navigator Gold or the FrontPage Editor that lets you edit a web page inside a display that looks exactly like the final online document will look. Compare this to an ordinary HTML editor, which shows the text with embedded HTML codes. The WYSIWYG editor hides the codes completely from the author or editor, yet still includes them in the final HTML output file.

# User Authentication

## Introduction

User authentication is the feature of most web servers that allows you to restrict access to the site to certain users or from certain locations in the network. The best place to look for information on controlling access is in your server documentation. However, the following procedures are traditionally used for servers based on the NCSA/CERN model. Please note that the term *folder* is equivalent to the term *directory* in UNIX systems.

## Restricting Everything at a Site

Suppose you want to do user authentication on everything at your site, so it can only be accessed by users *jsmith* with password *BoZo* or *jackm* with password *tea4two.* Find the user password file (such as *authuser.pwd*) in the server configuration folder (usually *conf*), then add the authorized user IDs and passwords to the file in the correct format. For instance:

```
jsmith:BoZo
jackm:tea4two
```

*Note:* Some programs actually provide a utility program such as *htpassword* that you can use to define these interactively.

Once you've defined user IDs/passwords, go to the server's access configuration file (such as *access.cnf*) and list the authorized user IDs between the <Limit> tags, for instance:

```
<Limit GET>
require user jsmith
require user jackm
</Limit>
```

Once access control is set up, the server will ask for a user ID and password whenever anyone tries to access the site. The users *jsmith* and *jackm* will be able to successfully enter a user ID/password and gain access to the site. All others will be denied access.

## Limiting Access to a Set of Files

If you have only a limited set of files to be restricted, place them in a separate folder (or series of folders) below the server document root, and make sure all your hyperlinks reflect the new path. Then create a hidden file in each folder that follows the server conventions. For instance, on a PC, the file might be #htaccess.ctl and on a UNIX system it might be .htaccess and the contents of the file might look like this:

```
AuthUserFile c:/httpd/conf/authusr.pwd
AuthGroupFile c:/httpd/conf/empty.pwd
AuthName Example
AuthType Basic

<Limit GET>
require user jsmith
require user jill
</Limit>
```

In this case, the first two lines show where the password files are located for user authentication or group ID authentication. (The *empty.pwd* file is just an empty file used here because group authorization is not needed.) The third line (AuthName) can be anything, and the fourth line must be included as is. The information between the <Limit> tags shows the authorized users with access permission.

## Authorizing Groups of Users

Instead of listing each user every time you want to create access authorization, you can define a set of users as being in a group, then limit the access by group name. First create a group file such as *authgroup.pwd* in the server *conf* folder. The format of a group definition is as follows:

```
groupname: user1 user2 user3
```

Then use the group name instead of the individual user names in the access control files. For instance:

```
AuthUserFile c:/httpd/conf/authusr.pwd
AuthGroupFile c:/httpd/conf/authgrp.pwd
AuthName ByPassword
AuthType Basic

<Limit>
require group groupname
</Limit>
```

Whenever anyone tries to access the protected site (or individually protected folders), the server will ask for the user ID and password. If the user ID is contained in the group ID file and the user enters a correct password, access will be allowed. Otherwise, all other access will be rejected.

## Limiting Access by Machine Location

If you want to restrict access to certain locations, or to open access to everyone *except* certain locations, you can do it for the entire site or just for specific folders. To apply the limitations to the entire site, edit the access.cnf file in the server configuration folder. To apply limitations to certain folders, edit or create the access control file (such as *#htaccess.ctl*) for that folder, as described earlier.

Within the access control files, access is controlled by the entries between the <Limit> tags. The following example denies access to any machine on the network, except the two named machines that are automatically allowed. Either IP address or hostname can be specified:

```
<Limit GET>
order deny,allow
deny from all
allow from machine1
allow from machine2
</Limit>
```

The next example allows access to anyone on the network *except* the named machines. Once again, either IP address or hostname can be specified:

```
<Limit GET>
order allow,deny
allow from all
deny from machine1
deny from machine2
</Limit>
```

# index

# ₃ATCH THE
# Technology Wave
## WILEY COMPUTER PUBLISHING

## Digital Money

DANIEL LYNCH &
LESLIE LUNDQUIST

In this in-depth executive briefing, CyberCash founder Daniel Lynch and new technology specialist Leslie Lundquist provide decision makers with an invaluable head start on the emerging world of Internet commerce. *Digital Money* explains the processes, issues, and strategic considerations of options now, or soon to be available. It helps you to understand the various ways in which your business can benefit from developing Internet transaction capabilities. And it provides answers to an array of practical considerations, such as how much it will cost you to set up and maintain a digital exchange system, what types of technologies and resources you will need to support it, which methods are most appropriate for your type of business, and many others.

**ISBN# 0-471-14178-X**
**Price $24.95 US/$29.50 CAN**
**paper 285 pp. 1996**

## The New Internet Business Book

JILL H. ELLSWORTH &
MATTHEW V. ELLSWORTH

*"If you're thinking about doing business on the Internet or even if your are already up and running, this book is a critical resource that you can't afford to be without!"*
—ENTREPRENEUR MAGAZINE

Everything you need to know about doing business on the Internet is in this book. Totally revised and updated, this best-selling guide gives you clear answers to all of your Internet business questions, including who is using the Internet, what are business and organizations doing on the Internet and the World Wide Web, where can you get Internet access and how do you actually use the Internet for business.

**ISBN# 0-471-14160-7**
**Price $24.95 US/$32.50 CAN**
**paper 512 pp. 1996**

## Internet Security for Business

TERRY BERNSTEIN,
GENE SCHULTZ,
ANISH BHIMANI &
CAROL SIEGEL

Talk of Internet security invariably strays to erecting firewalls to keep out hackers. But as businesses rely more and more on the Net to share information, firewalls alone may not be enough. Many of the most potent security threats lie behind their own lines. This book starts where the firewall books leave off and describes how to develop a complete and effective Internet security program. In addition to erecting a firewall, it describes how to secure specific services, such as e-mail, news, and file retrieval. And it addresses how to educate and train end-users to identify and respond to breach of security incidents.

**ISBN# 0-471-13752-9**
**Price $34.95 US/$48.95 CAN**
**paper 416 pp. 1996**

## The Internet Strategic Plan

MARTIN SCHULMAN

You're confronted with setting up and managing your company's Internet strategy and you've got to find the best system to keep every department happy. *The Internet Strategic Plan* is your solution. With the flexible, coherent, step-by-step procedures included in this book, you can effectively set up a customized Internet plan to meet your company's needs. With flowcharts, checklists and work sheets, every chapter will help you plan the stages of your Internet strategy—from identifying the key players and what information is needed to technical and network requirements.

**ISBN# 0-471-14275-1**
**Price $39.95 US/$48.95 CAN**
**paper 320 pp. 1996**